'Offering a lively and detailed account of the history of the English language from its origins to the present-day, informed by the latest linguistic theory, Dan McIntyre's *History of English* is an excellent introduction to the subject. Engaging with contemporary debates and with the language in all its fascinating variety, this book is an essential resource for students, teachers and all lovers of language.'

Simon Horobin, *Magdalen College, University of Oxford*

'This is a highly accessible and comprehensive textbook on the history of the English language. It allows students to explore all the major aspects of linguistic development in clearly related consecutive stages. Clearly, it is essential reading for university courses on the history of English and highly to be recommended.'

Thomas Kohnen, *University of Cologne*

D0220216

HISTORY OF ENGLISH

Routledge English Language Introductions cover core areas of language study and are one-stop resources for students.

Assuming no prior knowledge, books in the series offer an accessible overview of the subject, with activities, study questions, sample analyses, commentaries and key readings – all in the same volume. The innovative and flexible 'two-dimensional' structure is built around four sections – introduction, development, exploration and extension – which offer self-contained stages for study. Each topic can also be read across these sections, enabling the reader to build gradually on the knowledge gained. This revised second edition of *History of English* includes:

❑ a comprehensive introduction to the history of English covering the origins of English, the change from Old to Middle English and the influence of other languages on English;
❑ increased coverage of key issues, such as the standardisation of English;
❑ a wider range of activities, plus answers to exercises;
❑ new readings from well-known authors such as Manfred Krug, Colette Moore, Merja Stenroos and David Crystal;
❑ a timeline of important external events in the history of English.

Structured to reflect the chronological development of the English language, *History of English* describes and explains the changes in the language over a span of 1,500 years, covering all aspects from phonology and grammar, to register and discourse. In doing so, it incorporates examples from a wide variety of texts and provides an interactive and structured textbook that will be essential reading for all students of English language and linguistics.

Dan McIntyre is Professor of English Language and Linguistics at the University of Huddersfield, UK.

ROUTLEDGE ENGLISH LANGUAGE INTRODUCTIONS

SERIES CONSULTANT: PETER STOCKWELL

Peter Stockwell is Professor of Literary Linguistics in the School of English at the University of Nottingham, UK, where his interests include sociolinguistics, stylistics and cognitive poetics. His recent publications include *The Cambridge Handbook of Stylistics* (2014), *Cognitive Grammar in Literature* (2014) and *The Language and Literature Reader* (2008).

FOUNDING EDITOR: RONALD CARTER

Ronald Carter (1947–2018) was Research Professor of Modern English Language in the School of English at the University of Nottingham, UK. He was the co-founder of the Routledge Applied Linguistics, Routledge Introductions to Applied Linguistics and Routledge Applied Corpus Linguistics series.

TITLES IN THE SERIES:

Language and Media
Rodney Jones, Sylvia Jaworska and Erhan Aslan

Researching English Language
Alison Sealey

Stylistics, Second Edition
Paul Simpson

Global Englishes, Third Edition
(previously published as *World Englishes*)
Jennifer Jenkins

Pragmatics, Third Edition
(previously published as *Pragmatics and Discourse*)
Joan Cutting

Introducing English Language, Second Edition
Louise Mullany and Peter Stockwell

Language and Law
Alan Durant and Janny HC Leung

English Grammar, Second Edition
Roger Berry

Language and Power, Second Edition
Paul Simpson, Andrea Mayr and Simon Statham

Discourse Analysis, Second Edition
Rodney Jones

Practical English Phonetics and Phonology, Fourth Edition
Beverley Collins, Inger M. Mees and Paul Carley

For more information on any of these titles, or to order, please go to www.routledge.com/series/RELI

HISTORY OF ENGLISH

A Resource Book for Students

Second Edition

DAN MCINTYRE

 Routledge
Taylor & Francis Group

LONDON AND NEW YORK

Second edition published 2020
by Routledge
2 Park Square, Milton Park, Abingdon, Oxon, OX14 4RN

and by Routledge
52 Vanderbilt Avenue, New York, NY 10017

Routledge is an imprint of the Taylor & Francis Group, an informa business

First edition published by Routledge 2008

British Library Cataloguing-in-Publication Data
A catalogue record for this book is available from the British Library

Library of Congress Cataloging-in-Publication Data
A catalog record has been requested for this book

ISBN: 978-1-138-50071-6 (hbk)
ISBN: 978-1-138-50072-3 (pbk)

Typeset in Minion Pro
by Newgen Publishing UK

HOW TO USE THIS BOOK

This book spans over 1,500 years of linguistic history in little more than 230 pages and is therefore necessarily selective in what it covers. My aim has been to provide a basic introduction to the main themes and events of both the external and internal history of English, with the intention that, armed with this outline knowledge, you will be able to go off and explore for yourself the various stages of the language's development in more detail. Inevitably there are elements of the history of English that I have presented in a simplified form. For example, the shift from Old English to Middle English happened over an extended period and involved a degree of complexity that is beyond the scope of this book. Similarly, the process by which a standard written variety of English emerged has been the subject of much debate, which is presented here in a necessarily truncated form. There is also much more that could be said about the recent history of English. Nevertheless, to my mind it is more important for the beginning student to gain an overall picture of the key issues than to focus straight away on the complexities of English's development over time. I also took the decision that, although this book covers the history of English right up to the present day, its primary focus would be on the early history of English. The reason for this is that other books in this series include substantial discussion of recent change in the language, and of the development of world Englishes (see, for example, Stockwell 2007 and Jenkins 2015).

In keeping with the Routledge English Language Introductions format, this book is organised into four sections. Section A presents an external history of English, taking into account the main social, political, economic and cultural factors that influenced the development of the language from its earliest inception right up to the present day. Section B focuses more on the actual linguistic form of the language at each of its stages, as well as on some of the specific changes that took place and the attitudes towards English that have prevailed at various times. Section C provides exercises and activities to allow you to try out the knowledge and understanding you will have gained from reading sections A and B. I have provided commentaries on most of these exercises and these can be found at the back of the book. Some activities, however, are left open, to allow you scope to investigate the issue either alone or with your fellow students in class. Section D then presents a series of readings in the history of English, chosen to allow you to further the basic knowledge of the history of English that you will gain from sections A, B and C. Finally, in addition to the commentaries on activities provided at the back of the book, you will also find a short glossary of linguistic terms, a timeline of key events in the history of English, and suggestions for further reading.

CONTENTS

EXPLORATION

 EXTENSION

Commentary on activities

Glossary

Timeline

Further reading

References

Index

FIGURES AND TABLES

Figures

Tables

COMMON ABBREVIATIONS

BCE	Before Common Era (equivalent in dates to BC)
CE	Common Era (equivalent in dates to AD)
EModE	Early Modern English
GVS	Great Vowel Shift
ME	Middle English
OE	Old English
OED	Oxford English Dictionary
PDE	Present Day English
RP	Received Pronunciation

PHONETIC SYMBOLS

Below is a list of the most common phonetic symbols used throughout this book. These symbols are from the International Phonetic Alphabet, or IPA, and represent the phonemes of Present Day Southern Standard British English. Any symbols that do not appear in this list are explained in the section of the book in which they appear.

Vowels (monophthongs)

IPA symbol	Example	IPA transcription
iː	see	/siː/
ɪ	bit	/bɪt/
ɛ	bed	/bɛd/
æ	tap	/tæp/
aː	part	/paːt/
ɒ	top	/tɒp/
ɔ	law	/lɔː/
ʊ	put	/pʊt/
uː	loo	/luː/
ʌ	love	/lʌv/
ɜ	bird	/bɜd/
ə	about	/əbaʊt/

Vowels (diphthongs)

IPA symbol	Example	IPA transcription
eɪ	pay	/peɪ/
oʊ	toe	/toʊ/
aɪ	lie	/laɪ/
aʊ	cow	/kaʊ/
ɔɪ	boy	/bɔɪ/
ɪə	beer	/bɪə/
ɛə	pair	/pɛə/
ʊə	lure	/lʊə/

Consonants

IPA symbol	Example	IPA transcription
p	pot	/pɒt/
b	boy	/bɔɪ/
t	top	/tɒp/
d	dog	/dɒg/
k	kill	/kɪl/

IPA symbol	Example	IPA transcription
g	give	/gɪv/
tʃ	church	/tʃɜtʃ/
dʒ	judge	/dʒʌdʒ/
s	sad	/sæd/
z	zip	/zɪp/
ʃ	sheep	/ʃiːp/
ʒ	leisure	/lɛʒə/
h	house	/haʊs/
m	mouse	/maʊs/
n	no	/noʊ/
ŋ	sing	/sɪŋ/
f	fed	/fɛd/
v	van	/væn/
θ	thing	/θɪŋ/
ð	the	/ðə/
l	lit	/lɪt/
ɹ	rip	/ɹɪp/
j	yes	/jɛs/
w	wit	/wɪt/
ʔ	butter (when pronounced in British English as bu'er)	/bʌʔə/

ACKNOWLEDGEMENTS

I remain indebted to the many people who gave me advice on the first edition of this book. They are Dawn Archer, Carol Bellard-Thomson, Derek Bousfield, Beatrix Busse, Jonathan Culpeper, Robert Foot, David Gill, Ella Jeffries, Lesley Jeffries, Joanna Kopaczyk, Jessica Malay, Richard Marsden, Eszter McIntyre, Lauren McIntyre, Rocío Montoro, Sara Pons-Sanz and Peter Stockwell. In producing this second edition I have benefitted from the advice of a number of other people, to whom I am grateful. These include reviewers of the first edition who pointed out areas for improvement, and whose comments I have tried to address, as well as the reviewers of my proposal for the second edition. My colleagues Jim O'Driscoll and Hazel Price gave me advice on new sections and I am grateful for their insights. Ross McIntyre gave me advice on current colloquialisms in Australian English. I would also like to thank all the authors and publishers who generously gave me permission to reprint their work in section D. In particular, I am very grateful to Manfred Krug who went beyond the call of duty in providing help and advice on my abridgement of his work. Finally, the editorial team at Routledge have been extremely patient in waiting for this book and I thank them for their forbearance. The usual declaration applies: any errors are mine alone and if I have ignored anyone's advice, I only have myself to blame.

DM

Section A

INTRODUCTION
AN EXTERNAL HISTORY
OF ENGLISH

Sometimes when linguists talk about language they discuss it as if it is an actual substance – something that you can put under a microscope and examine, dissect in a laboratory, or take to pieces in a workshop. In some areas of linguistics, thinking about language in this way can be useful. When we study grammar, for instance, we often use the metaphor of dividing a sentence up into its constituent parts. Indeed, Crystal (1994: 6) talks about grammar as 'the business of taking a language to pieces, to see how it works'. Jeffries (2006: 7) goes further and suggests that 'the only real way to understand how language works is to get your hands dirty and pull it to pieces'. These statements use metaphors for language that see it as a machine. However, sometimes it is better to take a more realistic view of what language is like. Language is not a tangible substance. The outward expression of language might be speech, signs or written text but language itself cannot be separated from the people who use it. For its speakers, language has many different functions. It is, of course, a means of communicating with others. But it allows us to do much more besides. It provides a means of performing certain actions (e.g. offering someone a job, apologising, agreeing to marry someone, making a bet), it can be used to promote particular ideologies, and it is the means by which people communicate not just their ideas but their identities to others. One of the particularly interesting things about language is that it is constantly changing and developing. So too, of course, are the people who use it. It follows, then, that if we want to know how a language develops over time, inevitably we also need to know something about the society in which its speakers live and how historical events have affected them and their development. This is what we will concentrate on in section A of this book. Before we do this, however, it is useful to understand the distinction between the **internal history** of a language and its **external history**.

A language's internal history is a record of its linguistic development over time; for example, how its vocabulary, grammar and phonology have changed. Its external history is a record of its speakers and how they and their societies have developed. It follows that language change can be caused by both intralinguistic and extralinguistic factors (Samuels 1972).

In the case of the former, a change to one element of a language can cause the development of other related elements. For example, a change in the way that one vowel sound is produced can affect the sound of the surrounding vowels. (You can read about this aspect of the development of English in B4 and D4).

Extralinguistic change, on the other hand, comes about when external, non-linguistic events begin to affect the development of a language. For example, in the late 1980s, computer systems were developed that enabled the display of a background image on a computer screen. This image came to be referred to as *wallpaper* because of its decorative function. In effect, the pre-existing word *wallpaper* widened in meaning to refer to both the paper you use to decorate interior walls and the digital image that forms the background to a graphical user interface. That is, an external, non-linguistic event had an effect on the development of the lexicon. This is just one small example of how external events can affect language development. Section A of this book focuses particularly on the external events that impacted on the history of English.

A1 ORIGINS OF ENGLISH

The earliest form of English is **Old English (OE)**. Old English was derived from the Germanic languages of the Anglo-Saxons who settled in Britain, and most linguists agree that Old English emerged in the fifth century, around 449 CE. The language in this form was used for over 600 years, but during those 600 years, of course, it was constantly changing. By 1100, it looked and sounded very different to the language it had been in its earliest stages.

A1.1 The Isles before English

The English language emerged in the mid-fifth century CE on the island of Great Britain, the largest of the group of islands now known as the British Isles. The 'Great' in *Great Britain* is a reference to size, not status, and the term was used originally by the ancient Egyptian polymath Claudius Ptolemy to distinguish the larger island from its smaller neighbour to the west, which he called *Little Britain* (Toomer 1984: 88). In his book *Naturalis Historia* (*Natural History*), written in 77 CE, the Roman philosopher Pliny the Elder refers to Great Britain as *Britannia*, and the island group as a whole as *Britanniæ* (Pliny 77 CE: Book 4, Chapter 30). Pliny's term *Brittania* is Latin and likely derives from the Common Brittonic word *Pritanī*. **Common Brittonic** was a Celtic language spoken in Great Britain between 6 BCE and 6 CE. The asterisk indicates that this term is a linguistic reconstruction, i.e. a best guess at what the Brittonic word is likely to have been, based on the characteristics of languages that developed from Common Brittonic. Pliny notes that Great Britain was formerly known as *Albion*, a name that comes from Proto-Celtic, which is the ancestor language of Common Brittonic. One hypothesis as to the origins of the name *Albion* is that it was a development of the

Proto Indo-European stem *albho*, which means white. *Albion* may thus have been a reference to the famous white cliffs of the south coast of England.

It is important to understand that although the term *Great Britain* was in use long before the arrival of the Anglo-Saxons, it was not until much later that the countries of England, Scotland and Wales emerged as political entities. Likewise, the concept of a kingdom of Ireland did not develop until the seventh century CE. Before the Romans arrived, Great Britain was a geographical rather than a political entity, and its many indigenous tribes shared no unifying culture. What they did share, however, was a language.

The inhabitants of Great Britain and Ireland had been speaking Celtic dialects from around 2000 BCE (Cunliffe 2013: 249). This is not to say that they necessarily thought of themselves as Celts. The idea of a wave of Celtic immigration into Britain is largely a myth propagated by scholars in the seventeenth century. In reality, it is more likely that the Celtic language found its way to Britain by a combination of immigration and cultural diffusion (essentially the spread of cultural ideas from one society to another). Nonetheless, the **Britons**, as the *Anglo-Saxon Chronicle* refers to the indigenous people of Britain, were Celtic speakers. From around 6 BCE their language was Common Brittonic. By around 6 CE, this had developed into Welsh (spoken in the area that is now Wales), Cornish (spoken in what is now Cornwall) and Cumbric (spoken in the areas that are now northern England and lowland Scotland). In the far north of the island, in what is modern-day Scotland, the language spoken was Pictish, which some linguists consider to be related to Celtic. This area of the country had also seen an influx of settlers from Ireland, known as the Scoti or **Scots**. They spoke Goidelic, the ancestor language of Scots Gaelic, Irish Gaelic and Manx. This, then, was the sociolinguistic situation prior to the arrival of the Romans.

A1.2 The Romans in Britain

Where did English come from? The origins of English are usually dated to the arrival of the Anglo-Saxons in Britain in the mid-fifth century. But to understand what led to their arrival, it is useful to know a bit about events in Britain before they arrived.

At the beginning of the fifth century CE, Britain was an occupied country. Its occupiers, the Romans, had arrived in Britain in 43 CE, as part of an invasion force led by the Roman general Aulus Plautius, under the overall command of Emperor Claudius. The Romans had quickly subjugated the native Britons, who inhabited the areas we now know as Cornwall, Cumbria, Wales and parts of lowland Scotland. Also living on the island of Great Britain, in what is now eastern and northern Scotland, were the Picts. These were the descendants of Iron Age communities whose tribal designation gave rise to the Roman name for Scotland, *Caledonia*. The other inhabitants of Caledonia were the Scots, who originated from Ireland and who had settled in Pictish areas. Following the Roman invasion, then, the people in Great Britain feeling the effects of the occupation were the **Britons**, the **Picts** and the **Scots**, all living in disparate tribal groups and all speaking variant dialect forms of Common Brittonic and Goidelic (see the language family tree in C1 for an indication of how these languages relate to each other). The Romans brought with them Latin and, it is to be assumed, vernacular dialects of this language. (Your **vernacular** dialect/language is the one that you speak most naturally, i.e. your 'mother tongue'. The term is also sometimes used to refer to low-status varieties of a language.) This was not the first time the Latin language had been used in Britain. There had been a previous attempted Roman invasion in 55 BCE, led by Julius Caesar. This was not hugely successful and it took a further year and another invasion for Caesar to actually establish a settlement in Britain. Even so, Caesar achieved only moderate success and an occupation in any real sense did not occur until Emperor Claudius's invasion almost a hundred years later. Despite its success, Claudius's conquest of Britain did not go unchallenged. In 61 CE, for instance, Boudica (sometimes referred to as Boadicea), a native leader of the Britons, led a revolt against the occupying forces which resulted in the massacre of over 70,000 Romans.

Nevertheless, throughout their time in the country the occupying Roman forces established a firm ruling presence in most parts of Britain. The influence of the Romans was considerable. Major roads were built, towns and cities had bath houses, theatres and places of worship. Roman houses had water supplies and heating. Britain was beginning to look like the other provinces of the Roman Empire. A further indicator of this was the use of Latin, which was established as the language of officialdom. It is likely that Latin had a prestige value and was spoken not just by those for whom it was a first language but also by the upper-class native inhabitants of cities and towns. Latin, however, never supplanted the Common Brittonic language of the native Britons and it began to decline in use as a spoken language following the arrival of the Anglo-Saxons.

A1.3 The arrival of the Anglo-Saxons

At the beginning of the fifth century the Roman Empire was under threat and the Roman garrisons in Britain were withdrawn to Rome. By 410 CE the last Roman legion had left. The native Britons now found themselves facing something of a problem. During the Roman occupation there had been occasional attacks from the Picts and the Scots in the border regions, but the presence of the occupying armies had always been enough to suppress them. Nonetheless, the Romans had never managed to conquer Caledonia (modern-day Scotland). Now, with the Romans gone, the Britons found themselves open to increasingly frequent attacks from the Picts and the Scots and in the unfortunate position of not being able to adequately defend themselves. The Britons appealed to Rome for help, but Rome had problems of its own and was able to do little to help. As the situation worsened, Vortigern, described in Bede's *Ecclesiastical History of the English People* as a king (i.e. leader) of the Britons (see A1.4), made an appeal to the Germanic tribes of north-west Germany and Denmark for help in repelling the attacks. There was something of an irony in appealing to the Saxon nations, as the Saxons had made numerous attacks on Britain throughout the Roman occupation, causing difficulties for the occupying Roman armies (whose garrisons are likely to have included at least some soldiers of Germanic descent). Nevertheless, the Saxons agreed to come to the aid of the Britons and the first boatloads of Saxon warriors, along with two further groups, the Angles and the Jutes, began arriving in 449 CE. The **Saxons** came from north-west Germany, the **Angles** from the Danish mainland and islands, and the **Jutes** from northern Denmark. Collectively, these groups are known as the Anglo-Saxons.

Some older histories of English will describe what happened from 449 onwards as an invasion of Britain. This is not strictly true. For a start, the Anglo-Saxon newcomers were invited. Secondly, while it is true that once they had arrived they quickly subjugated the Britons, to talk of the Anglo-Saxons as invading Britain is to suggest a degree of organisation to the venture that was not there. The Anglo-Saxons were not a unified, invading army. They came in relatively small groups and continued to arrive throughout the sixth century. They succeeded in dispelling the Pictish and Scottish attackers and, once they had done this, decided to settle in Britain.

A1.4 English: what's in a name?

Much of what we know of the events of this period comes from the work of the Venerable Bede, a monk who lived and worked at the Jarrow monastery in the north-east of Britain. In 731 Bede completed his now famous *Ecclesiastical History of the English People*, which is a rich source of information about the Old English period. It is Bede who tells us that the Germanic 'invaders' were Angles, Saxons and Jutes, saying then that:

> They received from the Britons grants of land where they could settle among them on condition that they maintained the peace and security of the island against all enemies in return for regular pay.
>
> (Bede 1990 [731]: 63)

However, when interpreting Bede's work we have to be careful for several reasons. McCully and Hilles (2005: 51) point out that Bede was writing about the coming of the Anglo-Saxons almost 300 years after they arrived, with no first-hand records of these events. Bede wrote his history based almost entirely on stories that had been passed from generation to generation orally. Crystal (2005: 16) questions some of Bede's terminology and suggests that his description of the Angles, Saxons and Jutes as being 'nationalities' is not entirely accurate. Crystal explains that Bede's reference to three distinct communities is a simplification. Names for communities of people at the time did not necessarily equate to our modern concept of nations. Some groups would consist of people related by blood. Others might be considered a community because they grouped themselves together under a particular leader. And sometimes a community name might refer to a group (or groups) of people who had come together specifically for the purposes of attacking another group or defending themselves against attacks from others. The history of English is not as neat as it is often packaged!

So if the Anglo-Saxon population was made up of numerous different communities, how then did they come to be known collectively as the *English*? Why not the *Saxons*, for example? We might imagine that this is because the Angles were the more dominant of the groups who settled in the country. After all, *England* means 'land of the Angles'. However, it is not the case that there were simply more of the Angles than any other group. First of all, we have to remember that the idea of three separate communities (Angles, Saxons and Jutes) is an oversimplification. Bede himself sometimes uses the Latin terms *Angli* and *Saxones* interchangeably. *Angli*, then, could refer to groups other than the Angles. The Old English equivalent of *Angli* was *Engle*, so the name

Engla lande – clearly an early form of *England* – is derived from an Old English word which could, like *Angli*, be used to refer to any inhabitant of the country. Furthermore, the historian Peter Hunter Blair (1962: 12–13) suggests that the term *Angli Saxones* was used by some Latin writers to refer not to the Angles and the Saxons together, but to differentiate the *English* Saxons from what Bede called the 'Old Saxons' living on the continent. From the eleventh century onwards, then, Britain began to be referred to as *England*, though spellings of this word varied considerably until the fourteenth century.

Gradually, the Anglo-Saxons settled in England. It's not entirely clear how the Britons got on with the new inhabitants. We can assume that in some areas the Britons and the Anglo-Saxons might have lived together peaceably. But in the West Saxon area (along the south coast) there was considerable fighting as the settlers struggled to establish themselves. It is likely that some of the Britons from this area were forced out into nearby Cornwall, or perhaps into Wales (the name *Wales* actually derives from the Old English word *wealas*, meaning *foreigner*; hardly a very charitable way for the Anglo-Saxons to describe the native inhabitants of the country!) As the Anglo-Saxons asserted themselves, the civilisation that the Romans had created was gradually destroyed. One of the reasons for this, as Baugh and Cable (2002) point out, is that the Anglo-Saxons lived a different kind of life to the Romans, with the emphasis on hunting and agriculture. But by the seventh century, a number of significant settlements had become established. These were Northumbria, Mercia, East Anglia, Essex, Kent, Sussex and Wessex. Collectively, these seven kingdoms are sometimes referred to as the **Anglo-Saxon heptarchy** (see Figure A1.4.1).

The boundaries between these kingdoms were by no means stable and over the next 200 or so years, the balance of power fluctuated between them. Political power has always had an influence on the prestige of particular dialects (see Stockwell 2007: 16–17) and things were no different in Anglo-Saxon times. The effect of this on the developing English language was to raise to a position of prestige the dialect of whichever kingdom happened to be exerting influence at the time. We'll look at dialects in more detail in A2.

A1.5 Christianity reaches England

What we now call Old English emerged as the Germanic dialects of the Anglo-Saxon settlers converged over time. But Common Brittonic and Latin also had an influence on Old English (though of the two, Brittonic was significantly less influential). However, the influence of Latin did not come from the period of Roman occupation, even though Christianity had been introduced to parts of Britain during this period. There was no direct contact between Latin and Old English until Christianity was re-introduced to Britain in 597 CE by Augustine, a missionary sent by Pope Gregory I. Augustine's first success was baptising Ethelbert, the King of Kent, just months after arriving in England. No doubt he was helped by the fact that Ethelbert's Frankish wife, Bertha, was herself a Christian (the Franks were a Germanic tribe from around the Rhine, who eventually crossed into – and gave their name to – the country that is now France). Just four years later, Augustine became the first Archbishop of Canterbury. All things considered, the spread of Christianity was quick, and within a hundred years England

Figure A1.4.1 The Anglo-Saxon heptarchy (from Pyles and Algeo 1993: 98).

was a Christian country. (It should be noted, though, that many people continued to practise Christianity and paganism at the same time, not initially accepting the notion of Christianity as an exclusive religion.)

As Christianity spread, Latin was once again introduced to the country and became established as the language of the church and the language of learning. The effect on English was to infuse it with numerous Latin words, and so the vocabulary of English increased further.

A1.6 Viking raids

Although the Anglo-Saxons had succeeded in subjugating the native Britons, they themselves were not immune to attack. Between 787 and 850, Britain was the victim of a series of raids by Scandinavian aggressors. Later on, the raids increased in scale and in terms of the objectives of the Scandinavian invaders, and in time these groups settled in England too and exerted their own influence on the development of English.

The Scandinavian invaders of this period are commonly known as the **Vikings**, though the Anglo-Saxons called them the **Danes**. Initially, they carried out isolated attacks on towns and monasteries (the first being Lindisfarne in Northumbria in 793) for the simple purpose of looting. One of these raids, in 794, was on the monastery at Jarrow – the home of Bede.

The south of the country also suffered Viking raids but the greatest attack came in 865, when a large and well-organised Danish army, led by the memorably named Ivar the Boneless and his brother Halfdan, conquered East Anglia. (Ivar the Boneless and Halfdan were the sons of Ragnar Lothbrok, whose own name is no less memorable; James (2001: 221) translates it as 'Hairy-breeks' – or 'Hairy-trousers'!) Having conquered the greater part of the east of England, in 870 the Vikings attacked Wessex, where Ethelred was king. Initially, Ethelred repelled the attacks but just weeks later he was himself defeated. Ethelred died in 871 and was succeeded as king by his brother Alfred ('Alfred the Great'), who essentially paid off the Danish attackers. Five years later, though, the Danes were back. This time, however, Alfred was far better prepared and won a clear victory over Guthrum, the Danish King of East Anglia, who had led the assault. The Danes were pushed back from Wessex and Guthrum agreed to accept Christianity and was subsequently baptised. A treaty was drawn up in 886 whereby the Danes agreed to settle in a territory to the east of an imaginary line running diagonally from the Thames to Chester, which was to become known as the Danelaw. This territory was so-called because within it Danish law applied, as opposed to the West Saxon, Mercian and other laws and customs that applied in the west. The Danelaw extended from the east of England into the north. On the other side of the Danelaw, Alfred became the first King of the Anglo-Saxons.

Despite Alfred's victory over Guthrum, this was not the end of the Viking attacks. The famous Old English poem *The Battle of Maldon* tells the story of how, in 991, Byrhtnoth, an East Saxon leader, was defeated by a Viking army led by Olaf Tryggvason, who was later to become King of Norway. In 994, Tryggvason was joined by the King of Denmark, Svein Forkbeard, and together they continued the attacks against the Anglo-Saxons. Finally, in 1014, Svein drove the second King Ethelred (the great-great grandson of Alfred; often referred to as 'the unready', meaning unwise) into exile in Normandy and was crowned King of England. He died the same year and was succeeded by his son, Cnut. And so the Danes had finally gained power in England, and English was to be influenced by their language, Old Norse.

Old Norse had a significant effect on the development of Old English. Close contact between the Scandinavians and the Anglo-Saxons led to the borrowing of Old Norse words. In C2.2, for example, you can read about the influence of Old Norse on place names. Many now common lexical items also came originally from Old Norse, including such words as *take, die, wrong, call* and *law* (see C3.1 for more examples). Additionally, the <s> inflection on third-person present simple singular forms of the verb is a result of Scandinavian influence.

THE HISTORY OF ENGLISH OR THE HISTORY OF ENGLISHES?

There are many different varieties of English in Britain (and, indeed, across the world). These various forms of English are dialects. A **dialect** is a variety of a language which is distinct from other varieties of that language by virtue of particular lexical and grammatical selections that are not common to other dialects. For example, students of mine who are not from West Yorkshire often find it somewhat confusing (not to mention amusing) when they arrive in Huddersfield and find that there are words used here that seem unique to the region and, conversely, that words they might use at home are not recognised here. In Huddersfield, for instance, a *teacake* is a bread roll – an item that speakers from other regions might call a *cob*, a *breadcake*, a *huffkin* or a *batch*, to list but a few options. Dialectal differences also extend to grammar. I am originally from Yorkshire and when I went to university in Lancashire, my sister accused me (note the strong feelings often associated with particular dialects!) of 'betraying' my Yorkshire roots because I unknowingly started to use elements of Lancashire dialect when I spoke. For example, I would form questions differently – 'Do you not like carrots?' as opposed to 'Don't you like carrots?' (see Stockwell 2007: A2, B2, C2 and D2 for more on dialectal variation). Dialectal differences along these lines were also common in Anglo-Saxon times, though geography does not necessarily account for all the differences that existed, as we shall see. Just as there are different dialects today, so too were there different dialects of Old English.

A2.1 Old English dialects

The four main dialects of Old English which scholars have been able to determine are Kentish, West Saxon, Mercian and Northumbrian (the similarities between Mercian and Northumbrian mean that these two are sometimes grouped together and referred to as Anglian). Kentish was the dialect of the Jutes who had settled around Kent, West Saxon was spoken south of the River Thames, Mercian in an area extending from the Thames to the River Humber (but not including Wales), and Northumbrian, as the name suggests, by people living north of the River Humber. It is, of course, likely that there were more than these four dialects in use at the time. Our knowledge of Old English and its dialects is gleaned from a relatively small amount of data. Only around three million words of Old English text have survived (Crystal 2005: 34), so it is perhaps not surprising that scholars have only been able to determine four dialects with any confidence, especially when we consider that Anglo-Saxon culture was largely oral (though we might also say that is it impressive that scholars have managed to glean so much from such a sparsity of material). A further problem that scholars have, of course, is that they are trying to reconstruct Old English dialects from written manuscripts. Of course, written language can give us some insight into dialectal characteristics but, naturally, it can only give us a limited insight into what the spoken form of that dialect might have been. Some dialectal differences that existed may never have been recorded in writing. It is also worth remembering that at this time there would still have been no conception among Anglo-Saxon speakers of 'an English language' shared by all the inhabitants of a country. This is important because the definition of what constitutes a language is as much a political matter as a linguistic one. For example, if you are from the south of England you may find it extremely difficult to understand someone who speaks a strong Newcastle dialect; nevertheless, you would still consider them to be speaking English. However, imagine if the north-east of England were politically independent of the rest of the UK – and hostile at that. In such a circumstance, a London-based government might perhaps think very differently and consider Newcastle English to be a completely separate language. Politics, then, plays a large part in the definition of a particular variety as a language, and at this stage in the development of English the Anglo-Saxons were in no sense a politically unified people.

A2.2 The rise of West Saxon

Of the four dialects listed above, West Saxon was the most prestigious. Because of this, and the fact that West Saxon is the predominant dialect found in surviving manuscripts, most introductions to Old English (e.g. Hough and Corbett 2007; Mitchell and Robinson 2007) tend to concentrate on this dialect. But why was West Saxon viewed as prestigious? The answer to this is the same reason that particular accents and dialects are seen as prestigious in Present Day English (PDE): power. It has always been the case that the language variety used by the group that has a considerable degree of political and economic power will be viewed as more prestigious than those varieties used by less powerful groups. This was the case in Anglo-Saxon times too; though, as we have seen, the balance of power between the Anglo-Saxon kingdoms was in no way stable. During the late seventh and early eighth centuries, for example, Northumbria dominated both culturally and politically. This situation came about when in 633 Oswald, a Christian, became ruler of Northumbria. Although Christianity was by no means widespread in Britain before the arrival of Augustine, it had not entirely died out after the departure of the Romans and had survived in Ireland. An Irish monk called Columba had founded a monastery on the Scottish island of Iona in an effort to spread the faith to the Picts, and Oswald had been introduced to Christianity while on Iona in 616. As ruler of Northumbria, Oswald set about further spreading Christianity through the founding of churches and monasteries, such as those at Lindisfarne and Jarrow (the home, you'll remember, of the Venerable Bede). The monasteries were places of learning. Latin flourished once more as monks engaged in scholarship to disseminate their faith. Strong leadership and the success of the monasteries established Northumbria's political and cultural influence, which in turn would have increased the status of Northumbrian as an Old English dialect. However, the Viking raids of the late eighth century effectively put paid to Northumbria's political dominance. You'll recall that when the Vikings invaded they looted towns and monasteries. Among these were the monasteries at Jarrow, Lindisfarne and Iona, and the raids halted the advance of scholarship in these places.

Political and cultural power had not belonged exclusively to Northumbria though. Mercia too had some influence in the eighth century and texts survive that were written not just in Latin but also in Old English. Among these are Old English glosses of Latin texts. But Mercia was also to suffer at the hands of the Vikings, as described in A1.6. This left Wessex, under the rule of Alfred, as the remaining Anglo-Saxon stronghold, the power and influence of Mercia and Northumbria having declined substantially.

Alfred, as we have seen, managed to defeat the Danes (as the Saxons called the Vikings), who were pushed back into the Danelaw. However, since one of the consequences of the Viking raids was a decline in scholarship, owing to the attacks on the monasteries that were the great centres of learning at the time, in the years following these raids, the ability even among the clergy to read Latin had declined. Alfred, being politically very shrewd, recognised the importance of this ability; Latin, for instance, was the language used in Royal Charters to circulate instructions from the King – and, of course, if people were having trouble reading it, as Stenton (1955: 43) points out, then Alfred's legislation would not be widely recognised. Alfred therefore made the decision to revitalise learning and scholarship. He taught himself Latin but recognised as well the importance of having Saxon translations of Latin texts. He himself translated numerous works and it is thanks to his efforts at reform and the Anglo-Saxon manuscripts produced under his guidance that we know so much about Old English today.

Inevitably, the translations made by Alfred and his associates were in West Saxon. The importance of Wessex as a political and cultural centre meant that the West Saxon dialect attained a prestige that set it apart from other varieties. Furthermore, since copies of translations made in Wessex were often sent elsewhere in the country for further copies to be made, West Saxon became established as a kind of literary standard.

A2.3 Dialect boundaries

Of course, we have to be careful when speculating about the geographical boundaries of particular dialects. It was obviously not the case that there was a clear dividing line between areas where, say, West Saxon was spoken and areas where Mercian dominated. Indeed, there was likely to be a strong degree of overlap of dialects at the geographical borders between the Anglo-Saxon kingdoms. It is also the case that just because a text may exhibit characteristics of, say, the Mercian dialect, it does not automatically mean that it reflects that dialect in full. It was common for the monks who produced such texts to travel around from monastery to monastery, and as they interacted with people from other areas of the country it is inevitable that they would have picked up certain elements of other dialects. It is likely then that texts may contain elements of a number of dialects; for example, the copyist's own as well as elements he may have absorbed both from hearing the speech of people from other areas and from reading their variant spellings of particular words. The scribes who produced Old English translations of Latin texts under Alfred may not all have come from Wessex. Although they may have been influenced by the West Saxon dialect, it is also likely that a few of their own dialectal features found their way into the manuscripts they produced.

Furthermore, it has also been suggested that the dialectal differences apparent in some Old English manuscripts may be due in part to particular monasteries having their own styles of writing, almost like the individual house styles that publishing companies use now. Nevertheless, we can be confident that these styles must at least in part have been influenced by the dialect common to the region in which they were originally produced.

What should be clear by now is that when we talk about the history of English, we are really talking about the history of *varieties* of English. We may often concentrate on **Standard English** (and we'll look at the development of this form in A5) but we should be aware that there were and still are many different varieties of English in existence.

A3   LANGUAGE CONTACT IN THE MIDDLE AGES

Following the death of Alfred the Great, the West Saxons, under Alfred's heir, Edward, and later his grandson, Athelstan, managed to keep the Danes in check and retain the strength of Wessex. They even managed to take back areas of the Danelaw and in 937 Athelstan secured his most decisive victory over the Danes at the battle of Brunanburh. Following this, Athelstan had himself proclaimed King of the Anglo-Saxons and Danes (James 2001: 246) and it is now that we start to see the beginnings of a unified England.

However, this success was not to last (see A1.6). The Viking attacks of the late tenth century saw the Danes reclaim power, ultimately leading to Svein Forkbeard claiming the throne of England in 1014. This then passed to his son Cnut who ruled until 1035. Following Cnut's death, his son, Harthacnut, ruled from 1040, when he took over from his half-brother Harold Harefoot, until 1042. As Harthacnut had no son, the throne then passed to Edward, later to become known as Edward the Confessor. Edward was Harthacnut's half-brother. They had the same mother – Emma of Normandy – who had given birth to Edward while married to Ethelred the Unready (the great-great grandson of Alfred the Great). The result of Edward's accession to the throne was a restoration of the Saxon line (remember that Ethelred, Edward's father, was from Wessex) after many years of Danish kings.

Now, returning to the issue of language (all these kings get in the way!), what is significant about Edward the Confessor becoming king is that he had been brought up in Normandy as a result of his father's exile there. Consequently, when Edward took up the throne of England, he filled his court with French advisors. Indeed, the historian Norman Davies describes him as 'a Trojan horse' for the rising power of Normandy (Davies 2000: 232). Because of Edward's reliance on his French advisors, the French and English languages would have come into contact to a considerable degree. The influence of French turns out to be hugely important in explaining how English developed next.

A3.1   1066 and all that

Because Edward the Confessor's Royal Court included numerous French speakers, it is likely that even at this stage French was beginning to have an influence on English.

Words from one language would have been adopted into the other as French and English speakers attempted to communicate with one another. But the impact of French on English was to increase even further following Edward's death in 1066.

Edward died in January of that year and as he had died childless it was not exactly clear who his heir to the throne should be. Nevertheless, immediately after Edward's death, Harold Godwinson had himself proclaimed king. Harold's father, Godwin, had been one of Edward's most powerful earls. Indeed, Godwin had had significant influence over the running of the country, and upon his death, his son Harold had taken over that position as Earl of Wessex. Harold claimed that Edward had promised him on his deathbed that he would be his successor to the throne. As Harold was effectively ruling England anyway, it was not a huge step for him to proclaim himself king once Edward had died.

Harold, though, was not the only claimant to the throne. William of Normandy, a second cousin of Edward's, also wished to succeed Edward. The fact that he was a second cousin of the former king did not in itself make him a rightful heir. However, like Harold, William claimed that Edward had promised him the throne during a visit that William had made to England in 1052. The situation was complicated further by the fact that Harold had been shipwrecked off Normandy in 1064, during which time William had come to his aid in return for Harold promising to support him in his claim to the throne. At least, this is what William claimed. Harold maintained that he had been tricked into making this promise, and as it had been made under duress, probably felt no responsibility to honour it. This, then, was the situation that led to the infamous Battle of Hastings in 1066, and ultimately to the rise of French (or **Anglo-Norman**, as the invaders spoke) as a language of prestige in Britain.

The dispute over the throne of England left no option for William but to try to take the crown by force. In September 1066 he landed at Hastings with a formidable army. Harold's forces were badly depleted following their actions in the north of England to repel an invasion by the King of Norway, who was also keen to take the English throne (clearly England was hot property!). Nevertheless, when they arrived at Hastings they were able to take up a position on a hill above the Norman army, which gave them a significant advantage. It was only by pretending to retreat that William was able to lure the English down the hill, and once that had happened the battle was all but over. In the midst of the fighting Harold was killed (allegedly as a result of an arrow piercing his eye). And on Christmas Day, 1066, William of Normandy – William the Conqueror – was crowned King of England in Westminster Abbey. The French language had well and truly arrived in England.

A3.2 From Old English to Middle English

The Norman invasion of England had far-reaching consequences for the development of the English language. Of course, the language did not change overnight but gradually the variety of French spoken by the invaders (a variety which developed into what we now refer to as Anglo-Norman) began to have an influence that was to change English substantially and lead it into its next stage of development: Middle English. You can explore what Middle English was like in units B3 and C3.

We have already seen how, because of Edward the Confessor's Norman origins, the language of the Royal Court would have become dominated by French. This would have continued to an even greater extent under William the Conqueror, especially since so many of his advisors at Court would have also come from Normandy. Furthermore, the language of administration favoured by William would have been Latin, since this was what would have been used at home. So, Norman French became the vernacular language of the Royal Court and Latin the language of administration (and, of course, religion). One of the knock-on effects of this would have been to downgrade the status of English so that it lost a lot of the prestige it had gained under the Saxon monarchy.

The influence of Anglo-Norman (which is what Norman French developed into) would also have been felt further afield. One of the immediate consequences of William becoming king was his replacement of many English noblemen with his own Norman nobles (partly because William would have favoured his own men but also because so many of the English nobility had been killed at Hastings). According to *Domesday Book* (its name derives from the Old English word *dom*, meaning 'judgement'), which William had commissioned to record exactly what his new kingdom consisted of in terms of land and who owned it, by 1086 most landholders in England were Norman. In terms of linguistic consequences, this meant that Anglo-Norman would have gradually attained the prestige that English had formerly enjoyed, since it was now the language of the ruling class. But just how was Anglo-Norman affecting English?

In the immediate aftermath of Hastings, it should be said that the effect of Anglo-Norman on the majority of the native English population was probably very minimal. Kibbee (1991: 9) makes the point that out of a total population in Britain of 1.5 million, only approximately 20,000 were Normans (including the army). This amounts to just 1.3% of the population. Around 85% of Anglo-Saxons were peasant farmers but only around 0.35% of peasant farmers listed in the *Domesday Book* (1086) were Normans. We can conclude from this that in the countryside Anglo-Norman would have been neither heard much, nor used. Townspeople would have heard Anglo-Norman spoken much more than people in the country, though this very much depended on the area. For example, *Domesday Book* records that only 160 Normans owned houses in Norwich, out of a population of 6,000, with similar numbers in York (Kibbee 1991: 10). Hardly a majority. The situation was somewhat different in the south-east, where there was a stronger Norman influence. The extent to which English people would have experienced Anglo-Norman, then, would have depended on the amount of contact they had with the type of people for whom it was the vernacular language. For instance, traders in and around London were much more likely to come into contact with French speakers than farmers in the countryside.

The influence of French came from its prestige, a result of its association with the ruling class. One way in which French affected English was by English borrowing words from Anglo-Norman. This was the source of a lot of new vocabulary in English. In short, French began to affect English at many linguistic levels, including vocabulary, spelling, grammar and pronunciation. The extent to which French began to mix with English would have been increased by, for example, inter-marriage between French and English nobility. The children of such unions would have grown up bilingual and would have been likely to engage in code-switching (the sociolinguistic term for the mixing of two languages), resulting in the gradual addition of Anglo-Norman vocabulary to English. Trade, too, would have led people to mix languages, to borrow vocabulary and generally to be influenced by each other's ways of speaking and writing.

All of this development changed English to such an extent that linguists refer to the English of this period as **Middle English (ME)**. Middle English is usually said to refer to English from around 1100 to 1500. The reason Middle English is not dated from the arrival of William the Conqueror in 1066 is, of course, because change is never immediate and it would have taken several years for French to start having an influence on English. Linguists often make a distinction between Early Middle English (1100 to 1300) and Later Middle English (1300 to 1500). There are some clear linguistic differences between these periods and some of these can be ascribed to the wider social, political and cultural changes that were taking place at the time (see B3 for more details).

A3.3 The decline of French and the rise of English

Although in the years following the Norman Conquest the Anglo-Norman variety of French replaced English as the most prestigious language, this is not to say that English disappeared. Its status simply became downgraded. It went from being a language of officialdom, with a developing written standard, to once more being primarily a spoken language. Even so, it remained the language spoken by the majority of people in the country. However, its status was to rise again, following a number of events that led to a gradual decline in the use of French.

Among the first of these was King John's loss of Normandy in 1204. John was a descendant of William the Conqueror, and losing Normandy to the French meant that the English lost an important territorial connection with France. One of the long-term consequences of this was to generate a stronger sense of English identity among the nobility of England. This identity was bolstered by the actions of Henry III later on in the thirteenth century. Some of the English nobility began to accuse Henry of favouring those of his subjects who were of French descent. Henry responded by issuing a royal proclamation in English as well as French. In effect, this was a kind of propaganda, designed to emphasise Henry's commitment to his English nobility. As you can see, English is not just a means of communicating a message; here it was being used strategically to foster identity.

The use of English for this purpose increased during the fourteenth century. Between 1337 and 1453, the so-called **Hundred Years War** was waged between England and France. During this period, Henry V (who ruled from 1413 to 1422) began to use English to write despatches home from his campaigns. Again, this is an example of English being using for the purposes of propaganda. To write in French would have been to write in the language of the enemy. Using English emphasised the division between the English and the French and worked to create a greater sense of national identity.

All of these events led to the very considered use of English for particular political purposes. But another event that occurred during the fourteenth century led to an increase in the use of English that was not so obviously determined by politics. This was the **bubonic plague** or the **Black Death** as it is sometimes called. The bubonic plague had already swept across Europe and arrived in England in 1348. Its effect was devastating. Historians estimate that it killed around a third of the population of the country at the time. So how did this affect the development of English? One of the consequences of the drastic reduction in population was to reduce the country's work-force. Inevitably, this shortage of labour pushed up workers' wages as demand outstripped supply. This meant that the working classes were able to climb the ladder of social hierarchy and attain a level of prosperity that would have been impossible before the Black Death. And, as we have seen, the greater the influence a particular group has within society, the more likely it is that the language spoken by that group will be seen as prestigious. English was on the rise once again. However, it was an English that had been greatly affected by its contact with French and it remained the case that in some domains of life (e.g. religion), English was still not the dominant language used.

A3.4 Middle English dialects

In the Middle English period there was no established standard form of English such as there is today, either written or spoken. Middle English writers wrote as they spoke (Burrow and Turville-Petre 1996: 6). The upshot of this is that looking at Middle English writing can give us a clue as to the different dialects that were used at the time. Burrow and Turville-Petre (1996) distinguish five different dialects of Middle English: Northern, West Midland, East Midland, South East and South West. The divisions between these dialects can be seen in Figure A3.4.1.

The dotted lines between geographical areas are isoglosses. An isogloss is a boundary denoting the point at which a difference can be noticed in the use of particular linguistic items (e.g. particular spellings, pronunciations, etc.). Isoglosses are not absolute divisions, of course, as is explained in A2.3. At these boundaries we are likely to find more than one particular linguistic form being used (perhaps two different pronunciations of the same word, for example). A useful analogy is to imagine what would happen if you were to try and colour in the different sections of Figure A3.4.1 using watercolour paints. If you didn't wait for the paint to dry before starting on another section, you would find that the different colours would bleed into each other at the points where they touched. In effect, this is what happens linguistically at the points where isoglosses intersect.

A4 FROM MIDDLE ENGLISH TO EARLY MODERN ENGLISH

It should be clear by now how, in the history of English, external events have impacted upon the language and been causal in its development and change. Sometimes we can point to one event as being particularly significant (e.g. the Norman Conquest led to English coming into greater contact with French) but even in such apparently clear-cut scenarios, the reality is that a host of different occurrences – some linguistic, some

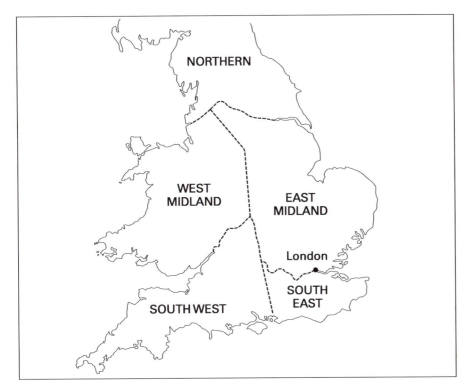

Figure A3.4.1 Middle English dialect areas (from Burrow and Turville-Petre 1996: 7).

non-linguistic – contrive to generate change in the language. This can be seen particularly in the development of Middle English into **Early Modern English (EModE)**.

The events that caused English to develop into a language that is much more similar to Present Day English are many and varied. Because of this, there is some disagreement among scholars about when Early Modern English might be said to begin and end. Again, we have to remember that boundary dates between linguistic periods are in no way markers of overnight change, but simply serve to indicate the points at which the language noticeably begins to alter. As a rough guide, Early Modern English might be said to begin around 1500, while the changes that were to affect its development into Present Day English were beginning to be felt around 1700. The reasons for this choice of dates will become clear once you have read about the various events that occurred in this period, which you will find in the rest of this unit and in A5.

A4.1 External influences on pronunciation

One of the key developments of English that occurred between the Middle English and Early Modern periods involved significant changes to the way in which certain vowel sounds were pronounced, a development which has come to be known as the Great

Vowel Shift. This occurred mainly between 1400 and 1750 and involved a gradual modification in the pronunciation of the long vowels in English. 'Long' in this sense refers to the duration of the pronunciation. For example, the word *sit* contains the short vowel /ɪ/, while the word *seat* contains its 'long' counterpart /iː/. (Try extending your pronunciation of *sit* – it should sound more like you are pronouncing *seat*.) In very simplified terms, what happened during the Great Vowel Shift was that the way in which people pronounced long vowel sounds altered and the long vowels in English were 'raised'. That is, the position of the tongue during the production of long vowel sounds changed over time so that gradually it moved closer to the roof of the mouth. The Great Vowel Shift thus had a considerable impact on the pronunciation of words and also on spelling, as we will see in A5.1, though it is not the case that every area of the country was affected in the same way.

You can read more about the linguistic complexities of the Great Vowel Shift in B4 and in the reading in D4, but since we are for the moment focusing on the external events that affected the development of English, it is worth considering the role that social factors might have played in causing it. Not surprisingly, this is a complex issue. The causes of the Great Vowel Shift have never been definitively established and there has been a considerable amount of disagreement between scholars. Nevertheless, one view, put forward by the sociolinguist William Labov, is that we can hypothesise about the causes of the Great Vowel Shift based on what we know about the causes of linguistic change in contemporary English. In the mid-1960s Labov carried out a groundbreaking sociolinguistic study of the varieties of English used in New York City (Labov 1966) and concluded that in terms of social groups the main driver of change in language was the middle classes. The British sociolinguist Peter Trudgill came to similar conclusions in his famous study of language use in relation to social class in Norwich (Trudgill 1974). In an article written in 1978, Labov suggests that the same might also have been true in the Early Modern period. The Great Vowel Shift may have been motivated by the merchant classes being influenced by varieties of English that they viewed as being particularly prestigious, and which they then either consciously or (more likely) subconsciously emulated. To understand the theory behind such a hypothesis it is worth quoting at length Labov's outline of the social process of sound change in language:

> A linguistic change begins as a local pattern characteristic of a particular social group, often the result of immigration from another region. It becomes generalized throughout the group, and becomes associated with the social values attributed to that group. It spreads to those neighbouring populations which take the first group as a reference group in one way or another. The opposition of the two linguistic forms continues and often comes to symbolize an opposition of social values. These values may rise to the level of social consciousness and become *stereotypes*, subject to irregular social correction, or they may remain below that level as unconscious *markers*. Finally, one or the other of the two forms wins out. There follows a long period when the disappearing form is heard as archaic, a symbol of a vanished prestige or stigma, and is used as a source of humor until it is extinguished entirely. If the older pronunciation is preserved in place names or fixed forms, it is then heard as a meaningless irregularity.

> (Labov 1978: 280)

Labov's hypothesis is useful in that it provides an external rationale for the sound changes that took place in this period. You can read more about the intralinguistic aspects of the Great Vowel Shift and the processes of internal change by which it occurred in B4.

A4.2 The translation of the Bible into English

One of the events that was to have an impact on the development of English in the Early Modern period was the publication of the Bible in English. In actual fact, there had been a number of translations produced before the definitive King James Bible of 1611, the first of which had been completed in the late Middle Ages. It is worth following the development of the Bible in English in order to assess its impact on English generally.

We have seen that during the Middle English period there were effectively three languages in use in England: French, English and Latin. French was the language of the Royal Court, English the language of the ordinary person in the street, and Latin the language of administration and religion. There was a clear hierarchy associated with the use of these languages. Only the educated would have been able to read and understand Latin and, at the time, being educated largely meant being a member of the clergy. Church services were held entirely in Latin and consequently few people would have had much beyond a surface-level comprehension of what was going on. It is easy to see how, for most people, the images and statues that adorned churches and cathedrals were of far more value in conveying biblical stories than the Bible itself. But the situation changed when John Wycliffe, an Oxford professor, produced an unauthorised translation of the Bible into English between 1380 and 1382. The translation of the Bible into English was to affect the English language in a number of ways over the Early Modern period and to comprehend the changes it is necessary first of all to understand the impact of Wycliffe's translation in the late Middle Ages.

Wycliffe's Bible was distributed around the country by the Lollards, an organisation of itinerant priests. One side-effect of this was an increase in literacy among common people. Literacy was not widespread at the time but people learned to read in order to be able to read Wycliffe's Bible for themselves. Nevertheless, not everyone was pleased by this development, particularly not the Church. In 1382, at Blackfriars in London, Wycliffe was put on trial by a Special Synod. He was found guilty of heresy, a parliamentary ban was imposed on his English translation of the Bible, and the arrest and prosecution of all Lollards was ordered. But this was not to be the end of the Bible in English. By the late 1300s, political events were shaping up that would affect the status of English and once more lead to its being used in the translation of the scriptures.

We have seen how, during the Hundred Years War with France, Henry V began to use English almost as a method of propaganda, for the purpose of establishing a common national identity that was at odds with that of the French. One of the ways in which he did this was to start using English to write his despatches home from his campaigns in France. Previously, these had all been written in French. Increasingly, English began to be used in government, and the fact that it was necessary for civil service documents to be understood as far apart as London and Carlisle was in part what gave rise to the emergence of a standard form of English that superseded rural dialects. The development of Standard English meant that the possibility existed to spread the word of God in English to even more people. The next major breakthrough in doing this came with the setting up of a printing press at Westminster by William Caxton in 1476. (We will explore the role of the printing press in the development of a standard form of English in detail in A5). Mechanising the process of book production meant that more texts could be produced than ever before, and Caxton's printing press also played a part in the eventual standardisation of English spelling. However, English translations of the Bible were still banned by parliament. Many in the upper classes worried about the difficulty of controlling the spread of ideas that the printing press had augmented. It was not until 1525 that someone else proved brave enough to attempt another translation of the Bible. This was William Tyndale.

Tyndale went one step further than Wycliffe by translating the Bible from the original Hebrew and Greek. Tyndale, too, was passionate about his translation. John Foxe, in *Actes and Monuments*, reports a heated argument between Tyndale and 'a learned man', during which Tyndale is reported to have said 'I defie the Pope and all his lawes' and 'if God spare my lyfe ere many yeares, I wyl cause a boye that dryueth þe plough, shall knowe more of the scripture then thou doest' (Foxe 1563: 514). The advent of the printing press meant that multiple copies of Tyndale's translation could be produced for relatively little outlay. Thousands of pocket-sized copies were printed in Cologne and smuggled into England. So fearful was the Church of the potential effects of Tyndale's translation that Henry VIII put the whole country on alert and many of the Bibles were intercepted. The Bishop of London went so far as to buy an entire shipment simply to destroy them. But Tyndale was not to be outdone. Using the profits from the sale of his Bible, he went on to produce an even better translation, this time of the Old Testament as well as the New Testament.

The influence of Tyndale's Bible was tremendous. It triggered the growth of literacy, with people learning to read specifically so that they could study the Bible in English. As Knowles (1997: 96) explains, 'Bible reading would be a strong motivation for learning to read in the first place, since it enabled readers to form opinions independently of the traditional authorities of church and state'. Tyndale's Bible gave us many words and phrases that we still use today.

Nevertheless, despite the reformation pre-empted by Henry VIII having split from the Roman Catholic Church to initiate the Church of England, Tyndale's translation of the Bible was still seen as heretical. In 1536 he was charged with heresy, strangled and then burned at the stake. Tyndale's last words were a prayer – that God might 'open the King of England's eyes'. It might have surprised Tyndale to learn that just three years later the King had indeed changed his mind. By this time, Henry had married his third wife, Jane Seymour, a follower of the new Protestant religion. She was instrumental in persuading Henry that a Bible in English was just what the new religion needed. Consequently, in 1539 Henry ordered the production of the first official English Bible, and every church in England was instructed to buy one. It was this 'Great Bible' (so-called because of its size) that was to be the basis of the King James Bible, or the 'Authorised Version', published in 1611. The writers of this text looked to Tyndale's and Wycliffe's translations in an effort to create the definitive English Bible, and in doing so they were responsible for many of the idiomatic phrases still in use today. Crystal (1995: 64) lists some of these as *to spy out the land* (Numbers 13), *the apple of his eye*

(Deuteronomy 32), *the skin of my teeth* (Job 19), *go from strength to strength* (Psalms 84), *the straight and narrow* (Matthew 7), *the sign of the times* (Matthew 16), *in the twinkling of an eye* (1 Corinthians 15), *filthy lucre* (1 Timothy 3), *rule with a rod of iron* (Revelations 2), and *out of the mouth of babes* (Psalms 8). The real impact of the King James Bible was to make English the language of religion in England. The days of English as a poor relation to Latin and French in terms of prestige were now gone.

The spread of ideas and the impact of the Bible both on literacy and on the development of English generally were greatly affected by the development of a standard form of English. In turn, the production of multiple copies of books reinforced this standard and helped in making it more widely recognised.

THE PROCESS OF STANDARDISATION   A5

The Early Modern period is generally seen as a period in which English underwent a process of standardisation. Of course, it is not the case that with the emergence of a standard form of the language dialect variation was lost. When we talk about Standard English, we are effectively concentrating on a written form of the language.

A5.1 Dialects and emerging standards

In the Old English period West Saxon had developed into a standard form of the language (at least for written literary texts). But for the majority of the Middle English period a standard variety (or even the notion of one) simply did not exist. It was only towards the end of the period that a standard form started to emerge. How this happened has been the subject of much debate by linguists. One early and influential account of this is that by Samuels (1963), who identifies four varieties of English in the fourteenth and fifteenth centuries that exhibit elements of standardisation. Samuels names and describes them as follows:

Type 1: Central Midlands Standard
This is the form of English that is found in those texts produced by the Wycliffite movement, such as the Lollard Bible referred to in A4.2. According to Samuels, 'until 1430, it is the type that has most claim to the title "literary standard"' (Samuels 1963: 85). It eventually died out towards the end of the fifteenth century.

Type 2: Early London English
This was in use up until the late 1300s and included characteristics of East Anglian dialects, suggesting that it was developed at least in part by writers originally from that area of England.

Type 3: London English

This form was in use from around 1380 to around 1425 and includes elements of a Central Midlands dialect. Some versions of *The Canterbury Tales* by the Middle English writer Geoffrey Chaucer are in this dialect, suggesting that this may have been the dialect preferred by him (though we should not discount the role of printers in deciding on the dialect in which a text was published and it is important to bear in mind that the first copies of *The Canterbury Tales* were scribal copies as opposed to printed texts).

Type 4: Chancery Standard

This was used in government documents from around 1430. (The Chancery was a royal court. 'Chancery Standard', therefore, is often used as a shorthand term for the variety preferred by the royal bureaucracy, though the category is perhaps not as distinct as its label would suggest, as we shall see.) It includes characteristics of Midlands and Northern dialects, suggesting that it was not solely a regional dialect from the London area, but that its development was also affected by writers from elsewhere incorporating their own dialect forms into this particular standard.

To illustrate the differences between London English (type 3) and the Chancery Standard (type 4), look at the differences in spelling of the following words (based on Samuels 1963: 89):

Type 3: London English	Type 4: Chancery Standard
nat	not
bot	but
swich(e)	such(e)
thise	thes(e)
thurgh	thorough

You will notice that the Chancery Standard spellings are much closer to (and in some cases, the same as) Present Day English spellings.

However, while it is sometimes claimed that Chancery Standard was deliberately cultivated by the Chancery (see Fisher 1996 for details of this argument), it is important to bear in mind that features associated with Chancery Standard did not necessarily originate from the Chancery itself. Research by Benskin (2004) suggests that Samuels's Type 4, although very common, was not the sole form of government English in use and that so-called Chancery Standard was not the fixed variety linguists have sometimes claimed it to be. As Benskin points out:

> Had Henry V's Signet clerks [Chancery scribes] really been concerned with institutional spelling norms, then the word *England* would surely have been a prime candidate for fixity, whereas their letters show at least seven variants: *Eng(e)lond*, *England(e)*, *Engeland*, *Ingelond*, *Ingeland*.
>
> (Benskin 2004: 21)

One Chancery writer quoted by Benskin (2004: 32) uses forms that are of a north midland variety. These include the spellings *sich* and *syche* (PDE *such*; compare these with Samuels's *suche*), *ich* (PDE *each*), *ony* (PDE *any*) and *mych* (PDE *much*). Another Chancery scribe uses the variants *soche* (PDE *such*), *hafe* (PDE *have*) and *gyf, gyve* and *yif* (PDE *give*), suggestive of a north-west midlands variety. Consequently, says Benskin (2004: 32), 'such cases do little to support the belief that Chancery, as a matter of policy, trained its clerks to write English of a certain type'. As he points out, 'The development of a written standard, even in the offices of government, was more complex and less determined than it has sometimes been made to appear, and government English is not the whole story' (2004: 36). Indeed, as Wright (1994) explains, the Chancery was not the only place in which the conditions necessary for a standard variety to emerge were in place. It seems likely, then, that other institutions than the Chancery would have played their part in the development of Standard English. The reason for this, as Crystal (2005: 232) notes, is that 'material emanating from the civil service, law offices, ecclesiastical bodies and business centres always operates with a rather special cachet'. He goes on to point out that since such material would generally have originated from London, it would be London norms of usage that were gradually spread around the country. To reiterate though, the important point is that not all of these norms would necessarily have originated from the Chancery. The insights of Benskin (2004), Wright (1994) and others (see, for instance, the papers in Wright 2000) challenge Samuels's (1963) original account of the development of a written Standard English, as well as that proposed by Fisher (1996), who argues that Standard English is a direct descendant of Chancery Standard. You can read more about this in B5.

A5.2 Caxton and the impact of the printing press

A key date in the development of a standard form of English is 1476, when William Caxton, an English merchant, set up a printing press at Westminster, now part of Central London. Caxton did not invent the press, nor was he the only printer operating in England at the time, but he had learned about the principles of moveable type while working as a printer in Bruges, Belgium, and quickly realised its business potential. What is significant about Caxton is that, unlike his competitors, he chose to publish books in English. This did much to establish the legitimacy of English as a language of learning (as opposed to Latin) as well as contribute to the development of a standard form, as we shall see. However, standardising the language was not a major concern of Caxton's. Indeed, some scholars (e.g. Scragg 1974: 64) have pointed out that, initially, printing actually caused problems for the establishment of consistency in written English. For example, the variety of different ways in which a word could be spelled was often useful for printers, who would add or subtract a letter in order to ensure that a line of type was justified on both margins. Added to this was the fact that because the technology that Caxton used had been developed abroad, he was forced to rely on the expertise of foreign compositors to operate it. These compositors had no training in English scribal techniques and were not familiar with the consistent spellings that the best of the London scribes (i.e. manuscript copiers) tended to use (Scragg 1974: 66). Consequently, the establishment of the print industry did little to standardise English spelling (at least not initially), never mind any other aspects of the language. Nevertheless, over the course of the sixteenth century consistency became more commonplace for various reasons. Caxton's protégé Wynkyn de Worde, who took over Caxton's press after his death, employed English compositors. And as printing overtook the manuscript industry, the orthographic conventions used by manuscript copyists were gradually transferred to the printing houses. By around 1650, a relatively fixed system of spelling was in use by printers (Scragg 1974: 67).

The impact of the printing press was huge. Mechanising the process of book production meant that more texts could be produced more quickly and for less cost than ever before. This made the rapid spread of ideas possible and the printing press played a huge role in the success of Tyndale's 1525 translation of the Bible into English. The rapid spread of books and pamphlets also meant the spread of the fixed spellings developed by the printing houses. However, it is important to note that this 'standard' was not necessarily a regional dialect. In some cases, the choices made by printers may have been little more than a 'house standard', in much the same way that modern publishers adhere to conventions that are entirely arbitrary – for example, advising authors to use <-ize> rather than <-ise> when spelling words such as *organize*.

A5.3 Dictionaries and grammars

Although throughout the Early Modern period a standard form of English gradually emerged, there were those who felt that a greater hand could be taken in the process of standardisation, and particularly in what was referred to as the 'fixing' of the language. In 1712 Jonathan Swift (the author of the satirical works *A Modest Proposal* and *Gulliver's Travels*) proposed that it would be valuable to 'fix' English, in *A Proposal for Correcting, Improving and Ascertaining the English Tongue*. There is an interesting presupposition here; namely that it is in fact possible to 'fix' a language in the sense of regularising and standardising it. It should be apparent by now that English, like any other language with native speakers, is constantly changing and evolving in response to external and internal stimuli.

Nevertheless, the calls from some quarters for the fixing of the language did at least reflect a growing need for some kind of description and explanation of the English language. English had not always enjoyed the same level of prestige as French or Latin, and because it had been primarily a spoken language during the Old and Middle English periods, no grammar books or guides to its usage had been produced – there had been no need. Now, though, the increase in the number of books in circulation caused by the use of the printing press led to a greater call for dictionaries and grammars of English. People wanted instruction on how to read English so that they could take advantage of the increasing number of texts available. Furthermore, since the Reformation, education was no longer controlled solely by the Church and English had begun to be used in academic circles (previously Latin had been the primary language of education). Consequently, there was a demand for schoolbooks that outlined the workings of English.

The first dictionaries of English were bilingual dictionaries, produced to allow the translation into English of Latin and French texts. Caxton himself produced an English–French dictionary in 1480. The first monolingual dictionary of English appeared in 1604 and was written by Robert Cawdrey. It was called *A Table Alphabeticall* and contained the definitions of around 2,500 words, though, unlike today's dictionaries, Cawdrey's focused entirely on what he called 'hard' words; i.e. he ignored words that he thought his readers were likely to have no problems in understanding. The words that Cawdrey focused on were those that had been borrowed into English from other languages, for example, Greek, Latin and French. It was not until later on that dictionary writers began to extend their remit. In 1691 Stephen Skinner produced *A New English Dictionary* in which so-called 'common' words were defined along with their **etymologies** (i.e. the histories of the individual words; for example, the languages they were derived from, etc.). John Kersey's identically titled dictionary was published in 1702 and contained the definitions of approximately 28,000 'common' words. With the understanding of language and linguistics that we have today, we can see that there are numerous problems with the works of the early dictionary writers; they were, for instance, extremely subjective accounts of the **lexicon** (the vocabulary of a language). Nevertheless, it is important not to be too critical of their efforts. Nowadays we take dictionaries for granted so it is easy to underestimate the enormity of the task that the early scholars set themselves. To produce a dictionary of a language without recourse to computer technology or the wealth of supplementary material that we have at our disposal today is admirable. Rather than be overtly critical of these early texts, we need to understand where their flaws come from. You can explore some of these issues in C4.

Easily the most impressive and most authoritative dictionary produced in the Early Modern period was that published by Samuel Johnson in 1755. Although Johnson realised fairly early on in the project that he had bitten off significantly more than he could chew (he notes in his preface to the dictionary that 'Every other authour [sic] may aspire to praise; the lexicographer can only hope to escape reproach' [Johnson 1755: preface]), it was still an impressive achievement. The dictionary was compiled over a period of nine years and contained definitions of almost 43,000 words. What made Johnson's dictionary especially noteworthy was the fact he used quotations from other texts to illustrate the meaning in context of the words he defined. Johnson also recognised that the changing nature of language meant that it was impossible to produce a dictionary that would be authoritative for all time. In his preface he says: '…no dictionary of a living tongue ever can be perfect since while it is hastening to publication, some words are budding, and some falling away[.]' (Johnson 1755).

As well as dictionaries, the Early Modern period also saw the production of grammar books. Where a dictionary defines the vocabulary of a language, a grammar explains its syntax; i.e. the 'rules' that govern the formation of meaningful sentences in that language. As with the dictionary writers, the writers of grammars were often simply wrong in some of their assertions. You can explore some of their misconceptions in C4. Nevertheless, the efforts of these scholars did much to promote consistency of usage in English (even if this was sometimes based on false premises) and to establish a standard form for written English.

A5.4 The boundaries of Early Modern English

It is perhaps harder to distinguish the boundaries of Early Modern English than it is to discern the points at which Old and Middle English can be said to begin and end. This is perhaps because Early Modern English does not seem so alien to speakers of Present Day English so it is harder to see the major differences between Early Modern English and Present Day English. It is also perhaps because we feel that we know a bit more about the Early Modern English period than earlier periods in history, and so it is harder to identify just one or two events that have affected the development of English. Clearly the Great Vowel Shift was of importance, as was the development of the printing press. The production of dictionaries and grammars also played a part, as did the economic and political climate that caused a standard form of written English to emerge. The point, of course, is that there is hardly ever just one event that causes a change in language. More often than not it is a combination of events, and this is true for all periods of linguistic history. Most historians of English suggest the boundaries of Early Modern English to be roughly 1500 to 1800. By 1500 the printing press would have begun to have some influence and the Great Vowel Shift would have begun to take effect. By 1800, Johnson's dictionary had become famous and the language was beginning to look and sound much more like the English we write and speak today. But, of course, such temporal boundaries are not hard and fast and change in language is happening all the time. For this reason, some linguists prefer to categorise this period of English differently. Barber et al. (2009), for instance, use the term **Modern English** to cover the period 1500 to the present day, subdividing it into Early Modern English (approximately 1500 to 1700) and **Late Modern English** (approximately 1700 to 1900). Late Modern English, they say, is distinguished by the Great Vowel Shift being completed, the loss of verb forms such as *loveth* and *lovest*, the disappearance of *thou* and *thee*, and the rise of the dummy auxiliary verb *do* (Barber et al. 2009: 211; you can explore some of these features in C5). Burnley (1992), on the other hand, designates Early Modern English as 1500 to 1800 and reserves the term **Modern English** for the period 1800 to 1920 (begging the question of how we describe the English of 1921 onwards). It is, of course, impossible to draw absolute boundaries between the periods and labels such as the ones described above are simply a convenience for talking about English's development. One further issue to bear in mind is that while boundary dates often reflect major developments in the standard variety of English, they don't necessarily correspond to developments in the regional dialects of English.

A6 COLONIALISM, IMPERIALISM AND THE SPREAD OF ENGLISH

We have already seen how during earlier periods Britain was effectively a trilingual nation, with English, French (in the form of Anglo-Norman) and Latin having varying degrees of status and being used in particular areas of life. This was in addition to the numerous Celtic languages (e.g. Cornish, Scots Gaelic and Welsh) that would also have been spoken in various parts of the country. So, the idea that languages belong to countries (i.e. English is the language of England, French the language of France, etc.) is a popular misconception. Indeed, English now extends far beyond England and is generally considered to be a global language. It was in the Early Modern period that the spread of English overseas began. This was as a result of **colonisation**, whereby British communities were established beyond the British Isles. These colonies were under the political control of Britain, and constituted part of the **British Empire**. In the reading in D6 you can find out more about this. For instance, colonisation can be achieved either through settlement or exploitation. Needless to say, in the case of the British Empire, both approaches were taken.

A6.1 English in the New World

The English had made a number of attempts to found colonies in America in the late 1500s and early 1600s, with settlements in Newfoundland and in what was later to become North Carolina (Jones 1995: 5). These early attempts failed and it was not until 1607 that a lasting colony was established in Jamestown, Virginia, on the east coast of America. In 1620 a further colony was established in what is now Plymouth, Massachusetts. The Puritan settlers who later became known as the Pilgrim Fathers arrived on the ship *The Mayflower*, fleeing religious persecution in England. These early settlers inevitably brought their own varieties of English to the New World. The Jamestown settlers originated from areas of Gloucestershire and Somerset, while the pilgrims of *The Mayflower* came from areas of the Midlands such as Lincolnshire and Nottinghamshire, as well as London and the surrounding areas of Essex and Kent.

By 1732, 13 British colonies had been established along the east coast of America. The British were not the only ones in the country though. The French had a significant presence in Canada, while the Spanish had settled in Florida. The Dutch had a colony along the eastern seaboard known as New Amsterdam which, when the English wrested control of it in 1664, was renamed New York in reference to the then Duke of York. In addition to settlers from Spain, France, the Netherlands and England, there were also immigrants from Ireland, Scotland and Germany. From 1619, there was also a rapidly increasing number of black African slaves brought to the colonies, initially to work on tobacco plantations. The presence of people from a multitude of backgrounds meant that the colonies were places of great linguistic diversity and it is easy to imagine new varieties of English emerging from the cultural mix.

In 1763, following a series of bloody conflicts, England seized control of Canada and the land east of the Mississippi River, as well as Florida, which Spain relinquished in exchange for Cuba and the Philippines. Britain had become the largest colonial power in the world. Because of the expansion of their American empire, the British quickly found it necessary to reform their colonial system in order to streamline the process of providing effective government and defence (Jones 1995: 37). The measures that were taken in pursuit of this goal (including increases in taxation and customs duties) were factors that contributed to the outbreak of the **American Revolution**, or the **War of Independence (1775–83)**. The war ended in 1783 and the Treaty of Paris recognised the independence of the United States. The first US President, George Washington, took office in 1789, following the ratification of the US constitution.

We have seen how powerful language can be in creating identities, both for individuals and for countries. In the USA, the integration of people from a wide range of backgrounds inevitably led to new forms of English. But moves were also made to actively develop a variety of English that was distinct from the standard form that was emerging in England, and that would demonstrate the uniquely American character of English in the US which would inevitably form some part of the identity of the new country.

What Samuel Johnson had done for the English language in England, **Noah Webster** did for English in America. Webster was born in 1758 and educated at Yale College, graduating in 1778. Following several smaller (though highly influential) works on English, in 1828 Webster published *An American Dictionary of the English Language*, which contained around 70,000 entries. Webster's dictionary had a major influence on American spelling and pronunciation but perhaps more importantly it played a significant role in establishing a linguistic identity for American English. You can explore some of Webster's ideas in more detail in C6.

A6.2 The expansion of the British Empire

Although Britain had lost its American colonies in the American War of Independence, this had done nothing to reduce the status of English as America's unofficial national language. The spread of English was to continue with the expansion of the British Empire into such places as Canada, the Indian subcontinent, Africa and Australasia.

The British position in India had come about as a result of the formation of the **British East India Company** in 1600, for the purposes of trade. The British initially established settlements in the Indian cities of Kolkata, Mumbai and Chennai (though typically they referred to these places using the xenonyms Calcutta, Bombay, and Madras) and ultimately India came under British control. British rule in India (the so-called **Raj**, derived from the Hindi word for 'rule') began in 1765 and lasted until 1947, during which time English was established as the language of administration and education. The universities set up in Kolkata, Mumbai and Chennai would have played a significant role in this, and part of the motivation for the introduction of English into the education system was to produce bilingual speakers who would be able to act as interpreters for the British (Kachru 1984: 355). However, Kachru (1984) explains that English was not necessarily imposed against the will of the local population. In the early years of the British presence in India, some of the local people had specifically asked that English be taught so that they would have 'access to the scientific knowledge of the West' (Kachru 1984: 354). As English became established in India it would also have come into contact with the variety of other languages (e.g. Hindi) and dialects used in the country, leading to spoken forms of English that may have differed substantially from the standard written form of English.

As the British Empire expanded, English also became the official language of administration and government in such places as Malaysia, Singapore and Hong Kong. British colonies were also established in South Africa, East Africa and West Africa. Alongside the standard varieties of English that were in use for official purposes, there also emerged language varieties which sociolinguists call **pidgins**. A pidgin is a language that arises when two or more different speech communities use their respective languages as the basis for a very basic language with a limited set of functions. For example, English-based pidgins were common along the west coast of Africa for the purposes of trade.

As a result of colonisation, English also found its way to Australia and New Zealand. In the case of Australia, the English language arrived when the British established a penal colony at Sydney in 1788. At the time it was felt to be a simple solution to the problem of overcrowding in English prisons. The settlement of New Zealand by the

British occurred later, in 1840. In contrast with Australia, New Zealand was settled as a free colony and attracted immigrants from southern England and from Scotland, many of whom were given assisted passage to help with the cost of the trip. As with the original settlers in the North American colonies, it is easy to imagine how the immigrants' dialects would have mixed and how, consequently, new pronunciations and new vocabulary would have emerged over time. There would also have been a certain amount of contact with the indigenous populations of the countries: Aboriginal Australians in Australia and the Maori in New Zealand. However, because of the differences in lifestyle between the settlers and the indigenous people, not to mention the often racist attitudes that prevailed among the immigrant populations, contact between cultures was limited (Eagleson 1984: 431). Consequently, as Eagleson explains, only a small number of words from the indigenous languages of Australia and New Zealand were borrowed into English.

By the beginning of the nineteenth century, then, English had spread across the globe as a consequence of the expansion of the largest empire ever. In the first half of the twentieth century, though, the British Empire began to decline. Nevertheless, by this time English was well established as a language used far beyond the boundaries of the British Isles. Furthermore, the spread of English would continue throughout the twentieth century and into the twenty-first. However, the mechanism that would turn English into a truly global language was not colonisation but a combination of technology, economics and politics.

MOVES TOWARDS PRESENT DAY ENGLISH   A7

By the beginning of the eighteenth century, English had developed to the stage where a present-day speaker of English would have little or no trouble understanding it. And from our perspective as speakers of twenty-first-century English, the difference between the language now and the language of 100 or even 200 years ago is undoubtedly not so great as the difference between Present Day English and Old English. This does not mean that English has stopped changing though (you can explore some of the ways in which English is continuing to develop in units B7 and C7). As we have seen, language is always in a state of flux. Throughout the nineteenth and twentieth centuries there were major social events that were instrumental in affecting the development of English – and not just the standard variety. What follows is a selection of some of the most significant events to have affected the course of English in Britain during the nineteenth and twentieth centuries (you may well think of more) as well as a summary of some of the developments that took place. In the next unit (A8) we will consider in more detail the current status of English beyond the British Isles.

A7.1 The Industrial Revolution

We have seen that in the Old and Middle English periods regional dialect differences in Britain were much more apparent than they are today. Part of the reason for this is that contact between regional communities was not as common as it is today. The relative isolation of rural communities meant that it was the norm for dialects to develop along different lines. The fact that speakers of these dialects mixed predominantly with other speakers of the same dialect meant that varieties were not exposed to outside influences in anything like the way that they are today. In the nineteenth and twentieth centuries this situation was to change significantly and consequently affect the development of dialects. In Britain, the **Industrial Revolution** was instrumental in causing the movement of people around the country, which led to dialects coming into much greater contact with one another than ever before, with resultant linguistic changes and developments. This had substantial effects on English in the nineteenth and twentieth centuries. Later, this contact between different varieties of English (both in Britain and beyond) would be caused by developments in communication technologies.

The Industrial Revolution began in the late 1700s when inventions such as Richard Arkwright's water frame (a machine for spinning thread, powered by a water wheel) transformed the textile industry in Britain. Almost in tandem with this, the **Enclosure Acts** of the 1700s, which prevented the grazing of animals on common land, had the effect of forcing many families from rural farming backgrounds into the cities in search of work. Almost inevitably, they found themselves working in the factories and mills that had sprung up as a result of the Industrial Revolution. This migration to the cities which continued into the nineteenth and twentieth centuries meant that people would encounter different accents and dialects, which would over time begin to have an effect on their own – perhaps generating new pronunciations and contributing vocabulary items and different grammatical structures. The sociolinguistic concept of **accommodation** is particularly pertinent here, describing as it does the process of unconsciously adjusting your own speech to more closely match that of someone else. The mass movement of people from the countryside to the cities placed them in situations that were ripe for accommodation to take place. Accommodation can affect lexis, pronunciation and stress patterns, and the mixing of dialects that took place in such situations began to blur the traditional boundaries of rural vernaculars, and urban dialect areas arose as a consequence of the new conurbations.

A7.2 The *Oxford English Dictionary*

The codification of English that had begun in the Early Modern period with the publication of grammars and dictionaries has continued right up to the present day. Perhaps because the *Oxford English Dictionary* (**OED**) is now something of an institution, many people are surprised to find that it was not published until relatively recently. Work began on the dictionary in 1882 and it was only in 1928 that the final volume was completed. Since then, there has been a second edition (published in 1989) and an electronic version (1992). Work on a third edition is ongoing, with regular updates published online. The OED was first proposed by the British Philological Society who saw the need for a comprehensive and authoritative dictionary of the English language. The first editor, James Murray, was appointed in 1879 and the project was initially intended to take just ten years. As it was, Murray died before the dictionary was finally completed. What made the OED stand out on its first publication was a combination of its sheer size (ten volumes comprising over 400,000 words) and its comprehensive nature. Each entry contained not just a definition but an **etymology** of the word in question (i.e. an explanation of the word's development over time), a guide to pronunciation, information about **part of speech** (whether the word was a noun, adjective, adverb, etc.), details of when the word was first used and quotations from published sources demonstrating the use of the word in context. The second edition of the dictionary built on this by taking fuller account of the variety of **World Englishes** in existence (e.g. Australian English, Singapore English).

A7.3 A spoken standard

In A5 we looked at the development of written Standard English, but the emergence of a standard accent did not occur in Britain until much later on. It is also the case that the spoken standard that emerged is not nearly as widely used as the written standard; indeed, there may be a case for reconsidering whether the term 'standard' is the best descriptor to apply to the accent.

The spoken variety that was eventually accepted as a standard accent is referred to as **Received Pronunciation** or **RP** ('received' in this case has the sense of 'accepted'). RP was a London accent associated particularly with the educated classes. The term *Received Pronunciation* was coined by the philologist and phonetician A. J. Ellis, in his 1869 book *On Early English Pronunciation*. The term was later popularised by the phonetician Daniel Jones, who used the accent as his model for describing the phonemes of British English speech, and defined the term *Received Pronunciation* more precisely than Ellis in his *English Pronouncing Dictionary* of 1917. The emergence of RP as a standard occurred later than the development of a written standard because the mechanisms by which it could be conveyed were not in place until the nineteenth and twentieth centuries. Whereas the development of written Standard English was greatly affected by the printing press and the ability to produce large quantities of uniform texts, the promotion of a standard spoken variety of English needed a different apparatus of transmission. The first part of this was the **Education Act of 1870**, which made a certain level of education compulsory for all children. Because of this, children were exposed to Standard English to a much greater extent than ever before, since this would be the variety reinforced by schoolteachers. The mixing of the middle classes and the upper classes in public schools also played a part in establishing RP as a standard (indeed, Jones's original term for describing the accent was *Public School Pronunciation*). The prestige associated with it led to many people adapting their own accents (either consciously or subconsciously) in order to avoid the stigma that was increasingly associated with regional pronunciations.

The prestige of RP was given a further boost when it was adopted by the **BBC** (the British Broadcasting Corporation, founded in 1922) in its early years as the accent of choice for its continuity announcers. In this, Jones played a further part, along with another professor of English, Henry Cecil Wyld. Both Jones and Wyld served as members of the BBC's Advisory Committee on Spoken Language, appointed to develop guidelines on pronunciation for BBC announcers. The appeal of RP was its prestige and its lack of association with any particular geographical area. Its use in broadcasting ensured its recognition by the vast majority of the population, though not necessarily its adoption. Part of the issue was that very few people spoke RP as their natural accent. Effectively it was a social accent as opposed to a regional one, and most people would simply not have come into contact with it beyond experiencing it via radio and television. The likelihood of it becoming the most prevalent accent in terms of number of speakers was, therefore, always low. Furthermore, it suffered from its upper-class connotations. During the latter half of the twentieth century attitudes began to change and nowadays it is quite common to hear regional accents used by radio and television presenters (though notice that most of the time the dialect used is Standard English; it is still rare to hear regional dialects).

RP, then, was never the most dominant accent in terms of the number of people who spoke it. It is usually estimated that only around 3% of Britain's population speak RP as a 'natural' accent. In fact, this percentage may now be even lower. If it seems somewhat unusual that we should consider RP to be a standard form of spoken English when it does not reflect how the majority of native speakers actually speak, then we need only consider the extent to which standard written English reflects how the majority of native speakers write. The answer is that it probably doesn't. This is not necessarily because people are unaware of standard forms, but because we all change our usage depending on the situation in which we find ourselves. It would be unusual if you were to write a job application letter in non-Standard English but it would not be at all unusual if you were to send a WhatsApp message or post on Instagram in a non-standard form. The point is that a standard variety does not necessarily equate to what the majority of people actually do most of the time. It is important to remember that language is about more than communication. The variety of English that we use says a lot about our identity. It is not the fact that RP has very few speakers that will result in its decline, but changing attitudes to what its usage connotes. In fact, it is better to speak of RP *developing* than *declining*. Accents, like dialects, change and develop over time and RP is no different. Many sociolinguists (e.g. Altendorf 2003: 163) believe that RP is taking on more and more of the characteristics of **Estuary English**, an urban dialect increasingly common in the south-east of England (see D4.2 for more information).

A7.4 The linguistic consequences of war

The twentieth century saw periods of bloody conflict and these as much as advances in technology and communication affected the development of English. War necessitates invention and one result of this is to contribute new words to the lexicon of a language. The First and Second World Wars did just this for English. Among the many new words (and old words with new meanings) listed by Baugh and Cable (2002) are *blitz, radar, blackout, machine gun, periscope, trench foot, beachhead, landing strip* and *foxhole*. More recent conflicts have added to this vocabulary. Examples include *grunt* as a term for a soldier (coined during the Vietnam War) and *WMD* (weapon of mass destruction), first attested in 1991 and coined during the first Iraq War. In addition to such lexical developments, however, we might also speculate that the large-scale movement of troops would potentially have had some effect on the dialects of individual soldiers as they came into contact with other groups of people who used English differently. This is in much the same way as economic migration during the Industrial Revolution affected rural dialects. Whether such effects were lasting (beyond the borrowing of particular vocabulary items) is more difficult to assess. Nonetheless, the impact of wide-scale troop movement also had a lasting impact on how English is perceived and used in the countries in which troops were stationed. In Japan, for example, as a result of the post-war strength of the US, American English is the dominant variety taught in English as a Foreign Language classes (Fukada 2010).

A7.5 Technology and communication

The nineteenth and twentieth centuries saw a boom in technological innovation. In the area of communication technologies this was to have a major impact on the development of English. 1840 saw the introduction in the UK of the **Uniform Penny Post**, a service which allowed people to post letters for the cost of just one penny (the equivalent of around 40p today). In 1898, this was extended to all countries in the British Empire, under a scheme known as the **Imperial Penny Post**. The system enabled letter-writers to communicate more frequently and more widely than ever before, with all the resultant exposure to new forms (words, spellings, structures) that we would expect of such an innovation. The result of both schemes was a huge increase in the number of personal letters sent.

The first **transatlantic telegraph cable** to work successfully was laid in 1868, allowing the rapid spread of news between Europe and North America. Because the British controlled a significant part of the telegraph network, English was established as a language for international communication.

The development of the **telephone** came shortly after. A patent was awarded to Alexander Graham Bell in 1876, though credit for the actual invention of the telephone remains disputed. Initially the telephone was primarily a communication device used by businesses. Its use in private households only became more common in the early twentieth century, though it was not until as late as the 1980s that the telephone became ubiquitous. A perhaps surprising impact of its invention was that it popularised the use of the word *hello* as a greeting. The *Oxford English Dictionary's* first attestation for *hello* as a greeting is 1853. The practice of saying *hello* when you pick up the phone was introduced by one of Bell's competitors, Thomas Edison. Had Bell had his own way, the standard greeting would have been *Ahoy*!

Radio was a much more pervasive mechanism for the spread of the human voice. Developed in the early years of the nineteenth century, radio came into its own in the twentieth and did much to assist the spread of the English language around the globe, particularly via the BBC's World Service broadcasts. **Television**, of course, had a similar effect. The **internet**, developed in the 1960s as a resource for the US military, was popularised via the **World Wide Web** in the early 1990s, and has been an immensely important vehicle for the development of English into a global language. It is to this latest development that we turn in A8.

GLOBAL ENGLISH AND BEYOND   A8

English has come a long way since its earliest inception in the Anglo-Saxon period. A unique combination of events has over time led to the development of numerous varieties of English and to the diffusion of these worldwide. Estimating the numbers of speakers of English worldwide is fraught with difficulties but even a conservative estimate would put the number of speakers of English as a first language at around 400 million (Crystal 2003), with many hundreds of millions more using it as a second language. English is now spoken in over 130 countries (ethnologue.com/language/eng), with Jenkins (2015:11) estimating around one billion speakers of English as a foreign language. Unsurprisingly, English is commonly referred to as a global language, but what does it mean to say this?

A8.1 English: a global language

We could say that English is now a global language simply by virtue of its being spoken by such a large number of people worldwide. However, while this may well be part of the definition, it is not an entirely satisfactory explanation. After all, there are many hundreds of millions of people who speak some variety of Chinese, yet it is English that is so often cited as *the* global language. Clearly, then, the notion of a global language is much more complex than simply being a language with a lot of speakers. In fact, we have already seen in relation to dialects how particular *varieties* of language become popular, and that is as a result of the relative power of their speakers (see A2.2). As Crystal says, 'Why a language becomes a global language has little to do with the number of people who speak it. It is much more to do with who those speakers are' (Crystal 2003: 57).

Crystal suggests that 'a language achieves a genuinely global status when it develops a special role that is recognized in every country' (2003: 3). For instance, English has been adopted as the official language (i.e. the language of government, law, etc.) of many countries, including, for instance, Ghana, Kiribati, Liberia and Uganda to name but a few. English is also taught as a second and foreign language worldwide. These are major contributory factors to why it is now seen as a global language. Nevertheless, we still need to account for why English has taken on these special functions that Crystal identifies. In part, we have covered some of the reasons already. The development of the British Empire and advances in communication technology have all played their part, as has the economic rise of the US following the Second World War. But to really understand what is meant when we refer to English as a global language, we need to know how all of these issues fit within the concept of globalisation.

Globalisation is a process that can be defined as 'the widening, deepening and speeding-up of worldwide interconnectedness in all aspects of contemporary social life, from the cultural to the criminal, the financial to the spiritual' (Held et al. 1999: 2). What this means is that communities all over the world are now connected to each other in ways that were not possible in the past. For example, I regularly communicate via email with colleagues in other countries and receive replies almost instantaneously – something that would have been impossible not so long ago. Television news provides immediate coverage of events going on in countries many thousands of miles away. It is often said that technology has made the world smaller. In fact, technology has connected what would once have been distant and remote communities and this gives us the illusion that we are physically (and sometimes, perhaps, psychologically) closer to such communities than might once have been the case. Furthermore, this 'connectedness' means that what happens in one area of the globe can have direct consequences for others parts of the world. For instance, a sudden bout of cold weather in the US can lead to an increase in demand for crude oil, with the knock-on effect of fuel prices rising in the UK. All of this happens because of the global connections that are now part of our everyday lives.

Now, if we go back to Held et al.'s (1999) basic definition of globalisation, it will be clear that in addition to the cultural and financial aspects of social life (and so on), there is also a linguistic aspect. And in addition to the worldwide connections that have developed in political and economic terms we can also recognise linguistic connections that have come into being as a result of these other developments. For example, the technological dominance of the US has had a major effect in making English arguably the most dominant language currently found on the World Wide Web. (It is difficult to assess in quantitative terms exactly how many of the billions of web pages out there are in English but a search for almost any term via a search engine such as Google reveals just how prevalent English is in comparison to other languages.) The economic dominance of the US financial markets has led to English being seen by many non-native speakers as a necessary language to learn in order to get a good job. In short, English has attained a level of prestige that makes it a highly influential language. But its influence is not a result of any kind of communicative superiority. Despite what lay opinion sometimes suggests, English is no easier or harder to learn than any other language, nor does it offer any greater communicative possibilities. What can be expressed in one language can also be expressed in another, even if not in exactly the same way. So, the reason that English has attained the level of prestige that it currently has is down to social and political reasons rather than linguistic ones. And it is globalisation, and the role that English-speaking communities have played in instigating this process, that has led to English developing the status that it currently has in the world.

A8.2 Globalisation and changes in English

The previous unit focused on how global events – technological, political, economic and social – have all led to English being seen as a global language. English is increasingly being used throughout the world as a **lingua franca**. A lingua franca is a language that is used for communicative purposes by speakers of different languages, often for very specific purposes such as business, commerce, education, etc. For example, Latin was the lingua franca of medieval Europe for such areas of life as religion and education. But in what ways have these latest global developments started to change English? It is, of course, impossible to make generalisations that are true for all varieties of English everywhere, but we can nevertheless make some observations about how some varieties of English have been or are likely to be affected.

Some aspects of globalisation have been responsible for the spread of Standard English. For example, many international organisations, such as the European Union, NATO (North Atlantic Treaty Organization) and the World Health Organization, have adopted English as an official language (sometimes alongside other official languages). International air travel necessitates a common language for air traffic controllers and that language is English. Electronic communication within the global academic community tends to be in English, as is most published research. In areas like these, Standard English is the norm but even so we might imagine that over time new standards will emerge. It is hard to imagine, for instance, the lasting adherence to entirely arbitrary linguistic 'rules' that advise against ending a sentence with a preposition (a practice that Winston Churchill famously said was something 'up with which I will not put') or splitting the infinitive (e.g. saying 'to quickly type' as opposed to 'to type quickly'). Such rules have no basis in linguistic reality, but more importantly serve no communicative purpose. It is highly likely that in areas such as government and academia we will see the development of a new Standard English. **World Standard English** might avoid the use of idioms (expressions that are common only to some varieties of English) and colloquialisms, and it might utilise particular pronunciations. The important point here is that it is not likely to be an Anglo-centric standard. The notion that English belongs to Britain and America is simply no longer true (if, indeed, it ever was) and we can fully expect to see other communities worldwide exerting an influence on the development of any new standard.

So, the rise of English as a global language may well end up affecting the development of Standard English. Nevertheless, it is highly unlikely to be the case that a World Standard English develops at the expense of regional varieties. In the same way that regional dialects of English are found within Britain, so too is it likely that 'international' dialects will emerge (indeed, there is evidence that this is already happening) as communities forge their own identities and start to use English in slightly different ways in order to achieve this. This might lead to particular grammatical forms emerging, or particular words developing.

In addition to standards and dialects, it is also worth considering the impact that globalisation has had on particular **discourses** of English. You can think of a discourse as the type of language used in a particular domain of life; for example, we can talk about the discourse of law, or the discourse of education. Where once we might have been able to see clear distinctions between particular discourses, now – often as a result of market forces – it is common to see discourses being mixed. So, for example, the discourse of education has (sadly) been infused with elements of a business discourse so that students are often referred to as 'consumers' or 'customers' and they and the people who work in education are referred to as 'stakeholders'. This may not seem like a particularly significant change but when we consider how language shapes our identities, it is easy to see how changing the norms of a particular discourse can lead people to develop new attitudes towards the domain of life that it relates to. If you are no longer a student but a customer, and if education is no longer a process but a product that you buy, does this imply that you are no longer bound to accept uncomplainingly the education that your university provides? The effects of changing discourses are complex and fascinating.

A8.3 Assessing the linguistic impact of historical events

Section A has attempted to provide a very broad outline of some of the non-linguistic events that have had an effect on the development of English from the Anglo-Saxon period to the present day. Needless to say, there are one or two cautionary points that it is worth reiterating. This historical outline, broad as it is, is necessarily selective. It includes those major events that are generally agreed to have been significant in the development of English, but it would not be possible to cover every such event in such a short space. If you go on to do some of the follow-up readings that are suggested elsewhere in the book, you will encounter other such events that you will be able to weave into the rough narrative history of English that section A has attempted to provide. (Indeed, some of these other events are covered in some of the readings in section D.) Another important point to bear in mind when getting to grips with the outline history of English is that not all events affect all *varieties* of English, and even in those cases where an event does impact on the language as a whole, it does not necessarily have the *same* effect on every variety. For example, the Great Vowel Shift did not affect every variety of English in the same way. The Industrial Revolution may well have had an impact on the language use of those people who found themselves migrating from the countryside to the towns, but for those who remained working on the land, the impact on their variety of English would have been much less. Finally, it is important to remember the distinction between written and spoken English. This may sound so obvious as not to be worth stating but it is surprising how often people can confuse the two when considering how particular events have affected the development of English. For instance, while the printing press clearly had a major effect on the emergence of a written standard, its effect on the spoken language was less important. While the world wars may have given rise to lots of new vocabulary that was common in everyday speech, not all of this would necessarily have found its way into written English. Read with a critical eye and when you come across an event that you think is significant in the history of English, before assessing its impact, ask yourself these questions:

❑   Would it have affected spoken English, written English or both?
❑   Would it have affected every variety of English; and if so, would it have affected every variety of English *in the same way?*

Finally, because the broad range of sociopolitical and cultural events in the external history of English can be overwhelming, at the back of this book you will find a time-line of key events. In effect, this forms a summary of section A. You may find this useful to refer to as you read sections B, C and D.

Section B

DEVELOPMENT
A DEVELOPING LANGUAGE

The aim of section B of this book is to give you a sense of what English was like at each of its various stages of development, from Old English to Present Day English, and to examine in more detail some of the linguistic and social elements responsible for the development of English. Clearly, it is not possible within the scope of this book for us to examine every feature of English's development over time, and so we will concentrate particularly on those characteristics of the language that allow us to distinguish it as, say, Old English or Early Modern English. The units presented here introduce some of the major aspects of the linguistic history of English. Once you have an overall picture in place of what English was like at its various stages of development, doing the suggested further reading will allow you to gain a wider knowledge and deeper understanding of these issues. As we look at the various forms of English we will also begin to examine some of the ways in which English has changed over time, something that you can follow up in section C.

Before we begin, however, I want to try and provide an answer to a question that students often ask about the history of English: how do you go about exploring linguistic change? It is all very well to compare a Present Day English text to an Old English text and note the differences but how do we trace the development of the language from its earliest origins to its current incarnation? Doing this involves answering two questions: (i) *how* did the language change and (ii) *why* did it change? It is usually easier to provide an answer to the first question than the second one.

To investigate linguistic change, linguists rely on three types of linguistic evidence: primary data, secondary data and linguistic reconstruction.

Primary data refers to records of actual language use from the time we are interested in. These might be tape recordings of mid-twentieth-century speech, personal letters from the Victorian era or poems from the Anglo-Saxon period. The point is that they show us how people at the time actually used language. For example, tape-recordings of mid-twentieth-century speech might expose differences between how words were stressed then and now; Victorian personal letters might offer insights into differences of syntactic structure; Old English poems might reveal semantic differences in vocabulary items. Of course, we have to be careful how we use primary data. One particular issue concerns genre. If we want to track the historical development of a particular linguistic feature with any confidence, we need to make sure that we are tracking its use in texts of the same type. Exploring the development of syntactic structures by comparing, say, Middle English legal texts (such as laws) and Early Modern English personal letters would not make much sense, for instance. This is because we would not know whether any differences we identified were really a result of historical change or simply a result of legal texts having different characteristics to personal letters. That is, genre is a variable (i.e. something that has the capacity to cause a linguistic difference) and to be confident in our results we need to ensure that we control it.

Secondary data refers to contemporary commentaries on language use. For example, dictionaries, grammar books and style guides all constitute secondary data, since they provide an insight into what people thought the language was like at that point in time. In George Puttenham's *The Art of English Poesie* (1589), for instance, the author makes the point that the sign of a bad poet is one who fails to choose words that properly rhyme. Puttenham says the following, by way of explanation:

> …as for example, if one should rime to this word [*Restore*] he may not match him with [*Doore*] or [*Poore*] for neither of both are of like terminant, either by good orthography or in naturall sound, therfore such rime is strained[.]
>
> (Puttenham 1589: 67)

Essentially, what Puttenham is telling us here is that in 1589, in his accent at least, the words *door* and *poor* did not rhyme with the word *restore*. This fact, combined with the double <o> in *door* and *poor*, suggests that in Early Modern English, the pronunciations /dʊə/ and /pʊə/ were common. (Note that some people still pronounce *door* and *poor* like this; we have to be careful when tracing the history of English not to assume that all varieties of the language develop in the same way). Secondary data can also reveal people's attitudes to language. You can find out more about this in the exercises in C4. Secondary data, then, are best thought of as conscious commentaries on language, while primary data are instances of its unconscious use.

The problem with relying on primary and secondary data is that the further back in time we go, the fewer examples of these we find. What we know about Old English, for example, is based on just three million words of primary data that have survived from the Anglo-Saxon period. For this reason, linguists are often forced to rely on **linguistic reconstruction**. This involves making educated guesses as to what the language was like at an earlier stage in its history, based on indirect evidence. For example, the Celtic word for Britain, **Pritanī* (see A1.1), is a linguistic reconstruction based on our knowledge of the languages that developed from Celtic. The Welsh word for Britain, for instance, is *Prydain*, and since Welsh is a descendant of Celtic we can assume that the Celtic word began with a /p/ rather than a /b/.

In addition to linguistic evidence from primary and secondary data and reconstruction, linguists can also consider non-textual evidence. Perhaps the most important is place names (see C2.2), which can sometimes be indicative of the origins of particular dialects. Crowley (1986: 104) explains that in the case of English they are important because 'they provide precisely localised phonological and lexical elements'. That is, variants of particular place name elements can indicate isoglosses, effectively demarcating earlier dialect boundaries. In addition to place names, Crowley (1986) also notes that in defining Old English dialects, inscriptions, such as those on the Ruthwell Cross and the Franks Casket (respectively, a stone Anglo-Saxon cross and a small whale's bone chest, both dating from the eighth century), and on coins, can also be of use. However, they are much less reliable as sources of information than textual data and can be used as supplementary evidence only.

As well as drawing on the types of evidence described above, historical linguists nowadays also make considerable use of the methodological techniques of corpus linguistics. Corpus linguistics is best thought of as a methodology for studying vast quantities of language data. Corpus linguistic software has allowed linguists to identify changes in the English language that would otherwise have been impossible to discover. For example, by searching corpora of 1960s and 1990s English, Leech and Smith (2006) show how the English modal verbs (*will, would, can, could, may, might, shall, should, must* and *ought to*) have been declining in usage significantly since the 1960s. You can read more about corpus linguistics in D7.1.

These then are the core types of evidence and methods used in the study of the history of English.

UNDERSTANDING OLD ENGLISH   B1

Old English (OE) is very different from the English that we speak and write today. It is not possible in the limited space available to teach you how to speak, write and understand Old English fully, though if you want to be able to do this well, there are plenty of excellent introductory books that will help you (some of these are listed in the Further Reading section at the back of the book). Fortunately, you do not need to be fluent in Old English to be able to grasp some of the main differences between Old English and Present Day English. The aim of units B1 and B2 is to make clear what some of these differences are and to give you a sense of what Old English is like as a language. In doing this, I may sometimes have made things appear simpler than they actually are. For example, there are more nuances to Old English pronunciation than the tables in B1.1 might appear to suggest. For the moment, this doesn't matter. My aim here is to give you a quick introduction to the basics of Old English. When you are comfortable with this, you can explore the language in more detail by consulting more advanced and specialist textbooks.

B1.1 Spelling and sound in Old English

Knowing how to pronounce Old English will sometimes help you to work out what a particular Old English word means. A word may look unrecognisable but may sound very similar to a modern English equivalent. Or, at the very least, it may remind you of a modern English word with which you are familiar. For example, if we pronounce the word *Angelcynn* as it would have been pronounced in the Anglo-Saxon period, we get a clue as to its meaning. You may be tempted to pronounce the first part of the word as the Present Day English *angel* (i.e. winged heavenly creature) but if I tell you that

Table B1.1.1 Old English graphs and associated pronunciations (based on Quirk et al. 1975: 10–11)

OE graph	Pronunciation	IPA symbol
ā	as in the <a> in *rather*	/aː/
æ	as in the <a> in *cat*	/æ/
ǣ	as in the French *bête*	/ɛː/
e	as in the <e> in *bed*	/ɛ/
ē	a longer form of <e> (say *bed* but extend the vowel sound)	/e/
i	as in the <i> in *win*	/ɪ/
ī	as in the <ee> in *deed*	/iː/
o	as in the <o> in *hot*	/ɒ/
ō	a longer form of <o> (say *hot* but extend the vowel sound)	/oː/
u	as in the <u> in *full*	/ʊ/
ū	as in the <oo> in *pool*	/uː/
y	try saying the <i> in *sit* but with your lips pursed; this sound is also similar to the <u> in French *tu*	/y/
ȳ	the same as the above but try extending the vowel sound	/yː/

the <g> is pronounced roughly as in *go* then you get a pronunciation that sounds like *angle* rather than *angel*. Now recall that in A1.3 we saw that one of the earliest tribes of settlers in Britain was the Angles, from whom the country name *England* developed. Knowing this, it seems plausible that the first part of *angelcynn* refers to the Angles – or the English. The second part of the word – *cynn* – may look rather less familiar. But again, if you know that the <c> is pronounced as it would be in the Present Day English word *cake*, and that the <y> is a vowel sound pronounced somewhere between <i> /ɪ/ and <u> /ʊ/, then the pronunciation of *cynn* may remind you of the perhaps more familiar word *kin*. *Kin* is now a somewhat archaic word but you will perhaps at least know that it refers to people (as in the phrases 'kith and kin' and 'next of kin'). If you do, then it is not difficult to work out that *angelcynn* refers to 'English people'. It is therefore worth investing a bit of time and effort in learning how to pronounce Old English.

In order to pronounce Old English words you need to know what sounds the individual letters of the Old English alphabet represented (see Table B1.1.1). You will recognise many of the letters because, following the introduction of Christianity, Anglo-Saxon scribes adopted the Roman alphabet that we still use today. You will also find that the sounds associated with the letters of the Old English alphabet have not changed much over the years. However, a few of the letters are different and have sounds that you might not expect and you will need to watch out for these. Below is a list of the letters that represented Old English vowel sounds, along with an indication of their pronunciation. In the tables that follow you will find the terms **grapheme**, **graph** and **digraph** rather than *letter*. This is because some sounds need more than one letter in order to be represented visually. The term **grapheme** refers to the symbol or symbols used to represent a particular **phoneme** (a phoneme is the smallest unit of speech; words are made up of combinations of phonemes). There are different sub-types of grapheme. A **graph** is one letter that represents one phoneme; e.g. the graph <m> represents the phoneme /m/. A **digraph** is a two-letter combination that represents one phoneme; e.g. the digraph <sc> represents the phoneme /ʃ/ in Old English. For those of you who are familiar with phonemic transcription, I have

Table B1.1.2 Old English digraphs and associated pronunciations (based on Quirk et al. 1975: 10–11)

OE digraph	Pronunciation	IPA symbol
ea	The symbol /ə/, found in the transcriptions on the right,	/æə/
ēa	represents a phoneme called schwa. It is the vowel sound	/ɛːə/
	at the beginning of the word *about* and at the end of the	
eo	word *sofa*. To pronounce the digraphs in the left-hand	/eə/
ēo	column, combine the pronunciation of the IPA symbols on	/eːə/
	the right.	

included the relevant IPA symbol. (The IPA is the International Phonetic Alphabet, a system of symbols for transcribing sounds; you can find a list of the phonetic symbols of Present Day Southern Standard British English at the front of this book). If you want to know more about the IPA, try reading unit A2 of Stockwell's (2007) *Sociolinguistics* book in this series, or, for a more in-depth introduction, Collins et al.'s (2019) *Practical English Phonetics and Phonology*, also part of this series. (NB: The horizontal lines above some of the graphemes in the following tables are called **macrons** and would not have been used by Anglo-Saxon scribes. They are used here as an aid to pronunciation by indicating vowel length).

Old English vowel sounds

You will notice that many of the vowel sounds are similar to modern English (especially if you are a native speaker of English who has a northern English accent!). The only really tricky ones are the sounds associated with <y> and <ȳ>, which do not have a real equivalent in Present Day English. Just remember that <y> and <ȳ> always represent vowel sounds, not consonant sounds. In addition to the vowel sounds listed above, you will also come across **diphthongs**. A diphthong is a combination of two vowel sounds that, when glided together, form a new sound. For example, if you take the vowel sound in *cat* /æ/ and run it together with the vowel sound in *put* /ʊ/ you will get the vowel sound in *south* /aʊ/. Try saying the vowel sound in *south* slowly and see if you can hear the two individual vowel sounds. The graphemes that represent diphthongs in Old English are shown in Table B1.1.2.

Now let's turn to the consonant sounds.

Old English consonant sounds

As with the vowels, many Old English consonants have the same phonemic value as in Present Day English. Table B1.1.3 shows the ones that differ significantly, and the digraphs that represent these sounds, plus those no longer used in Present Day English.

You will see from the tables that Old English made use of some letters that we no longer have in Present Day English. These are <æ> (ash), <þ> (thorn) and <ð> (eth). Additionally, although <w> was pronounced as it is in Present Day English, it was represented by the character <ρ> (wynn). The use of these additional letters and the digraphs of Old English was motivated by the fact that the Roman alphabet did not have enough letters to represent the variety of sounds in Old English. When you have

Table B1.1.3 Old English graphemes and associated pronunciations (based on Quirk et al. 1975: 10–11)

OE grapheme	Pronunciation	IPA symbol
c	usually pronounced as the <k> in *king* but as the <ch> in *<church>* when between or after vowels	/k/ or /tʃ/
f	as the <v> in *van* when between vowels or other voiced sounds, but as the <f> in *four* when at the beginning or end of a word	/v/ or /f/
g (sometimes written as ȝ)	usually pronounced as the <g> in *gold* but as the <y> in *yet* when between or after vowels	/g/ or /j/
h	as the <h> in *hand* when at the beginning of the word but as the <ch> in *loch* when in a medial or final position	/h/ or /x/
s	as the <z> in *snooze* when between vowels or other voiced sounds but as the <s> in *seven* when at the beginning or end of a word	/z/ or /s/
þ or ð (these letters were used interchangeably by most scribes)	as the <th> in *clothe* when between vowels or other voiced sounds but as the <th> in *thin* when at the beginning or end of a word	/ð/ and /θ/
sc	as in the <sh> in *ship*	/ʃ/
cg	as in the <dg> in *ledge*	/dʒ/

familiarised yourself with the letters and sounds in the tables above, practise your pronunciation by trying the exercises in C1.3.

B1.2 The vocabulary of Old English

Present Day English has borrowed vocabulary from many of the world's languages. Think about words like *chauffeur*, *government*, *gâteau* and *salary* from French; *pasta*, *balcony*, *ghetto* and *umbrella* from Italian; *wok* from Chinese; *rucksack* from German; and *coach* from Hungarian. Sometimes words come directly from one language or sometimes via another. *Coach*, for example, while ultimately from Hungarian, was borrowed into English from French. Once a word has been borrowed it becomes absorbed into the language to such an extent that we no longer see it as 'foreign'. In contrast, Old English contained far fewer borrowed words (though Latin was one source language) and was made up of predominantly Germanic vocabulary. Some Old English words are instantly recognisable and are still used in Present Day English, even if our modern spellings are sometimes slightly different. Examples include *gold* ('gold'), *saga* ('story' or 'narrative'), *candel* ('candle'), *ripe* ('ripe' or 'mature'), *stenc* ('stench' or 'stink') and *hunig* ('honey'). And some Old English words survive only in regional dialects of Present Day English; e.g. *nesh* ('afraid of the cold') in Northern English (from the OE *hnesc*); *whelp* ('puppy') in the north-east and north-west (from OE *hwelp*) and *oxter* ('armpit') in Present Day Broad Scots (from OE *ōhsta*).

Sometimes, though, what looks like a familiar word means something quite different in Old English. The word *drēam*, for instance, does not mean 'dream' but 'joy', 'melody' or 'music'. The word *grin* refers to a region of the groin rather than a smile, *þyncan* means 'to seem' not 'to think' and *sellan* is 'to give' not 'to sell'.

Old English made great use of **compounding** to form new words. This is the practice of putting two (or more) words together to form a new word. So, the word *sæ* ('sea') could be compounded with *grund* ('ground') to form *sægrund* ('seaground'; i.e. 'seabed'). *Eorðe* ('soil' or 'earth') could be added to *ærn* (meaning 'dwelling' or 'store') to form *eorðeærn* ('earth-dwelling' or 'grave'). The word *drēam* could be compounded with *cræft* (an 'art', 'skill' or 'science') to form *drēamcræft* ('the art of making music'). Similarly, *stæfcræft,* made up of *stæf* (meaning both 'stick' and 'letter') and *cræft* forms a compound noun that means 'grammar' ('the craft/science of letters'). Notice that in Present Day English we have replaced many of these compounds with words borrowed from other languages. Having a grasp of Old English vocabulary is as important as understanding its grammar. Indeed, Mitchell (1995) suggests that vocabulary is even more important than grammar in understanding Old English texts. You can find out more about Old English vocabulary in the reading in D1.1.

B1.3 Old English: a synthetic language

The main difference between Old English and Present Day English is that Old English is a **synthetic** (or **inflectional**) language whereas Present Day English is an **analytic** (or **isolating**) language. An analytic language is one in which the grammatical function of the words and phrases in a sentence (i.e. the 'job' that they do in the sentence) is indicated by the order in which they appear. For example, consider the following simple sentence:

1.   Oswyn shot Sigbert.

In this sentence, it is clear from the word order that Oswyn is the one who did the shooting and Sigbert is the person who was shot. In grammatical terms, Oswyn is the **subject** of the sentence and Sigbert is the **object** (the verb in this example indicates the action). If we reverse the sentence, we get a very different meaning:

2.   Sigbert shot Oswyn.

In this sentence, the change in word order signals a change in meaning. This time, Sigbert is the subject and Oswyn is the object. This is how the grammatical function of words in a sentence is conveyed in an analytic language. However, Old English is a synthetic language that marks grammatical function in a different way: the primary means of conveying the grammatical function of a word is by adding an ending to it. This ending is called an **inflection**. For example, imagine that Present Day English is not an analytic language but is, instead, a synthetic one. And let us imagine that the way the subject of a sentence is marked is by adding an <x> to the end of the word, and the way objects are marked is by adding a <z> to the end of the word. If this were the case, we would not need to put the words in the sentence in a particular order, as it would be clear from the inflection what job the word was doing in the sentence. For example:

3.   Shot Oswynx Sigbertz.

Here it is quite clear that Oswyn is the person who did the shooting because the word 'Oswyn' has the inflection <x>, which we have decided indicates the subject of the sentence. And it is equally clear that Sigbert is the person who was shot because the word 'Sigbert' has the inflection <z>, which we know marks the object of the sentence. Because we have these inflections, it is less important what order we put the words in. Providing they have an inflection, it will always be clear which is the subject of the verb and which is the object. For example, sentence (4) means exactly the same as sentence (3):

4.   Sigbertz shot Oswynx.

B1.4 Case, gender and number

In Old English, the grammatical function of nouns was indicated by an inflection on the noun in question. Inflections on nouns are sometimes called **case endings**. You may be familiar with case if you have studied a language such as German or Russian. In Old English, words that are the subject of a sentence are said to be in the **nominative case**. Words that are the direct object of a sentence are said to be in the **accusative case**. You can see how this works in Old English by considering the following (made-up) sentence:

5.   se wita hilpð þone bodan (The wise man helps the messenger.)

In the above example, the <a> ending marks the subject of the sentence and the <an> ending marks the object of the sentence. Hence, <a> is a **nominative case ending** or **nominative inflection** and <an> is an **accusative case ending** or **accusative inflection**. You will also notice that in the above example there are two different forms of the determiner (*the*). *Se* is the nominative form and *þone* is the accusative form. If a noun is in the nominative case then it must have the nominative form of the determiner in front of it. And if the noun is in the accusative case then it must be preceded by the accusative form of *the*. Because the information about the grammatical role of the nouns in the sentence is encoded in the noun itself and its accompanying determiner, we could alter the word order of our example sentence but retain the same meaning. So, sentences (5) and (6) mean exactly the same thing.

5.   se wita hilpð þone bodan (The wise man helps the messenger.)
6.   þone bodan hilpð se wita (The wise man helps the messenger.)

As well as being marked for grammatical function, in Old English words were also marked for gender. (You may be familiar with the concept of grammatical gender if you have studied a foreign language such as French or German.) The genders in Old English were **masculine, feminine** and **neuter**. In sentences (1) and (2), both the nouns are masculine and therefore are preceded by masculine forms of the determiner. If we change our example sentences slightly to include a feminine noun, then we also need to change the form of the article that goes before it:

7.   se cnapa lufode þā hlǣfdigan (The servant loved the mistress.)
8.   seō hlǣfdige lufode þone cnapan (The mistress loved the servant.)

In sentences (7) and (8) you can see that the form of the word *hlǣfdige* changes according to whether it is in the subject or object position (the <e> ending marks the nominative case and the <an> ending indicates the accusative). And because *hlǣfdige* is feminine, it has a feminine form of the determiner before it (*seō* if *hlǣfdige* is the subject and *þā* if it is the object).

Not all Old English nouns, though, have a different case ending for both the nominative and accusative. Consider example (9):

9. se cyning hilpð þone æðeling ('The king helps the prince.')

If we now make 'the prince' the subject of the sentence and 'the king' the object, we get the following:

10. þone cyning hilpð se æðeling.

If you compare (10) with (9) you will notice that *cyning* and *æðeling* have the same form in both the nominative and the accusative. In this instance, we have to rely on the determiners to tell us which is the subject and which the object. As you can imagine, as English developed and the case system started to break down, word order became ever more important.

So far we've looked at fairly simple examples. But there are more cases in Old English than nominative and accusative and so – surprise, surprise – Old English is more complicated than the examples above might suggest. The other cases are the **genitive case** and the **dative case**.

The **genitive case** indicates possession. In Present Day English we can indicate possession in various ways. We can use either a possessive pronoun (e.g. *his* or *her*) or an apostrophe followed by an <s> on the end of the noun; for example, *Dan's book*. Old English has possessive pronouns like Present Day English does but if we want to make a noun possessive in Old English then we need to add a specific genitive inflection. In the same way that the nominative and accusative cases are indicated with nominative and accusative inflections, the genitive case is indicated by a genitive inflection on the noun. Similarly, if a noun is in the genitive case and it is preceded by a determiner, we need to use the genitive form of that determiner. Consider example (11):

11. þæs mannes hund ('The man's dog.')

Here the genitive inflection <es> has been added to the noun *mann*, to indicate that this noun is in the genitive case, and the genitive form of the determiner – *þæs* – precedes it. The Present Day English word *Christmas* derives from the Old English form *Cristesmæsse* ('Christ's mass'), in which <es> is a genitive inflection that over the years people have stopped pronouncing (presumably because it is not a stressed syllable).

The **dative case** typically indicates the indirect object in a sentence. Here's an example of a sentence with an indirect object:

12.	The crusty old professor	gave	the students	a dull lecture
	subject	*verb*	*indirect object*	*direct object*

In example (12) there are two objects. The direct object is 'a dull lecture' (i.e. the 'thing' that is 'given') and 'the students' is the indirect object. There is a simple test you can do to decide which is the direct and which is the indirect object. You can put a preposition in front of the indirect object but you can't put one in front of the direct object:

13. The crusty old professor gave to the students a dull lecture.
14. *The crusty old professor gave the students to a dull lecture.

In Old English, indirect objects were in the dative case and, as with the nominative, accusative and genitive cases, there was a specific case ending to indicate this.

Finally, there was another element to Old English grammar that could affect the form of a word. This is **number.** This refers to whether a word is singular or plural (a distinction, of course, which remains in Present Day English). Unsurprisingly, the form of a word could differ depending on whether it was singular or plural. And, of course, the singular or plural inflection used would depend on the case and gender of the word in question, e.g.

15. seō hlǣfdige lufode þone cyning (The mistress loved the king.)
16. seō hlǣfdige lufode þā cyningas (The mistress loved the kings.)

B1.5 Old English verbs

Just as nouns in Old English inflect for case, gender and number, verbs inflect to mark person and tense.

In Present Day English, the only inflection for person is on the third-person singular form of the verb; for example, we say *I walk* but *he walks*. The irregular verb *to be* is an exception, with different forms for the first-person singular (*am*), second-person singular (*are*) and third-person singular (*is*). The origins of these inflections lie in Old English, which made use of different forms of the verb to mark person. For example, *ic singe* ('I sing'), *þu singest* ('you sing') and *hēo singeþ* ('she sings'). The third-person *eþ* form was common in southern dialects, eventually giving way to the northern <es> ending that survives in Present Day English. The second-person <est> inflection survived into Early Modern English but then fell out of usage (see B5.2).

To form the past tense form and past participle of most verbs in Present Day English, we simply add an inflectional ending <ed> (as in *walk/walked*). (The past participle is the form of the verb that is used after the auxiliary verbs *be* and *have*; see Table B1.5.1 for examples.) But notice that to form the past tense of a verb like *sing*, we don't add an inflectional ending. Instead we change the vowel – the past tense of *sing* is *sang*. In grammatical terms, *sing* is a strong verb while *walk* is a weak verb. Table B1.5.1 shows some more examples of weak and strong verbs in Present Day English.

As you will notice from Table B1.5.1, weak verbs form their past tense and past participle by the addition of an inflectional ending (notice that in speech this is pronounced either as /t/ or /d/). Strong verbs, on the other hand, inflect in a different way. To form the past tense of a strong verb, the vowel of the present tense form is changed. To form the past participle of a strong verb, either the vowel of the present tense form is changed or <en> is added.

You have already encountered some Old English verbs in the example sentences in B1.4. As in Present Day English, verbs in Old English were either weak or strong. However, there were more strong verbs in Old English than in Present Day English. Over time, many of these became weak through a process of regularisation.

Table B1.5.1 Weak (regular) and strong (irregular) verbs in Present Day English

Weak verbs			Strong verbs		
Present	Past	Past participle	Present	Past	Past participle
I *walk* to work.	I *walked* to work.	I have *walked* to work	We *eat* too much.	We *ate* too much.	We have *eaten* too much.
She *laughs* a lot.	She *laughed* a lot.	She had *laughed* a lot.	He *drinks* too much.	He *drank* too much.	He had *drunk* too much.
They *borrow* money constantly.	They *borrowed* money constantly.	They have *borrowed* money constantly.	You *sing* beautifully.	You *sang* a beautiful song.	You have *sung* beautifully.

VARIETIES OF OLD ENGLISH

In Present Day English we are used to the concept of different varieties of English. Some are regional (e.g. the Black Country dialect of the midlands of England, the Lancashire dialect, etc.) while some are national (e.g. American English, Singapore English, etc.). Perhaps because of the relative sparsity of Anglo-Saxon texts, it is sometimes easy to view Old English as one homogenous language. However, we need to be aware that in the Anglo-Saxon period, too, different varieties of English were used.

B2.1 Old English and Scots

In discussing the notion of Old English being used in Scotland, we need to add the qualification that in the Anglo-Saxon period there was little sense of English as a unified language. What we are really talking about is the extent to which a particular variety of Old English extended into Scotland.

We saw in A1.1 that the Scots were originally from Ireland and settled in what is now Scotland around 500 CE. Also present in Scotland at this time were the Picts, and it was not until 843 that Scottish and Pictish dominions were united by Kenneth MacAlpin, the first king of the Scots (Bugaj 2004: 25). As the language of the Picts gradually died out, the predominant language in Scotland became the Celtic language **Gaelic**. However, the Anglo-Saxon kingdom of Northumbria extended into the eastern lowlands of what is now Scotland, and so the Old English Northumbrian dialect would also have been common on the English–Scottish border. Bugaj (2004: 27) points out that the Viking raids of the ninth century in which Northumbrian settlements were attacked led eventually to the Northumbrian dialect being influenced by the Scandinavian dialects of the aggressors. A Scottish dialect of English emerged in the Middle English period, during the reign of Malcolm III of Scotland (1058–93) who used English as opposed to Gaelic as the language of his royal court, and whose wife, Margaret, was the great-niece of Edward the Confessor. Consequently, Gaelic never achieved the prestigious position it would have needed to survive as the language of Scotland. The importance of considering dialectal variety in the Old English period can be seen when we consider that contemporary Scots, 'a language continuum that ranges from "broad" Scots to "Scottish Standard English"' (Corbett et al. 2003: 1), developed ultimately from Anglian rather than Saxon varieties of Old English, which accounts for why Scots differs from Present Day English (Corbett et al. 2003: 4).

B2.2 Old English dialectal differences

You will have seen from B1.3 and B1.4 that Old English was relatively free in terms of word order. It should not be too surprising to learn, then, that most of the dialectal differences that can be noticed in Old English concern the sound of the particular variety in question (Marckwardt and Rosier 1972). Understanding these dialectal differences fully requires an in-depth knowledge of phonology. Nonetheless, it is possible to grasp some of the differences without too much difficulty if we concentrate on some straightforward examples.

An example of the kind of dialectal difference we encounter in Old English is that words which begin with an initial palatal consonant (a consonant produced using the palate – i.e. the roof of your mouth – as an articulator), such as /g/ or /k/, are followed by diphthongs in West Saxon but by **monophthongs** ('pure vowels') in other dialects. For example, West Saxon *giefan* ('to give') and *ceaster* ('castle') were *gefan* and *cæster* in Kentish, Mercian and Northumbrian (Marckwardt and Rosier 1972: 178). Marckwardt and Rosier (1972) also point out that some sound changes between the dialects affected the inflectional system of Old English. So, the fact that final <n> tended not to be pronounced in Northumbrian (unlike in West Saxon) may well have led to the impression of inflections not being present on particular words (as opposed to their being present, just not enunciated). Considering dialectal differences, then, can help in explaining long-term developments in the language.

One way of investigating dialectal differences is to compare texts which exist in more than one dialect. One such example is *Cædmon's Hymn*. In his *Ecclesiastical History of the English People*, Bede describes how Cædmon, a layman who worked on the estates of the Abbey of Whitby, in what was then Northumbria, was given the gift of poetry by God. The story goes that Cædmon left a feast early because he felt he would be unable to sing and entertain the assembled guests when his turn to do so came. He was subsequently visited in a dream by an angel who commanded him to sing about the creation of the world. Cædmon then found that he was able to sing beautiful poetry in praise of God. After telling the abbess of his new-found ability, Cædmon entered monastic life and became famed for his religious poems. *Cædmon's Hymn* is all that remains of Cædmon's work but what makes it especially interesting for historical linguists is that it exists in both the Northumbrian and West Saxon dialects. Here are the two versions, followed by a translation into Present Day English (the Old English versions are taken from Smith (1933) though I have removed punctuation that would not have been present in the original manuscripts):

> ### *Cædmon's Hymn* (West Saxon)
> Nu þe sculan herian heofonrices þeard
> metudes myhte his modȝeþanc

þurc þuldorfæder spa he þundra ȝehþilc
ece drihten ord astealde
he ærest ȝesceop ylda bearnum
heofon to hrofe haliȝ scyppend
middanȝearde mancynnes þeard
ece drihten æfter tida
firum on foldum frea ælmyhtiȝ

Cædmon's Hymn (Northumbrian)

Nu scylun herȝan hefaenricaes uard
metudæs maecti end his modȝidanc
uerc uuldurfadur sue he uundra ȝehuaes
eci dryctin or astelidæ
he aerist scop aelda barnum
heben til hrofe haleȝ scepen
tha middunȝeard moncynnæs uard
eci dryctin æfter tiadæ
firum foldu frea allmectiȝ

Cædmon's Hymn (Present Day English)

Now must we praise of heaven's kingdom the Keeper
Of the Lord the power and his wisdom
The work of the Glory-Father as he of marvels each
The eternal Lord the beginning established
He first created the earth for the sons [of men]
Heaven as a roof the holy Creator
Then the middle-enclosure of mankind the protector
The eternal Lord thereafter made
For men, earth the Lord almighty
                    (translation by Trapp et al. 2002: 2)

There are a number of observations we can make about dialect as a result of looking at the two different versions of the text above. At a very basic level, for instance, the different spellings suggest different pronunciations. We can note, for example, the tendency for diphthongs to be used in West Saxon where monophthongs are preferred in Northumbrian. Examples are *þeard/uard*, *bearnum/barnum*, *ȝesceop/scop* and *heofonrices/hefaenricaes*. In the West Saxon version we find the grapheme <þ> (sometimes replaced by <w> in modernised versions) where in the Northumbrian text we find <u> *or* <uu> (literally, double-u). And it would appear that in Northumbrian, <c> is used before <t> while in West Saxon it is <h>. We can also see in the Northumbrian text the origins of some present-day dialectal features. *Bearnum*, for instance, is the ancestor of the Present Day Scots *bairn* (child). The Northumbrian dialect contributed much to the development of Scots, which is just one reason why an awareness of dialectal variation is important if we are to account for the development of English over time. You can examine for yourself some of the other dialectal features of Northumbrian and West Saxon in C2, where you can also explore what place names can tell us about the Old English dialects.

B3 THE EMERGENCE OF MIDDLE ENGLISH

Units B1 and B2 should have given you some idea of what Old English was like as a language. They do not tell the full story, obviously, and to find out more about Old English you should do the follow-up readings in D1 and D2. Nevertheless, you should at this stage have enough of an awareness of Old English to be able to understand some of the changes that occurred in the Middle English period and afterwards. In this unit we will focus on the emergence of Middle English (ME), looking at what it was like, how it differed from Old English and what caused the changes that occurred between Old English and Middle English.

Linguists often divide up the Middle English period into Early Middle English (EME) (approximately 1100–1300) and Late Middle English (LME) (approximately 1300–1500). There are various reasons why this division is made. One reason is that in the second half of the Middle English period substantially more words were borrowed from French. Baugh and Cable (2002: 178) estimate that 40% of the French words borrowed into Middle English came into the language between 1250 and 1400. The enriched vocabulary of LME distinguishes it from EME. Another reason, suggested by Fisiak (1968: 10), is that from the fourteenth century onwards there was more of a move towards the development of 'a single national language', which was made possible owing to a variety of political, social and economic factors. This latter point reinforces one of the concerns of section A: namely, that the division of English into 'periods' is governed as much by non-linguistic factors as by linguistic ones, and that such divisions are essentially artificial. Language, as we have already discussed, is a process rather than a physical substance.

B3.1 The context of change

If English is your first language, you are perhaps likely to feel more at home with Middle English than with Old English. The vocabulary is more readily recognisable that that of Old English and the grammatical structure seems closer to Present Day English than Old English. Nevertheless, there are still significant differences between Middle English and Present Day English and, although to begin with it may seem easier to understand, in many ways Middle English is harder to get to grips with than Old English. This is in part because of the variety of dialects represented in Middle English manuscripts. There was no national standard form of English in the Early Middle English period and scribes wrote in the dialect of wherever in the country they happened to come from. Spellings and grammatical forms varied between dialect areas, and we can assume from this that pronunciation varied widely too. It is, then, impossible to describe a Middle English 'norm', since none existed. Variation and difference were characteristic features of Middle English at its early stage, and while variation is a feature of English at each of its stages of development, the difference is that in the Middle English period there was no standard form available for scribes to use. By comparison, in the Old English period a form of standardisation had taken place which saw the West Saxon dialect become the prominent written form (see A2.2). Indeed, such was its influence that this form was used beyond the regional boundaries of Wessex. Nevertheless, there are some general points that can be made about Middle English when compared to Old English, and these will be the focus of this unit.

In A3 we saw that one of the external events that contributed to the linguistic development of Old English into Middle English was the Norman Conquest of 1066. We must be careful, however, not to attribute linguistic change to this factor alone. The accession of William the Conqueror to the throne led to a rise in the number of French speakers in the country as William appointed his own nobles to prominent administrative positions, and French was eventually to influence English significantly, particularly its vocabulary (see B3.4). But the Norman Conquest did nothing to threaten the survival of English, since English remained the language spoken by the vast majority of the people, most of whom would have had no contact at all with the French ruling elite. English, while influenced by French, was also affected by the Scandinavian languages spoken by the Viking invaders, and a combination of factors was responsible for the development of Old English into Middle English (see B3.3 for example), a process which had started before the Norman Conquest.

What we see in the Middle English era is a period during which a number of languages were used in the country. French was the language of the ruling class, Latin was the language of the Church, and English was the everyday language spoken by the majority of the country's population (English as a written language had also been well established during the Old English period, though comparatively few people would have been able to read and write it).

B3.2 Spelling and sound in Middle English

In the absence of a written standard in the Middle English period, it is common to find considerable variation in the way that words are spelled. But while Middle English spelling may look anarchic, scholars have observed that certain spellings are common to particular regions. As a result of this, we can assume that these different spellings were attempts on the part of Middle English scribes to represent the way that such words would be pronounced. Different spellings therefore give us some insight into how the language was spoken in particular areas of the country (though you should bear in mind that this explanation makes the process of deciphering Middle English spelling seem deceptively easy; writers often used idiosyncratic spellings and sometimes varied the spelling of a particular word within a single sentence).

One major difference between Middle English and Present Day English pronunciation is that while in some Present Day English words we find silent letters, in their Middle English equivalents these letters would usually have been pronounced. In Present Day English, for example, we don't pronounce the <k> or the <w> in *knowledge*. In the Middle English equivalent, *knowlych* (one of a number of potential spellings, of course), these letters would have been pronounced. An exception is the pronunciation of words borrowed into Middle English from French, such as *honour* and *heir* whose initial letters are silent. But while this is a case of a French pronunciation being retained following the borrowing of the French word into English, for the most part, French influenced spellings rather than pronunciation. Some examples of how French scribal practices influenced English spelling in the Middle English period are as follows:

❑   The digraph <th> replaces <ð> to represent /θ/, though <þ> is still used by some scribes to represent this phoneme, particularly in Early Middle English, e.g. OE ðrinʒan ('to press') becomes ME thringen.
❑   <qu> replaces <cw> to represent /kw/, e.g. OE cwen ('queen') becomes ME queen.
❑   The digraph <ch> replaces OE <c> to represent the phoneme /tʃ/, e.g. OE cīld ('child') becomes ME chīld.
❑   The phoneme /ʃ/ is now represented by the digraph <sh> as opposed to the OE <sc>, e.g. OE sceran ('to shear') becomes ME sheren.

The changes introduced as a result of the influence of French conventions were not mere whims. For example, in the case of <ch> and <sh>, the <h> part of these digraphs indicated that the pronunciation of the preceding <c> or <s> was different from that which these letters normally indicated (i.e. /k/ and /s/ or /z/, respectively, as in cāndel, hūs and rīsen). In effect, the <h> was acting as a **diacritic**, an indicator of a different pronunciation. (In some languages diacritics are found above certain letters. In Hungarian, for example, the diacritic <ˊ> above <a> indicates that <a> is pronounced as in the English word hat. The absence of the diacritic indicates a pronunciation of <a> that is like the vowel sound in the word hot.) In the case of <ch> and <sh>, then, the <h> indicated that the digraphs represented, respectively, an affricate (as in the initial consonant sound of church) and a fricative sound, i.e. the kind of sound produced when air is expelled through a narrow space between the articulators (articulators are those vocal organs such as teeth, tongue and lips that we use in the production of speech sounds. You can find out more about this in B4.1). Try saying shhhhh or zzzzzz. The sound you produce will be a fricative.

In several instances, however, Middle English scribes misinterpreted the significance of <h>. For example, Present Day English words such as where and when, which all begin with initial <wh>, began in Old English with <hw>, e.g. hwǣr and hwanne. But by the Middle English period these words were being spelled with initial <wh>: whēr and whanne. The reason, according to Scragg (1974: 47), is that Middle English scribes assumed that in cases like these the <h> was working as a diacritic to indicate a fricative pronunciation of <w>; something like the final consonant sound in Present Day English loch. This was not the case though. The <hw> digraph did, in fact, sound something like a pronunciation of /h/ and /w/ in succession. Nevertheless, the graphs <h> and <w> were reversed in a misperceived attempt at regularisation. This explains why in some dialects of English – in Scotland, for instance – you will still hear words such as where and when pronounced with an initial /h/ sound.

A problem that arises out of the variation that is to be found in the Middle English dialects is how to conveniently describe Middle English pronunciation in the absence of a standard form. One option is to describe the sounds used by a particular writer whom we know to have written in a particular dialect. Horobin (2007) takes this approach and uses the writings of the famous Middle English poet, Geoffrey Chaucer, to reconstruct the typical pronunciations of the London English dialect. Tables B3.2.1 and B3.2.2 outline the vowel sounds of this dialect: monophthongs and diphthongs.

Table B3.2.1 Middle English vowels (monophthongs) (adapted from Horobin 2007: 57)

ME phoneme	ME spelling	Pronunciation	PDE phoneme	PDE example
/ɪ/	kyng, is	s*i*t	/ɪ/	king, is
/ɛ/	bed	b*e*t	/ɛ/	bed
/a/	nat	m*a*n	/æ/	cat
/ɔ/	oft	h*o*t	/ɒ/	hot
/ʊ/	but, sonne	p*u*t	/ʊ/ /ʌ/	but, sun
/iː/	wyf, wif	b*ee*	/aɪ/	wife
/eː/	mete	f*a*te	/iː/	meet
/ɛː/	mete	f*a*re	/iː/	meat
/aː/	name	f*a*ther	/eɪ/	name
/uː/	toun, town	g*oo*se	/aʊ/	town
/oː/	mo(o)d	v*o*te	/uː/	mood
/ɔː/	bo(o)t	h*oa*rd	/əʊ/	boat

Table B3.2.2 Middle English vowels (diphthongs) (Horobin 2007: 57)

ME	ME spelling	ME examples
/aɪ/	<ai, ay, ei, ey>	day, wey
/ɔɪ/	<oi, oy>	joye
/ʊɪ/	<oi, oy>	destroye
/aʊ/	<au>	taught, law
/ɔʊ/	<ow>	knowe
/ɛʊ/	<ew>	lewed
/ɪʊ/	<ew>	newe, trewe

For the most part, the consonants of Middle English are pronounced as they are in Present Day English. Some exceptions concern the pronunciation of the following graphemes:

❑ <c> retains the pronunciation /k/ but no longer has the pronunciation /tʃ/. (/tʃ/, as we have seen above, is instead represented by the French digraph <ch>.)
❑ <c> also now has the pronunciation /s/ in French loan words such as *protestacioun*.
❑ <gh> and <ȝ> are usually pronounced /x/ (similar to the final consonant sound in PDE *loch*) when they occur in a medial position in a word.
❑ <ȝ> is usually pronounced /j/ when it occurs as the initial letter of a word.

You can practise your pronunciation by reading aloud the texts in C3. But where your knowledge of Middle English sounds (especially vowel sounds) will really come in useful is in understanding the sound changes that occurred in the Early Modern English period. The so-called Great Vowel Shift is explained in B4.

B3.3 Changes in the system of inflections

As we saw in B1.3 and B1.4, the order of words in a sentence was much less important in Old English than it is in Present Day English, because Old English was a synthetic language as opposed to an analytic one. Hence, inflections conveyed grammatical information that in Present Day English is now indicated by other means, for example through syntactic structure and the use of prepositions. However, towards the end of the Old English period and throughout the Middle English period, this system of inflections began to break down and inflections became ever more scarce. Inflections didn't disappear completely (see B5.2) but by the end of the Middle English period the inflection system was substantially less complex than it had been in Old English.

What caused the loss of inflections in English? There are several potential explanations, outlined below. As you read through these explanations, bear in mind that it is likely that a combination of these factors was responsible (i.e. these are not necessarily competing explanations).

Changes in the sound system of English

Changes in the sound system of Old English were responsible in part for the reduced complexity of the inflectional system. Inflections became unstressed in speech, which had the effect of levelling the pronunciation of the vowels in these inflections. This simply means that the vowel sounds in inflections lost their distinctness. For example, consider the following forms of the Old English noun for *fish* in Table B3.3.1.

Read the words in Table B3.3.1 aloud. If you stress both syllables of each word equally you will hear a clear difference between the vowel sound of the different inflections. However, if you give primary stress to the first syllables of each word, the vowel sounds in the inflections will reduce to schwa and the different forms will sound much more similar to each other. Stressing only the first syllable of the words means that it becomes much harder to distinguish the type of inflection in the unstressed syllable. (And if you can't hear a distinction between the various forms then you are unlikely to produce the inflectional distinctions in your own speech.) Inflections would therefore have become gradually less important as a means of conveying important grammatical information, with a consequent reliance on word order (i.e. syntax) to fulfil this function.

Scandinavian influence

Language contact between the Danes and the Anglo-Saxons is another possible explanation for why inflections began to disappear from English. The root of a word in Old English was often remarkably similar to the root of the same word in Old Norse. The only difference was in the inflections that were appended to these words. Consider, for example, the inflected forms of the word for *hammer* in Table B3.3.2.

Table B3.3.1 Inflections for Old English *fish*

	Singular	Plural
Nominative	fisc	fiscas
Accusative	fisc	fiscas
Genitive	fisces	fisca
Dative	fisce	fiscum

Table B3.3.2 Inflections for Old English and Old Norse *hammer*

	Old English		Old Norse	
	Singular	Plural	Singular	Plural
Nominative	hamor	hameras	hamar	hamrar
Accusative	hamor	hameras	hamar	hamra
Genitive	hamores	hamora	hamars	hamra
Dative	hameras	hamorum	hamri	hōmrum

We can see the same issue in many other words, such as Old English *scipu* ('ships') and Old Norse *skip*; OE *brōþor* ('brother') and ON *bruðr*; and OE *freosan* ('to freeze') and ON *frjosa*. It will be apparent from the above examples that it was the inflections that were likely to be a barrier to mutual understanding. Getting rid of the inflections increased the likelihood of the Danes and the Anglo-Saxons being able to communicate effectively. This would have been especially necessary in areas such as the Danelaw (the territory to the east of an imaginary line running diagonally from the River Thames to Chester; see A1.6) where Danish and Saxon communities would have mixed. Consequently, this may well have been a contributory factor in the loss of inflections in English (though we should bear in mind that, as a result of sound changes in Old English, inflections were already becoming unstressed, as discussed in the previous unit).

The breakdown of the system of inflections led ultimately to English becoming an analytic as opposed to a synthetic language. As an example of the difference between Middle English and Old English, consider one of the example sentences from B1.4:

1. se cnapa lufode þā hlǣfdigan (The servant loved the mistress.)

In Middle English, this could have been expressed in various ways, for example:

2. þe ladde lovede þeo lafdiʒ.
3. þe ladde lovede þe lady.

Example (2) uses different forms of the determiner to mark the nominative and accusative, as in Old English. But during the Middle English period the different forms of the determiner were gradually replaced with just one form: *þe*. And because the ME nouns *ladde* and *lafdiʒ* have no inflections to indicate case, in example (3), where just one form of the determiner is used, we rely entirely on word order to determine the meaning of the sentence. (You will also notice different spellings in the two sentences, a common feature of Middle English.) By the end of the Middle English period, inflections on nouns had almost entirely disappeared and only one form of the determiner was used (Fisiak 1968).

B3.4 Middle English vocabulary

During the Middle English period, the lexicon of English increased substantially as a result of the borrowing of words from French, and Latin and Norse (of these, French had the most influence). The Viking invasions of the Old English period had also led to significant borrowing, and during the Middle English period many of these borrowed Scandinavian words became more widely used. Borrowing is made possible by language contact. Words can be borrowed directly from one language, or they may come via a second language. English had come into contact with Latin via the work of the early Christian missionaries, whereas contact with French came about both as a result of Edward the Confessor's French-speaking royal court and by the consequences caused by the Battle of Hastings of 1066 (see A3). It is also the case that certain conditions make borrowing more likely. For instance, Smith (2005: 16) suggests that the decline of inflections in the Middle English period made it easier to integrate words from other languages into English, as their forms did not need to be changed to the same extent. Unsurprisingly, the borrowed words often came from areas of life that the donor languages were specifically associated with. So, for example, Latin contributed many religious words (*pulpit, rosary, scripture, testament,* etc.) though this is not to suggest that this was the only semantic field from which vocabulary was drawn. French borrowings hint at the prestigious position of French speakers in England at the time: *prince, princess, virtuous, hostel, debt, cathedral, chivalry, magnificence, majesty.* Scandinavian borrowings such as *egg, knife, freckle, root* and *smile* suggest fairly close contact between the Scandinavians and the Anglo-Saxons. You can explore Middle English borrowings further in C3.

B4 SOUND SHIFTS

Because reading Early Modern English is closer to Present Day English in terms of grammar and vocabulary than Old English or Middle English, there is perhaps a tendency to underestimate some of the differences between the two, as well as the significant linguistic changes that occurred during the Early Modern period. Written Early Modern English seems closer to Present Day English because of the process of standardisation that occurred in the Early Modern period, and by the fact that the new standard that emerged was spread via the development of the printing press. But the Early Modern Period also saw major changes in spoken English, specifically pronunciation. In B4 and B5 we will examine these linguistic developments in spoken and written English.

B4.1 Speech sounds

One of the major changes to occur during the transition from Middle to Early Modern English was the so-called Great Vowel Shift, which affected pronunciation in many parts of the country and which led eventually to the pronunciations that we use in Present Day English. Although this was a linguistic phenomenon, it is outlined in A4.1 because of the social events that some linguists (e.g. Labov 1972a) have suggested were instrumental in causing it to occur (e.g. the fact that some accents came to be seen as particularly prestigious). In this unit I will concentrate on describing what happened linguistically during the Great Vowel Shift.

Understanding the Great Vowel Shift is made easier if you have a grasp of what happens physiologically when we produce speech sounds (and, obviously enough, vowel sounds in particular), so we will start with this. Then we will look at the changes in the pronunciation of the long vowels that occurred in the Early Modern period. Finally, when you feel comfortable with all of this, I would suggest that you move on to the readings in unit D4 in order to consolidate your understanding of the Great Vowel Shift as a whole and to explore its complexities in greater depth.

Producing speech sound

To produce speech sound, we expel air from our lungs which then passes through the **trachea** (sometimes called the windpipe) and the **larynx** (part of the throat), before leaving the body via the mouth or the nose. The particular sound that comes out depends on how we modify the airflow as it leaves our body. First of all, let's consider how we produce consonant sounds.

Producing consonant sounds

To produce a consonant sound, we use **articulators** (vocal organs such as the tongue, lips, teeth, etc.) to restrict the airflow in some way. If we use our lips as articulators we can create, for example, the sounds /p/ and /b/. To do this, we obstruct the airflow by keeping our lips tightly together. The build-up of pressure means that when we move our lips apart there is an explosion of air, creating what phoneticians call a plosive. In the case of /p/ and /b/, this is a **bilabial plosive**, since it is a plosive that is created as a result of using both lips as articulators (*labia* is the Latin plural of *lip* and *bi* means 'two'; hence *bilabial* means 'two lips'). The difference between /p/ and /b/ is that /b/ is **voiced** and /p/ is **unvoiced**. As air from our lungs is expelled it passes over the **vocal folds** (sometimes called the vocal cords). These are two bands of muscle stretched horizontally across the trachea. If the vocal folds are close together when the air hits them they will vibrate, creating a voiced sound. Conversely, if the vocal folds are open, the air will pass through them without causing them to vibrate, resulting in an unvoiced sound. To feel the difference, put your index and middle finger against your Adam's apple and say the sounds /p/ and /b/. When you say /p/ you should feel nothing; when you say /b/ you should feel the vibration caused by the vocal folds oscillating. All consonant sounds are either voiced or unvoiced and all are dependent on the airflow being restricted in some way. For instance, to produce the unvoiced phoneme /f/, we use our teeth and our lower lip as articulators. The air leaves the oral cavity (i.e. the mouth) through the gaps between the teeth and the lower lip. The articulators involved in producing the phoneme /m/ are the lips – as with /p/ and /b/. The difference is that the air leaves the body via the nasal cavity rather than the mouth. Remember, the common feature of all consonant sounds is that their production relies on our restricting the outflow of air in some way.

Producing vowel sounds

Vowel sounds are produced in a different way. To produce a vowel sound you do not restrict the flow of air from the body. Instead, the shape of the oral cavity and the position of the tongue within it determine the kind of vowel sound that is produced. Moving the tongue to a specific position within the mouth creates a resonating cavity within which a particular vowel sound can be produced. If the tongue is raised up in the mouth it leaves a small resonating cavity. If the tongue is moved towards the bottom of the mouth it leaves a larger resonating cavity. Try saying the sounds /i:/ (as in *meat)* and /a:/ (as in *bar*). Take notice of where your tongue moves to in your mouth as you say these sounds. When you say /i:/ your tongue is high up in your mouth. The resonating cavity in which the /i:/ sound is produced is small. Conversely, when you say /a:/ the tongue is low down in the mouth and you should feel that there is consequently a much larger space in which the vowel sound is produced.

Phoneticians make use of a trapezium-shaped diagram to represent the resonating cavity in which vowel sounds are produced (see Figure B4.1.1). **Close** vowel sounds are produced when the cavity is small (i.e. when the tongue is close to the roof of the mouth, or **raised**). **Open** vowel sounds are produced when the cavity is large (i.e. when the tongue is low down in the mouth). There are other factors that can influence the type of vowel sound produced. One is whether the resonating cavity is towards the **front** or **back** of the tongue. Try saying /i:/ and /u:/ (as in *boot*). You should feel that for both these sounds the tongue is high in the mouth. However, when you say /i:/ it should feel like the sound is coming from the front of the tongue while the /u:/ phoneme should feel like it is being produced from the back. This is because /i:/ is a front vowel while /u:/ is a back vowel. Another factor that can influence the type of vowel sound produced is whether your lips are **rounded** or **unrounded** when you produce the vowel sound in question. Say /i:/ and /u:/ again. Take notice of the position of your lips as you pronounce these sounds. When you say /u:/ your lips will be pursed. /u:/ is a rounded vowel while /i:/ is an unrounded vowel. Lastly, the length of a particular vowel sound is important in distinguishing it from others. Say /i:/ and /ɪ/ (as in *pit*). You should feel that these sounds are coming from roughly the same place within your mouth. Both are front vowels, and both are produced with the tongue close to the roof of the mouth (though the height of the tongue varies slightly between the two vowels). Additionally, both are unrounded. One of the main distinguishing features between these two sounds is that /i:/ is long while /ɪ/ is short.

You will see from Figure B4.1.1 that while some vowel sounds are produced with the tongue high up in the mouth and others with it low down, still other sounds are produced when the tongue is at a mid-point. The horizontal lines in the chart illustrate that different sounds are produced when the tongue is raised to the mid-open and mid-close positions as well. Additionally, while some vowel sounds come from the front of the tongue and others from the back, certain vowel sounds are produced from a resonating cavity in the centre of the mouth. These include schwa (see B1.1), /ɜ:/ and /ʌ/.

The vowel sounds represented in Figure B4.1.1 can be found in the following English words:

/i:/	meat, sleep, treat
/ɪ/	bit, tin, lip
/e/	bed, head, said
/æ/	cat, tap, pan

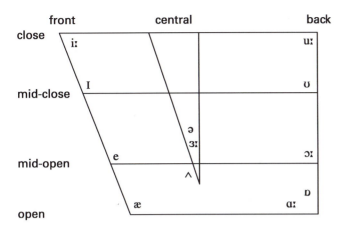

Figure B4.1.1 Pure vowels in English.

/ɑː/	rather, far, bar	
/ɒ/	hot, rock, mop	
/ɔː/	law, caught	
/ʊ/	look, cook	
/uː/	boot, shoot, loot	
/ə/	about, sofa	
/ɜː/	bird, hurt	
/ʌ/	cut, gun	(NB: Speakers of Northern English use /ʊ/ in those instances where speakers of Southern English use /ʌ/)

The sounds represented in Figure B4.1.1 are all pure vowels or monophthongs. Additionally, English also makes use of vowel sounds called diphthongs, which involve movement between one vowel position and another. For example, for many English speakers the vowel sound in the word *house* is a diphthong: /aʊ/. Producing the diphthong /aʊ/ involves the tongue moving between one position and another in the oral cavity. Figure B4.1.2 shows the direction of the tongue's movement during the production of this diphthong.

Of course, not every speaker of English would use the diphthong /aʊ/ in the word *house*. Accents vary, and in some parts of the north-east of England and in Scotland, the vowel sound in *house* would be closer to the pure long vowel /uː/. In fact, speakers of English who pronounce the word *house* as /huːs/ are demonstrating a pronunciation that would have been common in Middle English. We saw in B3.2 how Middle English pronunciation differed from that of Present Day English. It was the Great Vowel Shift that was the cause of many of these changes in pronunciation. What happened during the Great Vowel Shift was that the pronunciation of the long vowels was raised. That is, the Great Vowel Shift caused the long vowel sounds to be produced with the tongue higher up in the oral cavity than it would have been during the Middle English period. This resulted in changes to the seven long vowels of Middle English, including the **diphthongisation** (the process of a pure vowel becoming a diphthong) of some of them. We will see why in the next unit.

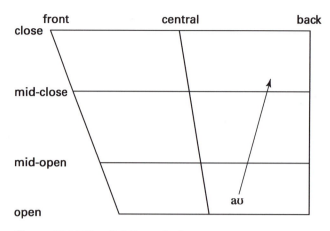

Figure B4.1.2 The diphthong /aʊ/.

B4.2 Changes in the long vowels

Once you have a basic idea of the movement of the tongue during the production of vowel sounds it becomes easier to grasp what happened during the Great Vowel Shift. The changes that occurred affected the seven long vowels in Middle English: /iː/, /eː/, /ɛː/, /aː/, /ɔː/, /oː/ and /uː/. Notice that not all of these vowels are represented in Figure B4.2.1, since some of these sounds are no longer used in Present Day Standard English (though some occur in regional varieties; e.g. /ɔː/ in a Lancashire pronunciation of *bored*).

Let's take a simple example of the kind of change that occurred during the Great Vowel Shift. The Middle English pronunciation of *name* would have been /naːmə/ and the Early Modern pronunciation would have been /nɛːm/. The vowel sound in the Early Modern English pronunciation is higher than that of the Middle English pronunciation. That is, when you pronounce the Early Modern English example your tongue is closer to the roof of your mouth than when you pronounce the Middle English example, thereby changing the shape of the resonating cavity inside your mouth that determines the vowel sound that is produced.

What is important here is that a change in the pronunciation of one long vowel has a knock-on effect on the other six. Essentially, the /aː/ vowel of the Middle English pronunciation was raised, resulting in it being pronounced as /ɛː/. So what, then, happens to the /ɛː/ vowel? The answer is that it too was raised so that it took on the quality of the /eː/ vowel. Then, as a consequence of this, the /eː/ vowel was raised to take on the quality of the /iː/ vowel. And what about the /iː/ vowel? As the highest front vowel there was nowhere for this to move to, and so the /iː/ changed into a diphthong: /əɪ/. This diphthong changed again to become Present Day English /aɪ/. So, the word *ride* would have been pronounced /riːd/ in Middle English and /rəɪd/ in Early Modern English, before eventually becoming /raɪd/ in Present Day English.

This deals with the front vowels. The back vowels, too, raised in a similar way. Aitchison (2001) summarises the movement of the long vowels diagrammatically

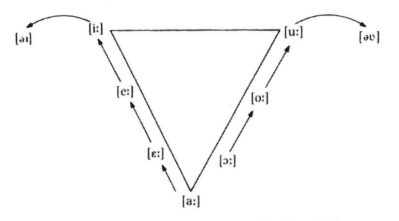

Figure B4.2.1 The Great Vowel Shift in English (Aitchison 2001).

(see Figure B4.2.1). Notice that, like the front vowel /iː/, the back vowel /uː/ raises to become a diphthong. In the Early Modern period this was /ɔʊ/, which eventually became /aʊ/ in Present Day English.

Figure B4.2.1 explains *what* happened during the Great Vowel Shift but it does not explain *why* it happened. In A4 we explored a potential social explanation for why people began to change the way that they spoke. But in addition to this we need a linguistic explanation for why the long vowels moved. Generally, linguists agree that the Great Vowel Shift was caused by a **chain shift**. Imagine the long vowels as links in a chain. As one part of the chain moves, so too do the other parts. There is, though, a further question, and this is whether one vowel sound was *pushing* the others into different positions or whether the converse was true; i.e. that one vowel was *pulling* the others into different positions. This is the difference between a **push chain** and a **drag chain**. You can explore these theories in more detail in D4.1.

B4.3 The Uniformitarian Principle in relation to the Great Vowel Shift

In A4.1 we saw that one potential sociolinguistic explanation of the Great Vowel Shift is Labov's notion that speakers were emulating the sounds they heard in prestigious varieties of English, just as there is evidence of this occurring in Present Day English. According to Machan (2003: 12), Labov's explanation is an example of the application of the 'Uniformitarian Principle'. Machan explains this as follows:

> Roger Lass [1980: 55] formulates the most general form of the principle in this way: 'Nothing (no event, sequence of events, constellation of properties, general law) that cannot for some good reason be the case in the present was ever true in the past.'
>
> (Machan 2003: 12)

Essentially, what this means is that if something is the case in the present, we can assume that in all likelihood the same was true in the past. For instance, in Present Day

English we have open vowels and close vowels, and so we can assume that earlier forms of English also had open vowels and close vowels (even though these may have differed from Present Day English slightly). Machan goes on to explain that the Uniformitarian Principle also extends to social aspects of language use:

> In principle, there is no reason that the Uniformitarian Principle cannot be extended from such issues of language structure to those of language use. Indeed, Suzanne Romaine inverts this principle and applies it directly to society and language, whereby the Uniformitarian Principle means that 'the linguistic forces which operate today and are observable around us are not unlike those which have operated in the past. Sociolinguistically speaking, this means that there is no reason for claiming that language did not vary in the same patterned ways in the past as it has been observed to do today' [Romaine 1982: 122–3].
>
> (Machan 2003: 12)

What this suggests is that we can assume the English of the past to have varied in the same ways as different varieties of English do in the present. We know that regional variation was commonplace but on the basis of the Uniformitarian Principle we can assume that social variation was commonplace too. That is, certain varieties and usages would have been seen as particularly prestigious and worthy of emulation. This, then, provides the support for Labov's theory of the sociolinguistic causes of the Great Vowel Shift.

B4.4 Consequences of the Great Vowel Shift

The obvious consequence of the Great Vowel Shift was that the pronunciation of the long vowels changed. But the Great Vowel Shift also begins to explain some of the peculiarities of English spelling. You will recall from A5 that one of the defining aspects of the Early Modern period was that it was an age of standardisation. During this time, the production of grammars and dictionaries of English increased substantially and significant efforts were put into standardising the spelling system. Previously, you will remember, spelling had been largely phonetic – that is, people spelled words in a way that reflected their own pronunciation in their own dialect. The problem, of course, was that all of this standardising was going on at a time when the spoken language was also undergoing significant change, as we have been looking at in this unit. A consequence of this was that the spellings that emerged as a result of the processes of standardisation often reflected the pronunciation of words *before* the Great Vowel Shift was complete. This begins to explain why in Present Day English there often appears to be no logical connection between the way that a word is spelled and the way it is pronounced. In fact, seemingly arbitrary spellings often reflect an earlier pronunciation. For example, the spelling of the words *mice* and *wine* reflects the fact that in the Middle English pronunciation the vowel sound in each was a pure vowel, or monophthong. Had the spellings of these words been fixed *after* the Great Vowel Shift had occurred, we might expect them to reflect the fact that both these words are now pronounced with the diphthong /aɪ/. *Mais* and *wain*, perhaps?

WRITING IN EARLY MODERN ENGLISH   B5

The Early Modern period saw the gradual emergence of a standard form of written English, which is often linked to the introduction of the printing press by William Caxton (see A5.2). The simple fact of there being a press in existence, however, does not in itself provide a full explanation for why a standard should emerge; as we saw in A5.2, Caxton's printing press was not the force for standardisation that we might assume it to have been. It also seems unlikely that Standard English is the result of a particular dialect having been adopted as a standard form, as Fisher (1996) argues when he claims that Chancery Standard is the dialect that gave rise to present-day Standard English. This is because the features that now form part of present-day Standard English can be traced back to a number of Middle English dialects, as Hope (2000) points out (see Figure A3.4.1 for an indication of dialect boundaries). This much is implied by Pyles and Algeo (1993: 141) when they say that the London English which gave rise to a standard form was 'essentially East Midlandish in its characteristics, though showing Northern and to a less extent Southern influences'. Because of this mixture of elements, it seems unlikely that this 'London English' really was a single distinct dialect.

If present-day Standard English did not develop from any single Middle English dialect then, we are left with the question of how exactly it did emerge. One way of exploring this issue is to consider Haugen's (1966) sociolinguistic explanation of the process by which standard varieties of a language develop. Haugen (1966: 110) suggests that there are four stages to the development of a standard. These are:

- [ ] selection of norm
- [ ] codification of form
- [ ] elaboration of function
- [ ] acceptance by the community.

The first of these stages involves the **selection** of a particular variety to become a standard form of the language. That is, the speech community in question has to choose a particular variety of their language to function as a standard. The next stage in the development is **codification**, during which the norms of the selected form are made explicit, usually by the production of printed materials and especially through grammars, dictionaries, style guides, spelling books and so on. The third stage in Haugen's process is the **elaboration** of the functions of the selected and codified standard. Haugen explains that since the selected and codified standard is 'by definition the common language of a social group more complex and inclusive than those using vernaculars, its functional domains must also be complex' (Haugen 1966: 108). What this means is that the newly emerging standard must be adequate for a variety of purposes. It must have the potential to be used by various classes of people and by different communities. It must be usable for a variety of different functions, including 'high' functions such as official communications and literary writing.

If a particular dialect has been selected, codified and elaborated then it stands a strong chance of becoming established as a long-term standard variety. Nevertheless, the final stage in Haugen's four-stage process is **acceptance** and requires that the newly developed standard be accepted by the speech community as a whole. That is, it must be seen to be a viable and useful form that offers something to its users, be this power, prestige or the opportunity for social and educational advancement.

While Haugen's four-stage process offers a neat way of thinking about how Standard English might have developed, it rather oversimplifies the process. As we have seen, Standard English is not the descendant of one single Middle English dialect. The selection stage, therefore, is not an accurate description of how Standard English emerged. However, rather than dispense with Haugen's framework entirely, we can revise it to take account of the nuances of Standard English's development. For example, Hope (2000: 51) suggests that the first stage of the process should not be seen as involving the selection of a particular dialect to function as a standard. Rather, it involved the selection of particular linguistic features from a range of dialects. Selection, therefore, is better thought of as *selections*. Similarly, the codification stage did not codify a particular dialect as a standard but instead codified the use of particular forms – which could be found in a number of dialects. Consequently, the Standard English that emerged is not a regional dialect but a social one. With regard to elaboration, Haugen's framework is again an oversimplification, with its suggestion that at this point in the process a standard had already emerged which writers then began to use for a range of high functions. In fact, as Scragg (1974: 70) points out, printers played a significant role in standardising spellings. As evidence of this, Scragg offers the following example, which shows the difference between the original manuscript and the printed copy of a translation of the Italian epic poem, *Orlando Furioso* by Ludovico Ariosto, from 1591:

Manuscript	*Printed copy*
Certes, most noble dames I ame so wrothe,	Certes (most noble Dames) I am so wroth,
with this vyle turke, for this his wycked sinne,	With this vile Turk, for this his wicked sin,
for speaking so great slawnder, & vntroth	For speaking so great sclander and vntroth,
of that sweet sex, whose grace I fayn would win:	Of that sweet sex, whose grace I fayn would win,

(Scragg 1974: 70)

The printed copy was produced by the printer Richard Field, based on the manuscript produced by Sir John Harrington. What can be seen from the printed version is that Field not only made changes to Harrington's spelling but to his punctuation too. In this respect, the printing industry may be seen to have played a role in the elaboration of standardised forms (that is, the adoption of standardised forms in literary writing was due in no small part to the decisions of printers like Richard Field). But this was not the only part that printing played in the development of a standard. To fully explain this, it is useful to incorporate into Haugen's framework some additional stages proposed by Milroy and Milroy (1999). One of these is **diffusion**. While codification refers to the writing and exemplification of rules for the use of the standard, diffusion refers to the spread of these rules. The role of the printing press in the development of Standard English includes the diffusion of codified forms through the printing of dictionaries, grammars and other guides to usage.

Milroy and Milroy's (1999) other additional stages are **maintenance** and **prescription**. The process of the standardisation of English, therefore, may be described as follows:

- ❑ *Selection*: linguistic features from a range of dialects are selected as standard forms.
- ❑ *Codification*: these forms are codified in early dictionaries, grammars and writing guides.
- ❑ *Diffusion*: the codified forms are spread via the printing press.
- ❑ *Elaboration*: the emerging standard forms are adopted in forms of writing that have a high social value.
- ❑ *Acceptance*: these standard forms coalesce into a social dialect that is accepted as valuable and viable by language users.
- ❑ *Maintenance*: the new standard is maintained by the printing industry.
- ❑ *Prescription*: further codification prescribes the standard and a prescriptive ideology preserves it.

The above description imposes a rough order on the standardisation process (e.g. as Hope [2000: 51] points out, 'prescriptivism is impossible until standardisation has done most of its work') though the reality is likely to involve overlap of stages.

It should be noted that the above description focuses on the development of a written standard, though Haugen's framework can be used to describe the development of a spoken standard variety too (see A7.3). Notwithstanding the complexities involved in the selection stage of the process, Haugen points out that '[t]o choose any one vernacular as a norm means to favor the group of people speaking that variety. It gives them prestige as norm-bearers and a headstart in the race for power and position' (Haugen 1966: 109). We will consider this issue of power and prestige in more detail in B6. Throughout the rest of this unit we will examine some of the characteristics of the newly emerging written standard in Early Modern English.

B5.1 Orthography in Early Modern English

At the beginning of the Early Modern period there was little consistency in spelling. The word *mother*, for example, might be spelled variously as *modir*, *modyr*, *moodre*, *modere* and *moder* (all of these forms can be found in the Paston Letters, a famous collection of family letters from the beginning of the Early Modern period). This inconsistency is also found in early printed books of the period. Scragg (1974: 66) puts this down to the fact that William Caxton, who had introduced the printing press in 1476, was likely to have been unfamiliar with developments in orthography during the fifteenth century, as he had spent much of this period away from England. Added to this, he initially employed foreign printers who were similarly unfamiliar with the developing standards of Chancery English. Over the Early Modern period, however, spelling conventions gradually became established and these orthographic norms mean that Early Modern English spelling is not as haphazard as it may at first appear to be. The following are some common features of spelling at the beginning of the Early Modern period:

❑ There are two forms of the letter <s> in use. The practice is to use <s> when the final letter of a word but <ſ> – sometimes called 'long s' – when the letter is word-initial or appears in a medial position.

❑ <u> can represent both the vowel sound /ʊ/ and the consonant sound /v/. <v> can also represent both the vowel sound /ʊ/ and the consonant sound /v/. Nevertheless, the usage is not arbitrary. <v> is used in word-initial position, whether the phoneme to be represented is /ʊ/ or /v/. Elsewhere, the norm is to use <u>. For example, *have* is typically spelled *haue*, while *up* is spelled *vp*. Present Day English, of course, treats <v> and <u> as distinct graphemes, a convention that began around 1630 as a result of continental influence (Barber 1997: 3).

❑ <i> tends to be used in places where in Present Day English we would use <j>. According to Barber (1976: 16), the letter combination <ij> – as in *diversifijng* – was the only instance in which the letter <j> would be used.

An additional point of interest about Early Modern English spelling is the use of <e> on the end of particular words. In the Early Modern period, final <e> in words like *name, moste* and *persone* would not have been pronounced in speech but fulfilled a number of different functions in writing. A summary of these (based on Görlach 1991: 47) is as follows:

❑ The use of final <e> was not arbitrary.

❑ Final <e> could indicate that the vowel sound in a word was long – e.g. in words like *name* and *nose*. Once established, this convention was applied to other words. So, for example, Middle English *cas* became *case, lif* became *life, wif* became *wife*, etc.

❑ The use of final <e> to indicate vowel length caused a problem in words like *writen* (PDE *written*). The <e> suggested that the vowel sound was long, when it was in fact short. The solution was to double the medial consonant, resulting in *written*.

❑ Final <e> was also used to differentiate between words that used <s> as a plural inflection on the end of the word and those in which <s> was simply the final letter. For example, adding a final <e> to *divers* indicates that the word is an adjective – *diverse* – not a plural noun. A similar example is *dens* and *dense*.

B5.2 Some grammatical characteristics

A number of grammatical developments take place during the Early Modern period. Barber (1997) covers these in detail. Here we will look particularly at what happened to the pronoun system as well as developments in the form of verbs.

Pronouns

Pronouns in Present Day English take different forms depending on a number of factors. The form of the pronoun depends on whether it is the **subject** or **object** of a sentence, or whether it is fulfilling a **possessive** function. (Broadly speaking, these three categories correspond to the nominative, accusative and genitive cases described in B1.4.) Other factors that determine the form of a pronoun are person (first-, second- or third-person) and number (whether it is singular or plural). We

Table B5.2.1 Pronouns in Present Day English

	First person	Second person	Third person
Subject			
Singular	I	you	he/she/it
Plural	we	you	they
Object			
Singular	me	you	him/her/it
Plural	us	you	them
Possessive			
Singular	mine	yours	his/hers/its
Plural	ours	yours	theirs

Table B5.2.2 Pronouns in Early Modern English (after Barber 1997: 152)

	First person	Second person	Third person
Subject			
Singular	I	thou	he/she/it*
Plural	we	ye	they
Object			
Singular	me	thee	him/her/it*
Plural	us	you	them
Possessive			
Singular	mine	thine	his/hers/his
Plural	ours	yours	theirs

*The original form of *it* was *hit*, which was in use until around 1600. The form *it* developed as a result of the initial /h/ being dropped in circumstances where *hit* was unstressed.

can summarise the different forms of the pronoun in Present Day English as in Table B5.2.1.

Notice that the form of the pronoun changes according to its grammatical function, i.e. the job that it is doing in the sentence. So, while the development of English over time is marked by a tendency towards regularisation and a reliance on word order to convey meaning, it is still the case that in Present Day English we sometimes change the form of a word in order to denote its grammatical function.

In Early Modern English, there were more forms of the pronouns than there are in Present Day English (Table B5.2.2).

You will see from Table B5.2.2 that there are some differences between Early Modern English and Present Day English pronouns. For instance, at the beginning of the Early Modern period, the gender-neutral singular possessive pronoun (in PDE, *its*) was identical to the masculine singular possessive pronoun *his*. The main difference between pronouns in Early Modern English and Present Day English, however, is the second-person forms. In Early Modern English, as in Middle English, the second-person pronoun changed form according to person, number and grammatical function. *Thou, thee* and *thine* are singular forms whereas *ye, you* and *yours* are plural forms. In Present Day Standard English there is no distinction between singular and plural forms and only the possessive form is different from the others. (Exceptions can be found in certain dialects – e.g. Dublin English and Liverpool English have a plural second-person pronoun, *youse*, and in American English we find a contracted second-person plural, *y'all* – i.e. *you all.*) However, as Leith (1997: 107) points out, the second-person forms also had a particular social meaning in Early Modern English. During the Early Modern period *thou* and *thee* and *ye* and *you* were marked for social status, and when used in this way *ye/you* could be applied as singular pronouns too. A person of higher social standing could address a person lower down the social hierarchy with either *thou* or *thee* and expect *ye* or *you* in response, since using *ye* and *you* showed a deferential awareness of that person's higher social status. Effectively, *ye/you* was a more polite form. Many languages still make a similar distinction and have second-person forms that are marked for politeness, though nowadays the factor that determines their usage is usually a person's age rather than their social class. French, for instance, has the forms *tu* and *vous*. *Tu* may be used between friends as marker of social solidarity, while *vous* is likely to be used by a young person speaking to someone older than themselves. Barber (1997: 153) explains that the *thee/thou–ye/you* distinction most likely developed in English as a result of French influence in the Middle English period). Similarly, Present Day German offers the option of using either *du* or *sie*.

Verbs

Throughout the development of English there has been a tendency towards **regularisation**. During the Middle English period inflections began to fall out of usage, though this was ongoing throughout the Early Modern period and it would be a mistake to assume that Present Day English is inflection-free. Present Day English verbs, for example, still inflect in the third-person present tense. We say *I walk* but *she walks, you drink* but *he drinks* (compare this with the past tense inflection <ed>, which is the same for first-, second- and third-person). Unsurprisingly, if we look at Early Modern English verbs we find a greater degree of inflectional complexity than in Present Day English. Consider, for example, the Early Modern English present tense forms of the weak verb *to walk* (see Table B5.2.3).

As you can see in Table B5.2.3, Early Modern English also included an inflection to mark the second-person singular form of the verb, in both the present and the past tense, which is something that does not survive in Present Day English.

It is also important to bear in mind that inflections varied according to dialect. For example, the singular present tense <eth> ending on third-person verbs was a southern inflection. In the north of England the singular third-person present tense inflection was <es>; e.g. *she walkes*. Notice that this is the form that survives in Present Day English. Barber (1997: 167) suggests that around 1600, this northern third-person inflection was considered less formal than its southern counterpart. So although the two third-person inflections denoted the same grammatical information, they conveyed different **pragmatic** information, in much the same way that the two Early Modern English forms of the second-person pronoun (*thou* and *ye*) conveyed different social implications.

The example in Table B5.2.3 is of a weak verb though the same inflectional complexity was present in Early Modern English strong verbs too. Table B5.2.4 is an example.

The inflection on the second-person singular form of the verb is something that we no longer have in Present Day English. Barber (1997: 165) suggests that it fell out

Table B5.2.3 Forms of the weak verb *to walk* in Early Modern English

	Singular		Plural	
	Present	Past	Present	Past
First person	I walke	walked	we walke	we walked
Second person	thou walk(e)st	thou walkedst	ye walke	ye walked
Third person	he/she/hit walketh	he/she/hit walked	they walke	they walked

Table B5.2.4 Forms of the strong verb *to give* in Early Modern English

	Singular		Plural	
	Present	Past	Present	Past
First person	I giue	I gaue	we giue	we gaue
Second person	thou giue(s)t	thou gau(e)st	ye giue	ye gaue
Third person	he/she/hit giueth	he/she/hit gaue	they giue	they gaue

Table B5.2.5 Strong and weak forms of the verb *to help* in Early Modern English

EModE base form	Strong past tense	Weak past tense
help	holp	helped
melt	molte	melted
swell	swole	swelled
climb	clamb/clomb	climbed

of usage when *ye/you* replaced *thou/thee* as the standard second-person singular pronoun in the seventeenth century, since there was no second-person inflection on the form of the verb that agreed with *ye/you*.

The process of regularisation also affected many of the strong verbs in Early Modern English. Many Early Modern English strong verbs regularised over time to become weak verbs. In some cases, however, verbs that are weak in Present Day English had both a strong *and* a weak form in Early Modern English. Some examples (from Barber 1997: 175) are given in Table B5.2.5.

B5.3 Expanding the lexicon

In B1.2 you can read about how new words were formed in Old English via the process of **compounding** (putting existing words together to form new words). In the Middle English period **borrowing** words from Latin and French was the principal means by which the vocabulary of English was expanded (see B3.4 for examples). In the Early Modern period, considerable disagreement arose among certain scholars concerning the most apt way of enlarging the lexicon of English. The disagreement occurred in the second half of the sixteenth century and centred on the appropriateness of expanding the vocabulary of English by borrowing words from Latin and other

Classical languages such as Greek. Some writers, such as Sir Thomas Elyot, believed that the expressive capability and status of the English language could be enriched by borrowing vocabulary from such languages. Other commentators felt that these loanwords were unnecessarily complex and that it was better to use 'simple' Germanic vocabulary. This disagreement has come to be known as **the Inkhorn Controversy**. *Inkhorn* is another term for *inkpot*, into which scholars would dip their pens as they wrote. Those writers who scorned the borrowing of Classical vocabulary described such loanwords as **inkhorn terms**, a disparaging phrase that conveys the belief that using such terms was a scholarly affectation. Sir John Cheke, a Cambridge scholar who was famously against the use of inkhorn terms, expressed his objections to the practice of borrowing Classical vocabulary in a letter of 1557:

> I am of the opinion that our own tongue should be written clean and pure, unmixt and unmangled with borrowing of other tongues, wherein if we take not heed by time, ever borrowing and never paying, she shall be fain to keep her house as bankrupt.
>
> (Cheke 1557, quoted in Johnson 1944: 115)

It may seem surprising that the 'inkhorn terms' to which Cheke and others were objecting included such now common words as *audacious, celebrate, clemency, compatible, contemplate, expectation, hereditary, insane* and *promotion*. Notice that commentators such as Cheke demonstrated an overtly prescriptive (and proscriptive) view of the development of English.

B6   THE DEVELOPMENT OF AMERICAN ENGLISH

The spread of English overseas from the late 1500s onwards necessitates a change in terminology when we talk about the language. Although *dialectal* variation existed in English from its earliest inception, from the point at which English begins to spread to other countries it becomes necessary to talk also about *international* varieties of the language. **American English** is one such example of an international variety that differs from British English (though it is important not to overstate the differences which, in the twenty-first century, are marginal owing to globalisation and the mixing of cultures that this has led to).

In this unit we will consider how English developed in America after the arrival of English speakers in what was then seen as 'the New World' (we will focus specifically on North American English and will look at other international varieties – or **World Englishes** – in B7 and B8). It is important to remember that the first British settlers in America would have spoken varieties of Early Modern English. Initially, then, varieties of English in America would have sounded like varieties of English in Britain. Over time, though, differences emerged as a result of numerous factors: contact with other languages, the influence of other cultures, power struggles, etc. The forging of a national identity distinct from that of Britain was also responsible for developments in the language.

B6.1 Causes of linguistic development in the American colonies

In A6.1 it is noted that the first British settlers in America came from a variety of places in England. London was just one of these. Additionally, settlers originated from such counties as Gloucestershire, Somerset, Lincolnshire, Nottinghamshire, Essex and Kent. What is particularly important here is that the early British settlers were drawn from the lower and middle classes of Britain, and consequently the English that was initially spoken in America included many regional dialectal features as opposed to being solely a form of Standard English. Cassidy (1984: 178) makes the salient point that 'people at the top of the social scale do not become colonists'. This is significant when we consider research in sociolinguistics which suggests that change and development in language is generally instigated by the middle classes.

Cassidy (1984: 179) goes on to suggest what some of the factors might have been that would have caused the development of English in the earliest American colonies. These include:

❑ *Numerical majority* – the dialectal forms that were most frequent in the colonies were the ones that were most likely to survive and develop into American English, i.e. the larger the group of settlers from a particular area of Britain, the more likely their regional dialect was to have an influence on what became the norm in the developing American English variety.
❑ *Prestige* – the linguistic forms used by community leaders would most likely have been viewed as prestigious and adopted into American English for this reason.
❑ *Lack of contact with Britain* – the influence of British English was, over time, reduced as a result of diminishing contact between the settlers and their homeland. Conversely, the experiences of colonial life were more likely to affect the development of American English.

In addition to these factors there is also the significant issue of language contact. In A3 you can read about the importance of language contact for the development of Middle English. Contact between English and other languages played a similarly important part in the development of American English. Languages and dialects that English came into contact with included those of the Native American Indians, as well as **Dutch**, **Spanish**, **French** and **German** (the languages of other immigrant groups in the country at the time).

B6.2 A developing standard

Reed (1967: 16) makes the point that because the early British settlers in America were not from the upper echelons of society (and hence, perhaps, not as well educated), it is likely that spoken language more than written language determined the standard form of American English that developed. The standard that gradually emerged was not as socially charged as, say, written Standard British English and Received Pronunciation, most likely because the social hierarchy of Britain had not been transplanted to the American colonies. In a study of contemporary American English, Toon (1984: 214) claims that 'in general, English in the United States is most uniform in the domain of syntax and most variable in pronunciation'. This is an observation also made by contemporary observers of American English in the 1700s (Marckwardt 1980: 70), though it is likely that this was overstated somewhat. Dillard (1985) puts this down to **dialect-levelling**, a process by which the characteristic features of dialects are gradually lost as dialects **converge** (i.e. speakers accommodate their language use to become more like other language users). Dillard explains that this dialect-levelling occurred from the beginning of the 1700s until well into the last quarter of that century (1985: 70) and that, within a generation of settlers, 'access to the levelled dialect was possible' (1985: 62). This rapid development came about in part because of the establishment of schools wherein children would be exposed to standard forms, as well as the peer pressure that caused colonial children to accommodate their language use to that of their classmates (Dillard 1985: 63). Nevertheless, by the end of the 1700s, dialectal diversity became more commonplace owing to contact with the frontier varieties spoken by immigrants from other countries (Dillard 1985: 71).

B6.3 'Archaisms' in American English

In the early years of the American colonies, in addition to the fact that American English was seen as remarkably uniform in terms of dialect, it was also often observed that it retained a number of 'archaic' forms of British English (the same claim is sometimes made today too). To a certain extent this was true, but it is necessary to exercise caution when investigating this. For example, it is not the case that forms of Early Modern English have been preserved in American English entirely without change (Marckwardt 1980: 71). And while it may sometimes be claimed that a particular word, grammatical structure or pronunciation in American English is an archaic form of British English, it is often the case that the form is still in use in dialects of British English other than Standard English (remember the necessity of considering varieties of English before making generalisations about linguistic change; see A8.3). Hence, some of the cited archaisms in American English are often simply forms which are no longer in use in Standard British English. 'Archaism' is perhaps not, therefore, the best term to use when describing these differences. As an example, here are some linguistic variables that are commonly cited as being archaic but which still survive in regional British dialects:

❑ Marckwardt (1980: 73) reports that the word *druggist* was used in England until around 1750, when it was replaced by *chemist*. However, *druggist* remained in use in the American colonies. Nevertheless, as Marckwardt points out, while *druggist* fell out of usage in the Standard British English of the time, it was retained in some dialects of Scotland. (In contemporary American English, while *druggist* may be used in the mid-West or on the East Coast, other dialects prefer *pharmacist*. Just to confuse things, you may find that *pharmacist* is now replacing *chemist* in some British English dialects. If you're a speaker of British English, which would you use?)

❑ In RP, *farm* is pronounced /fɑːm/ while in some accents of American English – that of New York, for example – it is pronounced /fɑːɹm/. The pronunciation of <r> in the latter example is an instance of what linguists call post-vocalic <r>;

i.e. the pronunciation of <r> after a vowel sound. Post-vocalic <r> can turn up in words like *car, hour, poor, wire, harm,* etc., and is sometimes cited as being an archaism since it used to be prevalent in British English but no longer is, despite being retained in many American accents. However, while it is true that post-vocalic /ɹ/ is no longer used in RP (according to Cassidy [1984: 201], it died out in the early seventeenth century in RP but was retained in the American colonies), it is still common in particular regional varieties of British English; for example, Lancashire. (Interestingly, the prestige value of post-vocalic /ɹ/ differs between British and American English, which reinforces the fact that the social 'value' of particular linguistic variables is determined entirely by non-linguistic factors; see Labov's famous study of New York English [Labov 1966] for more details.)

❑ Baugh and Cable (2002: 360) suggest that *mad* is used in American English to mean 'angry', which was its meaning in Early Modern English. The claim is that Present Day English *mad* now means 'mentally disturbed'. The problem, of course, is that seeing *mad* in American English as an archaism privileges Standard English in the history of the language and ignores the fact that *mad* to mean 'angry' is commonplace in some British dialects – e.g. Yorkshire English.

The notion of archaism as a trait of American English is, then, somewhat problematic. While it is true that older forms of English are preserved in American English, it is also the case that these forms continue to be used in British English dialects. The only sense, then, in which they are archaic is when compared against Standard British English; and to do this implies that Standard British English is the measure against which all other varieties are to be judged. The current status of English as a global language makes this an untenable position to take.

B6.4 The beginnings of African American English

So far we have been dealing with the developing English of immigrants to America from England. However, there is another variety of contemporary American English whose roots are not yet fully clear to linguists. This is **African American English (AAE)**, which has developed from the varieties spoken by the African slaves who were brought to work on plantations in the early seventeenth century. The debate about the origins of AAE has focused on whether it developed from the dialects of the early European settlers in America (as North American English did), or from **creoles**. Creoles develop from pidgins (see A6.2 for the definition of this term) and when a pidgin acquires native speakers – i.e. when the children of pidgin speakers use that pidgin as their first language – it is said to become a creole. Green (2002: 9) explains how some linguists have suggested that the first African slaves to arrive in America brought with them West Indian creoles (e.g. Jamaican Creole), which were then adapted and developed into AAE. This hypothesis is formed on the basis that AAE shares numerous patterns with Jamaican Creole (Green 2002: 9). The alternative view is that AAE is a development from the Southern dialects of the plantation owners. Green (2002) explains that recently the **creolist hypothesis** has been questioned and it has been suggested that AAE may have developed in much the same way as North American dialects, and that it is developments in the twentieth century that have led to its becoming significantly different from present day so-called white vernaculars (see Wolfram and Thomas 2002).

INTERNATIONAL ENGLISH

The global spread of English from the late 1500s onwards (see A7) has led to the emergence of numerous international varieties of English, or **World Englishes** (see A6 for the example of the early development of American English). In the limited space available it is impossible to provide a comprehensive survey of all of these varieties (though see Jenkins 2015 for a detailed introduction to World Englishes). What I will do instead is to focus on some of the characteristic features of just a few of these international varieties, in order to give a flavour of the variety of forms currently in use. We will consider how these varieties have emerged and what relationship they have with British English. As you read through the sections of this unit, bear in mind the notion that was introduced in A2.1 that the definition of a language is as much a political matter as a linguistic one. As Burchfield (1994: 13) points out, 'it must always be borne in mind that varieties of English, spoken at whatever distance, or however close up, are not discrete entities. [...] The similarities greatly exceed the differences'.

B7.1 Australian English

According to Trudgill and Hannah (2008: 21), there is little regional variation in Australian English. That is, dialects of Australian English have a tendency towards uniformity (though this does not discount the social variation that is to be found). Burridge and Mulder (1998: 38) suggest that this is because the settlement of Australia was by and large achieved as a result of Australian settlers sailing from New South Wales to other parts of the country. During this process of settlement whole groups of people might move long distances without coming into contact with other speech communities. This lack of contact had the effect of keeping the settlers' dialects relatively uniform; in effect, the English of the settlers in New South Wales was simply transferred around the country through a gradual process. In terms of accent, there are some obvious characteristic features of Australian English. Trudgill and Hannah (2008: 22–24) suggest the following:

❑ Use of schwa /ə/ in unstressed syllable where in RP the phoneme would be /ɪ/, e.g. *naked* /neɪkəd /, *David* /deɪvəd/, *honest* /ɒnəst/, *village* /vilədʒ/, *begin* /bəgɪn/.
❑ Use of non-rhotic /ɹ/ (see B6.3 for details of rhotic /ɹ/ usage – i.e. post-vocalic /ɹ/ – in American English).
❑ Intervocalic /t/ (that is, the pronunciation of /t/ between vowel sounds) becomes closer to /d/; e.g. *city* /sɪdiː/, *better* /bɛdə/ (this feature, though, is not as common or standard as in North American English).

❑ The /ʊ/ vowel has more lip-rounding than in 'English English' (i.e. the English spoken in England; try saying *put* with and without rounding and listen to the difference in the vowel sound).

❑ Use of /iː/ where in RP /ɪ/ is more common; e.g. *very* /vɛriː/, *many* /mɛniː/, *city* / sɪdiː/ (Trudgill and Hannah note that this feature is similar to southern English non-RP accents).

There are essentially two theories concerning how these distinctive features of the Australian English accent emerged. The first is that they are the result of dialect-levelling among the early settlers and convicts, many of whom came to Australia from the south-east of England and from Ireland and Scotland (note that one piece of evidence here is that the use of /iː/ where in RP /ɪ/ would be the more common phoneme is also a feature of southern English non-RP accents). Burridge and Mulder (1998: 37) explain that the early linguistic situation following the arrival of the first settlers would have been one in which a variety of dialects were spoken. As these converged, certain accentual features would have been lost and others consolidated, giving rise to distinctive features that would over time come to be associated with the new variety of English. The second theory, according to Burridge and Mulder (1998), is that London English (and particularly the **Cockney** dialect – the dialect of East Londoners) is the ultimate basis of the Australian English accent, while features from Irish and Scottish accents took effect later on.

In addition to distinctive phonetic and phonological features, Australian English also makes use of distinctive lexis. The following are extracted from a list put together by Trudgill and Hannah (2008: 26):

Australian English	English English
to barrack for	to support
bludger	a loafer, sponger
footpath	pavement
frock	dress
get	fetch
lolly	sweet
parka	anorak
station	stock-farm
station wagon	estate car
stove	cooker
stroller	push-chair
wreckers	breakers

Some of these examples are still relatively uncommon in English English (and other British varieties). *Estate car*, for instance, is still preferred over *station wagon* in British English. Some, on the other hand, *can* be found in British varieties of English. *Footpath*, for instance, which Trudgill and Hannah suggest is only used in English English to refer to 'a path across fields' (2008: 26), is commonly found as a synonym for *pavement* in Northern varieties of English. The problem, of course, is that it is difficult to make generalisations about differences between international varieties of English, since within all of these we also find variation based on a number of non-linguistic factors: geography, social class, the formality of the discourse situation, etc. You can explore these issues some more in C7.

B7.2 Indian English

The legacy of British colonial rule in India (see A6.2) is that English is now an official language in the country and the second language of a significant number of the population. While there is considerable variation in some aspects of Indian English, such as pronunciation (Trudgill and Hannah 2008: 133), there are other features which may be seen as typical of the variety. An example of one of these is the tendency towards regularisation in the formation of plurals of mass nouns. A mass noun is a noun that in Standard English is not countable; i.e. one which cannot be made plural by the simple addition of an <s> inflection (e.g. *hand* → *hands*) or by changing the vowel in the stem (e.g. *foot* → *feet*). An example of a mass noun is *bread*. In Standard English we cannot say 'I ate two breads'. Instead, we have to add a pluralising expression – 'I ate two slices of bread'. (Sometimes, mass nouns can become countable. A recent example which is particularly appropriate for us is the noun *English* to refer to the language. The explosion of international varieties has led us to talk now about World *Englishes*.) In Indian English, however, pluralising mass nouns by the addition of an <s> inflection is common, giving rise to such examples from Trudgill and Hannah (2008: 134) as:

aircrafts	Many aircrafts have crashed there.
fruits	We ate just fruits for lunch.
litters (rubbish)	Do not throw litters on the street.
furnitures	He bought many furnitures.
woods	He gathered all the woods.

Clearly, what is happening in these instances is that the rules governing the formation of plurals in Standard English have been regularised by the speakers of the Indian English variety. Over time this has come to be a common feature of Indian English and while it may be viewed as non-standard from the perspective of a speaker of British English, we have already seen that British English is no longer an appropriate benchmark (if, indeed, it ever was) against which to judge other varieties. In this case, what is non-standard in British English is standard in Indian English.

Another characteristic difference between Indian English and British English concerns the meaning of some modal verbs. Modal verbs are a type of auxiliary verb; that is, they always occur with a main verb and provide information that the main verb doesn't. In the case of the modals this extra information concerns the speaker's or writer's attitude to the proposition being expressed. For example:

You can go. (The modal auxiliary *can* indicates permission; *go* is the main verb.)
It could be true. (The modal auxiliary *could* indicates possibility; *be* is the main verb.)
You must answer! (The modal verb *must* indicates obligation; *answer* is the main verb.)
He should have tried harder. (The modal verb *should* indicates necessity; *tried* is the main verb; *have* is an additional auxiliary.)

You will notice from the above examples that in Standard Present Day British English the modals do not change their form according to person, number or tense (though this was not always the case) and that they express particular attitudinal perspectives. In Indian English this is also true, but the semantic information (i.e. the meaning) that the modals convey is often different from British English. Trudgill and Hannah (2008: 136) illustrate this with the following examples:

Indian English	*English English*
This furniture may be removed tomorrow.	This furniture is to be removed tomorrow.
These mistakes may please be corrected.	These mistakes should be corrected.

It would appear that in the Indian English examples the modal verb *may* has been interpreted by the speaker/writer as being a polite form and that this pragmatic function takes precedence over the semantic meaning.

Other grammatical features of Indian English that differ from Standard British English include the following (drawn from Trudgill and Hannah 2008):

Use of present tense as opposed to present perfect with durational phrases

Indian English	I am here since two o'clock.
English English	I have been here since two o'clock.

Lack of subject/verb inversion in direct questions

Indian English	What this is made from?
English English	What is this made from?
Indian English	Who you have come to see?
English English	Who have you come to see?

Unsurprisingly, it is also the case that Indian English has borrowed considerably from other Indian languages. Borrowed words include the following (drawn from Trudgill and Hannah 2008):

bandh	a total strike in an area
crore	ten million
durzi	tailor
hartal	a strike used as a political gesture
sahib	sir, master
swadeshi	indigenous, native, home-grown

Some of these words seem likely to have been borrowed in response to particular situations faced by speakers of Indian English during the colonial era. In addition to borrowings from other Indian languages, Indian English has also created new vocabulary by adapting existing British English words, e.g.:

appreciable	appreciated
backside	behind
biodata	curriculum vitae
hotel	restaurant, café
stir	a demonstration
tiffin	lunch

Some of these newly created words arise from changing the form of an existing word (e.g. *appreciable*), some change the meaning (*hotel*) and some change the degree of formality of the word in question (*stir* is perhaps more colloquial in British Standard English than in Indian English). You can explore the creation of new vocabulary in English in more detail in C7.

B7.3 Pidgins and creoles on the West African coast

Todd (1984: 286) points out that in those African countries where English is used as an official language, it is useful if we think of English as a language continuum. By this she means that English exists in a variety of forms – from pidgins and creoles through to second-language English influenced by the speakers' first languages, and local standards. In this unit we will concentrate on pidgins and creoles, since these provide further examples of how English has developed beyond the British Isles.

Pidgin varieties of English developed along the West African coast as a result of contact between the native inhabitants and European sailors and traders. (Indeed, Todd 1974 points out that many pidgins and creoles retain numerous nautical words as a result of their origins as coastal trading languages. She gives the example of *galley* as the term for a kitchen in Krio, a creole language in Sierra Leone.) This illustrates one of the key features of a pidgin, namely that it is a **contact language**. That is, it is no-one's first language but instead emerges to fulfil a limited set of functions for two or more speech communities that otherwise have no language in common. In B6.4 we discussed the notion of African American English emerging out of a pidgin. Pidgins need both a **substrate** language and a **superstrate** language. The substrate (usually the local vernacular) provides the grammatical structure while the superstrate provides the majority of the lexis of the pidgin.

Other key features of pidgins are **simplification**, **mixing** and **reduction**. Simplification involves both regularisation and loss of redundancy. Regularisation means the process of making irregular forms regular – for example, pluralising mass nouns by the addition of an <s> inflection (see B7.2, above). Loss of redundancy involves the deletion of linguistic elements that repeat information. For instance, a pidgin might not use the third-person present tense inflection on verbs since this is grammatical information that is conveyed by the third-person pronoun. Mixing refers to the tendency of pidgin speakers to incorporate elements of their own language – accent, grammatical structures, lexis, etc. – into the pidgin. Finally, reduction refers to the fact that pidgins have reduced function. That is, the simplification of the contributing languages in the process of **pidginisation** means that the pidgin is only useful for a limited set of functions; basic communication, for example, as opposed to, say, use as a language of administration or law.

This, then, is a pidgin, but in some cases further development takes place. If a situation arises where a pidgin becomes the first language of a speech community (as a result of children learning the pidgin as their mother tongue) it becomes a creole. The process of **creolisation** increases both the complexity and functionality of the language, resulting in increased expressive capability and greater capacity for use in numerous domains of life. What happens next to the creole depends on the particular society in which it has developed. If it has emerged alongside a standard language, it may develop in such a way as to take on more and more features of that standard.

Table B7.3.1 Pronouns in Cameroon Pidgin (Todd 1984: 7)

Subject	Object	Possessive determiner	Subject	Object	Possessive determiner
a	mi	ma	I	me	my
yu	yu	yu	you	you	your
i	i/am	i	he	him	his
i	i/am	i	she	her	her
i	i/am	i	it	it	its
wi	wi	wi	we	us	our
wuna	wuna	wuna	you (plural)	you	your
dɛm	dɛm/am	dɛm	they	them	their

If this happens, the creole is said to undergo **decreolisation**. Alternatively, it might remain as a creole. Once a creole has reached a certain stage of development it is also possible for it to generate new pidgins, in which case the whole process begins again.

Cameroon Pidgin well illustrates the concepts discussed above that are typical of pidginisation. For example, the pronoun system of Cameroon Pidgin (Table B7.3.1) demonstrates simplification via regularisation.

As will be apparent from the above table, a significant amount of simplification has taken place in Cameroon Pidgin. There is no indication of gender, for example, in the third-person pronouns, nor is there a distinction made between subject and object forms. In such varieties, contextual information becomes increasingly important for interpreting speaker meaning. Nevertheless, the simplification that is typical of pidgins is also governed by linguistic rules – it is not the case that anything goes. For example, Todd (1984: 5) points out that to form a negative statement in Cameroon Pidgin you put *no* in front of the verb. To give extra emphasis *no* can also be put in front of any nouns in the sentence, but without *no* before the verb the sentence is ungrammatical. So, as Todd (1984: 5) demonstrates, *No man no bin kam* ('Nobody came') is an acceptable sentence in Cameroon Pidgin while *No man bin kam* is not.

The mixing that is typical of pidgins can be seen in the vocabulary of Cameroon Pidgin, which utilises lexis not only from English but also from the local vernacular that forms the substrate. Todd (1984: 14) gives the following examples:

faɔn	chief
nchinda	chief's messenger
mbombo	namesake
ngɔmbi	spirit, god
birua	enemy
pulpul	grass skirt
akara	beancake
kaukau	sweet potato
fufu	pounded yam
kindam	crayfish

But while borrowing of words from the local vernacular is used as one means of extending the lexicon of a pidgin, communicative necessity means that this cannot be the principal source of vocabulary. **Calquing** is also used, a process in which 'ideas borrowed from the local cultures [are] expressed in English words' (Todd 1984: 15). Some examples from Todd include:

gud hat	sincere (literally, 'good heart')
krai dai	a wake, funeral celebration (literally 'cry die')
biabia mɔt	moustache, beard (literally, 'hair mouth')

Pidgins and creoles, then, demonstrate some of the means by which English has developed and spread globally.

B8 THE GLOBALISATION OF ENGLISH

Unit A8 describes the rapid globalisation of English over recent years. Considering English's current status as a global language it is interesting to speculate on how the language might develop in the future. In this final unit of section B we will consider some of the possibilities.

B8.1 Attitudes towards global English

Perhaps the first issue to consider in a discussion of the globalisation of English is the attitudes that people have towards English as a global lingua franca. Pennycook (2001) summarises some of the debate in this area, pointing out the difference of opinion that exists on the subject. For example, it is not necessarily the case that the spread of English globally is seen as a good thing. If you are a native speaker of English who has never considered the issue, this might surprise you. Surely, the spread of English globally provides numerous advantages? It makes travel easier, it makes international communication more straightforward, it provides more economic opportunities, etc. The answer, of course, is that it does – but not for everyone. If you are a native speaker of British Standard English you will enjoy all of the advantages listed above of English becoming a global language. But what if you are a speaker of an international variety of English that is not recognised as a standard? What if you do not speak English at all? From these latter perspectives the development of English into a global language is perhaps not as appealing. Bear in mind too that diversity is interesting in and of itself. Encountering other languages and cultures is an enriching experience.

A further argument against the global development of English is provided by Pennycook (2001), who cites Cooke's (1988) and Judd's (1983) assertions that English is a language of imperialism and that its global spread threatens the survival of many of the world's lesser-known languages. Their argument is that the prestigious position that English occupies results in people wanting to learn and use English in order to reap the economic advantages that it brings – and this inevitably leads to the downgrading of local vernaculars which, in a worst case scenario, can result in the dying out of languages. Crystal (2000) provides numerous arguments as to why we should be concerned by this. For example, languages are repositories of history. If we lose a language (that is, if it dies out entirely as opposed to simply developing) then we lose the history of the speakers of that language – especially if theirs was an oral culture. Furthermore, language provides a means of expressing individual identity; imagine how your sense of self would be affected if your native variety were to be displaced by a global language which you were then forced to communicate in. Would you still be able to express your identity in the same way? Not least of Crystal's (2000) concerns about the dying out of languages is simply that diversity is an essential part of our humanity. Experiencing difference allows us to understand ourselves better and to empathise with other viewpoints. If the consequences of the global spread of English threaten this, then this is something that should be a cause for concern.

There are, then, complex ethical and moral issues to be taken into account as English spreads globally. Managing the international spread of English requires careful and considerate language planning and policies. If you are reading this book as part of a course, you could debate these issues in class.

B8.2 World Standard English

We saw in A6 that it makes no sense to think of languages as 'belonging' to countries. English does not 'belong' to the English. World Englishes are not corruptions of a British 'norm' but complex and developed varieties in their own right (we saw in B7, for instance, that pidgin forms of English have grammatical rules just as Standard English does). Nevertheless, it is often the case that speakers of British English as a first language perceive international varieties as corruptions, partly out of a misplaced belief that diversification leads to a disregard for standards. As Crystal (2001) points out, though, the development of global English and all the varieties that constitute this *increases* the need for standard forms in order for speakers of World Englishes to communicate with one another. According to Crystal (2001: 58), what is particularly interesting about the future of global English is that speakers are likely to have to master at least two standard forms – what he calls **World Standard Printed English (WSPE)** and **World Standard Spoken English (WSSE)**. In fact, as Crystal explains, World Standard Printed English already exists insofar as Standard English is the common form used worldwide for writing in English. Only occasionally do we find national and/or regional variants in Standard English (for example, slight lexical and grammatical differences between American and British English) – and even in these cases the differences are not a barrier to comprehension. A World Standard Spoken English has not yet emerged but if it does Crystal (2001) surmises that it is likely to avoid such features as regionally based idioms and complex phoneme clusters, and to involve at least some degree of simplification. We already shift varieties according to particular contexts (I am writing this book in Standard English, for instance, though I may revert to my regional dialect when conversing with my family, as an identity marker). Perhaps we will see more of such shifting as global English develops further.

B8.3 Fragmentation or fusion?

What form might we expect English to take in the future? One conundrum concerning the future development of English is whether we can expect it to fragment – that is, to develop into numerous sub-languages that are not mutually intelligible – or whether, alternatively, we might expect it to develop to the extent where there are very few differences between international varieties of English. Crystal (2003) considers these possibilities and admits that with our current levels of knowledge about new varieties of English it is difficult to accurately predict the likelihood of fragmentation happening. He does, however, note that a number of factors might lead us to suppose that this is an unlikely scenario. The weight of material published in standard written English will continue to exert an influence on what is perceived as prestigious in terms of usage. Similarly, the ease with which it is possible to read and hear international varieties of English (via the internet, cinema, etc.) means that developing forms of English will not emerge in isolation from existing varieties. In this respect, mutual unintelligibility is unlikely to develop.

In fact, it is not necessarily the case that we need to consider the notions of fragmentation and fusion as mutually exclusive. In A8.3 I stressed the importance of considering how sociopolitical events do not necessarily affect all varieties of English in the same way. We have seen how English exists in numerous different forms – national varieties, regional varieties, social varieties, etc. It is also the case that individuals use language differently according to particular circumstances – the language you use at work or in the classroom may be very different from the language you use when out with friends. We might therefore expect the globalisation of English to lead to the fusion of certain varieties (a developing World Standard English such as that referred to above, perhaps) while at the same time retaining the diversity associated with particular local varieties of the language that are especially important for conveying identity. Burridge and Mulder (1998: 274) consider this possibility in their discussion of the related concepts of **conformity** and **diversity**. Conformity refers to levelling of difference in linguistic terms. Diversity is the opposite. Burridge and Mulder (1998) suggest that in many cases linguistic diversification is a reaction against conformity, pointing out how linguistic diversity emphasises the connection between language and identity. Developing particular localised varieties of English (even if speakers have command of several alternatives, as is likely) enables the assertion or reassertion of individual identities, which, as we have seen, is as important a function of language as communication.

Section C

EXPLORATION
EXPLORING THE HISTORY
OF ENGLISH

In this section you will find language data and exercises to help you investigate some of the major aspects of the history of English for yourself. Some of these exercises are designed to raise your awareness of the language as it was at its various stages of development, some concentrate on social attitudes towards usage, and others allow you to investigate specific aspects of linguistic change. A grasp of all of these elements is important in order to understand why English has developed in the way that it has. Each unit of section C broadly corresponds with the equivalent numbered unit in sections A and B, so if you find yourself getting stuck, re-read the corresponding A and B units and you should find these will help you to make sense of the issues raised here.

As you explore specific elements of change in English over time it is useful to keep in mind two questions:

1. At what structural level does the change occur?
2. What was the motivation for the change?

With regard to the first question, it is often useful to think about language as hierarchically organised. Figure C1 illustrates this notion by showing how the units of language combine to form progressively larger units.

The elements of the hierarchy are different depending on whether we are dealing with spoken language or written language. For example, in speech, morphemes are composed of phonemes, but in written language they are made up of graphemes. Nonetheless, linguistic change can occur at all of the levels in Figure C1. For example, the Great Vowel Shift (see B4 and D4) involved change at the phonological level; that is, a change in the sound system of English. The development of English into an analytic as opposed to synthetic language involved change at the sentence level; that is, a change in the syntactic structure of the language.

Having identified the level at which the change you are concentrating on has occurred, the next step is to consider question two and ascertain what caused the

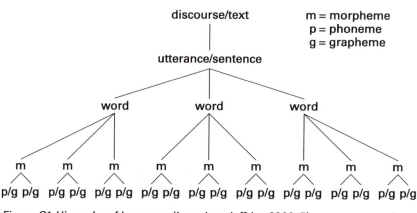

Figure C1 Hierarchy of language (based on Jeffries 2006: 5).

change to take place. In doing this it is important to remember that the levels in Figure C1 are interconnected and that change at one level can generate change at another. For instance, the syntactic development of English into an analytic language was caused by a sound change in Old English which led to the morphological inflections on the ends of words becoming unstressed in speech. This is an example of **internal change** – a development at one linguistic level causes further developments at others. Sometimes, though, linguistic development occurs as a result of external factors. For example, American English has borrowed numerous words from Native American Indian languages as a result of the contact between the Native Americans and the early settlers in America. Another external influence on the development of English was the introduction of the printing press, which led eventually to a standardised system of spelling.

One important level of change that the structural model in Figure C1 misses, however, is meaning (this is because meaning is not a structural element of language in the way that, say, morphemes are). The semantic meaning of words can change over time (for example, OE *drēam* originally meant 'joy' or 'music' before it took on its present meaning), as can their pragmatic meanings (consider the development of the EModE second-person singular pronouns). We will consider this issue further in C7.

In considering how and why change occurs in language, it is also useful to be aware of two concepts from historical linguistics. These are **actuation** and **propagation**. Actuation refers to the initiation of a linguistic change, though it is important to note that actuation is not necessarily a conscious process on the part of speakers. Actuation can be caused by a number of factors. One of these is gap filling, which is what happens, for example, during sound changes such as the Great Vowel Shift (in effect, when one phoneme moves position in the vowel space, it leaves a gap that is then filled by another phoneme; see B4.2 and D4 for more details). Another is regularisation. We can see this in the changes to the way that nouns are pluralised in English. In Old English, for instance, the plural of *ēare* ('ear') was *ēaran*, though this was later regularised to *ears* by the addition of the <s> inflection. Another cause of actuation is misperception. For instance, when Middle English scribes began spelling *hwǣr* ('where') and *hwanne* ('when') with an initial <wh> as opposed to <hw>, this was as a result of misperceiving the <h> to be a diacritic that indicated a pronunciation of the <w> as /x/. The aim was to bring the spelling in line with other words in which <h> functioned as a diacritic, such as *child*, where the <h> indicated a pronunciation of <c> as /tʃ/ not /k/. Other causes of actuation include creativity (e.g. the current use of *ship* as a verb to mean wanting two people to enter into a relationship) and the avoidance of redundancy (e.g. the change in meaning of *hound* to mean a dog kept for hunting, as a result of *dog* replacing *hound* as the general term for the animal). You can read more about causes of actuation in Culpeper and McIntyre (2015).

Actuation, or starting a linguistic change (whether intentionally or not), does not necessarily mean that the linguistic innovation in question will catch on, of course. For this to happen, propagation is required. Propagation refers to the spread of a linguistic innovation and happens as a result of contact between speakers. Propagation happens most easily within what are known as open social networks. The sociolinguistic concept of a social network comes from the work of Milroy (1987) and describes the structure of a speech community. A closed social network is one in which the members of a speech community all know one another and have little contact with other speech communities. By contrast, an open social network is one in which the members of the speech community (i) do not necessarily all know each other and (ii) have relationships with people belonging to other speech communities. Open social networks are by definition more exposed to new linguistic forms than closed social networks, meaning that propagation is more likely to happen within the former than the latter. Propagation can happen for two main reasons. The first is that speakers may adopt a particular linguistic innovation as a result of assuming it to have high prestige. This is what Labov (2001) calls 'change from above'. The second is that speakers may adopt a particular form simply because lots of other speakers are using it. This is what Labov (2001) calls 'change from below'.

THE ROOTS OF ENGLISH   C1

In this unit we will investigate the relationship Old English has with the languages from which it has developed, as well as the nature of Old English as a language in its own right. Bear these origins in mind as you investigate the language in its later stages of development as they will sometimes help you to understand where a particular word, structure or pronunciation has come from.

C1.1 Language family trees

Unit A1 outlines the number of languages that influenced the development of Old English. Celtic, Latin and Scandinavian all had an effect, however big or small, on the expansion of the Germanic dialects of the Anglo-Saxon settlers. One common way of representing the development of languages is to use a family tree to show the various relationships that exist between them. Figure C1.1.1 is a simplified family tree in which

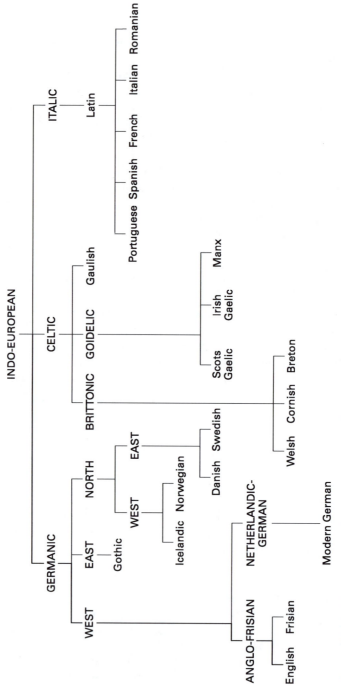

Figure C1.1.1 A language family tree for the Indo-European languages (adapted from Pyles and Algeo 1993: 68–9).

the bold line shows the linguistic development of English. If you trace the line back you can see that it is a language of West Germanic descent, which itself derives from a language called Indo-European. If we use the 'family' metaphor, English is the great-great-grandchild of the prehistoric Indo-European.

Activity C1.1.1

The family tree metaphor is useful for thinking about languages as it shows how languages group together because of shared characteristics. For example, you will rec- ognise that Spanish, Italian and Portuguese sound similar, even if you can't describe in technical terms why. This is because Spanish, Italian and Portuguese all derive from Latin – which is now considered to be a dead language (i.e. no-one speaks it as a first language anymore). However, family trees do not give the complete picture of a language's development. To think through this issue in a bit more detail, try answering the following questions:

1. What important elements of the development of Old English does the family tree not show? (Hint: think about the languages that Old English borrowed words from.)
2. Re-read (or read!) unit A1.1. Based on what you know of the earliest inhabitants of Britain (the Britons) and how they lived, how accurate is the family tree in reflecting the language they would have spoken?
3. English is often described as a living language, while Latin is said to be a dead lan- guage. Can languages really be dead or alive? How useful is this metaphor?

C1.2 The futhorc

In 597 CE, the Benedictine monk Augustine introduced Christianity into Britain (see A1.4). One of the most significant consequences of this was the development of a script for writing Old English, based on the Roman alphabet. Prior to this, the method of writing Old English was to use what are known as **runes**. The set of Anglo-Saxon runes is commonly known as the **futhorc**. This word is derived from the pronunci- ation of the first six runes of the set, just as the word *alphabet* comes from the Greek names of its first two letters (*alpha* and *beta*). There were approximately 32 runes in use during the Anglo-Saxon period (Symons 2016: 9). The first six runes, that spell the word *futhorc*, are as follows:

ᚹ	ᚢ	ᚦ	ᚠ	ᚱ	ᚲ
f	u	th	o	r	c

You will notice that the third rune, <Þ>, survives in Old English as the letter thorn <þ>. You should also recognise the origins of the some of the other letters of the English alphabet in the list of runes in Table C1.2.1.

Table C1.2.1 Runes of the futhorc

Rune	Pronunciation	Pronunciation notes
ᛈ	/f/	
ᚾ	/u/	
ᚦ	/θ/	
ᚠ	/o/	Similar to the vowel sound in *yawn*, if pronounced with full lip-rounding
ᚱ	/r/	A trilled /ɹ/
ᛕ	/k/	
ᚷ	/g/	
ᚹ	/w/	
ᚻ	/h/	
ᛏ	/n/	
ᛁ	/iː/	
ᚲ	/p/	
ᛡ	/j/	
ᛃ	/x/	
ᛣ	/ks/	
ᚻ	/s/	
ᛏ	/t/	
ᛒ	/b/	
ᛗ	/e/	Similar to the vowel sound in *way*, though not diphthongised
ᛗ	/m/	
ᚱ	/l/	
ᛢ	/ŋ/	
ᛞ	/d/	
ᛨ	/eː/	An elongated /e/
ᚨ	/ɑ/	
ᚫ	/æ/	
ᛦ	/y/	Similar to the pronunciation of <u> in French *tu*
ᛤ	/io/	
ᛐ	/æɑ/	
ᛚ	/k/	
ᛥ	/st/	
ᚸ	/g/	

Activity C1.2.1

If you look at the runes in the futhorc you will notice that they are largely angular in design compared to the curved letters of the Roman alphabet. Why do you think the runes were designed in this way?

Activity C1.2.2

One of the earliest surviving examples of Anglo-Saxon runic writing is found on the Ruthwell Cross, a stone cross dating from the eighth century, now located in Ruthwell Church in Dumfriesshire, Scotland. Below is an extract from the inscription on the cross:

ᛚ ᚱ ᛁ ᚻ ᛏ ᚦ ᚠ   ᚻ ᚠ ᛏ ᚱ ᚠ ᛞ ᛁ

Using Table C1.2.1, can you translate the inscription? Work out how to pronounce it first and then try to transliterate this pronunciation into Old English spelling (NB: The inscription represents four words). You may find it useful to consult an online dictionary of Old English once you have transliterated the runes. Try the Bosworth-Toller Anglo-Saxon Dictionary (http://bosworth.ff.cuni.cz) or the Old English Translator (www.oldenglishtranslator.co.uk).

C1.3 Pronouncing Old English

Familiarising yourself with how to pronounce Old English is helpful as a means of interpreting Old English vocabulary. Try the following activity for practice.

Activity C1.3.1
Using the pronunciation guide in B1.1, try pronouncing the following Old English words. Does your pronunciation help you to work out what each word means?

1. *wǣpen*
2. *forbēodan*
3. *swīnhyrde*
4. *tōdæg*
5. *dēaþ*
6. *blæc*
7. *steall*
8. *cirice*
9. *dægtīd*
10. *smiþ*
11. *wulf*
12. *scearp*
13. *mancynn*
14. *wulfas*
15. *ðornig*
16. *hors*
17. *drȳgan*
18. *ūpweard*
19. *hlaf*
20. *meolc*

C1.4 Case

In B1.3–1.5 we saw how case was more important in Old English than it is in Present Day English, and how nouns and determiners have to 'agree' – i.e. the determiner (if used) needs to be in the same case as the noun it precedes. Table C1.4.1 outlines the different forms of the determiner in Old English. You will also notice the form of the determiner

Table C1.4.1 Forms of the determiner in Old English

| | Singular | | |
	Masculine	Feminine	Neuter
Nominative	se	sēo	þæt
Accusative	þone	þā	þæt
Genitive	þæs	þǣre	þæs
Dative	þǣm	þǣre	þǣm
	Plural		
	Masculine	Feminine	Neuter
Nominative	þā	þā	þā
Accusative	þā	þā	þā
Genitive	þāra	þāra	þāra
Dative	þǣm	þǣm	þǣm

depends not only on its case but also on gender (whether the noun it precedes is masculine, neuter or feminine) and number (whether the noun is singular or plural).

Activity C1.4.1
Each of the following Present Day English sentences has one or more determiners missing. If you were going to use the correct Old English determiner, which would you need to fill the gaps? Use the Table C1.4.1 to work out which form is needed.

1. _____ king was tired (*king* is masculine).
2. _____ horse was strong (*horse* is neuter).
3. The king loved _____ queen (*queen* is feminine).
4. The king loved _____ swans (*swan* is feminine).
5. _____ king's swans were beautiful (*king* is masculine).
6. _____ queen gave _____ swans food (*queen* is feminine; *swan* is feminine).

Activity C1.4.2
Now try a similar exercise. This time we'll use a couple of sentences in Old English. These two sentences are extracts from an Old English version of a medieval romance, *Apollonius of Tyre*. You can find the text in Quirk et al. (1975: 15) and the word-for-word translation that I have given below each sentence is based on Quirk et al.'s more natural-sounding translation. For each sentence, I have given you the gender of the words that follow the determiner.

1. _____ōðer him andwirde ond cwæð: 'Swīga ðū[']
   (*ōðer* is masculine).
   (The other him answered [i.e. answered him] and said: 'You be silent'.)
2. Ðā ðā Arcestrates _____ cyningc hæfde _____ gewrit oferrǣd [...]
   (*cyningc* is masculine; *gewrit* is neuter).
   (Then when Arcestrates the king had the letter read [i.e. had read the letter].)

C1.5 An Old English riddle

Activity C1.5.1

The Exeter Book is a collection of Anglo-Saxon poetry that also includes a number of riddles (wordplay and punning in English is nothing new!). Here is Riddle 44, along with a word-for-word translation and a more natural-sounding translation:

Wrætlic hongað   bi weres þeo
frean under sceate   foran is þyrel
bið stiþ ond heard   stede hafað godne
þonne se esne   his agen hrægl
ofer cneo hefeð   wile þæt cuþe hol
mid his hangellan   heafde gretan
þæt he efe lang ær   oft gefylde

Something curious hangs   near the man's thigh
Under the lord's cloak   in front is a hole
It is stiff and hard   it has a good place
When the young man   his own garment
Above the knee lifts   he wants that well-known hole
With his hanging object   head to greet
That is of even length   often filled

Something curious hangs near the man's thigh, under the lord's cloak. In front is a hole. It is stiff and hard. It has a good place. When the young man lifts his own garment above the knee, he wants to greet that well-known hole, that is of the same length and which he has often filled, with the head of his hanging object.

What is being described?

REGIONS AND DIALECTS

C2

If we want to investigate different dialects or different international varieties of Present Day English, we can collect data directly from speakers of such varieties simply by recording examples of their speech (it may be costly and time-consuming, but theoretically at least it is fairly straightforward). Investigating different varieties of older forms of English is more difficult, of course, since we don't have access to spoken language or an abundance of evidence of how language was used in different contexts. Nevertheless, it is still possible to gain an insight into regional variation by looking at, for instance, texts which exist in more than one version. This is what we will concentrate on in this unit. We will also look at how place names provide evidence of different tribal settlements in Britain, which can also provide evidence for the origins of particular dialects.

C2.1 Dialectal differences in an Old English text

What we know about Old English dialects is as a result of studying texts that exist in multiple versions. The following activities give you the opportunity to try a comparative exercise of this kind.

Activity C2.1.1

Here are two versions of an Old English text (from Toon 1992: 432–3). One is in the West Saxon dialect and the other is in the dialect of Northumbria. Read the texts out loud and practise your pronunciation. Does this help you to recognise the text?

> **Version 1 (West Saxon)**
> fæder ure þu þe eart on heofonum
> si þin nama gehalgod
> tobecume þin rīce gewurþe ðin willa
> on eorðan swa swa on heofonum
> ūrne gedæghwamlican hlāf syle us to dæg
> & forgyf us ūre gyltas
> swa swa wē forgyfað ūrum gyltendum
> & ne gelǣd þu us on costnunge
> ac alys us of yfele

> **Version 2 (Northumbrian)**
> fader urer ðu bist in heofnum
> sie ðin noma gehalgad
> to cymeð ðin rīc sie ðin willo
> in eorðo suae is in heofne
> userne [ofer witlic] hlāf sel ūs todæg
> & forgef us usra scylda
> suae uoe wē forgefon usum scyldgum
> & ne inlæd usih in costnunge
> ah gefrig usich fro yfle

Activity C2.1.2

Re-read the texts closely and compare the West Saxon and Northumbrian versions. What differences do you notice between the two versions? Have any of the Old English words survived into Present Day English? If so, how have they changed? Have any of the Old English words been replaced by words borrowed from other languages?

C2.2 Place names

Studying place names can give us an insight into the geographical settlement of particular groups of people, including when such groups settled. Knowing this can help us in tracing the origins of English and can sometimes provide insights into the origins of particular dialects.

Cameron (1996) identifies two different types of place names: habitative and topographical. A habitative place name is one which denotes inhabited places such as farms, buildings, enclosures, etc. An example is *Lenham*, which is developed from a compound of the personal name *Lēana* and *hām*, the Old English word for 'village' (literally, 'Lēana's village'). Note that place names can be formed via compounding, in the same way as other words in the lexicon (see B1.2). Indeed, Cameron (1996) notes that many habitative place names are a compound of two elements; the first is often the name of a person or group while the second refers to the type of habitation. Another example is *Heckmondwike*, a compound of the personal name *Hēamund* and Old English *wīc* ('house', 'dwelling place' or 'village').

Topographical place names describe some feature of the landscape – either natural or artificial; for example, a tree, a ford, a river, etc. Again, compounding of elements is common and this gives us such names as *Bradford* (broad + ford), *Whitchurch* (white + church; 'white' perhaps in reference to white limestone), and *Millbrook* (mill + brook). It is also common to find personal names as the first element in a topographical compound. An example is *Huddersfield*, which derives from a compound of the Old English personal name *Hūd(a)* or *Hūdrǣd* and *feld*, meaning 'open land' (or 'field' in Present Day English).

What makes the study of place names useful in the history of English is that the elements of which they are made up reflect the variety of languages which have been spoken in Britain over the years. Understanding the etymology of place names can help us to see who lived where and give us some indication of how the country was settled. In terms of what place names contribute to our understanding of the development of English over time, Ekwall (1960: xxix) points out that they 'give hints as to the districts where a British population preserved its language for a comparatively long time'. Tracing the etymology of place names can show how the administration of particular places changed over time. For example, York derives ultimately from the Celtic name *Eboracon*, which itself comes from the word *Eburos* – which either means 'yew' or is a personal name (Reaney 1960: 24). *Eboracon* was then Latinised (the practice of re-spelling a word to make it sound and look more like Latin) by Roman settlers to *Eboracum*. Following the departure of the Romans from Britain, York came under the control of the Angles who began to use the name *Eferwic*. Reaney (1960: 24) explains that this was likely to be because in this period <b> had come to be pronounced as /v/. The element *Eber* was therefore likely to have sounded to Anglo-Saxon ears like *eofor*, the Old English word for 'boar'. The second element *wīc*, as we have seen above, could refer to a village, resulting in an Anglo-Saxon name meaning something like 'boar-village'. When York later came under the control of the Scandinavian settlers (see A1.6), the Danes once again adopted the existing name but spelled it in a way that reflected their own pronunciation – *Iorvik*. This then went through a series of spelling changes, including *Iork*, *ꝫeork* and *ꝫork*, before eventually becoming present-day *York* sometime in the thirteenth century. In this example, then, changes in the place name over time reflect wider political changes in society.

To investigate place names you need to be aware of some of the common elements and which languages they come from. Here are some of the most frequent elements and the languages from which they are derived:

Celtic elements

A few Celtic words survive as place name elements. Examples include *brocc* ('badger') in the name *Brockholes* ('badger holes') and *tor* ('hill') in the name *Dunster*. Many river names are of Celtic origin, including *Cray, Medway* and *Colne. Avon* as the name of a river is from the Celtic word for 'water', which also gives rise to the variant forms *Esk* and *Usk*. Cities with names that were originally Celtic include *Carlisle* (developed from the Celtic personal name *Luguvalos* plus Celtic *Cair* meaning 'city' or 'fortified place'), *York* (from *Eboracon*; see above) and *London* (from *Londinos*). As we have seen in the case of *York*, Celtic names were often Latinised by Roman settlers. *Londinos*, for instance, became *Londinium*.

Latin elements

Few Latin elements remain in English place names. Ekwall (1960) lists the following:

castra	a city or walled town, a Roman fort or camp (e.g. Lancaster, Lanchester; the similar-sounding element in names such as Doncaster and Manchester is OE *ceaster*, which is derived from the Latin element)
portus	a port (e.g. Portsmouth, Portland)
strat	street – i.e. a Roman road (e.g. Stratford, Streatham; *strat* was borrowed into OE, becoming *strǣt*)

In addition, Latin elements were added to some place names in later periods. For example, *Lyme* became *Lyme Regis* in the thirteenth century (*Regis* meaning 'king'). *Weston-super-Mare* acquired its Latin element (*super-mare* meaning 'on sea') also in the thirteenth century.

Anglo-Saxon elements

bury/burgh	fortified place (e.g. Loughborough, Canterbury)
bridge/brig	bridge (e.g. Cambridge, Stocksbridge)
cliff	cliff, rock (e.g. Wharncliffe)
dale	dale, valley (e.g. Borrowdale)
don	hill, down (e.g. Swindon)
ey	island (e.g. Walney)
field	open land (e.g. Sheffield, Wakefield)
ham	village, manor, estate, settlement (e.g. Rotherham, Rockingham)
hamm	enclosure, bend of a river (e.g. Higham)
ingas	people of (e.g. Hastings, Worthing)
ley	clearing, glade (e.g. Honley)
ton	farmstead (e.g. Bolton)

Some place name elements are confusing because of their similarity. For example, *ham* and *hamm* have different meanings but are often spelled *ham* in Present Day English. It is also common to find place names composed of more than two elements. For example, *Birmingham* derives ultimately from the personal name *Beornmund*, the *-ingas* element meaning 'people of' and *-ham* meaning 'village'; hence, 'the village of Beornmund's people'.

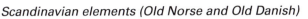

C2

Scandinavian elements (Old Norse and Old Danish)

beck	stream (e.g. Caldbeck, Sandbeck)
by	village, farm (e.g. Quarmby, Whitby)
carr	brushwood, marsh (e.g. Redcar)
rigg	ridge (e.g. Haverigg)
slack	shallow valley (e.g. Witherslack)
thorpe	farm, hamlet (e.g. Grimesthorpe)
thwaite	meadow, clearing (e.g. Slaithwaite)

French elements

A few place name elements can be attributed to French, such as *bel/beau*, meaning 'beautiful'. Examples of such names include *Beaulieu* ('beautiful place'), *Beaumont* ('beautiful hill') and *Beauchief* ('beautiful headland'). Occasionally we find French elements (e.g. the definite article) in place names, such as *Chester-le-Street* or *Chapel-en-le-Frith*. More commonly, French influence on place names is seen in the changed pronunciation of Anglo-Saxon forms. For example, the sound /tʃ/ at the beginning of the place name element *ceaster* did not exist in Norman French and so French speakers would commonly pronounce the sound as /s/. The legacy of this can be seen in the pronunciation of such place names as *Gloucester* and *Cirencester*. Finally, some place names include elements which are French personal names. Examples include *Melton Mowbray*, *Shepton Mallet*, *Aspley Guise* and *Drayton Beauchamp* (see Cameron 1996 for more of these).

You may have noticed from the above examples that in addition to place names sometimes being formed from more than two elements, it is also the case that place names are sometimes made up of elements from more than one language. An example is *Redcar* (OE *hrēod* 'reed' + Old Norse *kiarr* 'marsh'). We therefore have to be careful when investigating place names not to jump to conclusions about likely etymologies. Try to find out whether one element came first, or what reason there might be for a mixing of two languages in a place name. Think about what this might tell you about the social contact between different groups of settlers and what consequences this might have had for the development of English.

Activity C2.2.1

The place names Norfolk and Suffolk refer to 'Northern people' and 'Southern people', respectively, and reflect the geographical settlement of the Angles in the northern and southern parts of East Anglia. In a similar manner, Sussex means 'south Saxons'. Bearing this in mind, where else in the country are the Saxons likely to have settled? (Think about similar-sounding place names.)

Activity C2.2.2

Choose some British place names not listed above (perhaps places nearby if you live in Britain) and investigate their etymologies. An excellent resource for studying place names is the University of Nottingham's online *Key to English Place Names* (http://kepn.nottingham.ac.uk). Alternatively, use a dictionary of place names, such as Mills (1998) to do this. From what historical period do they originate? Which language(s) are they formed from? Can you identify any common elements? Do the names tend to be habitative or topographical, or do they derive from other sources (personal names, for example)? Can you make any connection between the place names you have investigated and wider social events referred to in section A?

C3 FROM OLD ENGLISH TO MIDDLE ENGLISH

The changes that were occurring towards the end of the Old English period eventually gave rise to a form of English that was markedly different from Old English. In this unit we will consider how the vocabulary of English was expanded as a result of borrowing words from other languages, and we will explore some of the characteristics of Middle English by looking at some extracts from Middle English texts.

C3.1 Loanwords

The rich vocabulary of English is a result of the extent to which it has borrowed from other languages during the course of its history. In the early part of the Old English period, borrowing was uncommon though some of the vocabulary of Old English was Latin in origin, having originally been borrowed into Germanic dialects before the arrival of the Anglo-Saxons in England. Following the Viking raids later on in the period, Scandinavian loanwords were introduced into English. During the Middle English period, borrowing as a source of new words increased and Latin and French loanwords entered English.

When investigating the borrowing of words into English, we need to be aware that words are not always borrowed directly. That is, a word may have been borrowed into English from French but the word in question may originally have been borrowed into French from Latin. An example of this is the word *charter*, which was borrowed into Middle English from the Old French *chartre*, which itself came from the Latin *charta*. It is also the case that the etymology of a word may be obscured as a result of changes in spelling. For example, *adventure* was originally borrowed into English from French (*aventure*), though the later addition of a <d> suggests a Latin origin. A similar case is *debt*, which is a French loanword (*dette*), though the later addition of a <b> suggests it too originated from Latin. In fact, it didn't and the <b> was added as a result of an etymological reinterpretation caused by the influence of Latin. Sometimes, suffixes on Latin loanwords were changed to more common French suffixes, thereby further confusing the origin of the borrowed word. For instance, the French suffix <ie> (which later became <y>) was often used in place of the Latin <ia>, giving rise to *letanie* ('litany'), *familie* and *custodie*. Below are some examples of loanwords borrowed into Middle English.

Scandinavian loanwords

In B3.3 we considered the reasons for the development of Old English into an analytic language and we saw that contact between groups who spoke different languages (or, at least, dialects) from one another was a major influencing factor in this. One such group was the Scandinavians. Unsurprisingly, the arrival of the Scandinavians led to the borrowing of numerous words from Scandinavian dialects into Old English. Although direct borrowing did not occur during the Middle English period, many of the words borrowed into Old English dialects found their way into the Middle English southern dialects. Of those still used in Present Day English that have a Scandinavian origin, Björkman (1969) lists, among many others, *anger*, *bask*, *booth*, the place name suffix <by> (see C2.2; <by> also survives in the PDE term *bylaw*), *carp* (as in 'to talk' or 'to brag'; still found in some regional British English dialects), *grime*, *husting*, *lug* (as in 'to drag/carry'), *meek*, *rotten*, *rugged*, *same* and *sly*.

French loanwords

Following the Norman Conquest of 1066, loanwords from French were gradually absorbed into English. Unit B3 explains how the division between Early and Late Middle English is in part determined by the number of French loanwords in English in these two periods, there being substantially more in Late Middle English. Serjeantson (1935) lists the following words, among many others, as being borrowed into English from French during the Middle English period (I have given you the PDE spellings): *capon, court, rent, ginger, justice, grace, bacon, chaplain, cardinal, mercy, purple, nunnery, acquit, debt, challenge, countess, tournament, chastity, cruel, dangerous, courtesy, feast, office, baron, sergeant, sermon, parliament, angel, merchandise, dungeon, baptism, humility* and *treason*.

Latin loanwords

In the Middle English period, Latin borrowings included the following: *implement, exorbitant, legitimate, simile, cardamon, diocese, memorandum, requiem, abacus, conviction, persecutor, redemptor, limbo, library, credo, Pater noster, comet* and *equator*.

Activity C3.1.1

Divide the French loanwords listed above into appropriate semantic categories (for example, you might choose 'food' as one grouping). Based on these categories, can you make any comment on the type of words that were borrowed from French? What does this suggest to you about the nature of contact between French speakers and English speakers? Now try the same activity for the Latin loanwords. Which spheres of life are represented by loanwords from Latin?

Activity C3.1.2

Among the many words borrowed into English from Scandinavian were the pronouns *they*, *their* and *them*. What do these words and the Scandinavian loanwords listed above suggest to you about the nature of contact between the Scandinavian settlers and the Anglo-Saxon groups already in England at the time of the Viking invasions?

C3.2 *The Canterbury Tales*

As a way into making sense of Middle English, let's have a look at a Middle English text. One of the most famous examples of Middle English is Geoffrey Chaucer's *The Canterbury Tales*, a collection of stories written in the fourteenth century and supposedly told by a group of travellers as they make a pilgrimage to Canterbury. Below is an extract from the beginning of 'The General Prologue', followed by a translation into Present Day English. Read the Middle English text and try to make sense of it before you read the translation.

Extract from 'The General Prologue'
Whan that Aprill with his shoures soote
The droghte of March hath perced to the roote,
And bathed every veyne in swich licour
Of which vertu engendred is the flour
Whan Zephirus eek with his sweete breeth
Inspired hath in every holt and heath
Tendre croppes, and the yonge sonne
Hath in the ram his half cours yronne,
And smale foweles maken melodye,
That slepen al the nyght with open ye
(So priketh hem nature in hir corages),
Thanne longen folk to goon on pilgrimages

Extract from 'The General Prologue' (PDE translation)
When April with its sweet showers
Has pierced the drought of March to the root,
And bathed every vein [of the plants] in such liquid
Of which power the flower is engendered [i.e. created]
When Zephirus, also, with his sweet breath
Has inspired [i.e. breathed life into] every grove and heath [i.e. field]
Tender crops, and the young sun
Has run half his course in the ram [i.e. Aries]
And little birds make melody [i.e. sing]
That sleep all the night with open eye
So nature pricks them [i.e. provokes them] in their hearts
Then folk long to go on pilgrimages

Activity C3.2.1
First, try reading the extract aloud using the guide to pronunciation in B3.2. Once you have done this, read the extract again and consider the following questions:

❑   In what ways does the language differ from Old English?
❑   What do you notice about the pronouns in the extract?
❑   What has happened to the meanings of *licour* and *foweles* over time?

C3.3 A Middle English *Pater noster*

In C2.1 you examined two different versions of the Lord's Prayer (or *Pater noster*) in Old English. Here is a version in Middle English taken from *The Pater Noster*, attributed to John Wycliffe, in Arnold (1871: 93–6):

> Oure Fadir þat ert in hevenes, halwid be þi name
> þi rewme come to þee
> þi wille be doon; as it is fulli doon in hevene so be it doon and in erþe
> To ʒive us oure eche days breed to day
> Forʒive us oure dettis, as we forʒive to oure dettouris
> Leed us not into temptacioun
> But, gracious Fader, delyvere us from alle yvel
> Amen

Activity C3.3.1

Compare the Middle English version of the prayer with the Old English versions in C2.1. What differences in grammar and vocabulary do you notice? What evidence is there that this is a text from fairly early on in the Middle English period?

CODIFICATION AND ATTITUDES TOWARDS ENGLISH   C4

In B4 you can read about some of the important sound changes that occurred in the Early Modern period. As we saw, one of the possible explanations for why such changes occurred is a social explanation; namely that attitudes towards particular varieties of speech may have caused speakers (either consciously or unconsciously) to alter their way of speaking. The important point here is that attitudes to language use can often determine its development. This is also true in the case of written language. Unit A5 outlines the importance of the printing press in the development of a standard form of written English, and as this standard variety developed so too did a desire to codify the language; that is, to write down the 'rules' that governed its use. A problem that can be seen in many of the early dictionaries, grammars and style guides, however, is that the writers of such texts tended to be prescriptive as opposed to descriptive. They were intent on explaining what people should and shouldn't do when they used English. In contrast, modern linguists simply describe how people use language. They do not judge this usage. The following activities allow you to investigate codification and attitudes towards English in the work of early writers on English usage.

C4.1 *A Table Alphabeticall*

The first monolingual English dictionary was Robert Cawdrey's *A Table Alphabeticall*, published in 1604 (see A5.3 for more details). From the perspective of modern linguistics, it is easy to be critical of the problems with such early work on the English language, and so it is important to remember the pioneering steps that such early writers on language were taking. Nonetheless, it is worthwhile considering the kinds of misapprehensions such writers had about the nature of language, since an understanding of these helps us to fully appreciate the capacity of language to develop.

Activity C4.1.1

The title page of Cawdrey's *A Table Alphabeticall* (Cawdrey 1604) contains the following statement:

> A Table Alphabeticall, contayning and teaching the true writing and vnderſtanding of hard vſuall Enaliſh wordeſ, borrowed from the Hebrew, Greeke, Latine, or Frenche, &c.
>
> With the Interpretation thereof by plaine Engliſh wordeſ, gathered for the benefit and help of all vnſkilfull perſonſ.

Bearing in mind the professed aim of *A Table Alphabeticall*, consider the extract from it below. What problems can you see with Cawdrey's definitions? Try comparing the extract with extract 2 from Johnson's dictionary of 1755. What information does Johnson's dictionary convey that Cawdrey's doesn't? What information is not present in either entry that you would expect to find in a Present Day English dictionary?

> Extract 1 – *A Table Alphabeticall* (Robert Cawdrey)
> *abjure*, renounce, deny, forfweare
>
> Extract 2 – *A Dictionary of the English Language* (Samuel Johnson)
> To ABJURE. v.a. [*abjuro*, Lat.]
>
> 1. To caſt off upon oath, to ſwear not to do ſomething.
>   Either to die the death, or to abjure
>   For ever the ſociety of man. Shakeſp. *Midſum. Night's Dream.*
>   No man, therefore, that hath not abjured his reaſon, and sworn allegiance to a preconceived fantaſtical hypotheſis, can undertake the defenc of ſuch a ſuppoſition. Hale's *Origin of Mankind.*
> 2. To retract, or recant, or abnegate; a poſition upon oath.

C4.2 English Orthographie

In C4.1 you considered some of the issues with the first monolingual dictionary of the Early Modern English period. Now let's consider a writing guide of this period. Owen Price's *English Orthographie* was published in 1668 and was aimed at both teachers and students. As with Cawdrey's dictionary, the title page (Figure C4.2.1) gives us an indication of the aims of the book.

Activity C4.2.1

Looking at the title page of *English Orthographie* (Figure C4.2.1), it is clear that Early Modern English spelling is on its way to becoming the Standard English that

á· 430.

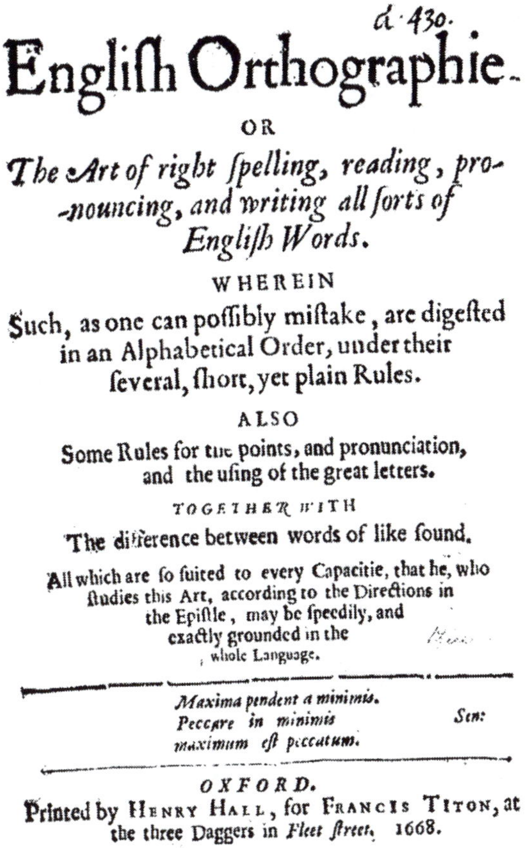

Englifh Orthographie.

OR

The Art of right fpelling, reading, pro--nouncing, and writing all forts of Englifh Words.

WHEREIN

Such, as one can poffibly miftake, are digefted in an Alphabetical Order, under their feveral, fhort, yet plain Rules.

ALSO

Some Rules for the points, and pronunciation, and the ufing of the great letters.

TOGETHER WITH

The difference between words of like found.

All which are fo fuited to every Capacitie, that he, who ftudies this Art, according to the Directions in the Epiftle, may be fpeedily, and exactly grounded in the whole Language.

Maxima pendent a minimis.   *Sen:*
Peccare in minimis
maximum eft peccatum.

OXFORD.

Printed by HENRY HALL, for FRANCIS TITON, at the three Daggers in *Fleet ftreet,* 1668.

Figure C4.2.1 Title page of Owen Price's *English Orthographie* (Price 1668).

is common today. What specific features of the text on the title page strike you as typical of Early Modern English? Can you note any differences in spellings and orthographic practices between this text and Present Day English? For example, what rules does Price appear to employ concerning when to use word-initial capital letters? When you have thought about this, read through Price's own explanation for his practices in this respect (Figure C4.2.2). Which rules are still used in Present Day English? Can you suggest reasons why some of these rules have fallen out of usage?

Activity C4.2.2

Read through the extract from the book in Figure C4.2.3, which is a series of questions and answers. What problems can you see with Price's answers to the questions he poses? What assumptions and misconceptions does he make? (NB: In the introduction, Price explains that he has 'syllabicated' words 'for the ease of a beginner' – i.e. he has hyphenated words to indicate the number of syllables in the word when spoken).

Of the great Letters.

Q. How do you know when to write the great letters?

A. *That must be a great letter, which is the first in*

1. *A proper name of a person, or place, as* Charls, England.

2 *The first letter in a Sentence, as the first let--ter in your writing, or the first after a period.*

3. *The first letter in a verse.*

4. *I, by it self is a great, I, as I am.*

5. *All those words that imply an emphasis, or what is remarkable, must be written with a great letter.*

Figure C4.2.2 Extract (a) from *English Orthographie* (Price 1668: 40).

Orthographie.

If this cor-rection of the letters will not sink into the block-i.h, or ignorant Teacher's head, let him go off to spelling.

Q. What is Or-tho-gra-phie ?

A. *Or-tho-gra-phie is an Art of right spel-ling, and wri-ting the let-ters*

Q. How are the l.t-ters di-vi-ded?

A. *The let-ters are di-vi-ded in-to vow-els, and con-so-nants.*

Q. What is a vow-el ?

A. *A vow-el is a let-ter which ma-keth a per-fect found of it self.*

Q. What is a dip-thong ?

A. *A dip-thong is two vow-els join-ed into one found, as meat not me-at, meet not me-et.*

Q. What is a con-so-nant ?

A. *A con-so-nant is a let-ter which ma-keth a found by the help of a vow-el, or a dip-thong.*

Q. How many vow-els are there ?

A. *There are six vow-els, a, e, i, o, u, and, y af-ter a con-so--nant.*

Q. How many con-so-nants are there ?

A. *There are twen-ty one con-so-nants.*

Q. When are the i, and u, made con-so-nants ?

A. *When a vow-el fol-lowes the, j, and v, in the same syl-la-ble they are made con-so-nants, as* Je-ho-vah ; *but when a vow-el fol-lowes them in a dif-fe-rent syl-la-ble, they are vow-els, as in in-ju-ri-ous, ver-tu-ous.*

Figure C4.2.3 Extract (b) from *English Orthographie* (Price 1668: 4).

C4.3 Problems with prescriptivism

In linguistics, being prescriptive involves telling people how they should use language – e.g. telling them that they should always use a capital letter at the start of a new sentence. Being proscriptive involves telling them what they shouldn't do – e.g. telling them that they should never end a sentence with a preposition. Being descriptive involves, obviously enough, describing how people use language – e.g. if we notice that people often end sentences in prepositions when they write, then we don't judge this as wrong; we simply record it as something that people commonly do in written language. It follows from this that a descriptive rule is simply a rule based on having observed what people do when they use language. A descriptive rule regarding Standard English, for example, is that we put an <s> inflection on the third-person singular form of the verb.

Activity C4.3.1

Prescriptivism and proscriptivism became increasingly common in the later part of the Early Modern period (in the 1600s, there were even calls for the establishment of an 'English Academy', along the lines of the French *Académie français*, that would provide rules of usage and 'protect' the language from so-called decline). Unfortunately, prescriptive and proscriptive views are also often heard today. Try to come up with answers to the following questions concerning the problems with prescriptive and proscriptive attitudes towards language usage. If you are reading this book as part of a class, discuss your answers with other students in your group.

❏ Why does it not make sense to take a prescriptive attitude towards usage? (Hint: think particularly about the focus of section A of this book and the nature of language itself).
❏ Is there any situation in which prescriptivism should be tolerated?

FURTHER ELEMENTS OF GRAMMAR IN EARLY MODERN ENGLISH

In B5 we looked at some of the grammatical characteristics of Early Modern English. In this unit we will consider some more of these and investigate some of the developments that have occurred over time.

C5.1 More on pronouns

In Early Modern English the second-person pronoun was socially marked (read B5.2 if you haven't already done so), as well as having different forms depending on whether it was first-, second- or third-person, singular or plural. A person's social status could be acknowledged in the pronoun you chose to address them with (compare, for example, *thou* and *you*).

Activity C5.1.1

Over time, the practice of marking social status through pronouns stopped. Why do you think this happened? It might help you to think through the issues if you imagine what it would be like if Present Day English still had socially marked pronouns. What problems might you encounter when using these? Would the mode of communication (speech or writing) influence your decision as to what forms to use? What might be the consequences of choosing the 'wrong' form? Can you see any advantages to this system? (If your first language is a language that marks status in pronouns – e.g. French or German – you will already have an insight into this.) Consider these issues and, if possible, discuss them with another student before reading the comments below.

Activity C5.1.2

When the tendency in the historical development of English has been towards regularisation, why do you think the personal pronoun system has not been regularised more than it has been?

C5.2 Gradable adjectives

Adjectives modify nouns – that is, they express the attributes of a noun. They can appear before the head noun of a noun phrase ('A *silent* film') or they can follow a verb and relate back to the noun phrase that is the subject of the sentence ('The film was *silent*'). Gradable adjectives are those that have comparative and superlative forms. For example, *big* (base form), *bigger* (comparative form), *biggest* (superlative form).

Activity C5.2.1

In Present Day English what are the grammatical rules that govern the formation of the comparative and superlative forms of the adjectives *small, heavy, light* and *friendly*? What about adjectives such as *beautiful, unpleasant, reckless, complicated, good* and *bad*? When you have worked this out, read through the following examples of Early Modern English. Identify the adjectives and then note the differences that you can see in how the comparative and superlative forms of the adjective were formed in Early Modern English.

> O yes, but I forgot. I have, believe it,
> One of the treacherousest memories, I do think,
> Of all mankind.
>
> (Ben Jonson, *The Alchemist*)

Brutus shall lead; and we will grace his heels
With the most boldest and best hearts of Rome.
(William Shakespeare, *Julius Caesar*, Act III, Scene I)

Arise faire Sun and kill the enuious Moone,
Who is already sicke and pale with griefe,
That thou her Maid art far more faire then she:
(William Shakespeare, *Romeo and Juliet*, Act II, Scene II)

In Belmont is a lady richly left,
And she is fair and, fairer than that word,
Of wondrous virtues.
(William Shakespeare, *The Merchant of Venice*, Act I, Scene I)

O, the most affablest creature, sir! so merry!
So pleasant!
(Ben Jonson, *The Alchemist*)

…transformed into the most uncleanest and variablest nature that was made
under heaven;
(Hugh Latimer, *Sermons on the Card*, 1529)

'Tis very true. O wise and upright judge,
How much more elder art thou than thy looks!
(William Shakespeare, *The Merchant of Venice*, Act IV, Scene I)

…there grew of necessity in chief price and request eloquence and variety of
discourse, as the fittest and forciblest access into the capacity of the vulgar sort.
(Francis Bacon, *The Advancement of Learning*, 1605)

This cannot be, except their condition and endowment be such as may content
the ablest man to appropriate his whole labour and continue his whole age in
that function and attendance.
(Francis Bacon, *The Advancement of Learning*, 1605)

…the grave is more easy for me than this dungeon.
(John Bunyan, *The Pilgrim's Progress*, 1678)

Activity C5.2.2

Read through the following list of adjectives (some are taken from Barber 1997: 146)
and discuss them with some other students. How would you form the comparative and
superlative of each? Do you all agree with each other? What factors might determine
the form you choose to use? What do your answers suggest about the future development of English?

pleasant
unhappy
subtle

common
stupid
gentle
friendly
simple
cruel
cloudy

C5.3 What did *do* do?

One of the distinguishing features of the Early Modern English period is the rise in usage of the dummy auxiliary *do*. The activities below will help you to explore its function.

Activity C5.3.1
Read through the following Present Day English sentences and decide what the function of the auxiliary verb *do* is in each case.

1. I do like coffee!
2. Do you like tea?
3. I like coffee but I do not like tea.

Activity C5.3.2
When you are confident that you understand the function of *do* in Present Day English, read through the following examples of Early Modern English. These have been taken from the Early Modern English section of the Helsinki corpus; details are available here: www.helsinki.fi/varieng/CoRD/corpora/HelsinkiCorpus/. (File names are provided below each example.) All of the examples would have been considered grammatically complete at the time. What differences do you notice between the use of *do* in Present Day English and its use in Early Modern English?

Did not christ lykewyse ascend vnto his father vnto the great mount of heuen?

(E1 1R SERM FISHER 1,317)

And why did'st thou tell so many Lyes then?

(E3 XX TRI LISLE IV 122C1)

What say'st thou? Prithee tell us what the Discourse was?

(E3 XX TRI LISLE IV 122C1)

"You saie well, sonne," quoth he; "I do not mislike that you are of conscience so scrupulous[."]

(E1 NN BIO ROPER 41)

I like not this Jury for our purpose, they seem to be too pitiful and too charitable to condemn the prisoner.

(E1 XX TRI THROCKM I,64.C2)

I say not this as if children were not to be indulged in anything[.]

(E3 IS EDUC LOCKE 52)

Well then, I pray, as we walk tell me freely, how do you like your lodging[?]

(E3 IS HANDO WALTON 213)

To whom speak you this? You tell me news I never heard of.

(E2 XX TRI RALEIGH I,207.C2)

ENGLISH IN THE NEW WORLD   C6

As English developed in North America, it was subject to contact with the languages of other settlers and with those languages of the Native Americans. Inevitably, these other languages had an influence on how American English developed. And as American English progressed into the eighteenth and nineteenth centuries, it became a powerful vehicle for the expression of national identity.

C6.1 Loanwords in American English

Contact with other languages inevitably led to the borrowing of words into the varieties of English spoken by the colonists. A selection of loanwords (drawn from Marckwardt 1980) includes vocabulary taken from the following languages:

French
pumpkin, brioche, chowder, praline, caribou, gopher, bayou, crevasse, flume, levee, rapids, cent, dime

Spanish
alfalfa, marijuana, mesquite, cockroach, coyote, mustang, chaparral, lasso, ranch, rodeo, stampede, enchilada, frijole, taco, tequila, tortilla, poncho, sombrero, canyon, sierra

Dutch
coleslaw, cookie, waffle, caboose, sleigh, stoop (meaning 'porch'), *boss, Yankee, dumb* (meaning 'stupid')

German
delicatessen, hamburger, pumpernickel, sauerkraut, schnitzel, pretzel

Activity C6.1.1

What semantic fields do the words above come from? Does this tell you anything about the nature of contact between the early settlers in America?

Activity C6.1.2

What reason would the early settlers in America have had for borrowing these words into English?

C6.2 The politics of spelling

As English continued to develop during the nineteenth century in America, so too did the attitudes towards its usage. As mentioned in Activity C4.3.1, during the Early Modern period in England, attempts were made by such literary luminaries as Jonathan Swift to 'fix' the English language; that is, to formulate a system of rules for so-called 'correct' usage. At the beginning of the nineteenth century, the American lexicographer Noah Webster took an opposing view to Swift and his companions and was more interested in radically changing the language rather than preserving it in the way that Swift and others had proposed. Webster's main concern was with the spelling system of English and his efforts to reform this sprang from his concern that there was an increasing divide between the spoken and written forms of the language (Simpson 1986: 58). In his *Compendious Dictionary of the English Language*, Webster expressed his views as follows:

> Every man of common reading knows that a living language must necessarily suffer gradual changes in its current words, in the signification of many words, and in pronunciation. The unavoidable consequence then of fixing the orthography of a living language, is to destroy the use of the alphabet. This effect has, in a degree, already taken place in our language; and letters, the most useful invention that ever blessed mankind, have lost and continue to lose a part of their value, by no longer being the representatives of the sounds originally annexed to them. Strange as it may seem, the fact is undeniable, that the present doctrin [sic] that no change must be made in writing words, is destroying the benefits of an alphabet, and reducing our language to the barbarism of Chinese characters in stead of letters.
>
> (Webster 1806: vi, quoted in Simpson 1986: 58)

Webster was clearly a man with strong opinions (and, it must be said, some wrong ones, including his extreme and somewhat erroneous view of the Chinese writing system). But his desire for reform was political as much as linguistic. He saw his efforts as contributing to the development of a growing American national identity, and the lengths to which he went are testament to how important language can be in expressing identity and personality. Webster's suggested reforms included an overhaul of the spelling system and his efforts in this sphere gave rise to some of the differences that still exist today between spelling in American and British English. Carney (1994: 475–6) summarises some of Webster's initial proposals for spelling reform as follows:

- Superfluous vowels, such as word-final <e>, should be removed; e.g. *definit, disciplin, doctrin, granit, imagin, maiz, nightmar, vultur.*
- Superfluous consonants should be removed; e.g. *chesnut, crum, diaphram, ile, thum.*
- Vowel digraphs should be simplified; e.g. *fether, lepard, cloke, juce.*

Some of Webster's proposals, such as those above, even he considered too radical to be accepted and when he published his *American Dictionary of the English Language* in 1828, he was careful not to make any proposals that might have been deemed too outlandish (after all, he would not have wanted to put people off buying his dictionary). Among the reforms that did become accepted in American English are the following (again drawn from Carney 1994: 475–6):

- Mass nouns spelled with <our> in British English are spelled <or> in American English, hence *armor, behavior, color, favor, honor, labor, odor, vapor, vigor.*
- British English <re> endings become <er> in American English, hence *theater, center, fiber, liter, meter.*
- The British English suffix <-ise> become <-ize> in American English, hence *capitalize, organize, naturalize, dramatize, analyze, paralyze.*
- British English <c> in nouns such as *defence, offence, licence, pretence, practice* is replaced in American English with <s>, giving rise to forms such as *defense, offense, license, pretense, practise.*
- The digraphs <ae> and <oe> in Greek and Latin loanwords are replaced in American English by <e>, e.g. *anaemia/anemia, anaesthetic/anesthetic, diarrhoea/diarrhea, encyclopaedia/encyclopedia, mediaeval/medieval.*
- Double consonants in unstressed syllables in British English are often single in American English, e.g. *traveler, counselor, worshiping.*

In addition to the above 'rules', American English also makes use of distinctive spellings of certain words. Carney (1994: 475–6) lists the following (British English examples are given first, American English equivalents second): *gaol/jail, tyre/tire, whisky/whiskey* (though note that in Irish English, the latter spelling is used), *plough/plow, cheque/check, draught/draft, kerb/curb.*

Activity C6.2.1

What is your opinion of Webster's spelling reforms? What advantages can you see to his simplified spelling system and what disadvantages? With regard to the future development of English, what potential problems can you see with attempting to reform spelling? (Think about the relationship between sound and spelling, and also the various different 'users' of English.)

C6.3 Early African American English

In B6.4 we considered the possibility of African American English having developed from creoles spoken by African slaves in America. Dillard (1992) sees this as a strong possibility:

Slaves coming to virtually any part of the East Coast in the eighteenth century are very likely to have known some version of Pidgin English. From the evidence we have, what was spoken in West Africa and at sea was rather similar to what was being used in the American colonies, and not just in the south.

(Dillard 1992: 65)

Krapp (1925) quotes the following extract from John Leacock's play of 1776, *The Fall of British Tyranny*, as an example of one of the earliest written representations of the speech of African slaves:

[Context: On board a British man-of-war near Norfolk, Virginia. The scene comprises a conversation between Lord Kidnapper and Cudjo, an escaped slave.]

Kidnapper: How many are there of you?
Cudjo: Twenty-two, massa.
Kidnapper: Very well, did you all run away from your masters?
Cudjo: Eas, massa Lord, eb'ry one, me too.
Kidnapper: That's clever; they have no right to make you slaves. I wish all the Negroes wou'd do the same. I'll make 'em free – what part did you come from?
Cudjo: Disse brack man, disse one, disse one, disse one, come from Hamton, disse one, disse one, come from Nawfok, me come from Nawfok too.
Kidnapper: Very well, what was your master's name?
Cudjo: Me massa name Cunney Tomsee.
Kidnapper: Colonel Thompson – eigh?
Cudjo: Eas, massa, Cunney Tomsee.
Kidnapper: Well then I'll make you a major – and what's your name?
Cudjo: Me massa cawra me Cudjo.
Kidnapper: Cudjo? – very good – was you ever Christened, Cudjo?
Cudjo: No, massa, me no crissen.
Kidnapper: Well then I'll christen you – you shall be called major Cudjo Thompson…
Cudjo: Tankee, massa, gaw bresse, massa Kidnap.

(Leacock 1776, quoted in Krapp 1925: 255)

Activity C6.3.1

What evidence is there in the speech of the character Cudjo to suggest that the author is attempting to represent a pidgin? (You may find it useful to read B7.3 if you haven't already done so). How reliable is data of this kind for tracing the development of African American English?

C7 PRESENT DAY ENGLISHES

In B7 we considered the development of international Englishes, or World Englishes as they are often called. Each variety of English has its own particular characteristics, as well as its own sub-varieties such as regional dialects, social dialects that are seen as particularly prestigious, etc. When English first began to spread beyond the shores of the British Isles the movement was very much one way. English went out into the world and developed in many different ways (see B7). But now that there are so many international varieties of English in existence, it no longer makes sense to think of the development of English as being a one-way process. It is no longer the case that all varieties of English are developments of British English. Some varieties of English, for example, have developed from American English, thus their connection with British English is indirect at most. This has consequences not just for the development of the variety in question but also for the sense of ownership that native speakers have about their language. For a person growing up in India, with no connection to the UK, and speaking Indian English as a first language, their Indian English variety is the norm by which they will judge other varieties. It makes no sense anymore to take an Anglo-centric view and see British English as a base form and all other varieties as deviations from this. And because the development of English worldwide is no longer a one-way process, it is also the case that the many international varieties can affect each other's development – in terms of lexis, grammar, pronunciation, orthography, norms of usage, etc. In this unit we will look at some of the ways in which English has developed in recent years. We will concentrate particularly on lexical developments, though in unit D7 you can also read about some of the recent grammatical changes in English. As you read through this unit, think about the issues raised in relation to your own variety of English.

C7.1 Unknown words from Australian English?

Lexical differences are one of the most obvious distinguishing characteristics of varieties of English. But to what extent are such differences really barriers to communication?

Activity C7.1.1

The following is a list of colloquialisms in Australian English taken from Trudgill and Hannah (2008: 26). The authors state that these colloquialisms are 'not known in EngEng' (i.e. English English). Read through the list. How many of the words and phrases do you recognise? How many of them do you use or are used in the variety of English that you speak? If you are a speaker of British English, do you agree with Trudgill and Hannah that these words are 'not known' in your variety? If you are familiar with any of these words, think about how you became familiar with them.

to chunder	to vomit
crook	ill, angry
a dag	an eccentric person
a drongo	a fool
to rubbish	to pour scorn on
a sheila	a girl
to front up	to arrive, present oneself somewhere
to bot	to cadge, borrow

hard yakka	hard work
to shoot through	to leave
tucker	food
a wog	a germ
a spell	a rest, a break
a park	a parking space
to shout	to buy something for someone (e.g. a round of drinks)
a humpy	a shelter, a hut
to chyack	to tease
an offsider	a partner, companion
a chook	a chicken
a larrikin	a young ruffian
to dob	to plonk (something down on something)
to fine up	to improve (of weather)
beaut	very nice, great
to retrench	to sack, make redundant
financial	paid up (as a member of a club)
interstate	in another (Australian) state

C7.2 Circles of English

Australian English is just one international variety of English among many. One particular challenge for linguists is how we account for the development of English internationally. One of the most influential descriptions of English as a global language is that proposed by Kachru (1982). Kachru argued that the global spread of English could be visualised as a series of concentric circles (see Figure C7.2.1). In the Inner Circle are those countries where English is the first language of the majority of the population. The model defines these as norm-defining countries, in that they influence the development of English in those countries in the remaining two circles. The Outer Circle countries are those where English is not necessarily the first language of the majority of the population but where English has some form of official recognition, perhaps as the official language of government. The English of the Outer Circle countries is norm-developing. Finally, the Expanding Circle countries are those where English is not a first language and has no official status but where it is spoken widely as a foreign language. Expanding Circle countries are 'norm-dependent'.

Activity C7.2.1
Kachru's (1982) famous diagram of global English as a series of concentric circles has been influential but has also been the object of criticism. What problems can you see with Kachru's conceptualisation of the global spread of English and of what relevance are these problems to accounts of the history of English?

C7.3 Enlarging the lexicon

Throughout the twentieth century the lexicon of English developed substantially. Contact between languages, such as that alluded to above, is one means by which this

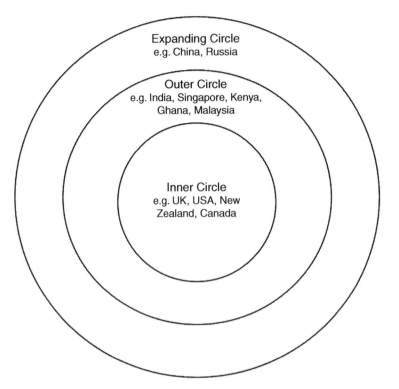

Figure C7.2.1 Kachru's circles of English model.

occurred. We have seen, for instance, that borrowing words is a popular way of introducing new vocabulary into English. Over time, English has borrowed from many
languages – Latin, Norse, Danish, French, German, Italian, Spanish, to name but a
few. But there are other means by which new words can enter the language. They
can, for instance, be created from the existing word-stock. One way of doing this is
through compounding, which we saw in B1.2 was greatly used in Old English. There
are, though, numerous other types of word formation. Read through the following
sections and as you do so, try to think of your own examples for each category.

Acronymisation
Acronyms are formed from the initial letters of some or all of the words in a particular phrase. Typically, the acronym is then pronounced as a word in its own right (as
opposed to pronouncing each constituent initial letter, which is the difference between
an acronym and an initialism). Acronyms are often found as names of organisations,
for example, *NATO* (North Atlantic Treaty Organisation), *HESA* (Higher Education
Statistics Agency), *BAAL* (British Association for Applied Linguistics) and *PALA*
(Poetics and Linguistics Association). It is also common to find acronyms developing
in institutions, where they are used as a form of shorthand among people familiar with
the full terms. Examples from my own university include *CAB* (Course Assessment
Board), *ASIS* (Applicant and Student Information) and *CATS* (Credit Accumulation
and Transfer Scheme). Note too how acronyms can be used to deliberately make it

difficult for people to understand what you are talking about. Large institutions tend to be very good at doing this! Acronyms you might encounter in everyday life include *ASAP* ('as soon as possible'), *DOB* ('date of birth'), *LOL* ('laugh out loud') and many others. Some acronyms become so well used that they are no longer recognised as acronyms, especially if in written language they are spelled using lowercase letters. Examples include *radar* (radio detection and ranging), *scuba* (self-contained underwater breathing apparatus), *laser* (light amplification by stimulated emission of radiation), *gif* (graphics interchange format) and *pin* (personal identification number). In the case of the latter, the fact that its status as an acronym is often forgotten can be seen in the way that people often use the phrase 'pin number'; the word number is, of course, technically redundant since this is what the <n> of *pin* stands for.

Derivation

Words are made up of **morphemes**, which are the smallest units of language that carry semantic information, i.e. information about meaning. Morphemes can be either **free** or **bound**. A free morpheme is a morpheme which can stand alone. For example, *bookcase* is a compound noun that is made up of two free morphemes, *book* and *case*, both of which are words in their own right. A bound morpheme is one which must always be attached to a free morpheme. The <s> ending on third-person singular verbs ('he walk*s*') is a bound morpheme, as is the <ed> that we put on the end of regular past tense verbs ('They walk*ed*'). These are examples of inflectional morphemes. Adding inflectional morphemes to the root of a word indicates a grammatical change (e.g. present tense to past tense) but it does not change the meaning of the word or the class that it belongs to. To do this we need to use derivational morphemes – or **affixes**. Affixes are another type of bound morpheme and affixation (the process of adding affixes) is a particularly common word-formation process. In English, affixes can be subdivided into **prefixes** and **suffixes**. Prefixes are found at the beginning of words and suffixes at the end. For example, the prefix <un> can be added to the adjective *happy* to form *unhappy*. If we then add the suffix <ness> we get a noun, *unhappiness*. If we add the suffix <er> to the verb *research* we get a noun, *researcher*. Derivation, or affixation, is responsible for the creation of a vast number of words in English, many of which become absorbed into Standard English. An example of the creative use of affixation can be seen in the words that arose out of the negative criticism that the fast-food chain McDonald's has received over recent years. As a result of this, the prefix *Mc* has come to be interpreted in some contexts as meaning 'low prestige' and people sometimes talk about *McJobs* (i.e. low-skilled jobs which afford little opportunity for career advancement) and *McDegrees* (i.e. university degrees considered to be of little worth).

Back-formation

Back-formation refers to the process of removing an affix from an existing word in order to create a new word. For example, the verb *televise* was created by removing the suffix from *television*. Similarly, the verb *burgle* was created by removing the suffix from *burglar*, *laze* was created from *lazy*, and *word-process* from *word-processor*.

Blending

Blends are formed by taking elements from two existing words and combining them to form a new word – in effect, 'blending' two existing words together. For example, *glamping*, a blend of *glamorous* and *camping*, is currently popular as a term for luxury camping. Not far from where I live there is an entertainment complex consisting of restaurants, cinemas, a bowling alley, etc., that styles itself *Centertainment*, a blend of *centre* and *entertainment*. A nearby shopping centre used to advertise itself as 'the land of *shoppertunity*', a blend of *shopper* and *opportunity*. The fact that it no longer does so is indicative of the pace of change in lexical development; blends can very soon seem dated. Some blends do get absorbed into Standard English though. Examples include *smog* (smoke + fog), *motel* (motor + hotel), *pixel* (picture + element), *malware* (malicious + software) and the sadly ubiquitous *Brexit* (British + exit). A particularly unusual recent blend (unusual because of its inherent paradox) is *anecdata* (anecdote + data), seemingly formed in an attempt to legitimise anecdote as a form of evidence; a *Guardian* article arguing that vacation rental websites are exacerbating the unaffordable housing crisis notes that 'Various studies support this idea, and there is also plenty of anecdata' (Mahdawi 2018).

Clipping

Clipping involves the deletion of syllables from a polysyllabic word. Examples include *prof* (professor), *lab* (laboratory), *flu* (influenza), *uni* (university), *pub* (public house), *bike* (bicycle), *phone* (telephone), *exam* (examination) and *wig* (periwig). *Advertisement* can be clipped to *advert* or the even shorter *ad*. Some clippings become so well established that we often don't realise that they are shortened forms of longer words. *Bus*, for instance, is a clipping of *omnibus* and *taxi cab* is a clipping of *taximeter cabriolet*. *Pram* (a clipping of *perambulator*) is an interesting example in that it loses the final three syllables and also the unstressed schwa that follows the initial consonant.

Coinage

Coinage is the creation of an entirely new word (i.e. a word with no relation to any existing word) and is a particularly rare type of word formation. Most coinages tend to be product names. Examples include *Kodak*, *Teflon* and *Xerox*. O'Grady and de Guzman (2006: 160) point out in relation to *Teflon* that the <on> suffix potentially makes the word sound more scientific because of the fact that this suffix is used in existing words like *phenomenon* and *automaton*. This may have been an influencing factor in its coinage.

Compounding

Compounding refers to the combining of free morphemes. The difference between compounding and blending is that compounding retains each constituent morpheme in full. Examples include *football* (noun-noun compound), *whiteboard* (adjective-noun compound) and *pushover* (verb-preposition compound).

Conversion

Present Day English words are remarkably versatile, as can be seen in the process of conversion. Conversion refers to the practice of changing the word class of an existing word to generate a new word. For example, we can use the noun *holiday* as a verb ('They holidayed abroad'), or the verb *ask* as a noun ('that's a big ask'). A recent example of conversion is the noun *meme* to a verb: 'It was a tweet that was immediately, and justifiably, memed and satirised' (White 2019). Conversion is a common process of word formation in Present Day English though it was not possible in Old English, since changing word classes in an inflectional language usually involves the addition of inflectional morphemes.

Onomatopoeia

Onomatopoeic words are lexical representations of particular sounds. A story in *The Times* newspaper about the return of the ITV news programme *News at Ten* began with the sentence 'The bongs are back'. The word *bong* in this context is onomatopoeic and represents the sound of Big Ben (the clock at the Houses of Parliament in London) striking, a sound heard at the beginning of every broadcast of *News at Ten*. Other examples include *buzz*, *crash*, *sizzle* and *cuckoo*.

The above categories describe instantaneous methods of word formation. But not all new words in English are formed in this way. A much lengthier process is **lexicalisation**. In simplified terms, lexicalisation is the process by which a phrase comes to be realised in a single word. For example, *nevertheless* was originally an adverb phrase with *less* as its head word, as in the first attestation in the OED, from 1382: 'Neuer þe lese withinne þoru vertu is all' (Wycliffe Bible). By 1400, the phrase was being spelled as a single word: *neuerþeles*. In this case, lexicalisation happens as a result of compounding. But of course it is not just in spelling that we see evidence of lexicalisation. The word *holiday*, for instance, is a noun-noun compound of *holy* and *day* (originally *hāligdæg* in OE) but evidence for lexicalisation can be seen in the reduction in vowel length in the first syllable from /aː/ to /ɒ/. This is indicated in the spelling *holidayes* from the Tyndale Bible in 1526. A still more complex example is *cupboard*. This derives from a noun phrase (*cup board*), compounded in Middle English as *copborde* (1380) and meaning 'A "board" or table to place cups and other vessels, etc. on' (OED). By 1555, the spelling had changed to *cobbarde*, suggesting that the /p/ of *cup* had assimilated to (i.e. taken on the characteristics of) the /b/ of *board*. Further lexicalisation is evidenced by later spellings which suggest that the *board* element has lost its full stress. These include *cubbard* (1591) and *cubbert* (1663). Present Day English *cupboard* then, is no longer a compound noun like *ironing board*, but has become fully lexicalised.

Activity C7.3.1

Urban Dictionary (urbandictionary.com) is a good source of new vocabulary in English. *Situationship* is a recent blend (of *situation* and *relationship*) to describe a relationship that is more than a friendship but not quite a romantic relationship. *Debtpression* is a blend of *debt* and *depression* and describes the negative feelings that arise as a result of being in debt. *Sexposition* is a blend of *sex* and *exposition* and describes the practice followed by some TV shows of spicing up otherwise dull plot information by conveying it in gratuitous sex scenes. These blends are often used in a tongue-in-cheek way but are they ever likely to become established in Standard English? Or are they more likely to fall out of usage? In what circumstances are blends absorbed into Standard English?

Activity C7.3.2
Here are some Present Day English words, along with their original forms. In the case of the first two, can you explain why the initial <n> was lost? In the case of the last one, can you explain why an initial <n> was added? (Hint: which form of the indefinite article would you use before the PDE forms?)

adder   (from OE *nædre*)
umpire   (from Old French *noumpere*)
nickname   (from ME *ekename*)

Activity C7.3.3
Sometimes more than one word-formation process can be identified in the development of a word. For example, the word *blitzkrieg* ('lightning war') was borrowed into English from German during the Second World War to describe the bombing raids on London. It was then clipped to *blitz* and has since widened in meaning so that it can now mean 'an intense campaign', as in this recent example from a news story on the Cheshire County Council website: 'Some 3,000 road signs and posts have recently been removed from highways in Cheshire as part of a blitz on unwanted signage'. *Blitz* has also undergone conversion to other word classes and can now be used as a verb ('to blitz' someone or something – i.e. to carry out a blitz) and as an adjective, in which case it has acquired a further meaning ('we were blitzed' – i.e. drunk). What new words have entered your variety of English recently? Which type of word formation was used to create them? Why were they created and how likely is it that they will survive to become an established part of the lexicon? Which type of word-formation process seems to be most common?

Semantic change
In addition to the word-formation processes described above, existing words can take on new meanings. Sometimes semantic **broadening** can occur, as a result of which a word's meaning becomes more general than it originally was. In Old English, for example, *hāligdæg* (PDE *holiday*) was a compound noun meaning 'holy day', though over time it has come to mean any period of rest from work. *Window* once meant simply an opening in a wall to let in light and/or air, whereas in Present Day English it also means a period of time ('a window of opportunity') and a work area on a computer screen. Another example of widening can be seen in the verb *to dial*. The verb is a conversion from the noun *dial*, which was borrowed from the Latin *diale* and was in use in Middle English to refer to a flat plate or disc marked with a scale of measurement (a *sundial*, for example). Following the invention of the telephone in the nineteenth century, *dial* came to refer to the movable disc that telephones used to have and which callers would move in order to make a connection to another number. The verb form *to dial* came into use to refer to the practice of moving this rotating

disc. Notice, though, that some people still talk about dialling a number even though nowadays most phones use touch-button keypads, with rotary dial phones being all but obsolete.

The converse of widening is **narrowing**. Just as some words take on more meanings, the meanings of some become more specific over time. *Liquor* originally meant liquid of any kind (see the extract from *The Canterbury Tales* in C3.2) though it now refers specifically to alcohol. The verb *to starve* which comes from Old English *steorfan* originally meant simply 'to die', though over time its meaning has narrowed so that it now means 'to die through lack of food', though in the Middle English period it meant 'to die as a result of cold'. (The Middle English sense is still used in some dialects of Present Day English.) Narrowing explains some seemingly odd uses of words in Present Day English. In the UK it is common at Christmas to eat mince pies, which are small round cakes filled with mincemeat. Mincemeat, though, is dried fruit, not meat as we would understand the word today (i.e. animal flesh). The use of the word *meat* to refer to a foodstuff that doesn't contain flesh stems from an earlier meaning of *meat* that meant food in general. This earlier sense also explains the Early Modern English word *sweetmeat*, meaning 'confectionery'.

Motivations for semantic change

Why do the meanings of particular words change over time? Williams (1975: 174) notes the influence of contact between languages in causing semantic change. He explains, for example, how Old English *deer*, which originally meant 'animal', changed to mean a specific type of animal as a result of the French word *beast* entering English. *Beast* also referred to animals generally but was viewed as more prestigious than the Old English term, thus forcing deer to take on a narrower meaning. Blank (1999: 61) points out that in tracing semantic change there are two aspects to consider. The first is the motivation that causes a speaker to innovate; that is, to change the meaning of a word. The second is the motivation that other speakers have for adopting the change. Some potential motivating factors for semantic change suggested by Blank (1999) are:

New concept

Technological innovation caused the semantic widening of *mouse* so that it now refers to the device used for moving a cursor on a computer (the motivation for using the word *mouse* no doubt stems from a physical similarity).

Sociocultural change

Concepts shift when we change society in some way. As a result, meanings of words may change too, e.g. when periods of exemption from work ceased to coincide solely with religious festivals, *holiday* (OE *hāligdæg*, 'holy day') broadened in meaning.

Close conceptual or factual relation

Close links between particular concepts can result in changes of meaning. For example, it is common for people to use the word *infer* when they mean *imply* (e.g. 'My teacher *inferred* that my essay was pretty bad'). To imply is 'to suggest without stating explicitly' whereas to infer is 'to draw a conclusion based on an implication'. In cases such as the above, the meaning of *infer* thus takes on the meaning of *imply*, especially if the context makes it clear which meaning is intended.

Emotionally marked concepts
Blank (1999) notes that certain emotionally marked domains such as death, sex, bodily functions, etc., are marked as taboo. As a result, euphemisms are often used in place of potentially embarrassing alternatives. Hence, the phrase 'he's passed away' uses the conceptual metaphor LIFE IS A JOURNEY to avoid using the verb *die*.

C7.4 Tok Pisin

In B7.3 we considered the development of pidgin and creole forms of English using examples from West African varieties. There are, of course, many other pidgins and creoles in existence. Tok Pisin ('talk pidgin') is the name of New Guinea Pidgin English. According to Romaine (1988: 122), it is likely that non-English speakers hearing Tok Pisin for the first time actually thought that what they were hearing was English – in fact, it is a combination of English (the lexifier) and a number of indigenous South Pacific languages (Sebba 1997: 25).

Activity C7.4.1
Below is an example of Tok Pisin taken from Romaine (1988: 122). The speaker is answering a question from Romaine about what his impressions of Tok Pisin were when he first heard it spoken. How much of the extract can you understand? Can you identify the words that are derived from English? When you have thought about this, read Romaine's translation.

> Mipela ting em tok bilong waitman ia. Mipela ting tok bilong waitpela. Bihain ol i tok em i tok insait long namel i tasol. I no bilong waitman. Mipela askim kiap ol kiap mipela askim kiap. Mi tok, 'Em tok ples bilong yu?' Em tok, 'Nogat'. Disfela tok pisin em i bilong yupela bilong Niu Guini. Mipela longlong. Mipela ting em bilong kiap ia bilong gavman, tok ples bilong en, nau. Nogat.

The Standard English translation would be:

> We thought it was the white man's language. We thought it was the language of white people. Then they said that there's only a little bit [of English] inside of it [i.e. Tok Pisin]. It's not the white man's. We asked the kiaps [Australian administrative officials]. We asked the kiap. We said, 'Is this your native language?' He said, 'No. This pidgin language is your language, a New Guinean language.' We were wrong. We thought it was the kiap's language, the government's language, their native language, but it wasn't.

Activity C7.4.2
Look back at the Tok Pisin extract. Using the translation, can you work out what some of the unfamiliar words mean? What does the suffix *pela* mean? What about the morpheme *yu*? What typical pidgin characteristics do you notice? (It may be useful to re-read B7.3 on the characteristics of pidgins).

C8 THE FUTURE OF ENGLISH

The rise of English as a global language raises many interesting questions concerning its future and the future of those languages that it comes into contact with and, in some cases, displaces. In this final unit we will consider some of the possible future developments for English.

C8.1 The cost of global English

The global spread of English is not without controversy. While English often brings economic advantage, it can also affect the relative status of other languages. In the case of English being used as an official language in countries where it is not (or was not traditionally) a native language (e.g. Ghana), this can create numerous problems. Some of these are discussed by Phillipson (1992: 35–6). Below is a summary of his main points:

❏ In countries where English is established as an official language, speakers of the indigenous languages of that country can become alienated as their national identity is threatened by the dominance of English.

❏ The dominance of English in former British colonial countries can lead the colonised people to 'internalize the norms of the colonizers' (Phillipson 1992: 36) – that is, to absorb the social, political and cultural views of the colonial power. This can result in the loss of local cultures and customs.

❏ The use of English in such countries sustains the dominance of the usually small governing elite.

Added to these problems, of course, are the issues discussed in unit B8.1, such as the fact that English often leads to the dying out of many of the world's lesser-known languages.

Activity C8.1.1

What might be done to alleviate the potentially damaging effects of the global spread of English? Is it possible to regulate the use of English across the world? If you had the power, what policies could you put in place to prevent English displacing local languages? What chance of success might such policies have? If possible, debate these issues in a group.

C8.2 Scare stories: declining standards

From time to time, stories arise in the press about the threat to literacy caused by the characteristics of text messaging and online communication. The implication is often that English is becoming debased because people no longer know how to use it 'correctly' (you can investigate the issue of prescriptivism in C4.3). A recent story in the British newspaper *The Mail on Sunday* picked up on this topic in relation to so-called 'textspeak'. Read the news article and then try the activity below.

OMG! How textspeak 'seriously harms teenagers' ability to develop language and grammar skills'
Julie Henry for the *Mail on Sunday*
Published: 23:43, 15 June 2019 | Updated: 01:59, 16 June 2019

- ❑ Experts say textspeak could harm teenagers' ability to develop grammar skills
- ❑ One study showed examples of texts sent by young people without any grammar
- ❑ One 13-year-old's message read: 'OMG ikr', meaning 'Oh my God, I know right'
- ❑ A 21-year-old's message to a friend said: 'Yo dude r u still coming to party Friday'

Textspeak is seriously harming teenagers' ability to develop language and grammar skills, experts warned last night.

The growing influence of text message and social media slang means many young people often use language without grammatical structure, and this could limit their opportunities in the future.

Professor Jane Mellanby, director of the Oxford Group For Children's Potential at Oxford University, said the ability to understand and use complex language was essential for academic attainment, leaving youngsters without these skills at a serious disadvantage.

Her research cited examples of textspeak, including a 13-year-old's phone message which read: 'OMG ikr', meaning 'Oh my God, I know right', and a 21-year-old's message to a friend: 'Yo dude r u still coming to party Friday.'

Prof Mellanby said: 'These sentences do not contain grammar, and certainly not complex grammar. For youngsters who already struggle with language structure, a reliance on textspeak could compound the problem.'

Primary school pupils are tested on language and grammar in SATs when they are 11.

National curriculum expert Tim Oates, said: 'This is really important stuff. We have a small window of time for young children to acquire complex grammar automatically from exposure. For those who have not acquired it, then it needs to be taught explicitly in school.'

Activity C8.2.1
To what extent should we be worried by stories like the one above? How likely is it that text messaging will affect the future development of English? What factors do you need to take into consideration in order to make an informed decision?

C8.3 Future developments in English

Predicting the possible future development of English is a perilous business, as many linguists have pointed out. A good summary of the problems involved in doing this can be found in Jansen (2018). Nonetheless, as we saw in C8.2, stories frequently turn up in the press about the likely future of the language; and usually such stories take a fairly pessimistic stance. While it is almost impossible to predict what will happen to English, then, it is a useful exercise to at least think through some of the issues that make this difficult to do. The following activities ask questions about three particular aspects of the possible development of English. Before you try to answer them, think about what makes it particularly difficult to predict the future of English.

Activity C8.3.1

One of the common features of the development of English over time has been its tendency towards regularisation (for example, the regularisation of plural inflections so that most nouns are pluralised by the addition of <s>, <es> or <ies>). Make a list of as many features of English as you can think of that have become regularised over the course of English's development. Think about this in relation to the structural levels of language described at the beginning of section C and the other elements of language that we have considered throughout this book:

Structure	phonology, morphology, lexis, syntax
Shape	graphology, orthography
Meaning	semantics, pragmatics

Would you expect the process of regularisation to continue? What other aspects of English may become regularised? Which varieties of English would be likely to be affected?

Activity 8.3.2

Another important issue in the development of English has been language contact. We have seen how English has been affected to a greater or lesser extent by all the languages it has come into contact with during the course of its history. As English continues its global spread, how might contact with other languages influence its continued development and how is contact with English likely to affect other languages? What might be the social, political and cultural consequences of such contact?

Activity 8.3.3

In what other ways might the development of English be influenced by the growth of new technologies? Consider this issue in relation to both written and spoken language.

Section D

EXTENSION
READINGS IN THE HISTORY OF ENGLISH

If you have already read sections A, B and C of this book you will be well aware that the history of English is long and complex. This relatively short book spans over 1,500 years of linguistic, social and political history. Not surprisingly, it is impossible for it to cover every aspect of the development of English throughout this time. Indeed, I have not attempted to do this. Instead, I have tried to provide enough of an overview of the language at each of its stages of development for you to be able to grasp the major aspects of its history, and to give you enough background knowledge to be able to go off and explore the history of English in more depth for yourself. To do this you will need to read widely. The eight readings in this section are intended to supplement the information contained in the rest of this book and to provide a springboard for exploring the topics covered in more detail. The readings vary in terms of type, length and complexity. Some are extracts from books and some are extracts from articles published in scholarly journals. Some deal with aspects of linguistic form while others are concerned with wider social events and how these impacted on English. In each case I have tried to choose readings that complement and expand on the material covered in sections A, B and C, and which also give a flavour of the wide range of approaches to the study of the history of English. In the 'Issues to consider' section that follows each reading, I have listed questions for consideration and, in some cases, particular activities to carry out. Where appropriate, I have provided a commentary on these activities, though many are open discussion questions. In considering your answers, re-read the corresponding units in sections A, B and C.

Except for the last one, all of the readings have been abridged. After you have read and feel comfortable with the abridged versions, I recommend tackling the full versions if you can get hold of them. And once you have finished section D, there is a list of further reading at the end of this book that offers advice on what to read next.

D1 VOCABULARY AND MEANING IN OLD ENGLISH

This first reading follows up specifically on the introduction to the linguistic features of Old English outlined in B1 and C1. The late Professor Christian Kay worked in collaboration with colleagues at the University of Glasgow (including Professor Michael Samuels, whose work on Middle English dialectology we discussed in A5.1) on a 40-year project that eventually resulted in the *Historical Thesaurus of the Oxford English Dictionary*. In this extract from her contribution to the book *English Historical Linguistics*, she explains the nature of the Old English lexicon. My reason for choosing this particular extract is that, although the structure of Old English grammar may seem initially confusing to learners unfamiliar with synthetic languages, vocabulary can sometimes pose much more of a problem than grammar (Mitchell 1995). The more you know about the Old English lexicon, then, the easier it will be to read Old English texts and understand the earliest form of the English language.

D1.1 Old English: semantics and lexicon

Christian Kay (reprinted from Bergs, A. and Brinton, L. J. (eds) (2015) *English Historical Linguistics*, pp. 313–25. Berlin: De Gruyter.)
[...]

3. The nature of the lexicon

Figures derived from *A Thesaurus of Old English* (Roberts and Kay 2000) give a total of around 34,000 separate word forms in Old English, less than half the number that might be found in a modern desk dictionary. The total rises to 50,700 meanings if polysemy and the occasional case of homonymy are taken into account. For comparison, *DOE: A to G online* (Cameron et al. 2007), which covers the first eight of the 22 letters of the OE alphabet, contains 12,568 headwords. In TOE, nouns predominate at just over 50%, followed by verbs at 24% and adjectives at 19%. The OE figures will undoubtedly change as editing of DOE progresses.

Any examination of the OE lexicon reveals its essentially Germanic character. Words often have cognate forms in other Germanic languages, for example modern German *Erde, See, Mutter, Fuss, gut*, or Swedish *jord, sjö, moder, fot, god*. The differences between cognate languages, and the differences between old and modern versions of the same language, show how word forms develop and diverge over the years.

Compared with Modern English, Old English contains very few words borrowed from foreign languages. When the Anglo-Saxons arrived in Britain, their language already contained some words borrowed from Latin through contact with Roman activities on the European mainland. These include *coper* 'copper', *strǣt* 'road', and *wīn* 'wine'. Following the conversion of the Anglo-Saxons to Christianity, Latin terms increasingly appear in the vocabulary of religion and education as well as in more general areas where new commodities, ideas or practices were introduced. From the several hundred words recorded, examples include *abbod* 'abbot', *sealm* 'psalm', *scōl* 'school', *discipul* 'disciple, student', *plante* 'plant'. Many individual plant-names, often for plants useful in medicine, were borrowed from Latin. Religious influences also came from France, and a few French loans are recorded late in the OE period, notably *prūd* 'proud, arrogant', leading to derived forms such as *oferprūt* 'haughty' and *woruldprūdo* 'worldly pride'. Native words, however, might continue to be preferred over synonymous foreign ones. *Discipul* was a relatively rare word in OE; the word used in the Anglo-Saxon Gospels and elsewhere was the native *leorningcniht*. They might also be more productive: unlike *plante*, native *wyrt* 'plant, herb' generates a host of compounds, such as *wyrtcynn* 'species of plant'.

A mere handful of words, perhaps around 20 in all (Hogg 1992a: 3), were borrowed into the general language from the Celtic-speaking people who already inhabited Britain. The best known of these are probably *brocc* 'brock, badger' and *āncor* 'anchorite, hermit'. According to Breeze, however, many Celtic loans in English remain to be discovered: he puts forward a case for, among others, OE *syrce* 'coat of mail' and *trum* 'strong' (Breeze 2002: 175–176). Less controversial is the fact that many place-names in certain parts of the British Isles are Celtic in origin. A more significant contact, linguistically at least, was with the Old Norse (ON) language of the Scandinavian Vikings, who raided, and later settled in, much of the east and north of the country. Unusually, and probably because of the cognate nature of the two languages and the fact that transmission occurred during everyday spoken interaction, Scandinavian-derived words replaced their OE counterparts in core areas of the language, resulting in Modern English words such as *take* (OE *(ge)niman*), *sky* (OE *lyft*) and the pronoun *they* (OE *hīe*). Often the cognate words were very similar in form, as OE *sweostor* and ON *syster*, the latter giving Modern English *sister*. Because such words were likely to have been restricted to casual spoken use in the early stages, only a few of them appear in the OE written record, but many more are found in early Middle English. Thus, *take* (OE *tacan*) is recorded in the OED late in the OE period, but *sky* is not listed until the 13th century, although it was probably in use before then.

A full account of foreign borrowings into Old English is given in Baugh and Cable (1993: 72–104) and Kastovsky (1992: 299–338). Words throughout this paper are generally given in the form found in Clark Hall's *A Concise Anglo-Saxon Dictionary* (1960); Clark Hall's brief definitions are also followed.

3.1 Lexical structure: affixation

Basic OE words tended to be short forms of one or two syllables. Stress fell on the root syllable, which was usually the first syllable. Grammatical information was conveyed by variable endings on words, identifying their role in the clause. Prefixes and suffixes were added to roots to create a variety of kinds of new words. In general, prefixes tended to change meaning, for example by negating or intensifying the root meaning, as in *oferfull* 'too full' or *mislædan* 'mislead'. Prefixes were often used to form verbs, for example *ūpflēogan* 'to fly up' and *āflēogan* 'to fly away, flee' from *flēogan* 'to fly'. Suffixes were used to create different parts of speech, such as the adverb *hearde* 'fiercely' from the adjective *heard* 'hard, fierce'. Many OE adjectives end in -*ful* (*caru/cearu* 'care, sorrow', *carful/cearful* 'sorrowful'), -*ig* (*wæter* 'water', *wæterig* 'watery'), -*isc* (*cild* 'child', *cildisc* 'childish'), -*lēas* (*līf* 'life', *līflēas* 'lifeless'), -*lic* (*sige* 'victory', *sigelic* 'victorious'). Common adverbial suffixes include -*e* (*dēop* 'deep', *dēope* 'deeply') and -*līce* (*dēoplic* 'deep', *dēoplīce* 'deeply'). Both -*end* and -*ere* were used to form agent nouns, as in *lærend* 'teacher' and *leornere* 'pupil, disciple'. Abstract nouns often end in -*dōm* (*wīs* 'wise', *wīsdōm* 'wisdom'), -*hād* (*cild* 'child', *cildhād* 'childhood'), -*nes* (*yfel* 'evil', *yfelnes* 'wickedness'), -*scipe* (*frēond* 'friend', *frēondscipe* 'friendship'). Other common Modern English suffixes, such as those in words like *emotion, magnitude, generous, generosity, social, sociable, sociability*, were adopted after the OE period from French or Latin.

One result of the frequency and flexibility of word formation in Old English is that we often find groups of words clustered round a shared root, as in the following words derived from *sorg* 'sorrow, distress': *sorgung* 'sorrowing', *sorgful* 'sorrowful', *sorgleās* 'sorrowless', *sorig* 'sorry', *sorgian* 'to feel sorrow', *unsorh* 'unsorry, free from care'. All of these affixes, except for the -*an* which indicates the infinitive form of the verb in *sorgian*, survive in Modern English, although particular forms and meanings may have been lost. For example, an adverb from the group, *sorglīce* 'miserably', survives into Middle English as *sorrowly*, with a last date in the 13th century, but of the adjective *sorglic* 'miserable', which might have survived in the same form, there is no trace beyond Old English. Likewise, there is no trace in the record of *unsorh* between Old English and the 20th century, where the OED finds three citations for *unsorry*. This may be an accident of collection, or may reflect the flexibility of prefixes such as *un*-, which speakers can use to invent new words as occasion demands.

Sometimes prefixes have little if any effect; *giefan* and *forgiefan*, for example, both mean 'to give', although only *forgiefan* develops the meaning 'forgive'. Many verbs may occur with or without the prefix *ge-*: *niman* and *geniman* both mean 'to take'. Such variation is sometimes summarized in OE dictionaries and grammars by bracketing the prefix, as in *(ge)niman*, and the *ge* is ignored for purposes of alphabetization.

3.2 Compounds

The root *sorg* also yields a number of characteristic OE compounds, where two independent words are joined to express a complex idea, as in *sorg* plus *cearu* 'care', yielding *sorgcearu*, meaning 'anxiety'. Compounding was a favourite way of creating new words in Old English, with the combination of two nouns, as in *sorgcearu*, being the most frequent type (Kastovsky 1992: 365). Other types include noun plus adjective (*nihtlang* 'night-long'), adjective plus adjective (*blæhæwen* 'light blue') and adjective plus noun (*ealdfæder* 'forefather'). However, as Hogg (1992a: 23–24) points out, we often cannot be sure from a manuscript, let alone a subsequent edition, whether one word or two was intended; possible solutions to this problem are discussed by Kastovsky (1992: 362–363), although it may be a problem which bothers modern readers, used to the consistent conventions of the printed page, more than it did Anglo-Saxon scribes. Compounds were used where Modern English is more likely to use a phrase, as in *sorglufu* 'sorry or sad love'. Sometimes they contained a good deal of information, as in *heorotsol* 'a stag's wallowing place' or *paddanīeg* 'an island populated by toads or frogs'. Many of them have disappeared from the language: we no longer express distress with *sorgword* 'sad words' or *sorglēoþ* 'sad song', but with the Latin-derived *dirge* or with *lamentation*, also from Latin but possibly entering English through French; these are first recorded in the OED in c.1225 and 1382 respectively (s.v.v. *dirge* n. and *lamentation* n.). The group centring on *sorg* thus illustrates in microcosm both how the OE vocabulary was structured and how the language has changed since OE times.

Many compounds, such as those above, are transparent in meaning, i.e. the meaning of the whole is obvious from its parts. Others, known as "kennings", are more opaque, relying on a metaphorical interpretation. Kennings, and compounds generally, abound in OE poetry and therefore refer to subjects often treated in poetry, such as emotions, epic voyages, and heroic deeds. Thus we find kennings for the sea like *swanrād* 'swan's road', *hwælweg* 'whale's path', and *fisces bæð* 'fish's bathing place' (which may be a phrase rather than a compound). If we look up expressions for 'ship, boat' in *A Thesaurus of Old English* (Roberts and Kay 2000: 331), we find 47 general words for the concept as well as 42 more specialized ones. Such a high degree of lexicalization, comprising both synonyms for the central concept and words for more specific concepts associated with it, indicates the importance of this concept in the culture of the time. Many of these words occur in poetry, often only in poetry. By far the most frequent metaphor is that of the horse, a common mode of transport on land at the time, shown in examples such as *brimhengest*, *merehengest*, *sæmearh*, *sundhengest* and *ȳðmearh*, where the first element means 'sea' and the second 'horse'. Some of these compounds also occur in more prosaic contexts; for example *sægenga*, meaning 'sea companion, ship' in the poem *Beowulf*, is used more literally elsewhere to mean 'sailor', while *sæhengest* means 'hippopotamus' as well as 'ship'. A vexed, and probably unanswerable, question about such words, as about synonyms generally, is whether an Anglo-Saxon speaker would be aware of their etymological differences and possible shades of meaning or would simply regard them as approximately synonymous and thus interchangeable in most contexts. Taken together with the frequent repetition of initial sounds, these examples also reflect the twin demands of Old English poetic style, alliterating stressed syllables and "elegant variation" through synonymy.

A comprehensive treatment of all aspects of word-formation can be found in Kastovsky (1992: 355–400) and the works cited there.

4. Innovation and change

All languages have ways of acquiring new words as the need arises. As we have seen in Section 1, Old English, like other Germanic languages past and present, favored using internal resources such as affixation and compounding for this purpose, but occasionally borrowed words from foreign languages. Since Old English was a predominantly synthetic language, using inflectional endings to express grammatical relationships, words could not usually be borrowed in the foreign form but had to be adapted to fit OE patterns, as when the Latin word *discipulus* 'a disciple' was adopted into Old English as *discipul*. Sometimes words from two sources existed side by side for a time. For example, alongside *discipul* we find native derivatives such as *leornere* 'learner' and compounds such as *leorningcniht* and *leornungmann* 'learningboy/man', the latter glossed in Clark Hall (1960: 216) as "used even of women". Sometimes the foreign word is effectively translated into Old English, reproducing the form of the loanword in what is termed a "loan-translation" or "calque". Thus the Latin word *patriarcha* 'chief father/bishop, patriarch' becomes OE *hēahfæder* 'high father'. By a similar process, Latin *sanctus* 'holy person, saint' becomes OE *hālga* 'holy one, saint', and *trinitas* 'group of three, Trinity' becomes *ðrines* 'threeness, Trinity'. It is typical of the history of English vocabulary that the OE terms were replaced in later periods by borrowing the Latin words which they had once translated. However, we do retain the expression *Holy Ghost*, OE *Hālig Gāst*, a calque of Latin *Spiritus Sanctus*, rendered somewhat strange to modern ears by the narrowing of meaning of the word *gāst* to refer to the particular kind of spirit we call a ghost.

One of the commonest, most economical (and least noticeable) ways of supplying a new word at all periods of English is to extend the meaning of an existing one, for example to embrace a new concept. Following the introduction of Christianity, concepts such as 'God', 'heaven' and 'hell' took on new meanings for the Anglo-Saxons but were expressed by words which had referred to similar concepts in the old religion: *God, heofon, hell*. The use of such familiar terms presumably made the new ideas more acceptable to potential converts, and illustrate the effect that cultural change can have on language.

4.1 Polysemy and homonymy

Various processes of semantic change can bring about the condition known as polysemy, where a single form has two or more distinct but ultimately related meanings either simultaneously or at different stages of a language's development. Sometimes a borrowed word already has more than one meaning, as in *torr* 'rock, crag' and 'tower, watch-tower', which had both meanings in the original Latin before the word entered Old English through Celtic. Two of the commonest of these processes of change are "narrowing" or "specialization", where a word's meaning becomes more restricted, and "pejoration", where the word comes to refer to something which is regarded as in some way inferior. For example, the OE word *fēond* meant both an enemy and, by a process of narrowing, the supreme enemy, the Devil. Likewise, the word *æppel* in Old English usually referred to any kind of fruit, as in *palmæppel* 'fruit of the palm, date', but there is evidence in the OE corpus of the beginning of a narrowing process to meaning the fruit we now call an apple. Narrowing often precedes pejoration. The word *cniht* basically meant 'a boy, youth', but came to refer to those performing roles commonly filled by boys, including the role of servant. In this case, the role was often at the relatively high social level of an attendant or retainer, resulting eventually in the modern word *knight*. However, in the case of *cnafa/cnapa*, meaning 'child, youth' and then 'servant', pejoration gave us ModE *knave*. The parallel processes of widening or generalization and amelioration are much rarer. An example of the former can be found in the word *hlāford* 'lord', which originally referred to the specific role of a lord within the Anglo-Saxon social system, but was extended more generally to people in authority, leading to compounds such as *hlāforddōm* and *hlāfordscipe*, both meaning 'authority'. This word also exhibits narrowing in its meaning of 'husband' and possibly amelioration as one of the many OE terms for 'ruler' applied to the Christian God.

Most semanticists distinguish between "polysemy", where new meanings are linked to old, and "homonymy", where two words just happen to have the same form through historical accident. There are very few homonyms in Old English, both because its vocabulary derives largely from a single source and because it is an inflected language, less hospitable to borrowed forms, which are a frequent cause of homonymy. DOE treats as homonyms the etymologically unrelated *fāh* 'at feud, hostile' and *fāh* 'variegated, stained, shining', but Healey (2006: 85–86) notes that the distinction is not always clearcut and can be deliberately exploited to create ambiguity. Possible occurrences of homonyms are often masked by the fact that modern editions of OE texts indicate vowel length by a diacritic; Anglo-Saxon scribes did not use such marks. Thus *ac* 'but' and *āc* 'oak' would have looked the same on the manuscript page, as would *sæl* 'room, hall' and *sǣl* 'time, season' or *broc* 'misery, affliction' and *brōc* 'brook'. Homonymy can cause ambiguity in understanding a text if both words make sense in a given context, which seems unlikely in these cases. However, much critical ink has been spilled over the interpretation of *gǣst* in line 2312 of the poem Beowulf, describing the first appearance of the dragon that will eventually kill the hero:

(1) *Đa   se   gǣst   ongan   glēdum   spīwan.*
     Then   the   ?   began   fire   to spew forth
     'Then the ? began to spew forth fire'

Is our mystery word an ironic use of *gæst* 'visitor, stranger' or is it *gǣst* 'demon, fiend'? The point is discussed in Hough and Corbett (2007: 120–124), who also note that Beowulf describes himself as a *gæst*, presumably 'visitor, stranger', in line 1800, while the monster Grendel is described as *se grimma gǣst*, presumably 'demon, fiend', in line 102. As modern readers, we can never be sure which meaning is intended in context; an Anglo-Saxon audience, listening to the poem rather than reading it, would have the difference in pronunciation to help them.

4.2 Metonymy and metaphor

Two other kinds of semantic change which lead to polysemy are metonymy and metaphor, which have been a focus of study in semantics generally since the pioneering work of Lakoff and Johnson (1980). Following their lead, most work on this topic has been done within the framework of Cognitive Semantics, which draws on both linguistic and psychological theories of meaning. "Metonymy", which many scholars consider to be the root of metaphor, usually occurs within semantically close areas of meaning when some aspect of an object or concept comes to refer to the whole, as when *fām* 'foam' or *wǣg* 'wave' are used as synonyms for 'sea', or *bord* 'plank, board' is used to refer to a shield, ship or table, all of which are made of boards. In "metaphor", words are transferred from one field of meaning to another, usually from concrete to abstract, as when *hāt* 'hot' from the field of physical temperature is transferred to the field of emotions, with meanings such as 'fervent, excited'. From a diachronic point of view, one of the most interesting aspects of metaphor is its persistence through time. Sweetser (1990: 32–40) analyses metaphors of sense perception deriving from physical concepts, such as 'grasping an idea' or 'seeing the truth', which can be traced back to Indo-European, claiming that "[d]eep and pervasive metaphorical connections link our vocabulary of physical perception and our vocabulary of intellect and knowledge" (Sweetser 1990: 21). In Old English many words transfer from a meaning of physical vision to one of mental vision, including *behealdan, besēon, lōcian, scēawian*, all with a literal meaning of *look at, gaze*, and a metaphorical one of *observe, regard, scrutinize*. Kay (2000: 284) comments: "The Vision group of words incorporates an even more fundamental metaphor, that of holding/grasping or possession. Thus *behealdan* presumably follows an etymological path from holding in the hand to holding in the eye (that is seeing), to holding in the mind, that is understanding [...] expressions for remembering include *(ge)healdan*, and *habban/niman/lettan on gemynde*". Both Trim (2007) and Allan (2009) offer further insights into the evolution of metaphor. A good deal of work on the development of metaphor and metonymy within various theoretical frameworks has been done by G. A. Kleparski and his students at the University of Rzeszów, for example Kleparski (1990).

Not all metaphors survive, however. In some cases, the metaphorical connexion remains even if it is differently lexicalized at various stages of a language, as when French *fine* replaces OE *ðynne* 'thin' in describing delicacy of perception. In other cases, the metaphorical connexion itself is lost, as happened to a group of metaphors for the body, mostly poetic compounds, where *bān* 'bone' is followed by a word denoting some kind of container, as in *bāncofa* 'chest', *bānfæt* 'vessel', *bānhūs* 'house', *bānsele* 'hall'. Containers and their properties, however, continue to supply metaphors, especially for the mind, as shown in an influential paper by Reddy on "The Conduit Metaphor" (Reddy 1979). Modern English examples include expressions like 'the thought entered my head', paralleled in Old English by uses of *cuman/irnan on gemynde/on mōd* 'come to mind, occur to one'; *hweorfan* literally 'turn', metaphorically 'turn the mind to'; *bewindan* literally 'wind, wind round', metaphorically 'revolve in the mind'. Such examples show the underlying continuity of human conceptual processes even when, as in the case of *hweorfan*, the word itself has been lost.

5. The nature of the evidence

Many of the problems encountered in studying the OE lexicon arise from the nature of the available data. Old English was spoken and written for over 600 years, with consequent diachronic, diatopic, and stylistic variation, but our evidence for such variation is patchy. Smith (1996: 17–19) notes how the survival of materials in the four generally recognized OE dialects, Northumbrian, Mercian, Kentish, and West Saxon, correlates with periods of historical importance for the areas concerned, and comments: "Apart from West Saxon, the dialect materials from Anglo-Saxon England are slight and fragmentary, and major parts of the country are almost entirely unrepresented (e.g. East Anglia)". The majority of surviving texts, including the considerable body of poetry, are in West Saxon, which flourished along with the kingdom of Wessex in the 10th and 11th centuries. Late West Saxon is widely used as a model in grammars and dictionaries, and has been chosen as "the preferred spelling for headwords in the *Dictionary of Old English* (DOE)" (Healey 2006: 78). However, as Hogg (1992a: 20) points out, while OE dialect features can be identified, "[...] there is almost complete social homogeneity between texts. Virtually every linguistic item we possess must have come from a very narrow social band indeed", that is the small number of literate people.

The extent of the problem of unrepresentativeness can be seen by a glance at the section below from TOE (Roberts and Kay 2000):

> 01.01.02.01.04.01 Marsh, bog, swamp: *gebrǣc, cwabba°, fenn, fengelād°ᵖ, fenhleoþu°ᵖ, fenhop°ᵖ, fenland, flēotham°, fynig, gyr(u), gyrwefenn°, hop, lǣc(e)ᵠ, mersc, merschop°, merscland°, mōr, mōrhop°ᵖ, mos, pidu°, polra°, sǣge°, slǣd, snæp°, strōd, strōdett°, sucga°, sumpt°, wæsse°, wereþ°*
> [...]
> Quicksand: *cwecesond°ᵍ, sandgeweorp°, sandrid°ᵍ* (Roberts and Kay 2000: 7)

It will be observed that the majority of words are followed by one or more superscript flags which give a rough indication of the currency of the words (as opposed to particular meanings in the case of polysemous words). These are 'o' indicating infrequent use, 'g' for words occurring only in glossed texts or glossaries, 'p' for poetic register, and 'q' for doubtful forms. The flags are explained more fully in Roberts and Kay (2000: xxi– xxxi) where the authors state: "The flags point to aspects of word frequency that should always be held in mind, given that the extant corpus of Old English is small and probably skewed in its representation of Anglo-Saxon vocabulary". Whereas the relatively small numbers of grammatical patterns in a language can be captured in a limited body of texts, parts of the larger and less stable corpus of lexical items may disappear wholly or partly from the record simply because the texts containing them are lost. In any lexical analysis, but especially in historical lexicology, frequency and context need to be taken into account. On the other hand, where evidence is scarce, any that survives must be of value.

One area where we have a relatively large body of surviving texts is poetry. Discussing traditional OE poetic diction, Godden (1992: 494) writes: "In both diction and syntax verse differs strikingly from contemporary prose and, one must assume, from contemporary speech". As well as the compounds discussed in Section 3.2 above, poetic diction included simplex words not found in prose, such as *Frēa* and *Metod* as terms for 'God', and *beorn* and *guma* as terms for 'man'. Such poetic words as *naca* 'ship', *gār* 'spear', and *wine* 'friend' have prose equivalents in *scip*, *spere*, and *frēond*. It is interesting, but perhaps not surprising, that the prosaic words, which are more likely to have been used in speech, are also more likely to survive into later stages of the language. It is also of interest that polysemous words could have both a poetic and a prosaic meaning. Thus Godden (1992: 498) notes: "[...] *lind* and *helm* are in general use in the senses 'lime tree' and 'helmet' but limited to poetry in the senses 'shield' and 'protector' ".

D1.2 Issues to consider

Activity D1.1
Although some borrowing of words from other languages (particularly Latin) happened during the Old English period, the predominant means of forming new words in Old English was compounding and affixation (see C7.3 for more details of these processes). Why were these word-formation processes more common than borrowing?

Activity D1.2
Here is a short extract from the Old English poem 'The Seafarer', which can be found in *The Exeter Book*, a tenth-century anthology of poetry from the Anglo-Saxon period (the extract is in the West Saxon dialect):

gielleð ānfloga,

hweteð on **wælweg**   hreþer unwearnum
ofer holma gelagu

(...the lone flier cries out / incites on to the sea the heart irresistibly / over the expanse of ocean)

Using the guide to Old English pronunciation in B1.1, can you translate the word in bold? What kind of compound is it?

Activity D1.3

As mentioned in A2.1, only a comparatively small number of texts have survived from the Anglo-Saxon period. These texts comprise approximately three million words of Old English; that is, we have only around three million words from which to determine the grammar and vocabulary of the Old English language. What kind of challenges does this pose to the historical linguist?

D2 CHANGES IN GRAMMATICAL GENDER

Old English was an inflectional language. But towards the end of the Old English period, inflections had begun to die out. As Merja Steenroos explains in this reading, the loss of inflections for grammatical gender (see B1.4) is one marker of the difference between Old and Middle English. But gender change didn't occur at the same rate in all varieties of Old English. In the Southwest Midlands, for instance, gender survived into Middle English, during which period it then gradually declined. This reading is an abridged version of a journal article by Steenroos that explores precisely how changes in grammatical gender occurred in the Southwest Midlands during the thirteenth century. It demonstrates how historical linguists go about studying such grammatical changes systematically.

D2.1 Order out of chaos? The English gender change in the Southwest Midlands as a process of semantically based reorganization

Merja Stenroos (reprinted from *English Language and Linguistics* 12(3): 445–73 (2008))

1. Introduction

One of the major changes that mark the traditional distinction between Old and Middle English is the loss of grammatical gender. [...] The aim of the present article is to trace the process of gender change within one text community, defined in terms of geography and time: the thirteenth-century Southwest Midlands. For most geographical areas, such a study would not be feasible because of the lack of surviving texts from the period of change. However, the Southwest Midland area provides plentiful material for a study of the gender change, due to a happy combination of circumstances: the late survival of grammatical gender in this area and a relatively large concentration of surviving Early Middle English texts. The material on which the present study is based consists of a group of twenty texts dated to the thirteenth century.

This paper focuses on the gender of personal pronouns in anaphoric use[1], the only category in which gender survives in Modern English.

[...]

It will be argued that a semantically based reorganization of gender assignment in anaphoric usage took place during this period. It is suggested that the main semantic patterns involved in this process are best described using the model of a 'hierarchy of individuation' [...]. According to this model, the assignment of gender to a noun reflects the extent to which it refers to something conceived of as individual and potentially active. Within this general framework, specific semantic categories may become strongly associated with particular genders. In Early Middle English, for example, it seems that the masculine gender becomes increasingly associated with human referents. It is further suggested that the patterns of Early Middle English gender assignment might form part of a direct line of continuation between the Old English system of grammatical gender and the postmedieval usage, with no need to assume an intervening period of confusion.

2. Grammatical gender in English: some preliminaries

[...] Grammatical genders are not defined on the basis of formal characteristics of the nouns themselves, but on the basis of agreement patterns shown by associated words, such as determiners or adjectives. While grammatical gender is often considered to have been 'lost' from English, some recent writers (e.g. Curzan 1999, 2003) have preferred to speak of 'gender change' rather than loss, reflecting the view that Present-day English, rather than being devoid of grammatical gender altogether, has 'pronominal gender' (Corbett 1991: 169–70).

The Present-day English use of pronominal gender is at first sight based on natural gender: *he* and *she* are used for human beings and for 'higher' animals of respective sex, while *it* is used for everything else. However, it is well known that pronominal usage in Present-day English is not as clear-cut as this. Higher animals and small children may be referred to as *it*, and it may also be used as a derogatory reference to an adult (Wales 1996: 160). Conversely, *he/she* may be used to refer to inanimates: as is well known, ships and cities are usually *she*. Such usages are more common in non-standard than standard speech. It may also be noted that gendered pronouns are in some cases used to refer to animate nouns regardless of sex: generic *he* for humans has persisted through centuries, while traditional usage at least in some varieties has generalized *she* for cats of both sexes.

[...]

It is now widely accepted that the core principle of gender assignment in human languages has to do with an 'animacy hierarchy' (Dahl 1999a: 99, 1999b: 577) or 'hierarchy or continuum of individuation' (Siemund 2008: 140), that is, the extent to which the referent of a noun is conceived of as an individual entity. [...] Siemund's classification, based on Sasse (1993: 659), focuses on well-definedness or individuality: at the one end of

---

1 The term 'anaphoric' is here used as a shorthand term referring to pronouns used for both anaphoric and 'cataphoric' reference, i.e. referring to nouns within the same text, whether they precede the pronoun or not.

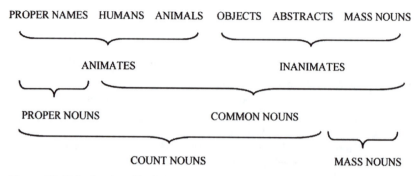

Figure D2.1 The 'scale of individuation' (cf. Siemund 2008: 140, based on Sasse 1993: 659).

the continuum are proper nouns, which denote a particular, defined human individual, and at the other end are nouns denoting fuzzy, uncountable substances (see Figure D2.1).

[…]

[A]n empirical study dealing with the semantics of gender in English historical texts must surely begin by asking what categories might be implied by the use of gendered personal pronouns, rather than assuming *a priori* that these categories will reflect prevalent conceptions of maleness and femaleness.

3. Grammatical gender in Old English and the process of gender change

Old English retained the three Indo-European genders, viz. masculine, feminine and neuter. They were reflected mainly, but not exclusively, as formal choices within the following categories: determiners, adjectives, some numerals, possessives and personal pronouns (anaphora).

Like most languages with gender, Old English combined semantically and formally based gender assignment rules. Words denoting humans were most often assigned gender in accordance with biological sex. This rule worked more regularly for males than females. Thus, all 32 noncompound words denoting males listed under the heading 'Humankind' in the *Historical Thesaurus of Old English* are masculine, while 23 out of 26 words denoting females are feminine.[2] A relatively large proportion of nouns could be assigned gender on formal grounds: so, nouns ending in -*a* would always be masculine (*guma* 'man', *assa* 'donkey', *wela* 'wealth'), while nouns ending in -*u* were often (although not always) feminine (*giefu* 'gift', *lufu* 'love' but not *sunu* 'son'). A recent study by Platzer (2005: 250–1), based on random samples of dictionary entries, shows feminine as the majority gender of nonanimate nouns, making up around 46 per cent of the total, with masculine making up around 32 per cent and neuter around 22 per cent.

From the tenth century onwards, the formal system of gender marking began to break down. This change was much earlier in East Midland varieties than in western or southern ones, gendered forms being retained longest in two particularly conservative

---

2 The exceptions are *mægden*, *wīf* (neut.) and *wīfmann* (masc.).

areas, the Southwest Midlands and Kent.[3] As the forms marking gender were case markers as well, the loss of case and gender formally makes up a single process. [...] [I]n the Southwest Midland area, formal distinctions were gradually lost over the thirteenth century; a crucial part of this process was the generalization of an indeclinable *the* as the definite article. By the fourteenth century, the only formal category that retained distinctive gendered forms was the third singular personal pronoun.

The formal loss of gender distinctions outside the personal pronouns was accompanied by major changes in the principles of gender assignment, often referred to as a change from 'grammatical' to 'natural' gender. Such a shift might be seen as an inevitable one: Howe (1996: 63) has suggested that pronouns are incapable of maintaining on their own, for any length of time, distinctions that are purely grammatical, i.e. that are not based on 'real-world entities' (Howe 1996: 61). As will be clear from the present material, the gender patterns in anaphoric reference were in fact changing alongside the loss of distinctions within the noun phrase, although the development within the two categories was far from identical. The assumption here is that the changes reflect a reorganization of the gender assignment system on a mainly semantic basis.

[...]

4. The present study: materials and methodology

The Southwest Midland area provides particularly promising material for a regional study of the English gender change. Compared with most other parts of England, the surviving texts from the period of change provide a fairly large corpus of texts. For the present purpose, the area is defined as consisting of Herefordshire and Worcestershire, as well as North Gloucestershire and South Shropshire. This area shows both a certain dialectal cohesion and a concentration of localized texts, many of which are interconnected, either textually, by manuscript association, or, less tangibly, by what seems like a shared audience or reference group. The last kind of interconnectedness is particularly notable in the case of the texts of the *Ancrene Riwle/Wisse*, the 'Katherine Group' and the 'Wooing Group'.

The corpus compiled for the present study consists of twenty texts dated to the period 1175–1300. They have all been localized in the area, on dialectal grounds, by Margaret Laing as part of her work on the *Linguistic Atlas of Early Middle English* (Laing and Lass 2007–). A full list of the texts, indicating the samples used, is given in the Appendix. The list also provides short name tags used to identify the texts in the examples below.

The corpus does not provide a range of text types of the kind possible to compile from later Middle English materials; it does, however, provide a good spread with regard to literary form, consisting of eleven verse texts and nine prose texts.

[...]

---

3 It is often taken for granted that the change happened early in the North as well (e.g. Millward 1996: 165); however, as there are virtually no surviving sources for Northern dialects between Old English and the fourteenth century, this can only be a guess.

Shorter texts are analysed in their entirety, while longer ones are analysed in samples of approximately 10,000 words. All instances of anaphoric pronouns referring to nonhumans have been collected (humans here including human-like beings such as the devil). Reference to humans is much more frequent than that to nonhumans, and the usage is predictable and regular over the entire material.[4] Because of this, pronouns referring to humans have not been collected systematically. For nonhumans, the total number of instances of anaphoric reference collected is 786, involving 178 different nouns as antecedents. Of these, inanimates make up 679 tokens involving 151 different antecedents. The remaining group (107 tokens; 27 antecedents) consists of nonhuman-like animates, that is, animals.

The great majority of the nouns referring to nonhumans are of Old English origin. There are only fifteen French loanwords, making up 8 per cent of the total of lexemes; in addition, there is one Latin word (*credo*) and two words of uncertain origin (*basket*, *cray*). There are at least twelve instances where the antecedent is uncertain or consists of more than one noun, and numerous instances where it is unexpressed or consists of a grammatical structure above word-level. The statistics presented below include only such examples as may be considered relatively unambiguous.[5]

[...]

5. The data

5.1 Animates

As far as is known, gender distribution in the animate category is at least partially semantically based in all languages that include gender as a category. A distinction based on male and female sex is very widespread when it comes to human referents, even though nouns referring to humans may have a grammatical gender that conflicts with the biological sex of the referent. Even in such cases, however, anaphoric refer-ence often agrees with the latter. According to the 'agreement hierarchy' postulated by Corbett (1979, 1991: 226), personal pronouns are more likely than attributive elements to show semantic rather than syntactic agreement. This reflects what Curzan (2003) has called the 'slippery' nature of anaphora – anaphoric pronouns do not simply refer to a particular word but also to things outside the text; in other words, there is no strict dividing-line between anaphoric and exophoric reference.

In the present material, anaphoric reference to nouns referring to grown-up humans and human-like beings consistently follows biological sex (or, in the case

---

4 This statement is possible, as I have read through the entire material and checked all references to humans, even though I have not collected them all as data.

5 Considering the nature of anaphoric reference, some of the examples used for the statistics might still have been interpreted otherwise by somebody else. There is also a slight possibility of circularity of argument, in that the researcher defining the antecedent of a pronoun will inevitably tend to use gender concord as a clue. However, it may be argued that the researcher is simply making use of the same kind of clues that the intended thirteenth-century reader would have used. At any rate, the number of questionable cases that may have entered the statistics is unlikely to be high enough to seriously skew the results.

of mythological or spiritual beings, culturally conventionalized gender). In cases of a conflict between grammatical and biological gender, Old English, like Present-day German, could show either syntactic or semantic agreement; however, as shown by Curzan (2003: 62), semantic agreement seems to have been preferred in the vast majority of cases. In the present material, anaphoric reference to grown-up humans is throughout semantically based, even when the pronoun follows very closely upon its antecedent:

(1) **Heo** slepeþ so faste **þ^t mayde suete** þat **heo** ne may nouʒt come ʒete
     'she is so fast asleep, **that sweet girl** (neut.), that **she** cannot come yet' (FB)

(2) Make bitere man as **wif** ded for **hire** child
     'make a bitter lamentation as a **woman** (neut.) does for **her** child' (Caius)

(3) Ouer soh seiden þat ʒunge [vif]mon; **hire** folweð mochel wisdom
     '**That young woman** (masc.) spoke very true [words]; great wisdom follows **her**' (LayAb)

The antecedent *child*, like *bearn* (both etymologically neuter), is referred to by *it* when it signifies a baby: *as wif ded for hire **child** … þe naued buten him ane & sið **hit** biuoren hire ferliche a-sterwen* 'as a woman does for her **child** … who has none but it/him and suddenly sees **it** die before her' (Caius). The switch to gendered reference generally takes place as the child reaches a point where it is viewed as an active individual; this may take place abruptly within the same sentence: *þis **child** weox … & al folk **hit** wes leof; þa **he** cuðe gan & speken …* 'this **child** grew and **it** was dear to all the people; when **he** could walk and speak …' (LayAa)

Generic *he* is used commonly: *muche fol were þe mahte to his bihoue hweðer-se **he** walde grinden* 'it would be a great fool, who could grind for his need wherever **he** wished' (AW). However, the three oldest texts of *Ancrene Riwle/Wisse* commonly use generic *she*, reflecting their specific female text universe: *euch schal halden þe uttre efter-þat **ha** mei best* 'everyone must keep the outer (rule) as best **she** can' (AW).

Virtually all human-like mythological or spiritual beings referred to, including *feond, deofel, engel* and *drake*, are referred to by *he: lucifer… þurh-þet **he** iseih* 'Lucifer … through what **he** saw' (NeroA). Most words for such beings were mas-culine in Old English; however, masculine reference is used also for words such as *wiht* ('being', OE neut.), when it refers to the devil: *þat foule **wiʒt** … **he** ne loueþ þe nout* 'that foul **being** … **he** does not love you' (D86). The OE feminine *nædre* 'snake, serpent' may be taken to illustrate the fuzzy boundary of the category 'human-like beings', as it may be interpreted as referring to the Devil either as a 'superhuman' (*he*) or in the shape of a serpent (*she*), and thus appears both with a masculine/neuter and feminine pronoun:

(4) Eue heold i parais long tale wið fle **neddre**; talde **him** al þe lecun (Cleo)

(5) Eue heold ine parais longe tale mid te **neddre** & tolde **hire** al flat lescun
     'Eve had a long conversation with **the serpent** in paradise … and told **him/it/her** the entire lesson.' (NeroA)

When referring to the animal only, *nædre* retains its Old English gender: *Nedre attreð … al þx **heo** priked* 'The **serpent/snake** poisons … everything that she stings' (Lam2).

The category of animals is on the whole the most regular one in retaining Old English gender. Most nouns referring to animals are of Old English origin, and they virtually always retain their Old English gender. Thus, *cat, dogge, hund, ile* [hedgehog] and *hare* are referred to using the masculine pronoun, while *culure* [dove], *hen* and *ule* [owl] are referred to as feminine. As with the reported present-day use of *she* for tomcats, biological sex seems to be unimportant in reference to animals. Thus, the falcon is masculine (following both its Old French gender and, it seems, a semantic association of large birds of prey with the masculine gender) even when engaged in emphatically nonmale activities: *þo hit bycom þat **he** hayhte & of **his** eyre briddes wrauhte* 'then it happened that **he** hatched and brought out chicks from **his** eggs' (J29).

Finally, like humans, very young animals tend to be referred to as *it*, irrespective of the gender of the antecedent: *þat fule **brid** … . þat pie and crowe **hit** to-drowe* 'the foul **chick** (OE masc.) … so that the magpie and crow tore **it** to pieces' (J29).

5.2 Inanimates: the survival of grammatical gender in the individual texts

When it comes to inanimate nouns, the first point to note is that much of the Old English gender system is retained in anaphoric reference. Approximately half of all native nouns that were masculine or feminine in Old English retain their gender in the majority of occurrences; this is true of 49 per cent of the masculine nouns and 52 per cent of the feminine nouns. At the same time, the spread of neuter *(h)it* is well under way: approximately one-third of the OE masculine or feminine nouns (38 per cent and 29 per cent respectively) are referred to by *(h)it* only.

The extent to which Old English grammatical gender is retained varies, at first sight, greatly from text to text. Figure D2.2 shows the proportions of historically 'correct' anaphoric pronouns referring to etymologically masculine and feminine nouns, arranged from the most conservative to the most advanced texts. For the sake of comparison, the proportions of historically correct definite articles (not including the unmarked masculine nominative singular forms) in the same texts are shown in a lighter shade.

It may first of all be noted that the most conservative texts (Layamon's *Brut*, the Tremulous Hand and Hand 1 of the Lambeth Homilies) show very high proportions (around 80–90 per cent) of explicitly marked gender forms in anaphoric reference; the first two also show very high proportions of gender marking in the definite article.

For most texts, however, the figures for anaphoric usage in the diagram are higher than those for the determiners, sometimes considerably so. The difference is particularly dramatic in the three earliest texts of the *Ancrene Riwle/Wisse*, all of which retain a high proportion of masculine and feminine anaphoric pronouns, but show few or virtually no remnants of gender marking within the noun phrase.

Three texts, *Floris and Blancheflur*, the Royal MS of the Katherine Group and the Worcester Sermon, show no gendered anaphoric usage at all. However, none of these texts shows many occurrences of anaphoric reference overall. Most texts that contain a reasonable number of occurrences do retain gendered usage: in fact, with the single exception of the Caius text of *Ancrene Riwle*, all those texts that contain more than fifteen occurrences of anaphoric reference to etymologically masculine or feminine nouns also show the OE gender being retained in more than 60 per cent of the occurrences.

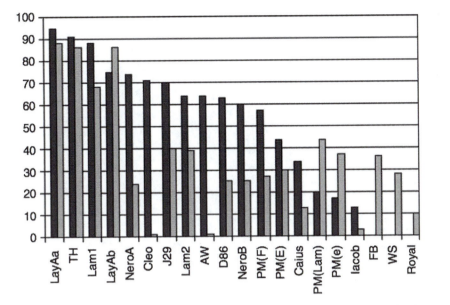

Figure D2.2 Comparison of percentages of (a) historically expected anaphoric pronouns for masculine/feminine inanimates, and (b) historically expected forms of the definite article (except masc. nom. sg). The former are shown in a darker shade. Descending order according to the retention of gender in anaphoric usage.

The differences between the texts do not appear to have any direct correlation with chronology. Figure D2.3 shows the data from Figure D2.2 rearranged chronologically. There seems to be no discernible pattern; on the contrary, some of the most conservative texts (most notably the Layamon texts and Jesus 29) belong to the end of the period.

This is true both of anaphoric reference and of gender distinctions within the noun phrase. It is suggested in Stenroos (in preparation) that this lack of correlation indicates a period of variable usage, during which formal gender marking within the noun phrase was optional or may have survived in local pockets. Around 1300, however, a critical threshold seems to have been reached with regard to gender within the noun phrase: as far as the present writer is aware, there are very few traces of it left in fourteenth-century texts.

In Stenroos (in preparation), three possible governing factors are suggested for the varying degrees of syncretism in the determiner system. Firstly, the six most conservative texts (Lambeth A and B, Layamon A and B, the Tremulous Hand of Worcester and the Jesus 29 miscellany) are localized within a fairly small area, suggesting a regional or local centre of very conservative usage. Secondly, with the exception of the Lambeth Homilies (some of which are translations from Old English), prose texts in general show fewer gendered determiner forms. Thirdly, there may be a significant correlation between the use of French loanwords and an advanced stage of gender loss within the noun phrase.

[...]

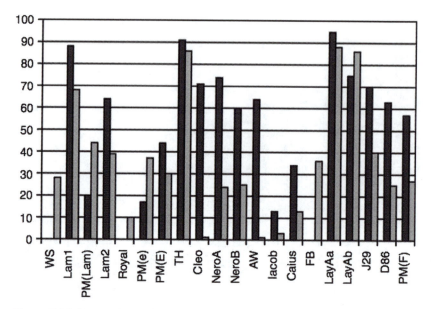

Figure D2.3 Comparison of percentages of (a) historically expected anaphoric pronouns for masculine/feminine inanimates, and (b) historically expected forms of the definite article (except masc.non.sg). The former are shown in a darker shade. Approximate chronological order.

6. Semantic reorganization

It now remains to ask whether the material simply shows a random spread of it, or whether any patterns may be discerned that would reflect a semantically based reorganization of gender assignment during this period. First of all, it will be worth asking whether those nouns that have shifted from masculine/feminine to neuter show any particular patterning. Such nouns, which appear wholly or almost wholly as neuter, are listed as follows:

> **Old English masculine:** *bigyrdel* 'purse', *bog* 'branch', *cnif* 'knife', *cyrtel, gar* 'spear', *hungor, leap* 'basket', *nama, pyff* 'puff', *pytt, scrift, stocc* 'stump', *swicdom* 'deception', *wa* 'woe', *wela* 'possessions'.
> **Old English feminine:** *behæs* 'vow', *betacnung* 'significance', *bliss, cuppe* 'cup', *dæd, fylð* 'filth', *higð* 'effort', *milts, rinde* 'bark, rind', *scamu* 'shame', *spræc, sihð, tidung* 'tiding'.

As in the list of nouns that show variable gender, given [...] above, a considerable proportion (eight out of twelve lexemes) of the etymologically feminine nouns that appear with a neuter pronoun are uncountable, either concrete (*fylð, rinde*) or abstract nouns (*bliss, higð, milts, scamu, spræc, sihð*). In addition, there are four abstract countable nouns (*behæs, betacnung, dæd, tidung*). Only one is a concrete countable noun (*cuppe*). The etymologically masculine nouns include a higher proportion of countable ones.

There seem to be certain semantic areas where nouns are particularly attracted to neuterness. Most nouns for property, something owned or won, were already neuter in Old English. A search under the category 'wealth' in the *Historical Thesaurus of Old English* (Roberts and Kay 1995) produces 34 simple or complex words[6] that can be used to convey the meaning 'property, goods', including specialized senses:

> **Neuter:** *āgen, ēad, feoh, gesteald, gestrēon, gōd, sceatt , þing*; (landed property) *lond*; (inherited) *ierfe*; (household goods) *inēddisc, ȳddisc, inorf*; (cattle) *orf*; (treasure) *sinc, gold, seolfor*; (equipment) *geþræc*; (worth) *(ge)weorþ*.
> **Feminine:** *āge, ār, faru, feorm, hæfen, wynn, æht*.
> **Masculine:** *begeat, wela*; (common property) *gemāna*; (treasure) *maþm*.
> **Feminine plural:** *frætwe*.
> **Variable:** (treasure) *gærsum* mn, *gærsuma* f, *hord* nm.

[...]

In general, most of the 28 nouns that in the present material appear to have lost their masculine or feminine gender seem to be either uncountable or denote things with a low degree of individuation. It might be held that the lexical set 'wealth', which seems to have become associated with neuterness at a very early stage, involves nouns with a particularly passive and unindividuated meaning. If this reflects a genuine tendency to assign gender on semantic grounds, it should then be expected that words that retain their masculine or feminine genders would have highly individuated referents. Leaving aside such nouns as retain their masculine/feminine gender only or mainly in the more conservative texts, this seems indeed to be the case. There are 21 nouns that regularly retain masculine/feminine reference even in the least conservative texts; these may be grouped into categories such as the following:

Abstract nouns, uncountable:

(6) þlurh eie-þlurles **deað** haueð **hire** inȝong

> 'Through the eyes **death** (masc.) makes **her** entrance' (NeroA)

[...]

Abstract nouns, countable:

(7) þeo oðer [**riwle**]...**Heo** teacheð...**þeos** is alse þuften

> 'the other [**rule**] (AF fem.)...**she** teaches...**this one** (fem.) is like a handmaid' (Cleo)

The human body and its parts:

(8) Iblesced beo eauer þos **hond**, for **ha** haued ytimbrid me þeo blissen of heuene

> 'blessed be always this **hand** (fem.), for **she** has built for me the joys of Heaven' (Caius)
> [...]

---

6 Compound words are excluded here, as they mainly involve the same simplex words in various combinations.

More abstract parts of man:

(9)   þin owene fles ... **He** flat sholde ben þi frend, He doþ þe raþest falle

'your own **flesh** (neut.) ... **He** who should be your friend, **He** is the first to bring you down' (D86)
[...]

The world:

(10)   of þe **worldes** meaðelunge ... of **hire** chaþe

'of the **world's** (fem.) speech ... of **her** chattering' (AW)
[...]

The sun and the moon:

(11)   þe **mone** bledeþ ... and geþ out of **hire** riȝte lawe

'the **moon** (masc.) bleeds ... and leaves **her** normal track' (D86)
[...]

Plants or fruits, viewed as individuals:

(12)   þe **lilie** myd **hire** fayre wlite ... Bid me myd **hire** fayre bleo þat ich schulle to **hire** fleo

'the **lily** (fem.) with **her** beautiful face ... Begs me with **her** fair countenance that I should fly to **her**' (J29)
[...]

Objects:

(13)   þe harde **rode** heue him ... luueliche bi-cluppede **hire**

'the hard **cross** (fem.) carried him ... lovingly (he) embraced **her**' (Caius)

Many of the nouns and categories included in the list [...] seem to appear with non-neuter pronouns in much later texts, at least occasionally. Most are here referred to by the feminine pronoun; the only examples of masculine gender are *appel* 'apple', *deð* 'death', *flesc* 'flesh', *muð* 'mouth' and *woruld* 'world'. In most cases (16 out of 21), the nouns retain their Old English gender; however, the following appear with a different gender: *deað*, *hope*, *flesh*, *mone* and *world*. In some of these cases, the gender may be influenced by a well-known and often personified Latin equivalent, suggesting a feminine personification of death and of the moon, and a masculine one of the world; similarly, the Latin gender may have reinforced the Old English gender of some words (*sawol*, *rode*). However, such an explanation, if feasible, could still not account for all the cases either of gender change or gender retention: the masculine gender of flesh and the retention of feminine reference to heart, sin and sun certainly cannot be explained in such a way.

There does, however, seem to be a semantic pattern. All antecedents involved seem to be viewed as clearly defined individuals, often (if not always) actively involved in an action.

[...]

This pattern would seem to be usefully illustrated with reference to a hierarchy of individuation, such as that used by Siemund (2008: 140). According to this model, as applied to different varieties of Germanic languages, the more individualized a concept the noun refers to, the more likely it is to be referred to with a non-neuter pronoun. Different varieties will vary with regard to the cut-off points between non-neuter and neuter:

> The proposal made here is that animate pronouns like *he* and *she* encroach upon this hierarchy from the left extending their domain of usage to the right while neuter *it* proceeds in the opposite direction, i.e. from right to left. It is claimed that pronominal usage in different varieties of English mainly differs with respect to the cut-off points defined on the scale of individuation. Some varieties effect a split between humans and animals, others between animates and inanimates while yet other varieties define the cut-off point between count nouns and mass nouns. (Siemund 2008: 4)

[...]

To summarize, it would seem that approximately the following prototypical system of semantically based gender assignment is emerging in the thirteenth-century Southwest Midland material:

Masculine: human males (post-babies), human generic,[7] 'superhuman' beings, some animals (post-babies)

Feminine: human females (post-babies), some animals (post-babies), inanimate objects and abstract nouns (perceived as individual)

Neuter: human and animal babies, inanimate objects and abstract nouns (not perceived as individual), mass nouns

The intention is, of course, not to suggest that such a semantically based system suddenly appeared out of nowhere to replace the more formally based Old English system. Rather, tendencies for semantically based gender assignment that were already there in Old English would have been strengthened, as potentially conflicting formal markers were lost. Thus, lexical sets denoting concepts with a low degree of individuation (such as 'wealth') tended to include many neutral words already in Old English. Similarly, the specific association of the masculine gender with humans would be bolstered by the

---

7 The use of masculine pronouns for generic human reference in the present material may to some extent reflect the largely male audience of formal, written texts; as noted above, the *Ancrene Wisse* uses feminine generic pronouns reflecting its predominantly female audience and text universe. It should be noted that singular generic 'they' appears as early as Old English (Curzan 2003: 70), and may have been more common in spoken language than written; it does not, however, seem to be used in the present material.

sheer weight of numbers: most anaphoric pronouns in Old and Early Middle English texts refer to human males, something that seems to be true of most texts produced in most English-speaking communities (see e.g. Wales 1996: 114).

List of primary sources

All texts were studied in diplomatic transcriptions made by Dr Margaret Laing for *A Linguistic Atlas of Early Middle English* (see Laing & Lass 2007–).
   [N.B. See Stenroos's original article for the full list of primary sources.]

D2.2 Issues to consider

Activity D2.1

In attempting to understand the change from grammatical to natural gender, Stenroos studies the Southwest Midlands dialect. What is her reason for choosing this variety in particular?

Activity D2.2

The 'animacy hierarchy' referred to by Stenroos in her article is an attempt to explain the principle by which grammatical gender is assigned in language. The more defined and individualised a noun is, the more likely it is to be referred to anaphorically with a masculine or feminine pronoun (as opposed to with a neuter pronoun). Assuming this to be the case, have a look at the following Old English nouns and their genders and decide what the most likely anaphoric pronoun would be to refer to their Middle English equivalents. For example, in Old English, the word *mūða* (estuary) is masculine. Its associated anaphoric pronoun is therefore also masculine (the equivalent of saying in Present Day English 'An **estuary** is an enclosed body of water. Rivers and streams flow into **him**'). Which anaphoric pronoun would a Middle English speaker have been most likely to use when referring to these nouns? Masculine/feminine or neuter?

   (i) foranhēafod (forehead), *neuter*
   (ii) bearn (bairn, i.e. child), *neuter*
   (iii) dor (door), *neuter*
   (iv) hōd (hood), *masculine*
   (v) wīf (woman), *neuter*
   (vi) bile (beak), *masculine*
   (vii) strǣt (street), *feminine*

D3 MEDIEVAL MULTILINGUALISM

In the British Isles, medieval society was characterised by a high degree of multilingualism. This is not to say that everyone was able to speak multiple languages; this ability is likely to have been concentrated among the higher social classes: royalty, government officials, the clergy, merchants, and the like. Certainly, the opportunity to formally study a second or third language would have been restricted to those from the upper echelons of society and those engaged in government and administration. But even if you spoke only English, you would have been keenly aware that you were a member of a multilingual society. It was not until the late 1530s, for example, that English began to be used in church services (Marshall 2017: 269). At the beginning of the Middle English period English was the vernacular language of the majority of the population, French was the language of the royal court and government, and Latin was the language of the church (see section B3.1). The relative statuses of these languages changed considerably between 1100 and 1500 but what we can observe in Early Middle English texts is a considerable degree of code-switching; that is, the mixing of different languages. It is important to remember that in the Middle English period there was as yet no sense of a standard form of English that was correct to the exclusion of other varieties. This tolerance of variation, coupled with the multilingual situation of the time, helps to explain why code-switching was accepted, though it does not answer the question of why writers engaged in it. In this reading, Herbert Schendl tackles this question by examining the function of code-switching in early English literature.

D3.1 Code-switching in early English literature

Herbert Schendl (reprinted from *Language and Literature* 24(3): 233–48 (2015))

1. Introduction
From the beginning of English literary tradition up to the modern period, multilingual texts have been well attested, though with varying frequency, distribution and function. [...] In this article, the strategy of mixing different languages within a single written text will be referred to as 'code-switching' [...] The use of this term also reflects my view that linguistic research into early multilingual literary texts should be seen as part of a larger field of historical code-switching research and should also profit from modern research into code-switching in multilingual speech. But one has to be aware of the specific sociohistorical context of early written code-switching and of its potential differences from present-day switching.

Code-switching in early English literature is a vast but under-researched field, of which the present study must take a necessarily panoramic view. It will focus on medieval England, whose complex linguistic situation gave rise to a great number of multilingual literary texts, with an emphasis on the functional-pragmatic aspects of code-switching, though the often neglected grammatical-syntactic issues will also be briefly addressed.

2. Medieval multilingualism and code-switching
Medieval England was a multilingual country, with a loosely diglossic situation between the 'High' language Latin and the Old English vernacular in the Anglo-Saxon period (up to about 1150). The introduction of French as a prestigious vernacular after

the Norman Conquest led to a trilingual situation in the Middle English period (c. 1150–1500), with close contacts between the three languages of literacy Latin, French and English at least in written texts (Hunt, 2011; Rothwell, 1994). The status and distribution of these languages, however, changed over time, and towards the end of the Middle English period, the balance began to shift to the emerging English standard language, which slowly established itself in more and more domains. Latin kept its high prestige throughout the Middle English period, though its distribution was slowly reduced. French, on the other hand, which had long maintained an important place as a language of administration and culture even when it was no longer a naturally acquired first language, became increasingly restricted to law and administration. [...]

As a multilingual practice, medieval code-switching is embedded in the wider context of societal multilingualism, which is reflected in different types of written expression. Most evidently, there are numerous monolingual texts in the three languages, which were 'composed and received in a multilingual network of allusions, undergirdings, expectations, resonances' (Wogan-Browne, 2009: 8), particularly in the many texts translated or adapted from Latin or French. Furthermore, some manuscript codices are compilations of monolingual texts in different languages, evidently assembled for a multilingual readership. With the widespread multilingualism of medieval England, it was also not unusual for authors to write texts in more than one language. A well-known medieval representative of such 'ambilingualism' (Hamers and Blanc, 2000) is the poet John Gower, whose oeuvre consists of works in Latin, French and English in fairly balanced quantity (see Machan, 2006).

Against this multilingual background, the occurrence of code-switching in numerous literary as well as non-literary medieval texts is in no way surprising and should be seen as two closely related expressions of the same phenomenon, namely a common discourse strategy attested in most multilingual speech communities. It is neither an exotic literary feature nor the result of insufficient linguistic competence.

In spite of many obvious similarities between medieval and present-day code-switching, the former has some specific characteristics, which have to be taken into account in our analyses:

i)   Latin and, by the late medieval period also French, were instructed languages of culture and administration, while English was for most authors and scribes a naturally acquired first language (cf. Lusignan, 2009: 21).
ii) The purely written nature of the data provides only limited information on code-switching in speech. However, the more oral character of medieval culture is reflected in 'the structure of language' (Fitzmaurice and Taavitsainen, 2007: 19) and medieval literature was often read to an audience (Lusignan, 2009: 30), two factors which may bring literary mixed-language closer to speech; however, it normally lacks the negotiation about the language of interaction typical of modern multilingual speech.
iii) The visual properties of multilingual texts form 'an integral part of the interpretation of the message' (Sebba, 2012: 2). This neglected aspect of medieval code-switching has recently been taken up by Machan (2011) and Jefferson (2013), who analyse the functions of contextual features (like page layout, underlining, boxing, colour and size of script) in different manuscripts of multilingual literary texts.

Such devices may differ between manuscripts of the same text and, like code-switching, often support and express the organization of a text.

When discussing code-switching in medieval literary texts, some specific characteristics of medieval literature should be borne in mind:

i)   It is heavily influenced by Latin, French and later also Italian models and many works are rather free translations or reworkings of foreign texts.
ii) Much of it is anonymous (at least up to the late 14th century), and we lack important information on linguistic variables such as authors, intended audience or readership, purpose of text, date and region of composition.
iii) Different manuscripts of the same text often differ substantially from each other, since scribes felt rather free to change their model.
iv) Much of medieval literature is in verse, and frequently stanzaic, which may have some bearing on patterns of code-switching.
v)   By modern standards, there is a lack of originality, which tends to 'give an effect of impersonality to [medieval] literature' (Baugh, 1967: 114). Extensive quotations, especially in Latin, were seen positively and not as a lack of artistic creativity.
vi) Medieval literature also comprises genres which are today regarded only peripherally as 'literature', such as religious, devotional and mystic treatises, historical chronicles and so forth; on the other hand, genres like the novel only developed later.

Because of the complex linguistic situation, code-switching considerably increased in the Middle English period in a range of literary and non-literary genres and text types. It reached its peak in the late 14th/early 15th century most likely due to the changing status of the three languages of literacy and the ongoing language shift from French and Latin to English in an increasing number of text types. Both the great variety in regard to functions and patterns of literary switching and some differences in regard to text types and genres make it reasonable to structure our discussion along these lines.

2.1 Functional aspects of medieval literary code-switching
[...] Medieval authors often use code-switching not only as a stylistic literary device, but also to express a variety of sociolinguistic and pragmatic functions. An analysis of these is often complicated by our insufficient knowledge of important sociolinguistic variables and some analyses have to remain tentative. There is, however, no doubt that a sociohistorical approach to multilingual texts can profitably supplement traditional literary interpretations. The following brief survey begins with shorter multilingual poems, then looks at some longer verse pieces and will conclude with a discussion of medieval drama.

2.1.1 Shorter multilingual poems
Code-switching in early medieval, that is, Old English, literature, is restricted to a few poems with very similar switching patterns from Old English into Latin (see Schendl, 1997: 54)[8]. However, their number drastically increases in the Middle English period

---

8 See the following representative line from *A Summons to Prayer*, where the Old English first half line is linked by alliteration to the Latin second one, resulting in a balanced distribution of languages: Geunne þe on life **auctor pacis** ['May he grant you in life a**the giver of peace**'].

and there are hundreds of bilingual and some trilingual poems dating from the 13th century to the end of the medieval period: political poems, love poems, courtly lyrics, and in particular religious poetry (including hymns and carols, see Wehrle, 1933). [...] Switching particularly occurs between English and Latin, though French is also well attested. The integration into verse or stanza is manifold and we find, for example, switching between half lines, full lines, refrain or cauda, as well as irregular switching (see Archibald, 2010: 277). Furthermore, switching fulfils a variety of functions and most of those listed in Gumperz (1982: 75–84) for living languages, such as quotations, reiteration, and interjections also occur in shorter medieval poems (see Schendl, 2001: 324–329). It is impossible to illustrate this diversity here, and I will only concentrate on some typical examples.

Political poems generally deal with political grievances or important political events. Code-switching in such poems tends to be irregular, is often quite creative, and frequently has the function to characterize a speaker, to set a particular scene or evoke a certain situation. In the *Song of the Flemish Resurrection* (early 14th century), both the French interjection used by a French knight addressing his king in (1) and the inserted French sentence spoken by a French nobleman in (2) serve to mark the speakers as members of a specific linguistic and social group, namely the French nobility fighting against the Flemish rebels (Schendl, 1997: 62–63).

1) Tho suor the Eorl of Seint Poul, **Par la goule Dé!** We shule facche the rybaus wher thi wille be,
    ['Then swore the Earl of Saint Paul, **By God!** / We will confront the rascals wherever they will be']
2) 'Sire Rauf Devel,' sayth the Eorl of Boloyne,
    'Nus ne lerrum en vie chanoun ne moyne,
    Wende we forth anon ritht withoute eny assoygne.'
    [**'We will not let alive chaplain nor monk**, / Let us go forward without any delay']

The short Latin quotations in *The Death of the Duke of Suffolk* (mid-15th century), on the other hand, set the scene for the poem: they are the beginnings of different parts of the 'Office of the Dead', which the bishops, supporters of the Duke of Suffolk 'perform on the execution of the duke' (Schendl, 2001: 326–327), a fact which is not explicitly stated otherwise:

3) Pray for this dukes soule þat it might come to blis, ...

    'Placebo', begynneth the bisshop of Herford.
    'Dilexit', for myn auauncement', saith þe bisshop of Chestre. ...
    'Si inquitates', saiþ þe bisshop of Worcetre,
    'For Iac Nape soule, **de profundis clamaui'**.

The individual switches in (1) to (3) carry specific meanings, that is, they have local function.
    [...]
One of the best-known trilingual *love poems* is *De amico ad amicam* with its equally multilingual *Responcio*, which form a fictional pair of letters (Putter, 2009: 397). Its second stanza is given under (4):

4) **Sachéz bien, pleysant et beele**
    That I am ryght in good heele
    Laus Christo!
    Et mon amour doné vous ay,
    And also thin owne nyght and day
    Incisto.
    ['**Be well assured, pleasing and beautiful one** / That I am really in good health /
        Praise be to Christ / **And I have given you my love** / And also thy own night
        and day / *I persevere*']

According to Putter (2009), the three languages of this poem represent different
registers: while French and English differ 'in the degree of communicative directness'
(2009: 407), the Latin cauda has a 'liturgical or scholastic ring' (2009: 400), and mirrors
its status as language of divine authority (see Section 2.1.2).

Code-switching is especially frequent in *religious poems* (including hymns and
carols), particularly from the 15th century. A productive writer of bilingual carols was
Charles Ryman, but most texts are anonymous. Switching patterns tend to be regular,
for example full Latin lines either regularly alternate with English lines or form the
refrain or cauda of the poem. Example (5) quotes part of an anonymous 13th-century
religious lyric with regular switches between lines.

5) Of on þat is so fayr and briȝt
    velud maris stella, ['**Like the star of the sea**']
    Briȝter þan þe day is liȝt **parens et puella,** ...
    ['**mother and virgin**']

Most Latin switches in religious poems are full or abbreviated quotations from the
Bible or from liturgical texts, which are often taken over from Latin hymns and lend
authority to the English text, which tells the story (Putter, 2009: 400); from a linguistic
point of view, these switches are 'prefabricated chunks', which may occur in more than
one text. They would evoke the original context or the full quotation for the clerical
audience, but would also be recognizable to people with little or no Latin.[9]

2.1.2 Longer verse pieces
[…] Many English romances are either systematic translations or reworkings of French
models. They sometimes use code-switching into French, particularly conventionalized
phrases such as *graunt merci* 'many thanks, thank you', *beau sir* 'fair sir' to characterize
a speaker as a member of a specific social group, in general of 'polite' society (e.g. in
Sir Gawain and the Green Knight; see also example (2) in this article). Similarly limited
and with specific local meanings are the switches in Chaucer's work. In his *Summoner's
Tale*, a friar occasionally uses French words and phrases in his speech as when he
rebukes his sick host with the words: 'O Thomas, *je vous dy*, Thomas! Thomas! / This
maketh the feend; this moste ben amended' (ll. 1832–1833). Here the function of the

---

9 The insertion of Latin biblical or other religious quotations was a well-established textual
   strategy in medieval writing, particularly common in non-literary religious texts such as
   sermons or treatises.

French phrase *je vous dy* 'I tell you' is to increase the friar's authority by showing his (rather limited) learnedness (cf. Putter, 2011).

Extensive code-switching of a different type occurs in [William Langland's] *Piers Plowman*, a work which deals with contemporary religious and social topics and whose author was evidently a highly competent multilingual. [...] Approaching the text from a sociolinguistic perspective, Machan (1994) interprets switching in *Piers Plowman* in the context of the diglossia between Latin as the High variety especially used in 'ideologically powerful institutions and discourses' and English as the Low variety. Competence in Latin is a sign of power and education, while ignorance of it 'is associated with "lewed" men' (Machan, 1994: 360). This is in line with the medieval view that only a person knowing Latin is 'litteratus', while everybody else is 'illitteratus' (Clanchy, 1993: 226–229). The attested violations of this linguistic use in the text are interpreted as reflecting the beginning collapse of the aforementioned diglossic situation (Machan, 1994: 363). Overall, code-switching in *Piers Plowman* is regarded as being 'largely ornamental', in other words stylistic, and not as being used 'to show solidarity with or social distance from an interlocutor' (Machan, 1994: 369).

Machan's analysis is partly refuted by Davidson, who, in a detailed discourse-analytical interpretation of the data, comes to the conclusion that code-switching often reflects 'discourse strategies in which each quotation envisions specific interlocutors; it may signal accommodation, inclusion as well as exclusion of interlocutors' (2001: 170) and thus frequently has 'local' meaning. Example (6) illustrate[s] such different discourse functions of Langland's code-switching.

In (6), the central figure of Will talking to his friar confessor uses two Latin switches, which he neither translates nor paraphrases, since this is 'in-group communication' with somebody knowing Latin. This is evident from the status of the addressee and the address 'ye lettred men' in the last line (Davidson, 2001: 153).

6)   For a baptized man may, as maistres telleth,
     Thorough contricion come to the heighe hevene –
     Sola contricio delet peccatum –
     Ac a barn withouten bapteme may noght be so saved –
     Nisi quis renatus fuerit.
     Loke, ye lettred men, wheither I ley or do not. (Piers Plowman *PP*, B.11.80–83)
     ['**Only contrition can blot out sin** / But a child without baptism may not be so
        saved / **Unless a man be born again** / Look, you learned men, if I lie or
        do not']

     [...]

For Davidson, the mixing strategies in *Piers Plowman* are motivated by 'the ingroup communication of clerks' (2001: 176, note 107), and the positioning of in-group and out-group speakers is established by their language choice.

In spite of their differences, both Machan and Davidson convincingly show that even in texts where speakers are mainly abstract allegorical figures and the Latin switches are mostly quotations, code-switching can have sociolinguistic and discourse-related meaning and that a linguistic analysis focusing on the functions of code-switching can bring new insights even into well-researched multilingual literary texts.

2.1.3 Middle English drama

Medieval drama only developed from the second half of the 14th century onwards and mainly deals with biblical and religious topics. It is traditionally divided into 'mystery' (or 'miracle') plays and 'morality' plays. Many individual plays of both groups show instances of code-switching, though to a varying extent (for a detailed discussion see Diller, 1997/1998).

There are a number of similarities between code-switching in medieval drama and in *Piers Plowman*, which are mainly related to the shared religious topic and the diglossic background of the texts:

i)   Most of the speakers are allegorical figures, mainly God and devils/demons.
ii)   Most switches are into Latin, the language of divine authority, and occur in the discourse between God (or his prophets) and Man (i.e. humanity), though there are some important exceptions (Diller, 1997/1998); switches into French are rare.
iii) Due to the central status of Latin as divine language and – from the point of religion – the only peripheral status of English as the language of the 'unknowing', the use of Latin is not just ornamental or stylistic, but has social meaning (Diller, 1997/1998).
iv)   The majority of Latin switches are quotations from the Bible or the liturgy, and thus 'prefabricated'. Full sentences and longer stretches of Latin predominate, though phrases and single words are also well attested.

One of the few differences between *Piers Plowman* and medieval drama relates to the audience or readership of the texts. *Piers Plowman* mainly addresses a clerical readership competent in Latin so that Latin switches are often not translated or paraphrased; for the mainly non-clerical audience of medieval drama, on the other hand, knowledge of Latin could not be generally expected, though many would have been familiar with the Latin liturgy. As a result, especially longer Latin switches in drama tend to be 'supported' by English translations or paraphrases.

The following examples from the popular morality play *Mankind* not only illustrate the switching types already mentioned, but also a number of unusual kinds of switching, such as the conscious use of 'bad' Latin. Most verbal exchange in medieval drama happens between *dramatis personae* or, less frequently, between *dramatis personae* and the audience or readership (Diller, 1997/1998: 507). But we also find code-switching in communication between the playwright and the reader/director (or the actors), namely in the – often elaborate – Latin stage-directions inserted into the text, where Latin thus has organizational, that is, text-structuring function, and – from the point of view of the playwright – indicates a change of addressee (cf. Davidson, 2001: 143):

7)   NEW GYSE, NOWADAYS. On hyse breche yt xall be seen, ... **Cantant OMNES** ['On his pants it shall be seen, ... **All sing**'] Hoylyke, holyke, holyke! (*Mankind*, 342–343)

      [...]

2.2 Syntactic aspects of literary code-switching

[...] [O]nly a few studies on medieval code-switching have dealt with syntactic aspects, most of them on the basis of non-literary texts (e.g. Halmari and Regetz, 2011; Ingham, 2011; Wenzel, 1994). Yet even on this restricted data we can refute the claim that historical code-switching only shows 'a limited range of constructions' (Gullberg et al., 2009: 23).

In regard to *Piers Plowman*, Machan (1994: 359) states that in no other medieval literary text do 'so many speakers change languages so pervasively at so many syntactic points' and emphasizes the similarities of its switching patterns with those found in non-literary medieval documents such as guild records and court rolls. Similarly, in shorter medieval poems, the length of switches ranges from single words to phrases, sentences and longer text sequences and involves a range of syntactic patterns (Schendl, 2000a, 2001).

The results of a surface-oriented, descriptive analysis of syntactic switching patterns in medieval shorter poems and bilingual ('macaronic') sermons were compared to frequency data from three modern studies of code-switching in Schendl (2000a). Though the medieval database of this study only comprised 478 instances of switches (239 from poems and sermons each), it showed that the differences between medieval and modern data were mainly due to the relative frequencies of specific patterns rather than to 'the presence or absence of specific features or types' (Schendl, 2000a: 82), even though there are some text-type specific properties. Table D3.1 gives the main syntactic patterns found in the corpus of medieval poems, sermons and those given in two of the three studies of modern spoken code-switching included in the original study, namely of English–German (Pütz, 1994) and English–Spanish (Poplack, 1980). Such analyses allow the establishment of empirically based frequency hierarchies for preferred switching patterns in historical code-switching, a desirable goal for future research.[10]

[...] A clear majority of switching in the two sets of medieval data as well as in Poplack's study occurs *between* major sentence constituents (NP, VP, PP), amounting to 94% and 82% respectively in poems and sermons, and 60% in Poplack's data. On the other hand, the poems show a higher frequency of switched noun phrases than the other data sets, but a much lower number of single word switches. A switching pattern found in the medieval texts but not in the spoken data analysed by Pütz and Poplack are non-finite switched clauses (see extract (8)), while 'emblematic switches' (interjections, tags, etc.) are quite frequent in modern speech (Poplack 29%, Pütz 10%), but extremely rare in the historical data (see (1) for an interjection in a medieval poem). These latter differences seem to be mainly due to differences in register, not to diachronic or systemic differences between the languages involved. (For further discussion of possible reasons for these differences and examples of the different switching patterns see Schendl, 2000a: 78–80.)

8) Ther they deyn a wonder thing,
    Feruentes insania
    ['There they did a dreadful thing, / **Raving in madness**']

More research on syntactic aspects of medieval code-switching along these lines is a clear desideratum and has been undertaken recently for medieval sermons by Halmari and Regetz (2011); however, it is still lacking for medieval literary texts.

---

10 For some methodological problems of such an approach see Schendl (2000b: 88). Even more problematic is the comparison of medieval written data with modern spoken data involving different language pairs and different registers. Thus the (partly incomplete) figures from the two modern studies can only serve as a very tentative first comparison of two different diachronic sets of data.

Table D3.1 Frequency of switched constituents in medieval and modern code-switching data (sources: Schendl, 2000a: medieval poems, medieval sermons, Latin/English; Pütz, 1994: English/ German; Poplack, 1980: Spanish/English)[1]

	Poems (E-L)	Sermons (L-E)	Pütz (E-G)	Poplack (Sp-E)
Constitutent	%	%	%	%
S(indep)	21.3	1.3	33.8	24.6
s(gover)	2.5	1.3		
S(dep) finite	6.7	2.6	1.6	
S(dep) non-finite	8.8	9.2	0	0
NP+VP/	6.3	15.1	0.9	
NP	30.5	8.8	2.5	11.4
VP	4.2	7.1	1.5	
PP	13.4	14.6	6.5	
Single words	2.9	20.5	38.0	19.2
Other types	3.3	19.7		
Total number	239	239		

Percentages are rounded. Abbreviations: S 'sentence', (in)dep '(in)dependent', gover 'governing', NP 'noun phrase', VP 'verb phrase', PP 'prepositional phrase'. Due to the often controversial status of 'inserted' single words, we have – like Pütz and Poplack – subsumed these in a special group 'single words', irrespective of their word class/syntactic function, but not included them under the respective NP, VP, PP to which they belong. For more details on the individual syntactic subcategories and illustrating examples see Schendl (2000a: 76–81).

3. Conclusion

Code-switching was a widespread multilingual strategy in medieval literature, showing a variety of functions, patterns and distribution. While it is restricted to poetry in the Old English period, it occurs with various functions in most Middle English literary genres, such as poetry, longer verse pieces and drama. The diglossic situation between Latin as the High variety and central language of divine authority, and English as the Low variety of 'lewed men' is frequently mirrored in the functions of the two languages in bilingual texts. French is more restricted in its use and function and often evokes the idea of polite society. Especially in *Piers Plowman* and in medieval drama, code-switching fulfils a number of socio-linguistic and discourse functions, but it is also used as a stylistic literary device in poetic texts. On the syntactic level, there is a wide range of switching patterns which mainly differ from those found in modern speech by their relative frequencies rather than by their presence or absence in a particular period. In view of the different status of the three languages of literacy Latin, French and English, and the fact that Latin and increasingly also French were instructed languages, it is not surprising that the three languages are kept clearly distinct in medieval literary code-switching and no specific type of mixed code developed in literary use. In general, medieval literary code-switching is marked by a high competence in the languages involved, though 'prefabricated chunks', mostly religious quotations, are also used extensively. All in all, medieval literary code-switching is an apt expression of a multilingual society and as such it is clearly linked to the numerous non-literary multilingual texts of medieval England, such as administrative and legal texts, sermons, letters and scientific texts. Furthermore, it is highly likely that in such a complex linguistic situation, spoken code-switching must also have been a frequent multilingual strategy. [...]

D3.2 Issues to consider

Activity D3.1
Based on your reading, make a list of some of the common functions of code-switching in the Middle English period. What was it used for?

Activity D3.2
The following is a short extract from one of the Paston Letters (see B5.1). The letter was written in 1426 by William Paston I to William Worstede, John Longham and Piers Shelton. What languages are used in this extract? Bearing in mind your answer to the previous question, why do you think the writer engages in code-switching? (Hint: consider the status of the addresser and addressee.)

> *Address*: A mez tres honnures mesitres William Worstede, John Longham, et Meister Piers Shelton soit donne.
>
> Right worthy and worshepefull seres and maistres, I recomand me to yow and thank yow with al my herte of the gret tendrenesse ye lyke to have of the salvacion of my symple honeste, preyng yow evermore of your good continuance.
>
> (Davis 1971: 1)

D4 SHIFTING SOUNDS

Unit B4 contains the background detail you need in order to grasp what happened during the Great Vowel Shift (GVS) of the late Middle English and Early Modern periods. The following reading provides more descriptive and explanatory detail regarding the shift. Manfred Krug presents a detailed description of the GVS and in addition considers why the process constitutes a shift and why it merits the label 'great'. The GVS is usually explained by reference to the notion of a chain shift, which functions as a model of how the GVS happened. In his chapter, Krug considers the evidence for which variant of the model (push chain or drag chain) is most plausible. Interestingly, Krug also discusses the history of GVS theories, arguing that Charles Darwin's work in evolutionary biology had a significant impact on the development of the push and drag chain models of the GVS that were formulated in the late nineteenth and early twentieth centuries, respectively. Krug argues that while this analogy with biology has undoubtedly been valuable to linguists by helping them to account for the GVS, it is also possibly constraining as a description of what happened.

D4.1 The Great Vowel Shift

Manfred Krug (reprinted from Bergs, A. and Brinton, L. (eds) (2017) *The History of English. Volume 4: Early Modern English*, pp. 241–66. Berlin: De Gruyter.)

[...]

2. Why "Great Vowel Shift"?

In the past three decades, research on the series of changes known as the "Great Vowel Shift" has centered on counterexamples and focused on why what happened to the ME (Middle English) long vowels should not be considered "great" or a "shift". This chapter will begin with a defence of the traditional label, although it is by no means the first to do so. In another recent handbook article, McMahon (2006) discusses in a systematic way the classic and partly interrelated five "problems" identified by Lass (1976) and Stockwell and Minkova (1988), around which most of the literature revolves:

(i) Inception: where in the vowel space did the series of changes begin?
(ii) Order: what is the chronology of individual and overlapping changes?
(iii) Structural coherence: are we dealing with interdependent changes forming a unitary overarching change or with local and independent changes?
(iv) Mergers: is the assumption of non-merger, i.e. preservation of phonemic contrasts, viable for language change in general and met in the specific changes of the GVS?
(v) Dialects: how do we deal with dialects which did not undergo the same changes as southern English or in which the changes proceeded in a different order?

After careful consideration of the issues and evaluation of the previous literature, McMahon concludes that while there is no simple answer to any of the above problems, the label "Great Vowel Shift" is justified beyond aesthetic and didactic grounds, certainly for the upper half, but probably also for the lower half, of the vowel space.

[...]

2.1 Why "great"?

In the late 19th century, linguists like Luick (1896: 306–307) were struck by the fact that all long vowels of the English spoken around Chaucer's time changed qualitatively in subsequent centuries. And the qualitative changes were so significant that for 17th century pronunciations new phonemic labels are necessary in order to avoid crude misrepresentations of the phonetic facts, certainly (but not only) for the predecessors of modern southern British English. For convenience and familiarity among the expected readership, my first reference point will be the accent that is referred to as "Received Pronunciation" or "RP" in its Present-day English (PDE) form, which – although supposedly supraregional – is essentially based on the pronunciation of educated southern British English speakers. Table D4.1 lists all ME long vowels and their PDE RP reflexes. Lexical exceptions as well as dialects and accents other than RP will be dealt with in later sections.

It is true that there exist northern English and Scottish dialects that have not participated in all of the changes sketched in Table D4.1. And yet the vast majority of modern native speakers of English worldwide have pronunciations that diverge in relatively minor ways from modern RP, notably so when their varieties are compared to early Middle English (that is, pre-GVS) pronunciations. In fact, many modern dialects can be shown to be conservative relative to RP and can thus be located somewhere on the paths from ME to RP (whose intermediate stages are specified in Table D4.2 and Figure D4.1 below). Consider, for instance, Edinburgh English dialects which are currently diphthongizing their reflexes of ME /uː/, /aː/ and /ɔː/ (Schützler 2009). This, of course, does not mean that RP is more advanced in the sense of "being

Table D4.1 Modern RP pronunciations of the ME long vowels with PDE Present Day English orthographies("C" stands for "consonant"; adapted from Barber 1997: 105)

	Middle English		Modern English (RP)	Example	Typical (and rarer) PDE spelling examples
(I)	iː	>	aɪ	time	iCe, -y, -ie, (i+ld; i+nd) tide, fly, pie (child, kind)
(II)	uː	>	aʊ	house	ou, ow mouse, how
(III)	eː	>	iː	see	ee, ie seed, field
(IV)	oː	>	uː	boot	oo, (oCe, -o) food, (move, who)
(V)	ɛː	>	iː	sea	ea, ei, eCe health, conceit, complete
(VI)	ɔː	>	əʊ	sole	oCe, oa, (o, oe) hope, boat, (so, foe)
(VII)	aː	>	eɪ	name	aCe make, dame

superior" or even a natural endpoint of diatopic or diastratic variation, as is immediately obvious from the fact that modern RP speakers – similar to Australian and New Zealand English speakers – are diphthongizing /iː/ again in words like *see, me, tea.* Just how complex the situation is can be seen in American English, which varies between [oː], [o] and [oʊ] for ME /ɔː/ in words like *go* and *goat*: depending on the history of a dialect, the monophthongal variants [oː] and [o] can be either progressive (i.e. monophthongizations of [oʊ]) or conservative (i.e. reflect one-step raisings from ME /ɔː/, as in most modern Scottish and Irish English dialects outside Edinburgh and Dublin; see also Section 3 below for discussion).

In any case, such evidence lends further support to the uniformitarian hypothesis (see Christy 1983), which most modern research on phonetic and phonological change is based on and according to which changes that are impossible today were impossible in the past because the same principles hold for changes irrespective of the period during which they occur. Lass (1997: 24–32) offers an illuminating updated account of the uniformitarian hypothesis, including the Uniform Probabilities Principle, which states that "the (global, crosslinguistic) likelihood of any linguistic state of affairs (structure, inventory, process, etc.) has always been roughly the same as it is now" (Lass 1997: 29). From this follows that present-day changes are in principle no different from historical ones and may thus shed light on the past.

Let us leave aside for a moment the question of whether or not the changes in Table D4.1 are interlinked and thus merit the label "shift" […]. Allowing for some simplification – as all models [and] theories must – the changes involved certainly meet the criteria for a number of strong labels in historical phonology. In the dialects that participated in the shift almost the entire English lexicon was affected by the changes in (I) to (VII). In other words, whatever the individual histories and intermediate stages, it is obvious that it was essentially phonemes that changed. We can thus label each individual change without oversimplifying too much an "unconditioned", i.e. "context-free" sound change that deserves to be called a "neogrammarian" sound change – though not in the strongest form of the hypothesis, which claims that sound change affects all words and all speakers of a speech community simultaneously, because some items (like *do, good*) were affected by the changes earlier than others (cf. Ogura 1987; Lass 1999a: 78 and the discussion in Labov 1994: Chapter 17 on sound change vs. lexical diffusion). Indeed, precisely the fact that some exceptions to the GVS can be explained by the existence of phonetic variants underpins the neogrammarian label: low-stress items like *and* or *my* [mɪ], as in *me mum*, for instance, simply had no long vowel because high frequency and low stress lead to vowel lenition (cf. Bybee 2003); and differences like *sane* vs. *sanity* or *divine* vs. *divinity* display a regular pattern, too (cf. McMahon 2007).

A conspectus of the current majority view of each ME long vowel's developmental path is offered in Table D4.2 and Figure D4.1.

Each arrow type (e.g. a sequence of arrows consisting of a dotted line) in Figure D4.1 represents one vowel trajectory, where the arrows with big arrowheads are part of the GVS and those with thin arrowheads are regarded by the majority of researchers as post-GVS developments. The changes of the ME vowels in the lower half of the phonetic space (the vowels given in brackets) start considerably later than those in the upper half. As was mentioned above, there is broad consensus in recent studies that at least the changes starting in the upper half, i.e. paths (I) to (IV), belong to the GVS or

Table D4.2 **Paths from Middle English long vowels to RP pronunciations**

Middle English									*Modern English (RP)*
(I)	iː	>	ɪi		>	əɪ	>	aɪ	
(II)	uː	>	ʊu		>	əʊ	>	aʊ	
(III)	eː				>			iː	
(IV)	oː				>			uː	
(V)	ɛː	>	eː		>			iː	
(VI)	ɔː	>	oː		>	oʊ	>	əʊ	
(VII)	aː	>	æː	>	ɛː	>	eː	>	eɪ

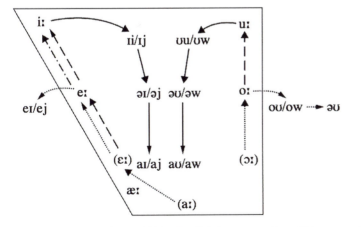

Figure D4.1 **Paths from Middle English long vowels to RP pronunciations (Great Vowel Shift and subsequent developments).**

"GVS proper" (Lass 1992, 1999, 2006; Labov 1994: 234; Stockwell 2002; Krug 2003a; McMahon 2006). Furthermore, variants like [ɪi/ɪj] and [ʊu/ʊw] of diphthongization stages are not purely notational in Figure D4.1. If Present-day English can serve as a guide, the phonetically most realistic assumption is that both pairs were essentially in complementary distribution: ME [ɪi] and [ʊu] would then be prototypical realizations in prepausal and preconsonantal contexts, while [ɪj] and [ʊw] are prevocalic prototypes serving to avoid hiatus. Finally, for the paths of ME /i:/ and /u:/ – (I) and (II) in Table D4.2 – some authors have used a more back first element for the modern RP vowels [aʊ] and [aɪ], namely [ɑʊ] and [ɑɪ], respectively, while others again have used inter-mediate stages [ʌɪ] and [ʌʊ].

In summary, for a number of reasons at least the epithet "great" seems justified for the series of changes under discussion here. Not a single long vowel of the major standard PDE varieties has remained in the position it occupied during the 14th cen-tury; the ModE reflexes differ greatly in quality from their ME ancestors and did so at the beginning of the 17th century, to which a number of authors date the end of the GVS (cf. Tables D4.3 and D4.4 for detail); the great majority of modern speakers – including modern speakers of English varieties that descend from dialects which did not participate in all GVS-related changes between 1200 and 1800 – command variants that are somewhere on the paths given in Figure D4.1. And finally, to con-clude on a utilitarian or didactic note, about half of the apparent mismatches between modern English orthography and pronunciation are related to the changes sketched in Tables D4.1 and D4.2. Once we have understood the history of the long vowels, such mismatches become more systematic and we can enhance considerably the chances for students of English to deduce the pronunciation from the spelling and vice versa.

2.2 Why a "shift"?

Hock (1991: 156) refers to chain shifts as "developments [...] in which one change within a given phonological system gives rise to other, related changes." Generally, two types of shift are distinguished: (i) "drag chain" (or "pull chain") shifts, which are motivated by the gaps resulting from a vacated space into which other, adjacent phonemes are pulled; (ii) "push chain" shifts, in which one phoneme encroaches onto an adjacent segment's phonetic space and thus causes the former occupant of this space to shift away (cf. Hock 1991: 156–157; Thomas 2006: 486; for a more detailed discussion of definitional issues involved in shifting).

Let us start from a bird's eye perspective and briefly list aspects that have been advanced in favour of chain shifting from an early date onwards. These usually exploit the notions of symmetry (front vs. back vowels) and gap or slot filling, which explains why the label of "shift" has been particularly attractive to researchers from a structur-alist background. Figure D4.1 illustrates the following points:

❑   The high vowels – both front and back – diphthongized, most probably via a cen-tral path involving nucleus-glide dissimilation (cf. Section 4 below).
❑   All non-high vowels – both front and back – raised, most probably via a peripheral path.
❑   Diphthongization occurred only for the two highest positions.

The question of timing is essential to determining whether the changes are interlinked and whether we are dealing with a "push chain" or a "drag chain" shift. So let us now turn to the question of when the changes shown in Table D4.2 occurred. It is, of course, impossible to pin down exact dates for historical sound changes, *inter alia* because (a) there exists a gap between writing and speech, (b) progressive pronunciations always coexist with conservative ones, and (c) modern sociolinguistic research into ongoing sound change has revealed that a complex network of social, stylistic, and regional factors plays a role in the distribution of the variants (as well as in the adoption of some of them in the eventual standard). Table D4.3 is a synopsis of previous scholarship (notably Stockwell 1972 and his subsequent work; Lass 1976 and his subsequent work; Faiß 1989; Görlach 1991, 1994; Barber 1997), all of which is essentially based on the interpretation of spelling evidence, rhyming conventions in poetry, dictionaries of rhyming words, as well as early modern English orthoepists' descriptions, such as those by John Hart (1551) or Alexander Gil (1619). Modern analysts generally assume that the pronunciations featured in Table D4.3 were common and stylistically unmarked in mainstream southern English speech around the dates given and that progressive dialects anticipate such pronunciations by at least fifty years. Table D4.3 suggests an early phase of interrelated changes from about 1300 to 1500 (some authors assume that the changes started about 100 years earlier). A second phase looks likely for the time between 1500 and the second half of the 17th century, when the first merger of two long vowels occurs, which leads to the homophony of *see* and *sea*. There can be little doubt that the first phase indeed constitutes a chain shift because the ME pairs /iː/ and /eː/ as well as /uː/ and /oː/ change in lockstep, and in each pair the latter supplants the former. This makes it almost impossible to deny a causal link (be that pushing or dragging). On closer inspection, it becomes clear that we are already dealing with two chain shifts in the upper half because the changes in the front and back are merely parallel, not causing each other – except if one wanted to invoke a general upward drift (the great vowel drift?) or a tendency towards parallelism. But it seems rather implausible to conceive of a reason why an upward drift in the back should trigger an upward drift in the front or vice versa. (Keeping this in mind, I will nevertheless, in line with the vast majority of researchers, continue to refer to these two parallel subshifts as one joint shift in order to avoid confusion.)

Whether or not we are dealing with one extended shift from 1300 to 1700 or with two independent subshifts in the upper and lower half of the vowel space (as, for instance, Johnston 1992 believes) depends, *inter alia*, on whether we see the raising of ME /ɛː/ (which would then set off the raising of ME /aː/) and the raising of /ɔː/ as

Table D4.3 Dating the changes of Middle English long vowels

	Middle English c.1300		c.1500		c.1600		c.1700		Modern English (RP)
(I)	iː	>	ɪi	>	əɪ	>	aɪ	≈	aɪ
(II)	uː	>	ʊu	>	əʊ	>	aʊ	≈	aʊ
(III)	eː	>	iː					≈	iː
(IV)	oː	>	uː					≈	uː
(V)	ɛː	>	ẹː	>	eː	>	iː	≈	iː
(VI)	ɔː			>	oː			>	oʊ > əʊ
(VII)	aː			>	æː > ɛː	>	eː	>	eɪ

interlinked with, i.e. motivated by the prior raisings from ME /e:/ to [i:] and /o:/ to [u:] respectively. This would be the most encompassing drag chain view of the Great Vowel Shift, where /ɛ:/ and /ɔ:/ fill the gaps left by the departure of the next higher vowels and ME /a:/ would be dragged into the position of /ɛ:/. The question of "Chain shifting or not?" therefore turns out to be definitional rather than factual in nature because the label is legitimate only if we allow time gaps of about 100 years as instances of gap filling (cf. also Guzmán-González 2003). The issue becomes a bit more complicated because the gap between the two subshifts can be closed if we take raisings by about half a step – ME /ɛ:/ to [ẹ:] and ME /a:/ to [æ:] – into consideration.

[...]

3. On the history of Great Vowel Shift theories

In order to improve our understanding of the origin and succession of GVS theories, it is useful to briefly consider their respective intellectual backgrounds. For dominant strands in the philosophy of science – in particular empiricism, positivism, and Darwinism – have had an impact on linguists who have directly or indirectly contributed to the discussion, be they neogrammarians, traditional dialectologists, Prague school and other functionalists, or modern sociolinguists and phoneticians.

[...]

3.1 Phonemes, species, and habitats

Most of this chapter was written in 2009, which happens to be the year marking the 100th anniversary of Jespersen's coining of the term "Great Vowel Shift". The roots of early GVS theories, however, can be traced back further, as the late 19th century had seen a major paradigm shift in the history of scientific thinking: in the middle of that century, Darwin's evolutionary theory had replaced earlier theories of the evolution of species. In the development of Great Vowel Shift theories, the analogy between biology and language must have seemed particularly appealing because both evolutionary biology and GVS treatments try to describe and explain change (on issues concerning evolutionary sciences and linguistic change, see also Guzmán-González 2005).

Now 2009 also celebrates the bicentenary of Charles Darwin's birth and at the same time the 150th anniversary of his ground-breaking work *On the Origin of Species*, which saw three editions within two years and as many as six editions until 1872. Chronological order and parallelism in reasoning suggest strongly that evolutionary thinking had spread from biology to other scholarly domains by the early 20th century, notably to the domain of language and language change. It is probably no coincidence, therefore, that about half a century after Darwin's (1859) first edition of the *Origin of Species*, the two most influential push chain and drag chain theories of the GVS were developed by Luick (1896) and Jespersen (1909), respectively. It should be emphasized, however, that this was by no means a new analogy, as venerable linguistic terms like "morphology" illustrate. Nor has this analogizing come to an end since, as can be seen from more recent theories related to evolution and biology as well as mathematical models (like dynamical systems or chaos theory) with applications to both biology and language (cf. McMahon 1994: Chapter 12; Lass 1997: 291–301; Schneider 1997; Croft 2000, 2006; Mufwene 2001, 2008).

In modern terms, both push chain and drag chain theories are essentially ecological niche accounts, in which – on the push chain scenario – one species drives a former inhabitant or competitor out of its habitat or – on the drag chain scenario – one species moves into a niche vacated by another species. Such an ecological theory has considerable appeal for sound change theories because of a number of possible analogies: vowels (like species) can be seen as competitors; vowel spaces of adjacent vowels are analogous to habitats; they may overlap and the spaces into which (say, 95% of) vocalic allophones constituting a phoneme fall may shift.

After a century of GVS theories, it seems, however, also necessary to reconsider some of the tenets underlying both push and drag theories that have perhaps for too long gone unchallenged. One general difference is that long stressed vowels (unlike species) rarely become extinct. Also, vowels can merge with neighbouring vowels – unlike species. The next section will discuss more concrete problems of early theories.

3.2 What's wrong with the push chain theory?

It is in particular Luick's push-chain theory which has a few serious logical flaws. Although Luick describes adequately a difference between the south (where both ME high vowels diphthongized) on the one hand and what are now conservative northern English and Scottish English dialects on the other (where the back high vowel did not diphthongize), the conclusion that the Great Vowel Shift must have been a push chain seems rash.

Adherents to push chain scenarios attribute the fact that northern varieties did not diphthongize their back high vowel to a missing back /oː/, which was fronted to /øː/ in northern dialects in the late thirteenth century (Smith 1996: 99–101; Johnston 1997: 69). Consider Luick's (1896) original formulation, which has a certain ring of circularity to it:

> [W]enn also mit einem Wort *ū* nur dort diphthongiert wurde, wo *ō* zu *ū* vorrückte, so ergiebt sich völlig zwingend, dass *ū* nur *deswegen* diphthongiert wurde, weil *ō* zu *ū* vorrückte und es gewissermassen aus seiner Stellung verdrängte. Wir sind also in den Stand gesetzt, eine causale Beziehung zwischen diesen zwei Lautwandlungen sicher festzustellen (Luick 1896: 78; emphasis original).

> In brief, if *ū* was diphthongized only in regions where *ō* raised to *ū*, then it necessarily follows that *ū* was diphthongized only *because* *ō* raised to *ū* and thus, as it were, pushed it out of its place. We are therefore in a position to firmly establish a causal relationship between these two sound changes [transl. MK].

South (and North before fronting of /oː/)		North after fronting	
iː	uː	iː	uː
eː	oː	eː øː	←□
ɛː	ɔː	ɛː	ɔː
aː		aː	

Figure D4.2 Southern and northern Middle English long vowel inventories according to Lass (1999a: 76).

D4

Lass (1999a) summarizes and refines the push chain position as follows:

> [N]o dialect has done anything to ME /e:/ like what the North did to ME /o:/, i.e. moved it 'out of position' before the GVS. And no dialect has consistent undiphthongised ME /i:/. This makes no sense except in the context of a chain shift beginning with the raising of the long mid vowels. A high vowel diphthongises only if the slot below it is filled by a raisable vowel when the shift begins. If the slot below the high vowel is empty (nothing there to push it out of position), there will be no diphthongisation (Lass 1999a: 76–77).

Both quotations show that the push chain scenario is explained *ex negativo*. The argument is that /u:/ did not diphthongize in northern dialects because there was no adjacent vowel /o:/ to push it out of its place. Although this theory seems intuitively plausible and has been described as "beautiful", the causal link is underdeveloped. For one, the situation was a great deal more complex than Figure D4.2 suggests (see the detailed discussion in Smith 2007: Chapter 6), and northern varieties had in fact developed long /o:/ in words like *throat* and *hope* prior to the GVS as a reflex of Middle English open syllable lengthening (Smith 1996: 99–101). The number of /o:/ words was obviously lower than in dialects that preserve Old English ō words like *food*, which is why scholars who want to save Luick's theory can with some justification speak of lower pressures in northern dialects.

There are more serious problems in the argumentation, however. First, from a strictly logical perspective, the back high vowel space has no explanatory power for what happens in the front vowel space and vice versa. In other words, if diphthongization occurs in the front, this does not entail that it must occur simultaneously in the back, even if this is what we find in southern Middle English dialects. Second, long high-vowel diphthongization can happen without concomitant raising of the next lower position, as many Present-day English varieties show (see Foulkes and Docherty 1999). Third, there are modern varieties that diphthongize /i:/ much more noticeably than /u:/, which may be rather stable or centralized (cf. modern RP or standard American English). All this suggests that high-vowel diphthongization in the front and back are (a) independent of each other and (b) independent of the existence of a lower pushing vowel. After all, long (or half-long) mid-high vowels exist only in some modern English dialects as allophones of the RP phonemes /eɪ, əʊ, ɔ:/ in words like *say*, *so*, or *force*.

A last problem for Luick's and Lass's push chain theories is that there is no *a priori* reason why only a mid-high back vowel /o:/ should be able to push /u:/. Although there may be a greater probabilistic likelihood for front vowels to raise along a front path, in principle, any adjacent vowel could have pushed /u:/ out of its position. Fronted northern ME /ø:/ could therefore have pushed /u:/ equally well as /o:/, because no long vowel was on the trajectory between /u:/ and /ø:/ in the relevant period either. Admittedly, the path from [ø] to [u] is somewhat longer than from [o] to [u], but if we consider the large phonetic space that other vowels travelled during and after the GVS, minor differences in spatial distance do not present a convincing argument for or against certain paths. This is particularly true for /ø:/ and /u:/, which are both rounded and thus rather similar from an overall articulatory point of view. In conclusion, if diphthongization of /u:/ does not happen in northern English varieties, the failure of this change to occur cannot be logically linked to the absence (or limited presence) of /o:/. The push chain theory in its current form is therefore to be rejected.

Notice that rejecting a causal link between /oː/-fronting and the absence of /uː/-diphthongization in the north does not entail an outright rejection of the push chain scenario. It is in principle possible for /eː/ and /oː/ to have initiated the shift in the south by pushing the higher vowels out of their habitats. But – and this is the last counterargument to Lass's justification of the push chain scenario – if two adjacent vowels change, it is not necessarily because an adjacent vowel pushes. It may be helpful to invoke the habitat analogy again: species /iː/ may prefer a new habitat for reasons independent of /eː/'s possible occasional inroads into its habitat. Other motivations for /iː/'s move may include a complex of factors like supply of water, food, and sun, all of which would be analogues to phonetic or other motivations for a vowel to change beyond a pushing neighbour. And there may finally be no apparent reasons at all for a vowel to change, not even a pulling neighbour, and yet it does change.

What, then is this chapter's conclusion regarding the inception problem? Lass (1976, 1999a) finds no evidence of a clear chronological order, while Stenbrenden (2003) appears to have found evidence of very early high-vowel diphthongization and thus supports the drag chain scenario. The present author also favours the drag chain scenario for the majority of dialects, one reason being uniformitarianism: many modern English dialects diphthongize their high vowels (see the synopsis in Krug 2003a) but have not (or not yet) raised their lower vowels. A second reason is that many northern English and Scottish dialects have followed or are currently following the diphthongization path of /uː/ (see the synopsis in Stuart-Smith 2003). Such dialects can thus be interpreted as conservative rather than as true exceptions to the GVS because adaptation due to contact with southern English as the sole explanation for the diphthongization can be excluded for these varieties on phonetic grounds (see Section 4). In addition, there is a strong historical and crosslinguistic argument against an explanation in terms of contact: there are many related as well as unrelated languages that – at different stages in the past 500 years – underwent high-vowel diphthongizations similar to those of the GVS. The contact situations of these languages and of the Middle English dialects that were affected by the GVS, however, are simply too diverse for contact with southern standard English to be considered as the sole or even major explanatory force. The ultimate jury on pushing and pulling may still be out, then, but perhaps such a verdict is not necessary. "English" is not and has never been a monolithic block and it seems quite conceivable that different dialects followed different routes (see, e.g., Knappe 1997 on the development of ME [x] in syllable-coda position). If one adopts this perspective, both the "dialect problem" and the "inception problem" lose some of their poignancy.

4. Motivating the Great Vowel Shift and avenues for further research

The question of why the changes known as the GVS happened is not often asked. In other words, accounts of motivation or causation are rare in the literature, unless we include the countless contributions to the inception issue (some of which are summarized in Stockwell and Minkova 1988) and *ad hoc* accounts for individual dialects under the rubric of explanations. It is in this area, therefore, that future research seems most promising and new insights can be expected from the digitization of medieval and early modern English texts. Social accounts of causation in the vein of Smith (1996, 2007), who capitalizes on the famous [...] argument of hyperadapting incomers (cf. Alexander Gil 1619), are also appealing but difficult to corroborate empirically in the absence of unambiguous historical sociolinguistic evidence or modern parallel cases.

[...]

If we subscribe to the drag chain scenario, then a hearer-based economy can be invoked for the subsequent filling of the high-vowel spaces, too. This follows from the functionalist principle of maximal differentiation, which was formulated and refined by Martinet (e.g. 1952) but had implicitly been utilized by historical linguists arguing for gap filling since at least the 19th century, including the GVS chain shift advocates from both camps. According to this principle, it is useful for languages to have the extreme positions /a, u, i/ filled to maximize the distance between the distinctive vowels in the available vowel space, and indeed there are very few languages that lack one of these three vowels (Ladefoged and Maddieson 1996). Researchers therefore speak of an "unbalanced system" when the two high vowel positions are empty and assume that they are likely to be refilled soon.

Language is the constant negotiation between hearer-based and speaker-based economies, so it would be surprising if speaker-based principles did not play a role in the GVS. Elsewhere (Krug 2003a), I have presented arguments in terms of speaker economy pointing in a similar direction as the principles and optimality-theoretic accounts cited above, thus strengthening the case for the drag chain scenario. The arguments presented involve phonetic factors that exploit the tense-lax opposition, hiatus avoidance, and the sonority hierarchy with its implications for high-vowel diphthongization. In essence, I argue that the instability of long high vowels is due to their relatively high production effort: since high vowels are more tense than low vowels and since pure [i] and [u] are more peripheral, their production (in particular when they are long) involves more muscular effort than that of lower vowels. Long high vowels are therefore assumed to be intrinsically prone to diphthongization, which is well supported not only by English but also by crosslinguistic evidence (Wolfe 1972: 131–134; Krug 2003a). The first stages [ɪi, əɪ] and [ʊu, əʊ] in high-vowel diphthongization along a central path are interpreted as lenition that is led by high frequency items, notably pronouns like *thou, I, my, thy*. A similar case for lenition has been made by Feagin (1994) for the monophthongization of /aɪ/ in southern American English, which seems to be led by the pronouns *I* and *my*. Such high-frequency items tend to develop progressive variants below the level of consciousness (Krug 2003b), which may be the impulse for a shift of a phoneme's prototypical realization and thus of its positional displacement.

[...]

In conclusion, I still tend to believe [...] that the most likely answer to the question of who triggered the GVS is: "You and me, basically; and maybe also *he* and *she*, or *us* and *we*. All of us essentially." But a lot more detailed socio-phonetic research and theoretical refinement will be necessary before we can turn this hypothesis into yet another theory that students of English historical linguistics should consider for memorization. Students might consider, however, discussing the many GVS-related hypotheses and debates mentioned in this chapter as heuristics for critically evaluating and better understanding the nature of linguistic change and theory building.

D4.2 Issues to consider

Activity D4.1

The Great Vowel Shift is not the only vowel shift to have occurred in British English. The contemporary variety known commonly as Estuary English, for example, is characterised by a shift in diphthongs compared to Received Pronunciation. The term Estuary English emerged in the late 1980s as a shorthand reference to an accent somewhere between London Cockney and a Standard English pronunciation, and was coined primarily because it was commonly heard around the Thames Estuary. Sociolinguists have cautioned against its wholesale adoption as a term, however, since it is suggestive of an entirely new variety, when in fact it simply refers to a change in particular Home Counties accents (see Trudgill 1999). Moreover, its features can now be heard beyond the Thames Estuary. Nonetheless, Aitchison summarises the vowel shift that characterises it as follows:

Don't be *mean*	→	Don't be *main* [mein]
The *main* road	→	The *mine* [main] road
It's *mine*	→	It's *moyne* [moin]
See the *moon*	→	See the *moan* [moun]
Don't *moan*	→	Don't *moun* [maun]
A little *mound*	→	A little *meund* [meund]
		(Aitchison 2013: 198)

Aitchison suggests that Estuary English was developed by teenagers. Why do you think it was this age group particularly who were responsible for the change, and what factors might have caused its spread to other social groups and geographical areas?

Activity D4.2

Table D4.4, taken from Culpeper and McIntyre (2015), is a summary of what happened to the long vowels of Middle English during the Great Vowel Shift.

Look at the example words in the column on the right. If you are a speaker of British English, how do you pronounce these words? Think also about other words that contain these vowel sounds. How do you pronounce those words? If you can, compare your pronunciations with those of someone from another part of the country. Do you

Table D4.4 Raising of the long vowels during the Great Vowel Shift

Middle English →	Early Modern English →	Present Day English →	Examples
[aː]	[ɛː]	[eɪ]	[naːmə] → [nɛːm] → [neɪm] name
[ɛː]	[eː]	[iː]	[mɛːt] → [meːt] → [miːt] meat
[eː]	[iː]	[iː]	[feːt] → [fiːt] feet
[iː]	[əɪ]	[aɪ]	[tiːdə] → [təɪd] → [taɪd] tide
[ɔː]	[oː]	[əʊ]	[rɔːb] → [roːb] → [rəʊb] robe
[oː]	[uː]	[uː]	[goːs] → [guːs] goose
[uː]	[aʊ]	[aʊ]	[huːs] → [haʊs] house

speak a variety of English in which the Great Vowel Shift was completed? Or does your accent retain earlier pronunciations? If so, consider what this tells you about how the Great Vowel Shift spread geographically.

D5 THE DEVELOPMENT OF A WRITTEN STANDARD

The Early Modern period in Britain saw the gradual emergence of a written standard. Not since the days of West Saxon in the Old English period had a particular variety of the language been adopted as a standard form. As we saw in A5, the development of print technology was a key driver in the process of standardisation, specifically the opportunities that it provided for the diffusion of standardised spelling. But as we discussed in B5, the printing press is not solely responsible for the development of Standard English. It is important to remember that language has a social function. And the way in which humans organise themselves into social networks (see the introduction to section C) has a major influence on the extent to which new linguistic developments are likely to spread among a speech community and be adopted by its members. In the article below, Colette Moore considers how the sociolinguistic concept of Communities of Practice might be integrated into accounts of the standardisation process. In particular, she considers the likely sociolinguistic situation towards the end of the Middle English period that gave rise to the standard variety that emerged throughout the period of Early Modern English.

D5.1 Communities of Practice and incipient standardization in Middle English written culture

Colette Moore (reprinted from *English Studies* 100(2): 117–32 (2019))

1. The study of variation and historical linguistics

Historical English language study has worked with many models to investigate variation. Typically, these models are developed for the study of present-day English and then adapted for historical research; though a diachronic perspective has certainly aided in the construction of better approaches to language variation.

The pioneering work in linguistic variation in the contemporary discipline of linguistics was done by the nineteenth-century dialectologists; we remember Edmond Edmont famously riding a bicycle around nineteenth-century French villages collecting the data that ultimately became the *Atlas linguistique de la France*, published in 1902 (Crystal 2007: 297). This dialect mapping methodology that these early linguists bequeathed us was an apt fit for Middle English manuscripts: all the little variations of orthography and morphosyntax in the existing manuscripts (e.g. the differing representations of the present-day pronoun 'she' as *scho, sche, heo*, etc) corresponded neatly to our growing sense of the geographic connections of the scribes or the texts. Dialect mapping culminated in the construction of the *Linguistic Atlas of*

Late Mediaeval English (1986), a stunning intellectual achievement that used texts of more certain origins as anchor texts to localise other less certain texts based on linguistic variables. The clear value of the mapping approach has meant that principles and interpretational significance have been fruitfully extended to other contexts and questions in medieval scholarship, as well – from Elizabeth Salter's models of 'interdisciplinary mappings' to the literary geography taken up by Beadle (1991), Scase (2007), and Lawton (2003) and recent mappings of language by Smith (2013), and geographical mapping of networks of relationships between manuscripts by Thompson (2007: 116) and Horobin (2011: 68).

As dialectology developed into sociolinguistics in the academy, more complicated models emerged for communities and the ways that different kinds of identity shaped linguistic practice. Linguists have used the phrase 'speech community' at least since Bloomfield (1933: 42) defined it as 'a group of people who interact by means of speech' (see also Gumperz 1968; Hymes 1974); Weinreich et al. 1968; Labov 1972b), and this concept of the speech community has been nuanced in different ways as an analytic tool over the past century. The model of social networks, for example – connections of people and the ways that they are tied together – was introduced to explain how groups of people encountered and adopted new variables (Milroy 1987, 2002). Networks turn out to be a really helpful way to approach social connections because we find trends across a variety of networks: for example that linguistic variables often spread more efficiently through the weaker links in a multiplex network than the stronger links. These sociolinguistic models of variation and methods of study have been adapted for historical research (Bergs 2000, 2005; Fitzmaurice 2000a, 2000b; Lenker 2000; Nevalainen 2000; Tieken-Boon van Ostade 2000). Models for understanding the connections between people, therefore, aid in understanding the process of language change.

The methods of sociolinguistics, of course, continue to evolve. Eckert (no date) describes twentieth-century sociolinguistic approaches as two waves of methodological investigation. In this interpretation, the 'first wave' was the quantitative study of variables according to large demographic categories (race, gender, class, age), and the 'second wave' was a more qualitative approach with participant-described categories (utilising more ethnographic methodology). Both the first and second wave focus on the speech community and examine local dialect features as they reflect local or regional practice. The 'third wave' for Eckert can be found in the growing examination of the social meaning of variation; the perspective has changed to emphasize styles rather than variables as associated with identity categories. Third-wave sociolinguistics, therefore, moves away from the dialect-based approach of the first two waves, casting variables as located in layered communities in which linguistic choices serve a social or stylistic purpose (Eckert 2012). Variation here does not merely reflect but also constructs social meaning and is a force in social change. Speakers are not passive 'carriers' of their dialects, but active shapers of their linguistic choice, and style, by extension, is not just a choice of words, phrasing, or pronunciation that presents different ways of saying the same thing, but contains ideological, social, and identificational meaning (Eckert 2012).

In Middle English studies, though, the strength of the tools and the force of the explanations of dialect geography/manuscript geography/literary geography have meant that our explanations for variation in Middle English have often begun and ended with regionalism. We know that other kinds of variation surely influenced the choice of orthographic and morphosyntactic options, but these are harder for us to talk about (especially given the fact that our surviving texts are in no way representative of the social distribution of Middle English speakers). Methodology, though, can be employed comparatively; we can use models from the present day when representation is fuller in order to better contextualise the tools that we have for approaching Middle English texts, and this helps us to theorise the gaps in evidence. This research addresses recent sociolinguistic models of communities of practice and how they apply to the creation of Middle English manuscripts, and then considers ways that these models are particularly promising for our understanding of standardising processes in Middle English.

2. Communities of Practice

The model of communities of practice was borrowed by sociolinguists from the social sciences; it was first developed in the early 1990s by anthropologists Lave and Wenger (1991) and drew upon Pierre Bourdieu's practice theory. The model has been elaborated for sociolinguistics by Eckert and McConnell-Ginet (1992), and it is described and applied in varying ways in ethnographic approaches (see reviews of the discussion in Meyerhoff 2008; Mendoza-Denton 2011). Three aspects are generally taken as central characterising features: mutual engagement, joint enterprise, and shared repertoire.

(1) **Mutual engagement** means that by participating in the community, members collaborate with one another, build relationships, and establish norms. These connections link the members as a social entity.
(2) **Joint enterprise** describes the way that through these interactions, members build a shared understanding of their activity. They continually negotiate this joint enterprise – it is also called the 'domain' of the community.
(3) **Shared repertoire**, lastly, refers to the way that through the practice, the community produces a set of communal resources used to enable the joint enterprise.

Lave and Wenger initially proposed communities of practice to describe how professional communities (they looked at tailors) induct and train new members and perpetuate set routines. The model describes many different kinds of shared enterprise, though: a quilting club can be seen as a community of practice, and so can an English department graduate admissions committee. The model also accommodates larger groups: connections of communities of practice who may no longer have as much direct contact – Wenger (1998: 126) calls these constellations of practice.

Wenger's original diagram for the operation of these three characteristic areas of communities of practice was modified and developed by Kopaczyk and Jucker (2013) to apply to research in English language history (see Figure D5.1).

Kopaczyk and Jucker (2013) delineate the kinds of community links and practices that elucidate the importance for English language history of the community of practice model. Their 2013 collection provides the first examples of how the model can illuminate work in the history of the English language across many periods, and other recent work has begun to draw upon the community of practice model (Timofeeva 2017; see also Grund 2017: 228).

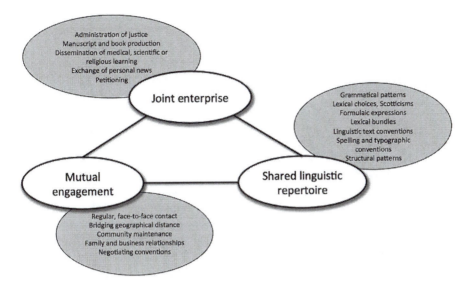

Figure D5.1 Communities of practice in historical research (Kopaczyk and Jucker 2013: 9).

2.1 *Communities of Practice in Late Middle English*

One aspect of the community of practice model that makes it particularly suited to the needs of Middle English scholars is the way that it fits what we are learning about the production of manuscripts. While speech communities and social networks are both frameworks for talking about spoken language, the community of practice model is particularly useful for talking about the early production of writing. Since our evidence of late medieval linguistic usage all comes by way of writing, of course, it is helpful for our linguistic models of early English to include particular perspectives on the production of writing.

While, in present-day English, general literacy encompasses many kinds of private and public writing, and writing is used as a tool for many different kinds of labour, in the medieval period, writing (at least the writing that produced our existing manuscripts), even if privately performed, was more often done for someone else: a commission of some kind. As such, it was a skilled practice performed by particular people with a particular social role (clerics, scriveners, scribes, and amanuenses). Whereas writing today has become a medium for other kinds of endeavours, then, in the late Middle Ages, much more so, writing was an endeavour in and of itself.

While it seems not unlikely that a relatively small group of specialists would have known one another and regarded their work as a joint enterprise, the details of the social connectedness of late Middle English scribes can be hard to establish using medieval records. Many early medieval manuscripts were the production of monastic scriveners, and it seems unquestionable that face-to-face communal practice was an aspect of these monastic scriptoria and that these are the product of communities of practice (Timofeeva 2017: 5). The production of lay manuscripts in the fourteenth and fifteenth centuries, though, leaves us with patchier evidence. Some sites are more clear: In the case of the Writers of Court Letter, for example, we have some records about connections in workplaces like the office of the Privy Seal, and we have some records of group connection. We also know that the clerks of Chancery and the clerks of the Privy Seal did not just work together, but even lodged together in *hospicia*, rented for them by the Chancellor (Mooney 2008: 193). Members of the book artisan industry in London, too, were part of a network; often born elsewhere, they were connected by the multiplex networks of book production that are evident in our records (Christianson 1989: 211).

Information about the connections between literary scribes is more speculative, but there are good reasons to believe that metropolitan manuscripts were produced by people who interacted with one another. Indeed, one of the features that Adams and Turville-Petre (2014: 220) use to characterise metropolitan manuscripts is their high level of corrections, indicating that the texts had some way of being passed around and checked against one another, and, further, that the affiliations of a manuscript serve to demonstrate 'the interconnections in that world of professional scribes.' Horobin (2009a) has described some highly corrected manuscripts as probable products of London, for example, the *Piers Plowman* C-text found in British Library Additional 35287. The manuscript contains many erasures and changes as well as words inserted with carets, making it clear that a later pass was made through the manuscript (by the original scribe or another), checking the manuscript against another one and making appropriate changes. This circulation points to a community that had a means for connecting.

Other recent scholarship has also been reconsidering the conditions of scribal pro-duction of manuscripts in ways that complement conceptions of communities of prac-tice. Doyle and Parkes's classic 1978 study on the production of copies of the *Canterbury Tales* and *Confessio Amantis* introduced the perspective that literary scribes either worked in small workshops of 1 or 2, or were essentially freelance operators organised by stationers (Doyle and Parkes 1978: 42). This notion of the scribes doing freelance literary copying to complement a bureaucratic scribal position has been developed by Mooney and Stubbs (2013: 4), whose recent book attributes links between several of the literary scribes and the Guildhall. While these proposals are still more specu-lative than conclusive (see Kerby-Fulton, et al. 2012: 77 and Edwards 2014), it is the kind of work that would serve to link the scribes to one another. If, indeed, Doyle and Parkes's Scribe B and Scribe D were attached to the Guildhall, then this would serve as evidence for the kind of mutual engagement characteristic of a community of prac-tice for literary scribes. Other recent scholarship in literary studies, too, has pointed to social networks for authorial composition, coteries of poets who composed their poetry partly in response to and in conversation with a community (Kerby-Fulton 1997: 111; Kerby-Fulton and Justice 1998). Although our focus is on scribal networks, it is relevant to consider the circles in which poets moved and to which they directed their work.

[...]

2.3 Shared repertoire

If we can successfully assign the framework of the community of practice with its mutual engagement and joint enterprise to some particular groups of scribes in late medieval England, then, the models would suggest that we could interpret their practices of writing English as 'shared repertoire.' What would casting writing practices as 'shared repertoire' look like in this context? In other words, what aspects of written language would be 'shared'?

Words are one candidate. There is, for example, some evidence that the religious dissidents called Lollards or Wycliffites employed a dedicated lexicon (Hudson 1981). Hudson cites Henry Knighton, an Augustine canon in Leicester as asserting that Wycliffites all shared 'one mode of speech;' she mentions phrases like *trewe men, pore men, it semeþ to many men, þus þenken many men* as examples of what such a mode might look like (Hudson 1981: 15). Barr (2001: 4–5) later examined anonymous Wycliffite texts and also found some patterns in the repetition of tropes and words like *pore* or *simple* and in words that incorporate stance on social structure, particularly lexical items that describe the second estate *vis-a-vis* the third estate (traits dealing with covetous ignorance, physical grotesqueness, lying, sloth) – basically, reappropriating terms that characterise anti-peasant discourses and applying them in anti-clerical contexts.

As a political move, this use of marked vocabulary can be a way to distinguish group members to one another – consider, for example, what is called in contemporary political discourse 'dog-whistle phrases,' the use of certain coded words that appear to mean one thing to the general electorate but that signal a particular political message (often a racist or xenophobic one which is more likely to be expressed obliquely) to a targeted subgroup. Wycliffism is an example of a kind of group identity that was legally or politically dangerous, and the use of words or phrases to covertly signal participation in the discourse was perhaps a useful kind of shibboleth. Targeting group identity does not have to be political, certainly: particular words can also signal membership in a social group. Cannon (2006: 82) uses the phrase *craft vocabularies* to describe identificatory lexical items used by different craft communities in late medieval England, for example. These kinds of jargon or identificatory specialised vocabularies could be part of a 'shared repertoire' of communities of practice.

Although these are examples of the ways that lexical items might be used as shared repertoire, words might not be the primary kind of shared practice. Since scribal communities are not typically responsible for composition, shared repertoire might be less likely to appear in lexicon, and more likely to appear in textual aspects that would be governed by writing practices: the morphosyntactic (word endings, pronoun forms), the orthographic (spelling conventions), or the organisational. The first two of these: morphosyntactic and orthographic choices are where we see the kind of variables that have constituted the conversation on incipient standardisation, so an investigation of 'shared repertoire' becomes in part an investigation of early standardisation.

3. Standardising processes

One of the more useful aspects of the communities of practice model might be how the 'shared repertoire' idea is applicable for early processes of standardising English. If shared repertoire is a set of communal resources used to enable the joint enterprise, then this set of communal resources is to be found in shared writing practice – especially shared practice in the little words and spelling conventions. The textual examples in the previous section, for example, have come from the Wycliffite texts, late fourteenth-century literary manuscripts like *Canterbury Tales* or *Confessio*

Amantis, and the Chancery documents: these all correspond, as it happens, to several of Samuels's types of incipient standards. Samuels, in his classic 1963 article, 'Some applications of Middle English dialectology' examines four clusters of shared writing conventions in Middle English manuscripts which have been the centre of the discussion of incipient standards in English. Type I texts include a group of Wycliffite texts from the mid to late fourteenth century, sometimes referred to as 'Central Midlands Standard', Type II texts are a group of mid-fourteenth century texts from the Greater London area or Essex (most famously the Auchinleck manuscript), Type III texts are a group of late-fourteenth century texts from London (most famously, the Hengwrt and Ellesmere manuscripts of the *Canterbury Tales*), and Type IV texts consist of government documents from 1430 and onwards (Samuels calls it 'Chancery Standard') (Table D5.1).

   Samuels's examples come from a model that is in need of updating. Half a century has passed since the publication of his article, but discussions about standardisation still point to his framework, which is really a loose sketch rather than a developed system and a correlation of the forms themselves rather than a description of dialects (Benskin 2004: 3). Medievalists await a more thorough and developed perspective on standardising processes in late Middle English. Fisher's (1996) thesis on Chancery English investigated aspects of the standardising impact of bureaucratic scribes and has been widely influential, but more recent scholarship regards him as weighting too heavily the sway of the clerks of Chancery (Benskin 2004). Sandved (1981) and Benskin (2004) have published shorter works on standardising processes, though not (yet) a larger project. The recent work on standardisation has come mostly through a collection of smaller studies like those collected in Wright's (2000) volume (see also Nevalainen 2012). Many scholars have sharpened the standardising model – Smith, for example, refines the thinking about the process of incipient standardisation by referring to 'focusing' rather than fixed practice: describing the way that usage converges upon shared variables rather than strictly adhering to a set of conventions (as we might in present-day 'Standard English') (Smith 1996: 66–8; see also Devitt's 1989: 74 discussion that increased variation precedes standardisation). Machan (2016) also refines the thinking about standardisation by pointing out that the one-way directionality of the model doesn't really work. I would like to link this process of focusing to communities of practice – that such focusing in the fifteenth century is a product of social organisation around the practice of writing.

   In the wake of Haugen's formative model of the process of standardisation, scholars of comparative standardisation have linked the development of standard language with institutions. Haugen delineated different stages in the process of language standardisation: selection (the identification of a norm), codification (the stabilisation of the

Table D5.1 Characteristic forms for Samuels's types of incipient standards in Middle English (from Hogg (2016: 1, adapted from Samuels 1963)

	Type I	Type II	Type III	Type IV
such	sych	suche	swich	suche
they	þey	hij	they	they
gave	Zouun	yafe	yaf	gaf
their	her	hire	hire	theyre

norm selected), acceptance (the process by which institutions and social groups implement the norm), and elaboration (the process by which the norms are disseminated across different genres and functions) (Haugen 1966: 251–2). These stages are not precisely chronological, though, and one is not completed when the next is begun. Each is ongoing, and we can see the continued workings of each stage. Codification in English, for example, while often discussed in relation to the Early Modern dictionaries and grammars, did not end after the Early Modern period: it is continually renegotiated and worked out for new audiences, genres, and media.

The infrastructure of English language practice did not always support all of Haugen's elements, however. Fully functional institutional attention to English usage practices did not develop in the medieval period; what we see instead of institutionalised language practices, I assert, are the products of pre-institutional communities of practice. Looking at it in this light highlights the social functionality: moving away from an understanding of early standardising as the product of an institution (a structural relationship) and instead focusing on it as the product of a group of people (a social relationship). The focusing of incipient standardising practices, therefore, comes from the more fluid authority that develops within groups – the authority of in-group negotiated practice rather than externally fixed practice. Constellations of practice, of course, are more formally structured, and the process of 'institutionalization' for constellations of writing practice occurs together with the standardising of their shared repertoire.

Just as evolutionary biologists look at the tiny pieces of the structure of an organism as evidence for the organism's evolutionary past, a linguist looks at the tiny pieces of orthography or morphosyntax as the products of a manuscript's past. But just as the small pieces of an organism's makeup could each be the result of numerous processes, it is not always clear which influences produced the surviving features of manuscripts. LALME typologies of scribal practice set out two poles of copying behaviour: literatim copying, wherein the scribe attempted to reproduce the language of the exemplar, and translation, wherein the scribe converted the language of the exemplar (Benskin and Laing 1981; see also LALME Vol. I). Scribes were regarded as being one or the other or somewhere in between. There are, however, a number of vectors that might influence the scribe's choice of forms. When a manuscript presents a particular scribal instance of the feminine singular pronoun, the use of *sche*, *scho*, *heo*, or *ho* could be a product of composition (signalling the region of origin of the author), or copying (signalling the region of origin of the text), or social identity (signalling the region of origin of the scribe), or social network (signalling who the scribe speaks to), or, as I here suggest, community of practice (signalling how the scribe participates in a social group for the production of written English).

These competing influences upon scribal choice of dialect forms have certainly been noted before, even providing layers of dialect variables in manuscripts. An early study by Smith (1988), for example, examines the manuscripts that have been attributed to Scribe D (by Doyle and Parkes 1978) and teases apart features characteristic of London and features characteristic of the South-West Midlands. Benskin and Laing (1981) have a fuller analysis of such *mischsprache* (dialect mixing). They mention the problem of regional features mixing with standardising features, 'To take but one example, *Mischsprachen* arising from contact with the written standard of the Central Midlands, and later of the Chancery, present frequently intractable problems' (Benskin and Laing 1981: 40). These are 'problems' if one is attempting to link manuscripts to patterns of regional practice, certainly, but region is not the only salient variable for morphosyntactic layering, and these mixed forms are not a 'problem' in the same way if one is looking for evidence of the influence of supralocal forms. Horobin (2003) describes these mixed forms as a reflection of register: that texts reflect not merely their regional origin, but also the register of language that they are written in. He points to an alternation in the spelling of SUCH in fourteenth and fifteenth-century London texts, for example, as indicating a register variation: the 'swich' spelling is more common in literary texts and the 'such' spelling is associated with legal documents.

I am here suggesting that such differences in register could also be seen as a product of community of practice. *Register*, a word describing formal variation between types of texts, could potentially have community of practice as a loose functional or social corollary. Such differences are not merely taxonomic; the shift in terms adds a social vector of practice to our explanations, a dimension that is a helpful corrective, since our explanations for variation and for shifts between incipient standards have all been based on regional dialect. Samuels, for example, posits that the reason for the shifts between his Type II and Type III in London had to do with immigration from the Central Midlands. While, this is certainly a possible reason for the shift and immigration is surely an influential factor, the demographic study on which he bases this claim is based on questionable data, as Wright established in a 1996 study (Ekwall 1956; Wright 1996). It shows, though, how immigration has been the first explanation for variation, and how sometimes we haven't explored anything further.

The advantage to employing the community of practice model is that it helps us to consider the development of regional norms for local communities of practice and their replacement (sometimes) with the supralocal norms of a larger constellation of practice. In the late medieval period, we can see the cultivation of incipient standards of communities of practice that are later replaced. Stenroos (2016) and Sandvold (2010) show a field survey from Barmston in the East Riding of Yorkshire that is written by four central scribes. Three of the scribes (called by Sandvold A, B, and D) used marked northern dialectal features. Scribe C, however, produced a half-sheet in the document that utilised supralocal features. These supralocal forms were apparently not perceived as a fit for the document, since it is followed by a rewritten version from Scribe D employing northern markers. Stenroos quotes an excerpt from the text written by C and contrasts it to the passage as written by D:

> C. Jn *primis* to begyne at **þe** west sid of **þe feld** nexste þe leye clos eu*ere* manes as **þey** lye

> D. Jn *primis* to begyn at **ye** west syde of **ye** sayd **feyld** next ye ley Clos of eu*ery* mannys as **thai** lye

> (to begin with, to begin at the west side of the [said] field nearest to the common grassland as they lie)

> (Stenroos 2016: 117)

Stenroos posits that the rewriting by scribe D suggests northern dialect was preferred as a functionally better choice. Another way to express this, I propose, is to regard scribe D's effort as the work of creating and reinforcing the shared repertoire of the documentary writers in East Riding.

In a discussion of standardisation, Nevalainen and Tieken-Boon van Ostade (2006: 311) suggest that register variation is one of the key factors that ultimately restricts the codification and generalisation of language standards. If, as I propose, communities of practice are a social counterpart to register, then, Nevalainen and Tieken-Boon van Ostade's observation might seem to contradict a link between communities of practice and standardisation. Instead, though, I think that their observation is an acknowledgement that in modern English (further along the cline of standardising practice than Middle English), communities of practice can provide a kind of wild card that pushes at the conformity of institutional standardising practices. The community of practice, then, can be paradoxically the locus for the standardising process and also the agent for its resistence. Communities of practice provide an alternate organising vector for individual choices in language that can result in localised conventions being regularised in ways that can either lead in the direction of new codification and standardisation or can present alternatives to an existing set of practices, possibly leading to their revision over time.

D5.2 Issues to consider

Activity D5.1
What is the particular value of the Communities of Practice model compared to notions such as *speech communities* and *social networks* in studying the standardisation process in English?

Activity D5.2
What problems does Moore see with using Haugen's (1966) framework for explaining the standardisation process in the case of English?

THE BEGINNINGS OF GLOBAL ENGLISH

D6

The reading in this unit is aimed at adding more detail to the accounts in A6 and B6 of the beginnings of English as a truly global language. Additionally, it supports the discussion in B7 of the concept of international English, particularly the notion of Englishes (plural). Mario Saraceni begins by describing two types of colonisation, both of which were undertaken by the British in pursuit of their imperial ambitions. These two types are related to Kachru's (1992a) concept of first and second diaspora in his account of how English spread globally. Having outlined the processes by which world Englishes came to be, Saraceni goes on to consider what secondary data (see the introduction to section B) from the time reveals about attitudes to international varieties of English in the nineteenth and early twentieth centuries.

D6.1 The story of the 'spread' of English

Mario Saraceni (reprinted from Saraceni, M. (2015) *World Englishes: A Critical Analysis*, pp. 59–64. London: Bloomsbury)

English everywhere

English is now habitually considered a global or an international language. With varying degree of fascination, such definitions are often accompanied by statistics showing the astonishing reach of the language worldwide. Estimates about the numbers of speakers of English are expressed comfortably in billions while lists of countries where English is a (co-)official language occupy entire pages (e.g. Crystal 2003: 62–65). All these numbers are meant to point at the uniqueness of English, and comparisons with other 'big' languages, such as Mandarin Chinese, Arabic and so on, are used to demonstrate its unrivalled level of global expansion.

English, the story goes, has achieved this unique and unprecedented status for a number of reasons. First and foremost, the initial spread of the language took place when the British began to build their empire. Subsequently, when the empire started to crumble towards the middle of the twentieth century, the rise of the United States as a global power ensured that the language kept, and actually boosted, its prominent position as an international language. Finally, due to the fact that it has become such an important international language, hundreds of millions of people around the world now feel the need to learn it, increasing the ranks of those who speak English as an additional language. Accordingly, impressive pieces of statistics are cited to illustrate the extraordinary status of the English language, such as that 'non-native speakers far outnumber native speakers' (Seargeant 2012: 100), or that '[t]here may now be more learners of English in China today than there are native speakers of the language' (Sonntag 2003: xi).

Indeed, in order to cope with such vastness, the omnipresent binary 'native speakers' and 'non-native speakers' is only one of the ways in which uses and users of English have been categorized. Terms and acronyms have proliferated. English has been called an 'international language' (EIL), a 'lingua franca' (ELF), a 'second language' (ESL), a 'foreign language' (EFL), additional language' (EAL) and so on. Users of English, in turn, have been defined in relation to those labels, for example, 'speakers of English as a lingua franca' and so on.

Apart from individual terms, full-scale descriptive models have been developed in order to better understand the 'spread' of English in the world. The best-known and most influential of such models is Braj Kachru's *Three Circles of English*. In this model, Kachru (1985: 12) identified 'three concentric circles representing the types of spread, the patterns of acquisition and the functional domains in which English is used across cultures and languages'. The three parameters are conjoined, in the sense that to each of the three types of 'spread' correspond a pattern of acquisition and a function of the language.

The kinds of language spreads that Kachru refers to, in turn, are linked to two types of colonization: settler and exploitation. Before examining the 'circles' model more in detail, therefore, it will be useful to provide a brief historical overview of these forms of colonization.

Two types of colonization

By and large, British colonialism manifested itself in two types of colonization: (i) settler and (ii) exploitation. In the former type, territories were incorporated to the empire primarily in order for the 'new' lands to be occupied by settlers from elsewhere (principally from Britain, but not exclusively). In the latter, the principal objective was to acquire raw materials and, often, slaves from the colonies.

Settler colonization

Settler colonization followed the great exploration journeys that took place between the fifteenth and the eighteenth centuries, during which Europeans 'discovered' unknown (to them) lands that they immediately saw as 'available' to be claimed in the name of their respective European crowns. The fact that those lands were inhabited was dealt with by the use of violent coercion and genocide. Additionally, the elimination of the original inhabitants was accelerated by the diffusion of diseases brought by the Europeans for which the indigenous populations had no natural defence.

So, for example, as a direct consequence of the arrival of the British in 1770. in Australia the Aboriginal population was reduced to a fraction of its original size within a relatively short period of time. As people from Britain (mainly prisoners initially) replaced the Aboriginals, so the English language replaced the Aboriginals' languages, which had become drastically reduced in size or completely extinct. By and large, this happened in North America and New Zealand too, where the (near-)disappearance of the original population and their replacement by the settlers caused the same to happen to local languages.

When the British Empire began to lose its pieces and the colonies to regain their independence, in countries which had been subject to settler colonization English remained the main (even if not necessarily the official) language of legislation, education, the media and every-day life for the majority of the population.

By contrast, in countries that had been at the receiving hand of exploitation colonization, the sociolinguistic situation was more complex colonization.

Exploitation colonization

Exploitation colonization was aimed at procuring raw materials and cheap labour. There was no wholesale replacement of populations. The colonists sought to secure deals with local rulers that would bring financial gain to the formers and personal power to the latter. In this way, the British acquired a large number of territories mainly in Asia and Africa in the eighteenth century. English was primarily a vehicle of communication between the British and the local ruling classes. Local languages weren't replaced, even though their prestige was lowered.

In much European imperialism, especially British and Dutch, the actual conquest and appropriation of territories were often carried out by trading companies, which had powers conferred onto them by their respective governments. The raison d'être of these companies was to find and gain control of strategic locations, especially along coastal areas, that would enable them to have access to natural resources, raw materials, spices, gemstones, slaves and so on for trading purposes. Through the operations of such companies, European imperial powers gradually seized larger territories, until by the end of the nineteenth century virtually entire continents were under their direct or indirect control.

The following passage, from an article published in the *London Times* on 8 January 1897, is highly illustrative. In it, the name 'Nigeria' was first suggested, by a journalist and commentator called Flora Shaw, for the territory that the Royal Niger Company had acquired largely through bogus 'treaties' with local rulers:

> In the first place, as the title 'Royal Niger Company Territories' is not only inconvenient to use, but to some extent is also misleading, it may be permissible to coin a shorter title for the agglomeration of pagan and Mohammedan states which have brought, by the exertions of the Royal Niger Company, within the confines of a British Protectorate and thus need for the first time in their history to be described as an entity by some general name. To speak of them as the Central Sudan, which is the title accorded by some geographers and travellers, has the disadvantage of ignoring political frontier-lines, while the word 'Sudan' is too apt to connect itself in the public mind with the French Hinterland of Algeria, or the vexed questions of the Nile basin. The name 'Nigeria' applying to no other portion of Africa may, without offence to any neighbours, be accepted as co-extensive with the territories over which the Royal Niger Company has extended British influence, and may serve to differentiate them equally from the British colonies of Lagos and the Niger Protectorate on the coast and from the French territories of the Upper Niger. Nigeria, thus understood, covers, as is well known, a thickly-peopled area of about half-a-million square miles, extending inland from the sea to Lake Tchad and the northern limits of the empire of Sokoto, bounded on the easr by the German frontier and on the west by a line drawn southwards from Say to the French frontier of Dahomey. The frontier lines have 10 years been the subject of discussion with our European neighbours on either side. The northern limit was definitely settled by the Anglo-French treaty of 1891; the eastern boundary was determined by the Anglo-German treaty of 1893; and certain vexed questions on the western frontier were for practical purposes brought to a close last year, when the Royal Niger Company completed in the neighbourhood of Bajibo the erection of forts which it judged necessary for the legitimate maintenance of its authority Within these limits Nigeria contains many widely-differing characteristics of climate, country, and inhabitants. Its history is ancient and is not wanting in dramatic elements of interest and romance.

There are various elements of interest here. First of all, the invention of the name 'Nigeria' at the end of the nineteenth century by a journalist from another continent is already indicative of the fact that the genesis of the country was quite different from that of, say, Italy or Germany in the same period.

Secondly, the frontier lines mentioned in the article were set by the British, the French, the Germans, in the same way as European colonial powers had done in the rest of Africa and in much of the rest of the world. So, the parties that must not be offended excessively by the coinage of the new name were Britain's European 'neighbours' that were engaged in the same looting of the African continent. The international conference held in Berlin in 1885 had precisely the purpose of settling disputes over borders dividing the various European possessions in Africa. The main preoccupation was to reach an agreement among colonial powers and, quite obviously, local African populations had absolutely nothing to do with the way their continent was being carved up in the heart of Europe. Ethnic, cultural and religious divisions were well known but were not taken into any account in what came to be known as the 'scramble of Africa'.

Significantly, the inhabitants of this newly defined and newly named territory of 'Nigeria' were described by Shaw as being of 'widely differing characteristics', just like the climate and the features of the land. Indeed, one of the distinctive marks in the ways in which the borders were drawn on paper by European colonizers was the inclusion, in the same territory, of people that were of different ethnicities, religions and, of course, languages.

Furthermore, the claim that Nigeria's history was 'ancient' was manifestly an attempt to legitimize this new entity as a country, *precisely* because Nigeria had in fact just been created. So, when the British Empire began to shrink, the colonies that were now granted independence became sovereign countries for the first time. There was no Nigeria (or any other of the newly independent countries) before British and European colonization.

It is for this reason that, when the time came for these countries to establish their own sovereign governments and legislation systems, some difficult decisions had to be made concerning, among many other things, the national language. The typical situation was one in which many different languages co-existed within the same country but none of them was spoken by a proportion of the population that would be large enough as to be representative of the entire country. Selecting any of these languages was bound to be met with hostility from the sections of the populations that didn't speak it.

Obviously, it wasn't simply a matter of linguistic allegiance. Linguistic divisions were a reflection of sociocultural and, frequently, ethnic and religious ones too. Tragic evidence of the depth of the disunity within populations that were suddenly part of the same country was the surge of civil wars fought by opposing factions that sought to achieve control and power in the country. Such wars, which continue to break out today, often led to secessions, like the Biafran war (1967–1970), in which the Igbo, in the south-eastern part of Nigeria, attempted (and, for a short while, succeeded) to establish a separate country for themselves.

It is evident how in such a situation the selection of one or another language as the national one would have meant granting special recognition to a particular group, with the inevitable strong resentment by the others. So, the policy makers of many governments ended up retaining the language of their former colonial masters. Accordingly, despite its cumbersome imperialist heritage, in most former British colonies English was at least seen as more neutral across the population than any other of local languages.

However, in this type of colonization English had been introduced in the colonies as an elite language, whose use was encouraged among, but restricted to, the higher classes, namely the top layer of society that the British dealt with directly. As Brutt-Griffler (2002: 89) explains:

> the British policy limited the number of students exposed to the formal teaching of English to meet the local demands for English-educated subjects of the empire. It left the bulk of the population to be educated in the local language or, at most, to acquire the rudimentary elements of the English language.

The poorer strata of the population had little or no access to English, which remained for them simply a foreign, unknown language. So this also meant that in the newly constituted countries, the national language was not really the people's language.

The 'Three Circles of English'

In relation to the two types of colonization described earlier, Kachru (1992a) coined the terms 'first diaspora' and 'second diaspora' describing the two ways in which English spread in the world. The former refers to the way in which English arrived and established itself as the national language in countries which were subject to settler colonization. The latter refers to the spread of English that occurred as a result of exploitation colonization, namely in countries where English became an additional (if elite) language, co-existing with local languages.

The Three Circles can be summarized as follows:

❑ The 'Inner Circle' refers to the 'traditional bases of English – the regions where it is the primary language' (Kachru 1985: 12) for the majority of people; these include places like the United Kingdom, the United States, Australia and so on.
❑ The 'Outer Circle' refers to countries where English arrived through the 'second diaspora' – and hence exploitation colonization – and where it is often a (co-)official language, playing an important role in education, the media and legislation; these include India, Nigeria, Singapore and so on.
❑ The 'Expanding Circle' includes regions where the presence of English is more recent and not linked to colonization but primarily to its status as an international lingua franca; these include Germany, Brazil, China and so on.

In relation to each type of spread, which is the main variable determining the 'circles', English has a different function in each of them. This, in turn, can be expressed in terms of depth and range of use. In the Inner Circle, English is the main or only language for the vast majority of the population of all social classes and is used for all types of activities, from the most public and formal (legislation, education, etc.), to the most private and informal (family, friends). In the Outer Circle, the depth and range of the function of English is a little narrower. The language has unequal penetration in society, being used more commonly by the higher social classes and less commonly by the poorer and less educated strata of the population. Also English tends to be limited to more official and formal situations, while local languages are more prevalent in more informal day-to-day activities. It is, therefore, a second or additional language. Finally, in the 'Expanding Circle' English has no historical presence in the society and is mainly used as a lingua franca for international communication. At the same time, the 'circles' are also associated to particular types of varieties of English. The Inner Circle comprises of *norm-providing* varieties, that is, varieties that 'have traditionally been recognized as models since they are used by "native speakers"' (Kachru 1985: 16). The Outer Circle includes *norm-developing* varieties, in which 'the localised norm has a well-established linguistic and cultural identity' (Kachru 1992b: 5), despite the inconsistency in the attitudes that speakers of such varieties have towards that norm. The Expanding Circle, finally, is *norm-dependent*, in the sense that no local norms exist and speakers of English in these settings rely entirely on Inner-Circle models such as British English or American English. As alluded to earlier, this has been by far the most influential model for the spread of English in the world. It is so well known and established that the terms designating the three circles have become standard phrases in the relevant literature and in academic conferences in the field.

The 'circles' model has important strengths. First of all, it has been an integral part of Braj Kachru's life-long academic endeavour to demonstrate the diversity of English. This is something that, especially in the earlier phases of his career, he often did in open contrast with other scholars in the field who maintained that it would be best for all speakers and learners of English to adhere to one of the two main varieties of the language: British or American. The three circles, in this sense, seek to represent the fact that English plays different roles and exists in different forms for different people in different places. The model symbolizes diversity, in opposition to rigid and immutable sameness.

Secondly, the clarity of the model has certainly contributed to its efficiency and immediacy. The inner-outer-expanding sequence is logical and memorable, while the circles are easily represented graphically. However, the simplicity of the model has also been the main source of the criticism that it has attracted.

    [...]

The 'prehistory' of World Englishes

Perhaps, the essence of the broad research area of World Englishes is in the pluralization of the noun 'English' (when referring to the language). The suffix -es encapsulates the spirit of this entire scholarly enterprise. There are more than one English in the world and they all deserve to be studied.

Although the genesis of World Englishes as an academic area can be traced towards the beginning of the 1980s (with earlier embryonic forms dating to the 1960s), the focus of this section is on what I call the 'prehistory of World Englishes'. This is because I wish to demonstrate how the 'seeds' of this broad school of thought can be found much earlier than the time when academic publications related to it started to flow.

American English sets the scene

One of the first (or, possibly, the first) recorded appearance of the noun 'Englishes' was in the headline of an article published in the *Baltimore Evening Sun* by American journalist and commentator Henry Louis Mencken, in 1910. The article was entitled 'The Two Englishes' and dealt with the differences between the American and the British varieties of the language. A few years later, between 1919 and 1921, Mencken published *The American Language*, one of the earliest quasi-sociolinguistic accounts of the American variety of English (Mencken 1921). The introductory chapter of that book included a very useful review of attitudes towards American English expressed at the time by American and British observers, both academic and not. What is particularly interesting is that the views reported by Mencken, as well as his own discussion of them, contain all the main ingredients of the debates, reflections and research that would later form the core of the World Englishes academic field.

Mencken relates two competing positions. One regarded American English as a corruption and degradation of the English language, and its users guilty of blatant disregard of its fundamental rules, purity and grandeur. The other saw it as an entirely natural evolution of the language, resulting from the new environment in which it had been transplanted.

Among the proponents of the former position, Mencken cites Thomas Hamilton, a British writer who recounts his travels in the United States at the beginning of the nineteenth century and describes, among other things, the language he finds there:

> The amount of bad grammar in circulation is very great; that of barbarisms enormous. ... the commonest words are often so transmogrified as to be placed beyond the recognition of an Englishman... The Americans have chosen arbitrarily to change the meaning of certain old and established English words, for reasons which they cannot explain, and which I doubt much whether any European philologist could understand. ... The privilege of barbarizing the King's English is assumed by all ranks and conditions of men.... I feel it something of a duty to express the natural feeling of an Englishman, at finding the language of Shakespeare and Milton thus gratuitously degraded. Unless the present progress of change be arrested, by an increase of taste and judgment in the more educated classes, there can be no doubt that, in another century, the dialect of the Americans will become utterly unintelligible to an Englishman, and that the nation will be cut off from the advantages arising from their participation in British literature. If they contemplate such an event with complacency, let them go on and prosper; they have only to 'progress' in their present course, and their grandchildren bid fair to speak a jargon as novel and peculiar as the most patriotic American linguist can desire. (Hamilton 1833: 232–235)

The classic ingredients of language prescriptivism and purism are all present in this citation. First of all, the use of the word 'barbarism' is possibly the most iconic. The sense of the word has always (i.e. not just in 'English') been associated to anything foreign and alien by reference to unintelligible speech, where of course 'foreignness' and 'unintelligibility' are both perceived from the subjective point of view of the person who refers to someone else as a 'barbarian'. In Hamilton's mind, the 'transmogrified' words that have become 'beyond recognition' to 'an Englishman' make Americans barbarians.

Hamilton clearly accuses them of unilaterally and unreasonably tainting something that isn't theirs, but is the property of the English people, of their king and of the nation's greatest poets. Indeed, his comments are about language only rather superficially. One key word stands out spectacularly: *patriotic*. What does (bad) grammar have to do with patriotism? Indeed, was Hamilton himself being profoundly patriotic in his tirade against American English? This adds two more elements that are recurrent in this type of rhetoric: language ownership and nationalism.

A third classic component in the discourse of language purism is a sense of fatal consequences looming in the near future if immediate action isn't undertaken to remedy the situation. Hamilton seemed to want to warn Americans that if they continued to modify the English language senselessly, they might end up linguistically isolated and no longer able to benefit from the privileges that came from sharing the language of British literature.

With regard to the second position, namely that the American variety of English was the consequence of natural evolution in a new territory, Mencken cites Thomas Jefferson who, a century earlier, in a letter dated 13 August 1813, wrote:

> I am no friend ... to what is called Purism, but a zealous one to the Neology which has introduced these two words without the authority of any dictionary. I consider the one as destroying the nerve and beauty of language, while the other

improves both, and adds to its copiousness. I have been not a little disappointed, and made suspicious of my own judgment, on seeing the Edinburgh Reviews, the ablest critics of the age, set their faces against the introduction of new words into the English language; they are particularly apprehensive that the writers of the United States, adulterate it. Certainly so great growing a population, spread over such an extent of country, with such a variety of climates, of productions, of arts, must enlarge their language, to make it answer its purpose of expressing all ideas, the new as well as the old. The new circumstances under which we are placed, call for new words, new phrases, and for the transfer of old words to new objects. An American dialect will therefore be formed; so will a West Indian and Asiatic, as a Scotch and an Irish are already formed. (Bergh 1903: 340)

Jefferson's words are strikingly congruous with the central ethos in World Englishes. This is particularly evident in the idea that English acquires new forms as it naturally adapts to different environments and that, accordingly, 'purism' is a concept which doesn't easily apply to language. What is even more remarkable is that his open-mindedness about regional variation in the English language allows him to predict the emergence of dialects in parts of the world that would later be categorized as Outer Circle and become the central concern in World Englishes literature. He continues:

But whether will these adulterate, or enrich the English language? Has the beautiful poetry of Burns, or his Scottish dialect, disfigured it? Did the Athenians consider the Doric, the Ionian, the Aeolic, and other dialects, as disfiguring or as beautifying their language? Did they fastidiously disavow Herodotus, Pindar, Theocritus, Sappho, Alcaeus, or Grecian writers? On the contrary, they were sensible that the variety of dialects, still infinitely varied by poetical license, constituted the riches of their language, and made the Grecian Homer the first of poets, as he must ever remain, until a language equally ductile and copious shall again be spoken. (Bergh 1903: 340–341)

Jefferson's ideas about language were incredibly modern in the way he regarded as enrichment what others would see as 'adulteration'. He was an intellectual but was, first of all, a politician. He was one of the 'Founding Fathers' and the third president of the United States as an independent country. His defence of the American variety of English, therefore, was inspired not only by his refined erudition and knowledge of other languages, but undoubtedly, by his profound convictions concerning the independence of the new country.

Indeed, Mencken's own book was itself a political statement as well as a linguistic account. Its very title, *The American Language*, which did without the word 'English' altogether, was unmistakably political.

That political independence had to be accompanied by linguistic independence was expressed extremely clearly by one of Thomas Jefferson's contemporaries: Noah Webster, the compiler of the *American Dictionary of the English Language* and popularly known as the 'Father of American Scholarship and Education'. As a lexicographer, Webster felt that it was necessary to reform the English Language, both to suit the American environment in which it was now found and to regularize its orthography. The way in which he expressed this necessity displayed a seamless mixture of linguistic and political concerns: 'As an independent nation, our honor requires us to have a system of our own, in language as well as government' (Webster, 1789: 20).

A few lines later, he elaborated on the divergent paths that the American and the British versions of English were on:

> ... several circumstances render a future separation of the American tongue from the English, necessary and unavoidable. ... These causes will produce, in a course of time, a language in North America, as different from the future language of England, as the modern Dutch, Danish and Swedish are from the German, or from one another: Like remote branches of a tree springing from the same stock; or rays of light, shot from the same center, and diverging from each other, in proportion to their distance from the point of separation. (Webster, 1789: 22–23)

Making use of the LANGUAGE IS A PLANT metaphor, Webster emphasized both the same origin of American and British English and the different branches that they now represented. Again, it wasn't just a matter of linguistic distance:

> Great Britain, whose children we are, and whose language we speak, should no longer be our standard; for the taste of her writers is already corrupted, and her language on the decline. But if it were not so, she is at too great a distance to be our model, and to instruct us in the principles of our own tongue. (Webster, 1789: 21)

Here, besides the inextricable link between political and linguistic autonomy, Webster interestingly uses the 'corruption' argument against Britain and British English. What he advocates, therefore, is not only that a separate American variety of English should be documented and codified, but also that this was made even more urgent in order to preserve the language from the decline that it was subject to on the other side of the Atlantic.

Indeed, Webster was himself a purist. In his view, American English had to be not only distinct from the distant and inexorably corrupt British English but also as internally uniform as possible, and hence devoid of any variation. It was important, therefore, to 'demolish those odious distinctions of provincial dialects, which are the objects of reciprocal ridicule' (1783: 5) and to 'diffuse an uniformity and purity of language' (p. 11).

D6.2 Issues to consider

Activity D6.1

Why is population number an unreliable statistic to use for calculating how many people speak English worldwide?

Activity D6.2

Saraceni refers in his chapter to a book by H. L. Mencken, entitled *The American Language*, and notes that its title constitutes a political statement. What assumptions does the title of Mencken's book make about the nature and development of English in America?

STUDYING RECENT CHANGE IN ENGLISH   D7

Historical perspective makes it easy to perceive differences between Present Day English and, say, Old English. It is also quite clear that Middle English, and even Early Modern English, is substantially different from the English that we speak and write today. But trying to work out how English has changed more recently, and within a shorter time-frame, is harder. Answering the question of how Present Day English has developed over the last 60 years or so would be impossible to do simply by comparing a text from the late 1950s with a text from today. Unlike the differences between Old English and Present Day English, the differences between the English of 60 years ago and now are not stark enough for us to identify confidently without recourse to much more data. This is where the methodological technique of corpus linguistics comes in. Corpus linguistics is a computational methodology for identifying patterns in large databases of language. Consequently, it offers a useful set of methods for historical linguists interested in more recent change in English (though corpus techniques are now routinely used for studying all periods of the history of English). In this reading, Bas Aarts, Joanne Close and Sean Wallis investigate how British English changed between the late 1950s and the 1990s, deploying corpus linguistic techniques to do so. Specifically, they look at how the modal verbs *shall* and *will* have changed. While this may seem a very small feature of language to consider, it is only by carrying out such focused studies that we are able to build up a bigger picture of how the language has developed over time. In addition to the findings they reveal, one of the particularly valuable aspects of Aarts et al.'s report of their work is the space they devote to outlining their working practices. It is this commitment to openness that makes it possible for other linguists to try and replicate their results. This is an important step in increasing the confidence with which we can make claims about English's development.

D7.1 Choices over time: methodological issues in investigating current change

Bas Aarts, Joanne Close and Sean Wallis (reprinted from Aarts, B., Close, J. and Wallis, S. (eds) *The Verb Phrase in English: Investigating Recent Language Change with Corpora* (2014), pp. 14–45. Cambridge: Cambridge University Press)

1. Introduction

The fact that English is changing is immediately apparent to a modern reader of, say, eighteenth- or nineteenth-century literature, or indeed to a teenager speaking to an elderly relative. However, as Mair (2006: 15–21) points out, anecdotal evidence for linguistic change is unreliable. The systematic study of language change requires large, evenly balanced and reliably annotated corpora with texts sampled over a period of time. These considerations are accepted by many linguists working on current changes in English. However, with regard to methodology we observe that within the field of diachronic corpus linguistics there are still a number of issues that generate a certain amount of discussion and debate.

One of these concerns the issue of variability. Bauer (1994: 19) highlights the importance of this concept in studies of language change when he states that 'change is impossible without some variation'. Variation within a set of linguistic choices, including the idea that there may be 'competition' between these variants, is fundamental to studies in current change. In this chapter we will argue that an important methodological task for corpus linguists studying language change is to focus on linguistic variation where there is a choice. Many factors are likely to influence the use of particular words, phrases or constructions. If we wish to study and explain variation found in a corpus as being the result of factors affecting variation over time, then we need to eliminate as many potential alternative sources of variation as possible. This, we contend, calls for a restricted definition of the variants involved in a perceived change, and a consideration of any 'knockout' contexts, i.e. contexts where variation may be impossible, or constrained in a different manner to the general case.

We use the Diachronic Corpus of Present-Day Spoken English (DCPSE) as a database. This corpus is unique in two important respects: it contains spoken English exclusively and is fully parsed, and as such is suitable for studying current change in English from the late 1950s to the early 1990s. It complements other resources, including major historical corpora of writing, notably A Representative Corpus of Historical English Registers (ARCHER) which contains written texts sampled from the late seventeenth to the late twentieth century, as well as corpora of earlier speech derived from written sources such as A Corpus of English Dialogues (CED; Kytö and Walker 2006) and the Old Bailey Corpus (Huber 2007). In the next section we briefly present the functionality of DCPSE.

2. The Diachronic Corpus of Present-Day Spoken English

The Diachronic Corpus of Present-Day Spoken English (DCPSE) [...] spans a time period of approximately thirty years and is composed of material from spoken English. DCPSE is composed of speech samples collected between the late 1950s and the early 1990s, and it allows us to monitor grammatical changes during this period. In this chapter we will present data on the alternation between *shall* and *will* [...], with a focus on [...] methodological issues raised [...]. Before showing how this can be done with DCPSE we will discuss a few general features of the corpus.

DCPSE was released by the Survey of English Usage (SEU) in 2006. It contains 464,074 words of orthographic (word-for-word) transcriptions of English speech taken from the London–Lund Corpus (LLC)[11], and 421,362 words of spoken data from the British Component of the International Corpus of English (ICE-GB; Nelson, Wallis and Aarts 2002).[12] These are sampled in matching text categories, so there is approximately the same quantity of face-to-face conversation (for example) in both

---

11 The LLC is the spoken part of the Survey of English Usage Corpus, founded by Randolph Quirk in 1959. It contains 510,576 words of 1960s spoken English, is prosodically annotated, and has been used – and continues to be used – by many scholars for their research.

12 ICE-GB is composed of both spoken and written material from the 1990s. It contains textual markup, and is fully grammatically annotated. All the sentences/utterances in the corpus are assigned a tree structure.

PU	CL	SU	NP	NPHD	PRON		
	main ▷				pers ▷	-------	I
		VB	VP	MVB	V		
			montr ▷		montr ▷	-------	think
		OD	CL	SU	NP	NPHD	PRON	that
			depend ▷				dem ▷
				VB	VP	MVB	V	's
					cop ▷		cop ▷
				CS	AJP	AJHD	ADJ	fascinating
					prd ▷		ingp
						PAUSE	PAUSE	< >
							short

Figure D7.1 An example tree diagram, *I think that's fascinating* (DI-A02#28).

portions ('subcorpora'). Two caveats are in order. The LLC subcorpus is distributed over a longer period of time (twenty years) than the ICE-GB subcorpus (three years), and texts are not evenly distributed by year.

DCPSE includes mostly spontaneous spoken English, such as face-to- face conversations, telephone conversations, various types of discussions and debates, legal cross-examinations, business transactions, speeches and interviews. As it is generally assumed that changes in English propagate themselves in the first instance through spontaneous discourse, we would argue that DCPSE is ideal for the study of current change. Whereas written corpora contain text genres which allow for editorial correction, DCPSE consists entirely of orthographically transcribed utterances. Immediate self-correction is explicitly marked, so that repetitions and word partials can be excluded from searches. The small proportion of scripted speech that is included is transcribed, rather than the script reproduced.

The spoken transcription is divided into putative 'sentence' utterances, termed 'text units'. Every text unit is then given a full grammatical analysis in the form of a phrase structure tree using a grammar based on Quirk, Greenbaum, Leech and Svartvik (1985) and exemplified in Figure D7.1. DCPSE contains over 87,000 such fully analysed text units. These trees were produced by automatic and manual parsing methods and were then extensively cross-checked. [...] The result is a corpus of spoken English which allows a high degree of confidence in the reliability and completeness of the grammatical analysis.

The question arises of how to search this forest of over 87,000 trees. Our ICECUP software (International Corpus of English Corpus Utility Program; Nelson et al. 2002) is designed as a platform for exploring the corpus and obtaining results. Linguists can search for lexical strings, wild cards, etc., and – importantly in grammatical studies of current change – tree patterns. ICECUP contains a powerful query system, termed Fuzzy Tree Fragments (FTFs). FTFs are 'sketches' of grammatical constructions that can be applied to the corpus to obtain an exhaustive set of matching cases. Figure D7.2 shows an example of an FTF which matches all instances of a VP followed by a subject complement (CS). This FTF matches the three nodes highlighted in Figure D7.1 above.

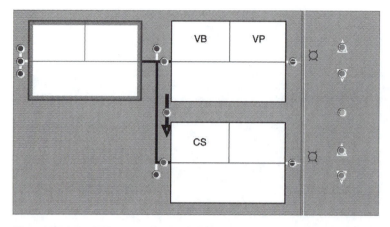

Figure D7.2 An FTF created with ICECUP, matching the highlighted nodes in Figure D7.1.

Respecting the fact that linguists disagree about grammar, ICECUP allows users to experiment with the best way of retrieving the grammatical phenomena they are interested in, using the Quirk-style representation in the corpus. The interface is designed to let linguists construct FTFs, apply them to the corpus, identify how they match cases in the corpus, and refine their queries. One can also select part of a tree structure and construct an FTF query from that fragment in order to find how a particular lexical string is analysed, and then seek all similar analyses.

ICECUP offers a range of search tools based around this idea of an abstract 'FTF' query, including a lexicon and 'grammaticon'. DCPSE is an unparalleled resource for linguists interested in short-term changes in spoken English [...]

3. A case study: the alternation shall versus will

3.1 Background

Modal verbs have attracted a lot of attention in the current change literature and *shall* and *will* are no exception. In 1964 Charles Barber wrote:

> [T]he distinctions formerly made between *shall* and *will* are being lost, and will is coming increasingly to be used instead of *shall*. One reason for this is that in speech we very often say neither [*will*] nor [*shall*], but just ['*ll*]: *I'll see you tomorrow, we'll meet you at the station, John'll get it for you.* We cannot use this weak form in all positions (not at the end of a phrase, for example), but we use it very often; and, whatever its historical origin may have been (probably from *will*), we now use it indiscriminately as a weak form for either *shall* or *will*; and very often the speaker could not tell you which he had intended. There is thus often a doubt in a speaker's mind whether *will* or *shall* is the appropriate form; and, in this doubt, it is *will* that is spreading at the expense of *shall*, presumably because *will* is used more frequently than *shall* anyway, and so is likely to be the winner in a levelling process. So people nowadays commonly say or write *I will be there, we*

will all die one day, and so on, when they intend to express simple futurity and not volition. (Barber 1964: 134)

Similarly, David Denison has remarked that:

> During the latter part of our period [1776–present day] … in the first person SHALL has increasingly been replaced by WILL even where there is no element of volition in the meaning. (Denison 1998: 167)

Comments such as these may lead us to expect that investigating the trajectory of such a change is straightforward. However, from these two quotations alone a number of interrelated issues arise. These are: (i) the status of the variants; (ii) their syntactic behaviour; and (iii) the intended meaning of the clause. In the following discussion, we will address each of these issues.

3.2 Mair and Leech's work on written English

Recently, Mair and Leech (2006: 327) reported frequency statistics for the perceived decline of the use of *shall*. Their data are based on raw frequency statistics of *shall* and *will* in written British and American English (henceforth BrE and AmE, respectively) from the 1960s and 1990s using the 'Brown family' of written English corpora (LOB, F-LOB; Brown, Frown […]). Counts include verb and negative contractions: e.g. *won't* and *'ll* are included under *will*.

Table D7.1 shows that, comparing four one-million-word corpora, the frequency of *will* appears to decrease by 2.7 and 11 per cent in the BrE and AmE corpora, respectively, and the use of *shall* by almost 44 per cent overall in both BrE and AmE corpora.

Mair and Leech employ a […] log-likelihood test to compare absolute frequencies against the overall word count to confirm that this fall in *shall* is statistically significant.

However, […] this statement simply tells us that *shall* is significantly less frequent as a proportion of words in the later data set. This is not particularly instructive […] because there may be many causes of this particular decline. It is possible that the opportunity for speakers to utter *shall* changed (for example, due to variation between text samples), rather than that *shall* declined in use when speakers had the opportunity. What we ideally wish to know is whether *will* is replacing *shall* in circumstances where the writer is in a position to choose.

[…]

Our experimental data should ideally be restricted to include only cases in contexts where *will* and *shall* are interchangeable. In what follows we outline a number of 'knock-out' contexts, attempting to focus on those cases where *will* and *shall* are true

Table D7.1 Decline in the use of *shall* in written corpora, LOB/F-LOB and Brown/Frown (after Mair and Leech 2006)

	British English				US English		
	1960s	1990s	*d%*		1960s	1990s	*d%*
will	2,798	2,723	−2.7%	*will*	2,702	2,402	−11.1%
shall	355	200	−43.7%	*shall*	267	150	−43.8%
Total	3,153	2,923	−7.3%	Total	2,969	2,552	−14.0%

alternants and can therefore be said to represent a choice. In addition to declarative cases, *shall* and *will* can appear in interrogative and negative constructions.

1) a.   Interrogatives: *Shall we go to the park?* vs *Will we go to the park?*
    b.   Negatives: *I won't/will not go to the park* vs *I shan't/shall not go to the park.*

However, the semantics of the interrogative cases are distinct from the declarative cases, different usage constraints may apply, or use may be sensitive to genre. Another concern is that the negative cases include the increasingly archaic and informal *shan't*. We therefore chose to concentrate on the base form in positive declarative utterances, and exclude these 'knock-out' contexts.

In Section 2 we discussed the fact that every text unit in DCPSE is given a tree analysis and we can use Fuzzy Tree Fragments (FTFs) to identify cases conforming to a particular structure. To extract declarative cases, we limit cases to where *shall* and *will* are classified as auxiliaries following a subject NP. This will retrieve from the corpus all cases of *shall* and *will* preceded by a pronoun or a noun phrase subject and exclude instances of subject–auxiliary inversion. [...]

A second, similar, FTF was used to retrieve instances of *shall/will not* and these cases were then subtracted from the results. We exclude all negative cases, including *shall not/shan't/will not/won't*. For now, we also exclude the contracted form *'ll*. Results are summarised in Table D7.2.[13]

We evaluate the alternation with a [...] χ^2 test. The χ^2 figures in the bottom row are equivalent to goodness-of-fit χ^2 tests against the total.[14]

The final column contains three figures: the percentage swing *d%* from LLC to ICE-GB for *shall* out of the total [...], the [...] φ effect size measure[15] [...] and the [...] χ^2 result. The results show a significant change between the two subcorpora, and that most of the variation over time appears, perhaps unsurprisingly, to be attributable to the decrease in the frequency of *shall* [...].

If we analyse the figures for *shall* and *will* for British English presented by Mair and Leech (see Table D7.1) using the same method we obtain the results in Table D7.3.

These results are significant, but the effect size measures (*d%* and φ) are lower than in our spoken data in Table D7.2 (in other words, the change is smaller, but still sufficiently large to be judged 'significant' given the data available). The question we might ask therefore, is, are the results significantly different?

To answer this question we used a further test. Wallis (forthcoming) defines a 'statistical separability' test to compare the results of two [...] tests. This finds that the results are significantly separable at a 0.05 error level, so we are justified in claiming that our experiment obtains a significantly stronger result than that obtained using

---

13 The contracted form *'ll* and negative cases are excluded. Note that *d%* represents the percentage swing of *shall*. Cramér's φ is a similar measure, but is calculated across both *shall* and *will* – it measures the size of the *shall/will* alternation (0 = no change over time and 1 = complete change). It is particularly useful for comparing results.

14 Values in bold are significant at $p < 0.05$ (if they exceed 3.841). The figures on the bottom row indicate whether a particular value (*shall*, *will* etc.) significantly changes over time. The 2 × 2 result simply tells us that 'a change is taking place', but does not tell us where this is happening. High individual χ^2 values indicate cells which have unexpected values.

15 NB: An effect size measure indicates the size of the difference between two data-sets.

Table D7.2 χ^2 for *shall* and *will* between ICE-GB and LLC (spoken, positive and declarative; bold is significant for $p < 0.05$). The contracted form *'ll* is excluded

(spoken)	shall	will	Total	χ^2 (shall)	χ^2 (will)	Summary
LLC (1960s)	124	501	625	15.28	2.49	$d\% = -60.70\% \pm 19.67\%$
ICE-GB (1990s)	46	544	590	16.18	2.63	$\phi = 0.17$
Total	170	1,045	1,215	31.46	5.12	$\chi^2 = 36.58$

Table D7.3 χ^2 for *shall* (+*shan't*) and *will* (+*'ll, won't*) between LOB and FLOB (written) (data from Mair and Leech 2006)

(written)	shall+	will+'ll	Total	χ^2 (shall+)	χ^2 (will+'ll)	Summary
LOB (1960s)	355	2,798	3,153	15.58	1.57	$d\% = -39.23\% \pm$ 12.88%
FLOB (1990s)	200	2,723	2,923	16.81	1.69	$\phi = 0.08$
Total	555	5,521	6,076	32.40	3.26	$\chi^2 = 35.65$

Table D7.4 χ^2 for the simple lexical auxiliary verb queries for *shall* and *will* between ICE-GB and LLC, all cases, i.e. excluding the contracted form *'ll*

(written)	shall+	will	Total	χ^2 (shall)	χ^2 (will)	Summary
LLC	193	812	1,005	13.87	2.39	$d\% = -48.88\% \pm 16.46\%$
ICE-GB	91	836	927	15.04	2.59	$\phi = 0.13$
Total	284	1,648	1,932	28.91	4.98	$\chi^2 = 33.89$

Mair and Leech's method for written data. However, it is not clear whether this fact derives from the exclusion of 'knock-out' contexts, a focus on spoken rather than written material, or simply the different ways in which the corpora were sampled. To investigate this, we modify the experimental design in a series of steps and repeat the separability analysis.

First, we apply Mair and Leech's data collection method to DCPSE. It turns out that the results obtained from our spoken corpus are very similar to their FLOB/LOB results. Changing the corpus does not change the result. The issue therefore seems to concern 'knock-out' contexts.

Staying with our lexical queries, we now eliminate cases of *'ll*. We find that these results are significantly distinct from Mair and Leech's, but are not significantly different from those obtained with FTFs. The results are summarised in Table D7.4.

Results obtained from our spoken data are consistent with those obtained from the written corpora FLOB and LOB. However, if the contracted forms are removed the *shall/will* alternation increases in strength. The use of FTF queries focusing on declarative and positive cases is more restrictive still, but does not obtain a stronger result than this.

[…]

When can the alternation take place? Until now we have assumed that all cases of declarative *shall* and *will* can alternate. Here are two examples where the alternation is unproblematic.

2) a.   *...who <u>shall</u> remain nameless* (DI-B04 #208) → *...who <u>will</u> remain nameless*
    b.   *now Svevo I <u>shall</u> refer to him henceforth* (DL-J02 #240) → *I <u>will</u> refer to him henceforth*

However, some replacements sound awkward to our modern ears. A small number (up to eight) appear to be formulaic, and the alternation may be less likely simply because the word selection is determined by quotation. Thus it is impossible to replace *shall* with *will* in the formulaic *ye shall be saved* (DL-J01 #49) without changing the purpose of the utterance.

A number of linguists have argued that *shall/will* alternation is likely to be more restricted than this. Coates (1983) reviews modal meaning in two 1960s corpora (the Lancaster Corpus and the LLC), and argues that second- and third-person subject *shall* is only found in cases of obligation – a rare meaning for *will*. Similarly, Collins (2009) investigates meaning in a 1990s corpus based on ICE-GB, ICE-AUS and US data. He finds few cases of second-person *shall* and, in the third person, almost exclusively deontic *shall*. In expressions of futurity, he casts doubt on whether a traditional prescriptivist rule (*shall* to be used for first person, *will* for second and third) is being followed.

Mindful of these observations, we decided to limit our search to cases where the subject is the first person. [...] The results are shown in Table D7.5.

[...]

In our declarative data from DCPSE, second- and third-person *shall* is rare (below 7 per cent of cases) whereas the majority of cases of *will* (around 86 per cent) are in the second and third person. This tends to support the argument that with second- and third-person subjects *shall* is rarely an alternative to *will*, even if *will* substitutions are deemed to be acceptable. However, Table D7.5 shows that in first-person cases, if *'ll* is excluded, far from being a residual usage, *shall* is in the majority across DCPSE.

[...]

3.3 Plotting trends over time

DCPSE date-stamps each spoken recording with the year that it was made. As our evidence suggests a decline in the use of *shall* over time, we can plot this trend on a year-on-year basis. We plot *shall* against two baselines: against the uncontracted *will* and against *will* plus the contracted form *'ll*. In so doing we revisit the concept of what we called the 'true rate' of alternation.

In carrying out a plot over time, we introduce an additional potential source of variation, because the number of texts per year and the sampling conditions under which they were obtained are not evenly balanced in each annual subcorpus. However, the advantage of considering our data as a time series – compared to the contingency table

Table D7.5 χ^2 for *shall* and *will* between ICE-GB and LLC (spoken, first-person subject, declarative), excluding the contracted form *'ll* and negative cases

(spoken, 1st ps subject)	shall	will	Total	χ^2 (shall)	χ^2 (will)	Summary
LLC	110	78	188	1.32	1.45	$d\% = -30.24\% \pm 20.84\%$
ICE-GB	40	58	98	2.53	2.79	$\phi = 0.17$
Total	150	136	286	3.85	4.24	$\chi^2 = 8.09$

Table D7.6 Frequency and probability data from DCPSE reflecting a declining use of *shall* over time as a proportion p(*shall*) of the set of alternants {*shall, will*} (left) and {*shall, will, 'll*} (right), following first-person subjects (non-VP-final)

Year	shall	will	Total n	p(shall)	Year	shall	will+'ill	Total n	p(shall)
1958	1	0	1	1.0000	1958	1	3	4	0.2500
1959	1	0	1	1.0000	1959	1	5	6	0.1667
1960	5	1	6	0.8333	1960	5	9	14	0.3571
1961	7	8	15	0.4667	1961	7	40	47	0.1489
1963	0	1	1	0.0000	1963	0	4	4	0.0000
1964	6	0	6	1.0000	1964	6	17	23	0.2609
1965	3	4	7	0.4286	1965	3	16	19	0.1579
1966	7	6	13	0.5385	1966	7	24	31	0.2258
1967	3	0	3	1.0000	1967	3	17	20	0.1500
1969	2	2	4	0.5000	1969	2	32	34	0.0588
1970	3	1	4	0.7500	1970	3	3	6	0.5000
1971	12	6	18	0.6667	1971	12	21	33	0.3636
1972	2	2	4	0.5000	1972	2	15	17	0.1176
1973	3	0	3	1.0000	1973	3	3	6	0.5000
1974	12	8	20	0.6000	1974	12	23	35	0.3429
1975	26	23	49	0.5306	1975	26	165	191	0.1361
1976	11	7	18	0.6111	1976	11	38	49	0.2245
1970	0	0	0	?	1970	0	5	5	0.0000
1990	5	8	13	0.3846	1990	5	33	38	0.1316
1991	23	36	59	0.3898	1991	23	246	269	0.0855
1992	8	8	16	0.5000	1992	8	138	146	0.0548

approaches thus far – is that we can adjust for the differences in LLC and ICE-GB sampling periods. The LLC portion, while nominally described as '1960s', was sampled over a period from 1958 to 1977, whereas ICE-GB was recorded between 1990 and 1992.

Table D7.6 shows data for first-person *shall* vs *will* by year on the left-hand side. For each year, p(*shall*) is the fraction of cases of *shall* out of the total *n*. On the right-hand side we carry out the same procedure for *shall* vs *will*+*'ll*. Data retrieval involves [...] subtracting negative cases.

First, we plot *shall* against a baseline set {*shall, will*} in Figure D7.3. We employ a scatter-plot to record the probability (*p*) of *shall* rather than *will* being selected by a speaker, against the year the material was recorded. The dotted lines represent the upper and lower estimated trend lines and the crosses represent the mid-points of the LLC and ICE-GB data.

The vertical 'I'-shaped error bars express the Wilson confidence interval for each data point. A large confidence interval means a greater level of uncertainty.

Where samples are tiny (as here), confidence intervals will be extremely broad. The LLC data in particular is a 'cloud' from which no real trend can be inferred (hence two questionable trend lines).

The problem with this graph is the spread of data. Perhaps a better strategy with this data set is to aggregate years together into five-year periods. Note that we are not really expecting to see an annual steady decrease in the use of *shall*, rather we are attempting to estimate the rate of change over the period. We can group data into half-decades as indicated in Table D7.6, and plot the results in Figure D7.4. The trend becomes clearer as a result.

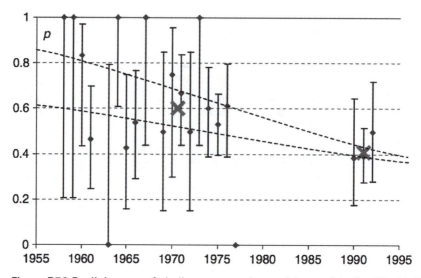

Figure D7.3 Declining use of *shall* as a proportion *p* of the set {*shall, will*} with first-person subjects, annual data, with Wilson intervals (I-shaped 'error bars') make it difficult to infer a single trend line (hence the upper and lower estimated trend lines indicated by the dotted lines.) 'X' marks the centre-point of each subcorpus.

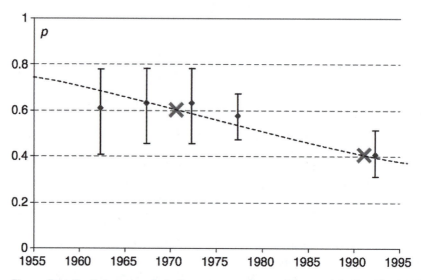

Figure D7.4 Declining use of *shall* as a proportion *p* of the set {*shall, will*} with first-person subjects, half-decade data ('1960' = 1958–62 inclusive, '1965' = 1963–7, etc.)

Putting Figure D7.4 into words: in declarative first-person contexts, *shall* appears to be being replaced by *will*, with *shall* falling from around 60 per cent of cases in or around 1970, to about 40 per cent by the early 1990s. This suggests a switch from one dominant form (and therefore what speakers might consider to be the default choice of modal auxiliary verb) from *shall* to *will* over this period.

These results may also tie in with Collins' (2009) observation that the traditional prescriptive rule regarding preference for the first-person usage of *shall* did not appear to apply to his 1990s data. If this is the case then it could be that the almost total dominance of *will* in second- and third-person usages is undermining this rule.

[...]

3.4 Modal meaning

In our discussion of *shall* and *will* we have not addressed the issue of modal meaning. We have assumed that *shall* and *will* compete regardless of their meaning. However, work by Smith (2003), Leech (2003), Leech et al. (2009) and Close and Aarts (2010) suggests that this is unlikely. It is therefore necessary in our investigation of *shall* and *will* to investigate the level of competition according to semantic classification. This is also necessary if we are to reach any conclusions about reasons for change in the modal system.

All first-person positive declarative instances of *shall* and *will* (but not *'ll*, which was omitted for reasons of time) were therefore manually coded according to whether the modal expressed Root or Epistemic meaning. We follow the classification system proposed in Coates (1983) whereby the Root meanings of *shall* include 'obligation', 'intention' and 'addressee's volition' (typically found in interrogatives, which were not included here), while Epistemic refers to 'prediction' (1/4 'futurity') (Coates 1983:185). With respect to *will*, the Root meaning includes 'willingness' and 'intention' (both of which can be subsumed under the heading 'volition') and Epistemic meanings include 'predictability' and 'prediction' (Coates 1983:169–70). Illustrative examples from the DCPSE corpus are as follows:

3) Root:
    a. *I've got some at home so I shall take it home.* (DI-A18 #30)
    b. *I will answer you in a minute.* (DI-B30 #293)

4) Epistemic:
    a. *So I shall have roughly from the twenty-ninth of June to the eighth of July on which I can spend the whole of that time on those two papers.* (DL-B01 #62)
    b. *It's certainly my long term hope that I will have some kind of companion...* (DI-B53 #0257)

According to Coates (1983: 170), there are many cases of 'merger' found with *will* which makes coding difficult. In particular, in active clauses with an agentive subject and an active verb which is not progressive or perfective it is often difficult to decide whether *will* refers to a future event which is likely to take place (Epistemic meaning), or whether the subject is indicating an intention to carry out an action (Root meaning). The examples provided in (5) are ambiguous: in (5a) it is unclear whether the speaker intends to do half as much work or whether his statement is to be interpreted as '*it is inevitable that (in the future) I will have no choice but to do half as much work*', and in (5b) *will* is ambiguous between intention and prediction (future).

5) a. *So I said, 'this just means I shall do half as much work', and he said, 'very well'.* (DL-B16 #224)

    b. A: *Are you going to stay at that house then?* (DL-B30 #39)
        B: *Well, I will be for the next couple of months.* (DL-B30 #40)

Table D7.7 Distribution of semantic types of *shall* and *will* in first-person positive declarative utterances in DCPSE

	Source corpus	Root %		Epistemic %			Unclear %		Total
shall	LLC	33	30.84	72	67.29		2	1.87	107
	ICE-GB	22	59.46	14	37.84	←sig	1	2.70	37
will	LLC	44	55.70	28	35.44		7	8.86	79
	ICE-GB	37	66.07	14	25.00		5	8.93	56
Total		136		128	↑sig		15		276

Note. Percentages are quoted of the total for *shall* and *will* in each row. Significant results of 2 × 2 χ^2 tests (at $p<0.05$ level) applied to the Root and Epistemic columns (Total row), and to the *shall* and *will* rows (column) are indicated by 'sig'.

Obviously, coding is a subjective exercise, and this raises problems when comparisons between results from different studies are compared. This is unavoidable.

Our results are summarised in Table D7.7.

Investigating the distribution of semantic types as a proportion of the total reveals a shift in the use of *shall* over time. The overall fall in *shall* appears to be due to a sharp decline in the number of cases of Epistemic *shall*, over 80 per cent of which appear in the earlier subcorpus.

Our results lend support to the argument that change in the modal system is related to the semantics of the modal auxiliaries (see Leech 2003; Smith 2003; Leech et al. 2009; Close and Aarts 2010). Specifically, we observe a sharp decline in Epistemic *shall*.

Table D7.7 contains three variables (source corpus, lexical item and modal meaning). In order to break down this three-way design we select two variables and subdivide the data by the third.

First, let us consider alternation over time for the Root and Epistemic subsets. Root and Epistemic *shall/will* alternation are analysed in Tables D7.8 and D7.9, respectively.

Root *shall/will* is stable and the results are not significant. However, the alternation for Epistemic *shall/will* is statistically significant: indeed, out of the choice of *shall* and *will* in Epistemic contexts, *shall* declines in use as a proportion of the total by an estimated 30 per cent (although note the large confidence interval). This analysis separates out Epistemic *shall* from the baseline (Epistemic modals). The fall in *shall* is therefore not simply attributable to the sharp fall in Epistemic modals from 100 to 28: rather, we have evidence for a shift in use from Epistemic *shall* to *will*.

[...]

Overall, Table D7.7 appears to indicate that Root *shall* had already declined to a 'rump' by the 1960s, and the numerical decline in Root *shall* in our data is not significant. Our analysis identifies a secondary decline in usage of Epistemic *shall*, taking place in spoken British English between the 1960s and 1990s. Returning to the comment made by Barber (1964: 134) that the 'distinctions ... between *shall* and *will* are being lost', we suggest that the decline in Epistemic *shall* is actually making *shall* and *will* more distinct (or, to put it another way, making *shall* more marked).

Table D7.8 Analysis of change over time for first-person declarative Root {shall, will}

Root	shall	will	Total	χ² (shall)	χ² (will)	Summary
LLC	33	44	77	0.11	0.08	d% = -12.99% ± 38.83%
ICE-GB	22	37	59	0.15	0.10	φ = 0.06
Total	55	81	136	0.26	0.18	χ² = 0.32ns

Note. The results are not significant and the overall change φ is small. Percentage swing d% represents the change over time in the proportion of cases of *shall*. This is not significant ('ns': the confidence interval is bigger than the estimated change).

Table D7.9 Analysis of the first-person declarative Epistemic {shall, will} alternation set over time

Epistemic	shall	will	Total	χ² (shall)	χ² (will)	Summary
LLC	72	28	100	034	0.71	d% = -30.56% ± 27.33%
ICE-GB	14	14	28	1.23	2.52	φ = 0.19
Total	86	42	128	1.57	3.23	χ² = **4.80os**

Note. *Shall* declines from being the majority Epistemic modal in the LLC '1960s' data, to being equal in frequency to *will* in the ICE-GB subcorpus. The results are significant ('s' = significant) and the overall change φ is substantial.

An examination of the percentages of *will* and *shall* synchronically shows that, in the 1960s data, two-thirds of cases of first-person *shall* were Epistemic, whereas around 55 per cent of cases of *will* were Root. The decline of Epistemic *shall* means that around 60 per cent of cases of *shall* during the 1990s were Root – a similar proportion to *will*. If we also consider cases of *shall* and *will* in second- and third-person contexts, we find that the vast majority of cases of *will* (around 80 per cent) in both time periods were Epistemic. A possible explanation for the decline of first-person Epistemic *shall* signalling 'prediction', therefore, is simply that a dominant alternant, i.e. Epistemic *will*, is spreading from second- and third- person contexts to the first person.

[…]

4 Conclusions

[…] Our initial results for *shall* vs *will* demonstrated a significantly greater change than that found in Mair and Leech's data. By carrying out a small number of intermediate experiments and comparing their results, we narrowed down the difference to the exclusion of 'knock-out' contexts of interrogative and negative cases, and finally, second- and third-person subjects. We also showed how it was possible to plot the fall in the use of *shall* over a time series, revealing an apparent shift in dominance from *shall* to *will* between 1960 and 1990.

By examining modal meanings we found that the fall in *shall* was attributable wholly to Epistemic *shall*, with Root cases remaining stable over time. Extending the alternation experiment to include *'ll* and *be going to*, both in non-VP-final position, permitted us to identify that the fall in *shall* was robust and held up when cases of *'ll* were included with *will*. […] With the exception of modal semantics, where manual coding was necessary, our experiments exploited the parsed corpus to obtain results.

D7.2 Issues to consider

Activity D7.1
In assessing whether a linguistic form is declining, what is the problem with simply comparing its frequency in two datasets?

Activity D7.2
How confident would you be in using corpora of around one million words in size (e.g. the Brown family of corpora) to assess change in English over time?

D8   ENGLISH IN THE FUTURE

The question of what English might look and sound like in the future is one that has exercised the minds of a number of linguists over the years. Trying to make reasonable predictions about English's future development is in some sense a bit like trying to engage in linguistic reconstruction; but instead of taking what we currently know about a language and using this to work out what it must have been like in the past, instead we are taking what we currently know about a language and using this to work out how it is likely to develop in the future. David Crystal's article, below, is in part a response to an article written in the same issue of *World Englishes* by Modiano (2017) and it would certainly be useful to read that one too. But Crystal's article can be read as a standalone piece of work. Modiano's article speculates about the likelihood of Britain's exit from the European Union sparking a new form of 'Euro-English'. Crystal's article considers the likelihood of this from a number of perspectives.

D8.1 The future of new Euro-Englishes

David Crystal (reprinted from *World Englishes* 36(3): 330–35 (2017))

All over the world there is clear evidence today of the 'dynamic polymodel' that Modiano (2017) takes as his starting point in his insightful and stimulating paper. Innumerable research projects have given formal shape to many of the so-called 'new Englishes'. Every country that has introduced English (which today surely must mean all countries) – whether as an official, semi-official, or special-regional-status language, or simply as the first or second language taught in schools – has begun to adapt it, and these adaptations have increasingly come to be codified in regional dictionaries, as Modiano points out. These adaptations have also come to appear in creative writing – novels, poems, plays – as well as in the press and on the Internet. At the same time, the more formal situations in these countries, such as international written communication in science and technology, have retained the norms of traditional standardized English, whether British or American. The result has been multiglossia: local spoken informal, local spoken formal (for instance, the British standard), local written informal, and standardized written English (again, for example, British).

Today I am perfectly happy to talk about Swedish English, French English, Chinese English, and so on, alongside more well-recognized notions of Australian English, Ghanaian English, and the like. By this I mean 'the kind of English I am going to encounter when I speak the language with fluent English speakers in Sweden, France, etc.'. I don't care whether these speakers are L1 or L2. The critical question is: what English do I need in order to understand them, and they me? In the distant days when a single variety of English was the pedagogical norm, there was no issue. But the whole point of new Englishes (as well as old ones) is that they express local identities, and the forces that promote identity are by their nature in conflict with the forces that promote intelligibility, both within nations (in the form of accents and dialects) and between them. So, just as I have become multidialectal in British English (given my life experience in Wales, Liverpool, and elsewhere), so I have become multidialectal in world Englishes (given my travelling encounters around the globe), even though my ability to use the regional variety of a particular country may be more passive than active. I often tell the story of my first experience of American English, when in line in a diner I was asked 'How do you like your eggs?' and I replied, confused, 'cooked', not knowing US egg terminology (such as 'once over easy'). I am fluent in Egg now (and, you will note, from *line* and *diner*, in other lexical areas too).

So what is it that gives me that sense of local English identity when I visit a country? It is chiefly a mix of local accent and lexicon, along with pragmatic and sociolinguistic factors (such as politeness norms), and some grammatical differences. I have illustrated these elsewhere (Crystal, 2012, 2016a), but the main factor is cultural identity, manifested in the vocabulary, idiom, and encyclopedic knowledge taken for granted by the speakers. Just as anyone encountering British English has to work out what is meant when someone says *It was like Clapham Junction in there* or *Those shoes are very Bond Street*, or appreciate the effect when someone says *To drive or not to drive – that is the question*, so I have to work out what is going on when people from Sweden, France and other countries say equivalent things. What is the equivalent of Clapham Junction in Paris, or Bond Street in Stockholm? Swedish English, for me, is primarily that: the cultural knowledge I need to have to make sense of what Swedish people are saying when they speak English to me in Sweden. Most of the time, our shared world experience will allow the conversation to continue without any confusion, but as soon as the topics become at all local (and deal with topics like sport, politics, food, travel) it does not take long before a lack of local knowledge in the foreigner manifests itself, and communication breaks down.

This is the perspective in which we need to examine the future of Euro-English. I totally agree with the spirit of Modiano's paper: Euro-English has every chance of developing into a new English in its own terms, and Brexit could make this more likely. But this will only happen if the conditions are right, and the chief condition is a self-awareness of cultural identity. So here is my first question. He writes: 'what would be required for the establishment of Euro-English need not be any different than what has transpired elsewhere'. Really? In all other new Englishes we have a political unit whose cultural identity after independence is clear. Can that unified cultural identity be claimed for the EU? There is little point in talking about a linguistic identity for the EU if there is no certainty about that. What are the shared cultural characteristics that would motivate such a development? This now ceases to be a linguistic argument and becomes a discussion about the relationships between countries and the political future of Europe. Modiano's case depends on a certainty which cannot be assumed at present, with all the talk of Grexit, Frexit, and what have you. The spectre of linguistic vetoes is on the horizon.

Then there are the consequences that stem from the existence in member states of their individual local cultural linguistic identities in English. He writes:

> When continental Europeans use culture-specific terms they indicate their reluctance to fastidiously mimic the lexical choices thought to be those of an idealized L1 user of a prestigious Inner Circle variety, and instead, in so doing, celebrate the linguistic characteristics of their own social group.

Agreed. But this celebration is country-focused. The social groups are Dutch, Swedish, French, and so on. Is there any real notion of an EU 'social group' – one that displays sufficient solidarity (in the sociolinguistic sense) to motivate shared linguistic norms? At present, judging by the examples in his paper, the only evidence for this would be Eurospeak jargon, which is characteristic of written English and in-house spoken discussion. Idiom is his other example, but here he sees a problem:

> [C]ontinental Europeans seem apparently less keen to use idiomatic phrases, something which otherwise exemplifies the speech of Inner Circle users of English. It is possible that continental Europeans are aware of the fact that because such language use is often to some extent esoteric, idiomatic phrases, when utilized in international contexts, may not be comprehended by everyone present and for that reason are not good communication.

Agreed again. But the problem of idiom (which is a subset of the cultural issue) is not restricted to Inner Circle users. All new Englishes have their own lexicon of expressions, not used outside their own culture, and these now compete with traditional British or American English expressions. It is not too difficult for an L2 speaker of British English to avoid using British cultural expressions; they are going to be immediately noticed. It is much more difficult for an L2 speaker from, say, France, to avoid using French cultural expressions – usually, because native speakers do not realize how culturally idiosyncratic their own speech is. They can be surprised when someone from another culture asks what they mean. I've even seen this happening among native speakers. I was present when an American lecturer, having used the idiom 'that was from out of left field', was put into a state of confusion when someone in the room (from Britain) asked what he meant. It had never occurred to him that his non-US audience would not be familiar with baseball.

If there is 'a continental European enterprise, with its own unique characteristics', then certainly, it would be right to codify it. So what are those characteristics?

The term Euro-English best suits those continental Europeans whose speech is not decidedly based on any one Inner Circle variety but is nevertheless characterized by influences from standardized English as well as their native tongues, and where there is a propensity to use culture-specific features common to the manner in which English is used as an L2 in continental Europe, when and where such usage is situationally appropriate. Along with the regional accents of European English, the most salient feature is lexical usage.

The first two factors are clear: standardized English (whether British, or American, or the increasing mix that Modiano notes) and L1 influences (which would include my cultural point above). The third is less clear: 'common to the manner in which English is used as an L2 in continental Europe'. We lack the descriptive studies to be able to say with any certainty what this is, or what the 'situationally appropriate' settings are. Even if we restrict the evidence to lexical usage, there is little to go on, and my experience is that there is far less uniformity among continental Europeans than he suggests.

In October 2016 I was invited to give a lecture to the combined forces of EU translators and interpreters at the European Parliament in Luxembourg, streamed through to Brussels, on the same topic as Modiano's paper. Several heads of department were present, and made contributions to a panel. It was clear from what was said that this was a rare meeting: everyone is so busy that they hardly ever get the chance to have joint discussions, and thus to find out what everyone else is doing, with respect to the kind of English being recommended for EU use. And what came across loud and clear were the differences, rather than the similarities. Yes, codification will come, 'if Europe chooses to uphold a European standard for lexical use, grammar, spelling, and punctuation'. But what I saw was enormous variation in practice, and in the discussion that followed my paper the reasons for this variation were clear.

There was, first of all, a recognition that whatever Euro-English is, it is different in speech and in writing. Then, within each of these headings, the participants recognized that there were differences in informal and in formal settings. Within each of these, but especially the latter, they made a further distinction, between in-house and out-of-house usage (the latter usually meaning: for the general public). And within each of these, they acknowledged there was a distinction between personal and shared usage. All of this was seen in a synchronic frame of reference: this is how we use language *now*. But when discussing the reasons for the differences, a diachronic frame of reference immediately came to the fore: a typical comment about why a department used a particular word, spelling, punctuation, or grammatical construction was that 'we've always done it that way'. Clarity vs convention, as one participant put it.

Another factor, whose influence varied across departments, was the question of responsibility. If a political figure in the EU insists on a particular usage, should this be accepted in the written record, even if it is idiosyncratic? As one participant put it: 'do we serve the speaker or not?' Although every department strives for consistency, this can be disrupted through individual differences (and where the 'individuals' are politically powerful people). There was certainly no unanimity over how to treat contentious usage, such as whether to use abbreviations, whether to explain technical terms, whether to use *they* as a singular, the distinction between *like* and *as*, or whether to use *you* or *we* in a report. Many of the examples cited by participants were to do with grammar rather than lexicon. Grammar – and style in general (see below) – was evidently in the forefront of their minds far more than vocabulary. There was a general bored tone of 'not again!' when examples like *subsidiarity* came up.

The conclusion, which everyone in the hall seemed to accept, was that there was no Euro-English, only Euro-Englishes. It was also evident that the various stylistic distinctions were not being viewed as clear-cut oppositions; rather there was a spectrum of usage, as informal gradually became formal, and so on. None of this is news to linguists, but stylistic hierarchies of this kind, and the associated sociolinguistic gradations, were evidently unfamiliar to many of those present.

Several drew attention, but with some embarrassment, to one of the most difficult features of cultural expression: the overall 'feel' of the English that a particular L2 speaker produces. The example was given of whether the 'flowery' nature of French expression in English should be maintained, or whether it should be replaced by more everyday language. The contrast between Romance and Germanic style was clearly a concern. It reminded me of a time in the 1980s when I was asked to develop a new series of short encyclopedic treatments (of such topics as philosophy, religion, and science) for the Scottish firm of Chambers. They were to be commissioned from English authors. Then Chambers was taken over by Group de la Cité , who publish Larousse. They already had such a series, in French. Obvious solution: simply translate these into English, and save a lot of time and money. But it proved impossible: the translation samples were unusable – not because of the quality of the translations, which were accurate enough, but simply because the way in which the subject was being approached, the kind of analogies being used, and suchlike were distinctively French. As one board member put it: we want 'down-to-earth' treatments – he meant, displaying the kind of Anglo-Saxon empiricism that he felt was lacking in the French texts. New English texts were accordingly commissioned. It is very difficult to be precise about these things, without causing insult, so I could see why the participants at the Luxembourg symposium were reluctant to talk about it. But any future notion of Euro-English will need to be brave and address the matter.

I would underline Modiano's point about the importance of the global economy: if the EU wants to trade with the rest of the world, and become more outward-looking, then it will have to respect global linguistic realities. English, as he says, is 'an integral component of globalization'. And this sense of 'belonging to a global community', especially present among young people, makes it self-evident, at least to me, that his conclusion is correct: 'UK membership in the Union does not have any bearing on the decision among continental Europeans to use English'. His other big point is also critical, with member states having made 'considerable investments in English, and are not prepared to participate in EU affairs in other languages'. I agree with his conclusion – 'When the dust settles, there is every reason to believe that English, because of its utility, will have the same role within the EU as it maintains today' – but I wonder about 'with the exception that there will be a noticeable lack of L1 users of English present to influence the direction English is to take in the days and years ahead'.

Is this so? I do not know what will happen, with respect to the numbers of British people currently employed in this field in Europe. 'Presuming that nearly all of the British subjects working in the interpretation and translation services lose their jobs, which is the only rational deduction one can make'. Really? Experience, linguistic and editorial skills, and familiarity with the EU machine, count for a great deal, I learned in Luxembourg, and these would be extremely difficult to replace. What about the opposite presumption: assuming they stay in post? They would presumably continue to operate as they do now – which is with many different practices. Some do indeed follow a British standard. One departmental head said he liked to edit according to the standards of the *Financial Times*. When he said this, others immediately jumped in citing other British models, and the issue of American influence on British English came up straight away. But even if the Brits did leave, would it follow that EU members 'will not have colleagues whose L1 intuitions can easily be accessed when assistance is needed'? I can access any number of L1 intuitions at the click of a mouse. Indeed, virtual speech communities, meeting via Skype (or the like) are in many respects a great deal easier to work with than trying to arrange a face-to-face meeting.

It may well be that 'the very processes that make possible the emergence of a second-language variety will be more pronounced and move forward at a quicker pace without the presence of L1 users who feel compelled to defend what they believe is a more "correct" rendition of the language'. But given that: (a) there is considerable difference of opinion about what counts as 'correct' among the L1 speakers; (b) several of them are much more flexible in their linguistic views than Modiano's paper suggests; and (c) their opinions are governed by factors that are outside their control, I don't think the presence or absence of a few Brits, or a change in the legal status of the UK, is going to make the slightest difference. A Euro-English will continue to develop, informally and erratically, in the way it has already done. The debate surrounding Irish and Maltese (both of which have English as an official language alongside their identity languages) is thus somewhat irrelevant, whether or not 'some member states may insist that they have the right to have more than one official language'. And of course, both Irish and Maltese English (as opposed to 'British English') already exist, in the cultural sense I outlined above.

But there is one big problem, and Modiano raises it when he writes: 'I feel that it is imperative that we encourage teacher trainees to promote in their school teaching a spoken language which is compatible with the written language' – thinking especially of 'higher education, scientific publishing, and in the working world'. He is optimistic. He claims that 'What we are witnessing in the English of mainland Europeans is a spoken usage which does not conflict more or less dramatically with the challenges of mastering written English when compared to other speech communities with similar demographic profiles'. Frankly, I have not witnessed it, and I'm not sure how this could actually happen. Standardized written English is essentially the language of print, observable around the world with minor variations (US vs UK spelling and punctuation, in particular), thereby guaranteeing mutual intelligibility; it may of course be spoken, in formal settings. It contrasts with the evolving spoken norms that are part of the new (or old) Englishes, expressing local identity; these may of course be written, especially in informal settings. The features that identify these Englishes are a combination of phonology (both segmental and non-segmental), orthography, lexis, grammar, and pragmatics, and they make for a considerable distance between speech and writing, in any variety (including British and American English). Euro-English will be no different.

What I *have* witnessed, impressionistically (again, we need descriptive studies) is the emergence of a different kind of Euro-English that has nothing to do with the corridors of power in the EU. My daughter lives in Amsterdam, and has many expat English-speaking (as L1) friends. When they talk together I hear all kinds of differences which are not part of her (and presumably their) original idiolect. Their intonation and rhythm are different, a touch more staccato (but not syllable-timed). They use expressions such as *For sure* (meaning 'absolutely, yes'). Theirs is a Euro-English too, and one that is very different from formal written English – for example, they code-switch in a way that would be completely unacceptable to my EU audience.

In short: if we stay with a monolithic conception of Euro-English, we cannot have it both ways. Either it is going to be systematically distinctive in speech compared with other varieties, in which case it will be very different from written standardized English. Or it will be close to the latter, in which case it will lose much of its spoken individuality. Only a multiglossic recognition of Euro-Englishes can resolve this dilemma, but how one turns this into confident professional practice we have yet to see. At least the issue is now being recognized. It will be interesting to see how things develop, in this new sociolinguistic space.

D8.2 Issues to consider

Activity D8.1
In his article, Crystal turns on its head the notion that international varieties of English are variant forms local to particular countries. Instead, he suggests that, say, Australian English refers to the cultural knowledge that you need in order to make sense of what an L1 speaker of English in Australia is saying to you. What kind of cultural knowledge would be necessary in such a case?

Activity D8.2
Notwithstanding the difficulties of predicting the future of English (see C8.3), how might Crystal's claim as to the importance of cultural knowledge be used to consider how English might develop in the future?

Activity D8.3
In terms of social attitudes towards English, what is the likely effect of a steadily increasing number of people speaking English as a second or foreign language?

Activity D8.4
Based on your reading of Crystal's article, how likely to do you think it is that a Euro-English will emerge?

COMMENTARY ON ACTIVITIES

C1.1.1

1. The family tree misses out quite a lot of important information in the development of Old English. We know, for example, that Old English borrowed a large number of words from Latin, but the family tree suggests that English did not have any contact with Latin at all. Similarly, the family tree shows no contact between English and Celtic, or English and the Scandinavian languages. Later on in the development of English, French had an important effect on the language (see C3); but again, the family tree misses this out completely.
2. The family tree gives the impression that all languages can be traced back to a single, overarching language. But this 'top-down' view gives a false impression of how languages develop. We know, for instance, that the Britons lived in fairly disparate communities, perhaps often far apart from each other. The idea that all these communities would speak in exactly the same way therefore seems a bit farfetched. It is more likely that they spoke various dialect forms of Brittonic. But the language family tree does not show up the contribution that dialects make to a language's development.
3. When we talk about a language being 'dead', we mean that it is no longer spoken as a first language by anyone. This metaphor suggests that languages are living entities. But languages are not born and they do not die. A language only 'dies' when the last of its speakers dies (or, in fact, when the last but one of its speakers dies; after all, if you're the only remaining speaker of a language, who are you going to talk to in that language?). Consequently, using the 'family' metaphor to describe languages might be misleading in that it can lead to incorrect assumptions about how languages are created. It's important to remember that a language is not a tangible thing. The development of a language is to a large extent affected by the development of its speakers, and the society in which they live. A language family tree does not take account of this.

C1.2.1

Runes were typically engraved into stone or carved on wood or bone. It is much easier to carve angular letters than curved ones.

C1.2.2

The runes are transliterated as *krist wæs on rodi*, which means *Christ was on [the] cross*. *Rood* is the Old English word for *cross* and survives in the word *Holyrood* ('Holy cross'), the name of the area of Edinburgh where the Scottish parliament is located. Parts of the text on the Ruthwell Cross can also be found in the Old English poem *The Dream of the Rood*.

C1.3.1

1. *weapon*
2. *to forbid*
3. *swineherd*
4. *today*
5. *death*
6. *black*
7. *stall* (for cattle)
8. *church*
9. *daytime*
10. *smith* (as in *blacksmith*)
11. *wolf*
12. *sharp*
13. *mankind*
14. *wolves*
15. *thorny*
16. *horse*
17. *to dry*
18. *upward*
19. *loaf*
20. *milk*

Were you right? Did any (parts) of the words cause you problems? If so, why was this?

C1.4.1

1. *se*
2. *þæt*
3. *þā*
4. *þā*
5. *þæs*
6. *sēo* and *þǣm*

C1.4.2

1. <u>Se</u> ōðer him andwirde ond cwæð: 'Swīga ðū[']'.
2. Đā ðā Arcestrates <u>se</u> cyningc hæfde <u>þæt</u> gewrit oferrǣd […]

C1.5.1

It's a key, of course. What were you thinking?!

C2.1.1

You may have recognised the text as you read it aloud. It is the Lord's Prayer, sometimes called the *Pater noster*, or the *Our Father*. (If you're not familiar with the Present Day English version, look it up. You will be able to find it easily on the internet).

C2.1.2

You will notice spelling variations (e.g. *willa/willo*, *rīc/rice*, *heofonum/heofnum*, *nama/noma*), which are likely to be indicative of pronunciation differences between the two dialects. We can be reasonably confident of this because despite the prestige of the West Saxon variety, the concept of standardised spelling was not established to the extent that it is today. Toon (1992: 30) notes that <o> before the nasal consonants <m>, <n> and <ng> is indicative of the Anglian dialect, sometimes used as a superordinate term for Northumbrian and Mercian. Additionally, we can identify different pronouns. Compare, for example, West Saxon *ūre* and Northumbrian *usra* for 'our'. The latter survives in Yorkshire English as possessive *us* ('Forgive us us sins'). You will also notice two different words for the same concept (i.e. *gyltas* and *scylda*, both meaning 'guilt' or 'sin'). Now if we consider distinctions between Old English and Present Day English, these include register differences. Here, certain words have been replaced in Present Day English by words that have their origins in other languages. For example, the Church of England's current version of the *Book of Common Prayer* offers two variants of the Lord's Prayer, one of which says 'forgive us our *trespasses*' while the other says 'forgive us our *sins*'. *Trespass* is from Old French whereas *sin* is from Old English. Germanic words often have more informal connotations than words of Latin origin, which is presumably why the Church of England has chosen to replace the word *trespass* in the more modern version of the prayer.

C2.2.1

Think about the place name *Middlesex*, which translates as Middle Saxons.

C3.1.1

When we talk about vocabulary we can make a distinction between open-class words (also called lexical words) and closed-class words (often referred to as grammatical words). Open-class words include nouns (e.g. *chair, happiness, boxes, silence*), verbs (e.g. *go, ran, followed, is*), adjectives (e.g. *red, heavy, apparent, interesting*) and adverbs (e.g. *slowly, suddenly, fast, carefully*). In the closed-class category we find conjunctions (e.g. *and, but, if*), prepositions (e.g. *on, at, in, under*), auxiliary verbs (e.g. *may, must, should, will*), determiners (e.g. *the, a, this, some*) and pronouns (e.g. *he, them, us, you*). Most of the loanwords above are open-class words as, indeed, are any new words that are coined in Present Day English.

You will probably have noticed that the loanwords from French relate to spheres of life that would have been dominated by those high up in the social hierarchy. So, for instance, there are words relating to law, government, administration and finance. Latin, as the language of the church, inevitably contributes a substantial number of religious words, as well as providing vocabulary relating to the arts and sciences, which is further indication of the areas of life in which it was used.

C3.1.2

The Scandinavian loanwords appear to come from spheres of everyday life. Furthermore, the words borrowed from Scandinavian include the pronouns *they, them* and *their* – closed-class words. For closed-class words to be borrowed into English suggests very close contact between Scandinavian settlers and Anglo-Saxons, and the borrowing of these words was likely also to have been motivated by the similarity between the languages of these two groups.

C3.2.1

Did you find it difficult to understand the extract? My guess is that although there may have been particular words that you struggled with (*soote, holt, corages*, perhaps?), in general you will have found it easier to make sense of than the Lord's Prayer in C2.1. Middle English seems much closer to Present Day English than Old English. Nonetheless, there should be elements of the language that you recognise as being clearly developed from Old English. For example, some of the verb forms include Old English inflections: *slepen* (from OE *slæpen*), *maken* (from OE *macian*) and *goon* (from OE *gegangen*). You may also have noticed that *whan* is now spelled with initial <wh> as opposed to the initial <hw> of OE *hwanne* (see B3.2). With regard to the pronouns in the extract, *his* is not masculine as you may initially have thought. It is actually the gender-neutral singular possessive pronoun (what in Present Day English would be *its*); it just happen to be identical to the masculine form at this point (see B5.2). In terms of vocabulary, Middle English borrowed extensively from French, as we saw in B3.4. Evidence of this can be seen in the extract: *perced, licour, vertu, engendred, inspired, cours, melodye, corages* and *pilgrimages* are all French loanwords. What you may have noticed about *licour* and *foweles* particularly is that over time they have narrowed in meaning. Whereas *licour* originally meant any form of liquid, it now refers solely to strong alcoholic drinks. And *foweles*, meaning birds, now refers specifically to birds that are eaten as food. This narrowing of meaning is considered in more detail in C7, where we concentrate on the formation of new words in English.

C3.3.1

The presence of the letter thorn indicates that this is a text from early in the Middle English period; it has not yet been replaced by the digraph <th>. With regard to syntax, you should notice that word order is much closer to Present Day English than the Old English versions in C2.1, with fewer inflections. The influence of French can be seen in some of the constituent word of the text. For example, *dettis* ('debts') has replaced OE *gyltas* and *temptacioun* has replaced OE *costnunge*.

C4.1.1

Cawdrey's aim in his dictionary was to define so-called 'hard' words and to be successful in this he needed to be confident that his readers would be able to understand the synonyms (words of similar meanings) he used to define the target word. *Abjure* comes from Middle French and is defined using *renounce* and *deny*, which also come from French, and *forsweare*, which is of Old English origin. Whether French-derived words would have been helpful to define another French-derived word depends on how well known they would have been to the reader. At the very least, we can assume that this was a dictionary aimed at an already fairly well-educated speaker. An additional issue is that although Cawdrey's dictionary was aimed at educated readers, there would still have been a problem if Cawdrey's definitions of 'hard' words were hard words themselves; i.e. not known by the reader. What the entries from Cawdrey's dictionary lack is an indication of how the target word is used in context. Johnson's dictionary goes much further towards explaining this by providing quotations containing the target words. Johnson's dictionary also gives the language from which the target word was borrowed, and takes account of the two senses of the target word. It was in all respects a phenomenal achievement for one person. Additional information that you might expect in a Present Day English dictionary would include a phonetic transcription indicating the pronunciation of the word and, potentially, pragmatic information about the context in which the word is usually used.

C4.2.1

You should notice that Price employs long <f> in word-initial and medial positions but 'short' <s> at the ends of words. While this may have been a useful convention in handwriting (allowing the reader to clearly discern the beginning and end of words), there is much less need for it in printed texts, so it is easy to see why this convention fell by the wayside. Price also appears to use word-initial capitalisation for emphasis, rather than as a rule to be applied to every noun.

C4.2.2

An interesting point about the extract from Price's book is the presupposition inherent in his definition of orthography as 'an Art of right fpel-ling, and wri-ting the let-ters'.

The presupposition, of course, is that there is indeed a 'right' (i.e. 'correct') way of spelling and writing in English and that anything other than this is wrong. As we saw in B5, this is a notion that did not exist in the Middle English period when variation was a defining feature of written language. Similarly, there was considerable freedom of choice for writers during the Early Modern period (see, for example, C5.2 and C5.3). Towards the end of the Early Modern period, however, the pendulum was swinging in the opposite direction and standardisation was being actively promoted. Sometimes, though, the pursuit of a written standard was based more on prescriptive rules than on descriptive ones. In the case of English Orthographie it would seem that there is an attempt at descriptive rules, though these are not always useful.

Price's attempt to provide some ground rules concerning English orthography is admirable yet runs into difficulties from the outset. This is because he does not differentiate clearly between letters and sounds. In answer to his question 'What is a vowel?', Price explains that it is 'a let-ter which mak-eth a per-fect found of itfelf'. The problem is that a vowel is primarily a feature of speech, not writing (see B4.1 for an explanation of how we produce vowel sounds in English). What Price means is that a 'vowel' in written language is a grapheme which may be used to represent a vowel sound. Furthermore, his explanation that a vowel 'mak-eth a per-fect sound of itfelf' does not provide enough explanatory detail for us to understand what he means. What is 'a perfect sound'? We can see when we look at his next question ('What is a dip-thong?') that what he means by 'vowel' is a monophthong, but this is only really clear if you already know what a diphthong is. (Notice that his definition of a diphthong relies on the reader understanding what a vowel is, thereby resulting in a circular definition!). Price's confusion of letters with sounds continues in his last question and answer, in which he explains that there are six vowels. A more accurate answer would be that there are six letters with which we can represent vowel sounds (there are many more than six vowel sounds in English).

In general, it seems that Price views writing as primary, as opposed to speech. Because of this, he runs into difficulties when trying to explain such concepts as vowels and consonants. Nevertheless, it would appear that Price is at least attempting to provide a description of standard practice (as can be seen in his explanation of when to use capital letters). He is also sympathetic towards students whose teachers may have been using the book in class; in a marginal note next to the extract above, he writes: 'If this correction of the letters will not sink into the blockish, or ignorant Teacher's head, let him go off so spelling'! (Price 1668: 4).

C4.3.1

Despite what prescriptivists would like to think, language change is inevitable and cannot be stopped. Think, for example, of how language contact, such as that between the Anglo-Saxons and the Danes, leads inevitably to linguistic developments. Prescriptivists often simply do not understand the ways in which languages develop over time. Prescriptive attitudes are also usually based on mistaken beliefs, such as the notion that splitting the infinitive is wrong. These are nothing more than simple stylistic preferences. It is also the case that prescriptivist attitudes are often revealing of underlying prejudices with regard to class and education; that is, prescriptivist attitudes go beyond complaints about language. With regard to situations in which prescriptivism might be tolerated, despite the fact that there is no linguistic basis for such attitudes, we need to be aware that certain elements of usage invoke strong feelings in some people. For this reason, it is useful to be aware of what constitutes appropriate language for the situation. For instance, using features of regional dialect in a job interview may not be a good idea if the job in question relies on an ability to communicate with people from a range of different cultures. In such an instance, an ability to use Standard English is clearly useful. Language education, therefore, should be focused on exploring the effects of particular usages in particular contexts, rather than on prescribing certain forms. And in practice, we all shift between varieties, registers and styles all the time.

C5.1.1

Leith (1997: 107) points out that pronouns are directly associated with social interaction and suggests that because of this, we are perhaps especially sensitive to their effect in conversation. Although it is probably impossible to state definitively the reasons for the decline in the use of socially marked pronouns in English, we can at least speculate on some possible explanations. One likely problem, of course, is that you would not necessarily have always known which pronoun was the right one to use. Embarrassment or even offence might be caused if you referred to someone as *thou* and they were expecting *you*. Leith (1997) suggests that this might have been a particular concern for the middle classes. Whereas the upper classes were sure of their position in society, the middle class was more fluid (having money often bought you a place among the middle classes, even if you were of humble origins). Consequently, it was not always easy to tell who was deserving of the more polite *you*. A safer option was to use the polite form regardless of the social status of the person you were talking to. Notice that this explanation relates to the sociolinguistic notion of the middle classes being the major drivers of change in language (see A4.1). A further explanation is suggested by Barber (1997: 155) who explains how the Quakers (a religious group) favoured the use of *thou* rather than *you* owing to their egalitarian ideals. Leith (1997: 110) suggests that this may have led to *thou* becoming stigmatised as the pronoun of choice for the religious fanatic, resulting in non-Quakers favouring *you*.

C5.1.2

One possible answer to this question is to consider it from the perspective of gender. The loss of grammatical gender in English, which had begun towards the end of the Old English period, did not result in the complete regularisation of the pronoun system, as you might have expected it to. One of the reasons for this is that while Old English had grammatical gender, this was largely in alignment with natural gender (see the reading in D2.1 for more information). Hence, the masculine and feminine pronouns survived. The Old English neuter third-person pronouns *his* and *him* were identical to the masculine pronouns, and gradually became associated with males, hence were preserved though no longer considered neuter. It is interesting to note that in recent years, the concept of non-binary gender (that is, being neither male nor female) has started to have an impact on the development of the personal pronoun system in English, as many non-binary people choose to be referred to as *they* rather than *he* or *she*. While singular *they* dates back to the fourteenth century, it has tended to be used when the antecedent is unspecified; e.g. '*An artist* should always know what *they* feel about a topic'. This, though, is changing, with usages such as the following becoming increasingly common: 'I spoke to *Sam* last night and asked *them* if *they'd* like to go out for dinner.'

C5.2.1

There are two ways of forming comparative and superlative adjectives in Present Day Standard English. For adjectives of one syllable (or those of two syllables which end in <y>, <ow> or <er>, e.g. *friendly, narrower, cleverer*), the practice is to add an inflectional morpheme: <er> for comparatives and <est> for superlatives. Hence, *small, smaller* and *smallest; heavy, heavier* and *heaviest; light, lighter* and *lightest; friendly, friendlier* and *friendliest*. This, of course, is a relic of English's past as a synthetic language. In Old English, for instance, the comparative and superlative forms of the adjective *glæd* ('happy') were *glædra* and *gladost*. (Note that a few adjectives are irregular, such as *good, better, best* and *bad, worse, worst*.) For polysyllabic adjectives we don't add an inflection but rather use an adverb: *more* for comparatives and *most* for superlatives. Hence, *beautiful, more beautiful* and *most beautiful; unpleasant, more unpleasant* and *most unpleasant*. If you deviate from these grammatical rules – for example, by saying *more small* or *complicatedest* –prescriptivists would accuse you of being wrong and descriptive linguists would note that you were using non-standard forms. What you should have noticed from the Early Modern English examples in Activity C5.2.1, however, is that the rules governing the formation of comparatives and superlatives in Present Day Standard English do not appear to hold for Early Modern English. Instead, we find polysyllabic superlatives formed with <est> (*treacherousest* and *variablest*), monosyllabic comparatives formed with the addition of an adverb (*more fair*) and double superlatives (*most affablest*). We might note that in some circumstances, the use of the double superlative is perhaps employed by the iambic pentameter of the verse. Very briefly, iambic pentameter verse consists of ten syllables with every other syllable stressed, as in the line from *Julius Caesar*, 'With the most boldest and best hearts of Rome'. Using the double superlative in this example makes the line fit the ten syllable structure (even though in performance the grammatical words *the, and* and *of* are unlikely to be stressed). However, the fact that double comparatives and superlatives were used in literary writing suggests that they were not seen as ungrammatical (at least, not to the point of impairing meaning). Furthermore, we also find them in non-literary prose ('the most uncleanest and variablest nature'). Barber (1997:147) suggests that there may have been a stylistic difference between the <er/est> and *more/most* forms. He suggests that <er/est> forms may have been considered colloquial whereas *more/most* forms might have been deemed more formal. Nonetheless, he admits that, in general, Early Modern English writers were pretty much free to decide which form to use.

C5.3.1

The first sentence would be grammatically complete even without the verb *do*. The function of *do* in this example is to add emphasis to the speaker's assertion that he/she likes coffee.

In contrast, without *do* the second sentence would be grammatically incomplete (at least, in Standard British English). Generally speaking, yes/no questions are formed by inverting the subject and the verb from the position they would be in if we were making a statement. For example, to form a yes/no question out of the statement 'She is writing a letter' we invert the subject *she* and the verb *is* (that is, we swap them around). This gives us 'Is she writing a letter?' However, if the statement from which the question is derived does not contain an auxiliary verb (*be* or *have*), or if the main verb is not *be* or *have*, then we need to insert *do*. For example, the statement 'They enjoy hiking' does not contain an auxiliary verb and so in Present Day English we cannot simply invert the subject and verb to form a question. 'Enjoy they hiking?' is ungrammatical in Standard English. In such a case we don't invert the subject and verb; we simply insert *do* before the subject, as in 'Do they enjoy hiking?' In this respect, *do* is often referred to as a 'dummy' auxiliary.

In the third sentence, *do* is used to form a negative statement. Again, without *do* the statement would be ungrammatical.

C5.3.2

As with the formation of comparative and superlative adjectives, there was a greater freedom of choice for Early Modern English writers in how they formed negative statements and yes/no questions. In some of the examples in Activity C5.3.2 the auxiliary *do* is used exactly as it is in Present Day English. Sometimes, though, it is not used at all, leading to sentences that would be considered grammatically incomplete in Present Day English. For example, the syntactic structure of the question 'And why did'st thou tell so many Lyes then?' would be acceptable in Present Day Standard English (even though some aspects of morphology, spelling and lexis would be different). On the other hand, the statement 'I like not this Jury for our purpose' would be considered grammatically non-standard or, at least, archaic.

C6.1.1

What is interesting about these loanwords is, as Marckwardt (1980) points out, that so many come from the semantic field of food. Marckwardt (1980: 62) hypothesises that this suggests 'pleasant but commonplace social contacts', though it is difficult to arrive at this conclusion solely from examining loanwords. We would be on safer ground simply to acknowledge that food played an important part in the contact between different cultures in the early years of the American colonies.

The loanwords listed above in Activity C6.1.1 are from immigrant groups within America at the time. Another group of people who contributed significantly to the lexicon of American English were the native inhabitants of the country: the Native

American Indians. A selection of American Indian loanwords (again, from Marckwardt 1980: 30) is as follows:

Trees, plants, fruits
catalpa, hickory, pecan, persimmon, sequoia, squash
Foods
hooch, pemmican, succotash, supawn
Animals
chipmunk, moose, muskrat, opossum, raccoon, skunk, terrapin, woodchuck
Amerindian culture
powwow, totem, papoose, squaw, moccasin, tomahawk, kayak, tepee (tipi), wigwam

C6.1.2

Marckwardt (1980) notes that these loanwords vary in the extent to which they have been absorbed into American English. Some words, like *moccasin* and *kayak*, are used internationally, while others are known only in particular areas of America. Others have little reference beyond the American Indian culture they are taken from (e.g. *tomahawk*). It is likely that such words were borrowed by early settlers to describe foods, plants and animals that they had no experience of in their own cultures. It should also be noted that these words were not borrowed in the form that they now take. Most have been spelled differently, often to reflect early settlers' struggles to pronounce the original forms. For example, Marckwardt (1980: 33) explains that *squash* is a shortened form of the Narrangansett word *askutasquash*, while *racoon* is a corruption of *arakunem*.

C6.2.1

On the surface, it is easy to see why a reformed spelling system seems an attractive idea. We have seen how English spelling often represents older pronunciation (see B4.4) and how, consequently, there sometimes seems to be little connection between the spelling of a word and its pronunciation. We might quibble and say that, for instance, Webster's simplification of *cheque* to *check* makes the noun ambiguous with the verb (*to check*), but such ambiguities are easily resolved in context (plus we have no difficulty in interpreting the meaning of these terms in speech, despite the fact that they sound alike). The more important issue with spelling reforms such as Webster's is that the rules suggested are often as inconsistent as the existing practices. Carney (1994: 53) points out, for example, that if we are going to simplify the spelling of nouns that in British English end in <re> (e.g. *theatre* becomes *theater*) then, logically, we ought also to change the spelling of those nouns that end in <le> (e.g. *battle* should be spelled *battel*). This, though, has not happened. An even more important issue is the fact that accents vary and one person's pronunciation of a word can be very different to another's. For example, in some accents of American English, <r> following a vowel is pronounced whereas in other accents it is not; so *car* may be pronounced /kaːɹ/ or /kaː/. It is not possible to represent all these accentual variations in the spelling of a word – this would require a different spelling for some accents, a practice which would contradict the purpose of having a standardised spelling system. Any spelling system, then, is always likely to favour some accents and disadvantage others.

C6.3.1

Clearly there are attempts in the extract above Activity C6.3.1 to represent a non-standard form of speech via non-standard spellings. For example, the spelling of *every* as *eb'ry* suggests a pronunciation of /v/ as /b/ and the apostrophe suggests the elision of the middle syllable. *Eas* appears to be a rendering of *yes* and suggests a pronunciation of this word that begins with a diphthong (/ɔa/ perhaps?) rather than the palatal approximant /j/. In terms of grammar we can note the use of the object pronoun *me* rather than the standard *I*. The line 'Me massa name Cunney Tomsee' lacks a gentive inflection on *massa* and the verb *is* is missing before *Cunney Tomsee*. The line 'me no crissen' lacks an auxiliary verb and includes a simplified form of negation. No doubt you will be able to spot other examples of this kind. There is, then, the suggestion of the simplification and mixing that is a feature of pidgins. Of course, we need to exercise caution in drawing conclusions from such data, since it is fiction as opposed to naturally occurring language and it is a representation of a variety rather than a phonetic transcription. However, the choices the writer has made in representing the speech of an African slave do at least give a suggestion as to what might have been some common features of this variety.

C7.1.1

There will always be words in particular varieties of English that are not familiar to speakers of other varieties. To Trudgill and Hannah's list we could add *sook* ('sulky'), *grommet* ('a young surfer'), *gronk* ('an idiot') and many more. But despite what Trudgill and Hannah claim, I would be very surprised if you speak British English as a first language and have not heard of at least some of these colloquialisms. There may be some that you didn't know at all (*hard yakka, a humpy* and *to chyack*, perhaps?) but I suspect that you will be familiar with most of the others, even if you don't use them yourself. In response to the question of how you might be familiar with these words, there are a variety of potential explanations. Some are obvious contractions – e.g. *beaut* – which, even if you don't use yourself, are not difficult to interpret. Some are, in fact, common in British English, if not in exactly the same form. *Tuck*, for instance, is a colloquialism for *food* in some contexts (did your school have a tuck shop?) and is clearly related to *tucker*. Some words, on the other hand, have entered British English as a result of contact with Australian English. One way in which this happened was through the syndication of Australian TV shows to UK channels in the late 1980s, particularly soap operas such as *Neighbours* and *Home and Away*, whose contemporary settings and characters were a perfect conduit for colloquial Australian English. In this respect, international varieties of English influence British English (which, of course, is itself just another international variety) just as much as vice versa. And in this way English will continue to develop. It would seem that when Trudgill and Hannah claim that the above words are 'not known in EngEng', what they actually mean is 'not used', but even so we would need to qualify this by saying something like 'not used in standard written British English'. Such words may not form part of our active vocabulary (the store of words that we frequently use) but they are almost certainly part of our passive vocabulary (the store of words that we are familiar with though don't use ourselves). The issue of usage is particularly important since although international varieties may share words, where they often vary is in how such words are used. For example, the short form *beaut* may sometimes be used in British English, though only as a noun (e.g. 'That's a beaut!'). In contrast, the Australian Corpus of English shows how it is common in Australian English for *beaut* to be used as an adjective (e.g. 'It's beaut, isn't it?'; 'he made my brother a real beaut dingo').

C7.2.1

One problem with labels such as Australian English, Singapore English, etc. is that they perpetuate a view that certain forms of English belong to particular nation states. That is, the three circles model is primarily concerned with geography rather than usage. Furthermore, the notion that Inner Circle countries are norm-defining is a very Anglo-centric view. Consider, for instance, someone who has grown up speaking English as an L1 (i.e. first language) in Kenya, with no contact at all with people in an Inner Circle country. The notion that such a person's English should be judged in relation to the norms of the Inner Circle seems not only illogical but disparaging. There are other issues too. The model does not account for speakers who are bilingual or multilingual, for whom the notion of an L1 is complex. Nor does it account for the proficiency of speakers, which can vary enormously. Although there are problems, then, with Kachru's model, it has been enormously influential for what it hypothesises about how English spreads. Furthermore, it has influenced a range of other models that aim to address the problems discussed above. For a summary of these, see Jenkins (2015: 12–21).

C7.3.1

A new word is more likely to enter the standard language if it fills a lexical gap. Hence, blends which do this are more likely to catch on. *Pixel* is a good example of this, as is *Brexit*, both of which explain a complex concept in a single lexical item. By contrast, the concept described by a blend like *situationship* is less complex, and the blend seems more a result of a creative impulse. The morphological characteristics of blends also seem likely to affect the extent to which they are adopted. I would say that *debtpression* is unlikely to catch on because (a) the first syllable is a full free morpheme, and (b) the assimilation of /b/ to /p/ in natural speech is likely to result in a pronunciation that is closer to the existing word *depression*, thereby losing what made the blend distinctive.

C7.3.2

In the case of *adder* and *umpire*, the initial <n> has been reanalysed as belonging to the indefinite article. In the case of *nickname*, the <n> of *an* has been reanalysed as being the initial consonant of the word that follows.

C7.4.2

Some of the vocabulary may initially look unrecognisable but on closer inspection is clearly derived from local pronunciations of English words; for example, *ting* ('think'), *tok* ('talk'), *nogat* ('no good'), *gavman* ('government'), *ples* ('place'), *bilong* ('belong'). In this respect we can see how English is acting as a lexifier language. Romaine's Standard English translation also allows us to work out the grammatical function of some of the Tok Pisin words. The word *waitpela* is translated as Standard English 'white people', suggesting that *pela* is a suffix meaning 'people'. In fact, a literal translation of *pela* is 'fellow' (deriving from a localised pronunciation of the word), but since *waitman* is translated as the singular 'whiteman', we can work out that *pela* can act as a plural marker – so *waitpela* means 'white people' and we can note that *pela* has undergone semantic widening. From this we can work out that while *yupela* is translated as 'your', the literal translation is 'you people' (the natural-sounding translation takes into account the preceding verb *bilong*). This in turn suggests that *yu* is likely to be a second-person pronoun. Indeed, *yu* turns up in the phrase 'Em tok ples bilong yu?' Because we know that *yupela* divides into two morphemes, we know that *mipela* must divide this way too (i.e. *mi-* and *-pela*). And because this is translated as 'people', we can work out that *mi* on its own is likely to be a singular first-person pronoun (literally *me*, i.e. *I*). In fact, Romaine translates 'Mi tok' (literally 'me talk') as 'we asked', though this is likely to be because her translation takes account of the situational context of the speaker's story (i.e. a group of people hearing Tok Pisin for the first time) to provide a more natural-sounding translation. No doubt you will be able to work out more of the Tok Pisin words using a similar deductive process, though the pidgin characteristics of the language should already be clear. The majority of the vocabulary is taken from English. Simplification is evident in the way that the pronoun system uses a minimum number of forms and marks plural pronouns by compounding the singular form with the suffix *pela*. Past tense forms of the verb are avoided – for example, 'Em tok' ('him talk') translates as 'he said'. Note too how the simplification extends to the avoidance of irregular forms: 'Em tok', despite being a third-person present tense form, has no third-person marker on the verb (i.e. *tok* as opposed to **toks*). We therefore see both regularisation and a loss of redundancy (since the pronoun indicates the third person there is no need to indicate this again on the verb). Mixing is apparent in the way that phonological characteristics of the substrate languages of Tok Pisin influence the pronunciation of the English words that Tok Pisin makes use of. For instance, the long vowel in *talk* is short in Tok Pisin (the spelling *tok* suggests /tɒk/) and the labio-dental /f/ of *fellow* becomes bilabial /p/ in *pela*. Note how this short account of a small extract from a pidgin illustrates the variety of ways in which English can develop once it comes into contact with other varieties in a specific sociocultural setting.

C8.2.1

Scare stories such as that from the *Mail on Sunday* are fairly common in the press. But to believe that the techniques of text messaging are likely to affect the development of both the English language and literacy is to ignore the fact that, as we saw in A8.3, technological innovations do not necessarily affect every variety of the language. Added to this is the fact that within each variety of English are a series of different registers; that is, language variations caused by particular social circumstances. For instance, in a job interview we tend to use a fairly formal register, whereas talking in the pub with friends will involve a much more informal style. In the former situation we would tend to use Standard English (because of the 'prestige' that people cannot help but attribute to particular varieties) while in the latter situation we might be more likely to revert to a regional dialect, especially if this is shared with the other speakers. Prescriptivists tend to forget that we change the way we write and speak depending on the circumstances we find ourselves in. Using text-message shorthand is clearly inappropriate for writing, say, an academic essay because it is not versatile enough to be able to handle complex ideas and arguments, and because the extensive use of acronyms and abbreviations relies on the reader understanding all of these, which may not necessarily be the case. However, for the purposes of communicating quickly with someone who you know will understand the short forms that are commonly used, text-message shorthand is quite clearly appropriate. Similarly, while dialect forms are perfectly appropriate when talking in an informal situation with people from the same speech community as you, Standard English is much better when addressing, say, a group of people for whom English is a second language, because it is a variety that is commonly known internationally. So, the first mistake that prescriptivists make when bemoaning such forms as text-message shorthand is to forget that people are able to handle many different registers and varieties and that changes to one of these do not necessarily affect the others. If students are routinely using so-called 'textspeak' in schoolwork then the issue is not so much that text messaging is affecting the development of English (for this to happen the changes would need to affect other groups of people too), rather that such students need help in mastering the more appropriate registers of English available to them. But the article in question is about teenagers' use of textspeak in text messages – where it is clearly appropriate!

The second issue with the article concerns the claim by the journalist that textspeak is harming teenagers' 'ability to develop language and grammar skills'. The claim from the academic quoted in the article that the cited text messages do not contain grammar is clearly nonsense (we cannot, of course, discount the possibility that the academic was misquoted). For example, the text 'OMG ikr' contains an interjection (*OMG*, i.e. 'Oh my God'), a subject (*i*, i.e. *I*), a verb (*k*, i.e. *know*), and a question tag (*r*, i.e. *right?*). These clausal elements may be conveyed through two acronyms but they are clearly still present, otherwise the receiver of the message would have no chance of understanding it. Moreover, it would be impossible to formulate such a message without an implicit understanding of the syntax of English sentences. Textspeak, in this example, simply serves as a shorthand way of conveying the proposition in question. Similar techniques of shorthand are used in myriad other forms of communication, such as computer languages, morse code, semaphore and so on, yet no-one ever claims that these communicative practices lack grammar. As is so often the case, it seems that the complaint about teenagers' use of textspeak is motivated by a prejudice against particular stylistic tendencies. The article offers no evidence at all that using textspeak affects teenagers' ability 'to develop language and grammar skills'; indeed, the examples cited in the article demonstrate that these skills are clearly in existence. In short, while it is important for people to be versatile when it comes to using the appropriate register for the situation, there is no sense in which textspeak is having a detrimental effect on the English language. Hence, the only cause for concern about articles such as this one is that they perpetuate damaging myths about the nature of language.

C8.3.1, C8.3.2 and C8.3.3

It is always very difficult to make predictions about the future of English, because so many external and internal factors can affect its development, as we have seen throughout this book. Any consideration of likely developments, then, is always contingent upon a particular set of circumstances. For example, our predictions as to what we might expect to see by way of future regularisation in, say, British English, will be dependent on the sociopolitical and cultural situation and whether this changes significantly or remains the same. If, for instance, conservative education policies were to be replaced by more liberal ones, we might expect to see some level of change in what is considered acceptable in Standard English. Singular *they*, for instance, might stand more chance of being accepted as a common and usual pronoun, or the possessive apostrophe might be deemed an unnecessary complexity (after all, we manage perfectly well without an oral equivalent to the apostrophe in speech). If the current situation does not change though, we can expect a more vigorous defence of supposedly traditional usages. Of course, these predictions concern just one area of life and one form of English; other varieties will continue to develop regardless of education policies. Considering how English might affect and be affected by other languages as it continues its global spread is also fraught with risk. Again, any predictions we make would need to be grounded in a particular sociopolitical situation; that is, before we can make any such predictions, we would need to assume a particular situation to be the case. For instance, if America continues to be the dominant global economic power, how might this affect the development of English? What if China overtakes the US economically? Finally, with regard to the possible influence of new technologies, we need to be careful about over-predicting their influence. In this respect, it is worth returning to the two points made at the end of section A: always consider (i) whether a sociopolitical/cultural change is likely to affect the spoken language or the written language, and (ii) whether it is likely to affect all the varieties and registers of the language or just some of them.

D1.1

Because Old English is a synthetic language, it is difficult to borrow words directly from other languages without needing to change their form in some way. This is necessary in order to make it possible for them to take the inflections needed to convey their function in a sentence. For this reason, the language-internal processes of affixation and compounding were much more common ways of forming new words.

D1.2

Wælweg translates as 'whale-way'. The compound is an example of a kenning. Kennings convey meaning through metaphor and 'whale-way' may thus be interpreted as *sea*.

D1.3

Grammatical patterns are perhaps easier to determine from the surviving corpus of Old English texts because there are fewer of them compared to lexical items. In contrast, the extant Old English texts give us only a partial view of the Old English lexicon. It is likely, for example, that many words that were common in speech were not recorded in writing (particularly given that literacy was not widespread beyond the clergy). We also need to consider the issue of register. As Kay (2015) explains, a large proportion of the surviving Old English texts is poetry. And the poetic register is very different from everyday language. Consequently, we need to bear in mind that the vocabulary we find in such texts is unlikely to be indicative of everyday speech. Relatedly, we should also consider the social status of the writers of the surviving texts. The simple fact of being literate tells us that they would have belonged to a privileged class. The voices of those lower down the social scale are comparatively unrepresented in Old English texts. Relatedly, although scholars have been able to identify four dialects of Old English (Northumbrian, Mercian, Kentish, and West Saxon), we can surmise on the basis of the Uniformitarian Principle (particularly Romaine's 1982 conception of this; see B4.3) that there would have been many more than are represented in those texts that survive.

D2.1

The Southwest Midlands dialect is useful to study because it retained grammatical gender for longer than other varieties. This provides the opportunity to see gender change happening in Middle English. It's also the case that, compared to other areas, a relatively large number of Middle English texts have survived from the Southwest Midlands. The more data we have (and the more this data is representative of the variety in question), the more confident we can be in the generalisabilty of the study's findings.

D2.2

During the Middle English period, the concept of natural gender gradually replaced grammatical gender. In very basic terms, following the principle of the animacy hierarchy, we would expect that by the end of the Middle English period nouns that refer to animate entities will be referred to with masculine or feminine pronouns (e.g. *he* and *she*), and those that refer to inanimate entities will be referred to with neuter pronouns (e.g. *it*). With this in mind, this is what happens to the nouns you considered:

(i) *Foranhēafod* (forehead) is not an animate noun. In Middle English it therefore takes a neuter pronoun, just as in Old English. This description of the Prioress from 'The General Prologue' to *The Canterbury Tales* is an example: 'But sikerly she hadde a fair **forheed**. **It** was almost a spanne brood, I trowe'.

(ii) *Bearn* (bairn, i.e. child) is an animate noun referring to a human and consequently is referred to with the appropriate masculine or feminine pronoun (as opposed to the neuter pronoun of OE).

(iii) *Dor* (door) does not change its pronominal reference in Middle English as, in terms of the animacy hierarchy, it is an inanimate object and therefore requires neuter anaphoric reference. Here's an example from 'The Miller's Tale': 'Ther nas no **dore** that he nolde heve of harre, Or breke **it**, at a renning, with his heed.'

(iv) The Old English masculine *hōd* (hood) takes neuter anaphoric reference in Middle English, as in this description of the Summoner from 'The General Prologue': 'But **hood**, for jolitee, ne wered he noon, For **it** was trussed 40 up in his walet.'

(v) As natural gender replaces grammatical gender, *wīf* (woman) is referred to anaphorically with *she*.

(vi) *Bile* (beak) takes neuter pronominal reference in Middle English, as in this extract from 'The Nun's Priest's Tale': 'His **bile** was blak, and as the jeet **it** shoon'.

(vii) Likewise, so too does *strǣt* (street), as in this example from 'The Prioress's Tale': 'And thurgh this **strete** men myghte ride or wende, For **it** was free and open at eyther ende.'

D3.1

Code-switching in Middle English texts has a variety of purposes:

- ❑ It occurs when writers quote from texts written in other languages.
- ❑ It can be used to signify a change to a different register.
- ❑ The use of a particular set phrase can trigger the reader's contextual knowledge of, for example, the text from which that phrase is taken.
- ❑ Conventionalised phrases such as French greetings can be used to signify that that the writer (or the character using the phrase) belongs to a particular social group.
- ❑ It can be a marker of in-group identity.
- ❑ It can be a marker of education.
- ❑ It can indicate a degree of power.

D3.2

Although Paston writes his letter in English, he addresses it in French. This functions to indicate his high social standing and degree of education.

D4.1

Sociolinguistic research has demonstrated that the middles classes are often the drivers of change in language, as they subconsciously emulate (or try to emulate) the linguistic behaviour of the social class that they aspire too. Young people too are often the drivers of linguistic change, though for different reasons. In their case, the decision to adopt particular linguistic forms is often part of a desire to distinguish themselves linguistically from the generation above as a means of projecting a distinctive identity. This is likely to be the reason why it was this group of speakers particularly who propagated Estuary English. In terms of its geographic spread, language contact is is the explanation here, with speakers of Estuary English moving between geographic areas. Propagation by media such as TV and radio has also been a factor.

D4.2

If you are a speaker of British English and live in Britain, you may find – depending on where you come from – that your variety of English retains some pronunciations that were common before or during the Great Vowel Shift. A Lancashire pronunciation of *road*, for example, is likely to be closer to /rɔːd/ than /rəʊd/. It will be clear, then, that the Great Vowel Shift did not affect all varieties of English to the same extent. This is important to note, because it is often the case that histories of English overlook what happens to regional varieties. The Great Vowel Shift is often used to demarcate Early Modern English and Late Modern English, for example (see Barber et al. 2009: 211), but this doesn't make much sense if we observe that the Great Vowel Shift didn't actually run to completion in all varieties of the language.

D5.1

The concepts of speech communities and social networks are ideal frameworks for investigating spoken language. But because the data we have from the Late Middle English and Early Modern English periods is written language, these concepts are of limited use. Additionally, the standardisation that happened in the Early Modern period was of the written language rather than the spoken language. Because of this, the Communities of Practice model makes a better tool for investigating the issue, since it applies equally to the production of writing.

D5.2

Moore notes that not all of the elements of Haugen's (1966) framework are applicable to the process of standardisation as it happened during the Late Middle English and Early Modern English periods. For example, the concept of acceptance does not apply in quite the way that Haugen suggests, since institutions (such as the Chancery) were not the propagators of standard forms to the degree that has sometimes been suggested. Rather, acceptance of standard forms happened among groups of people rather than institutions.

D6.1

Population numbers are problematic as a means of calculating how many speakers of English there are in the world for a variety of reasons. First of all, this calculation requires a reliable model (e.g. Kachru's Circles of English model; see C7.2) of which countries use English. And as we have seen, there are problems with assessing this. Second, simply counting people does not tell us anything about their level of language ability. For example, although Kachru's model tells us that in Expanding Circle countries people speak English as a foreign language, we would need to develop a clear measure of what it means to do this before we can count them as speakers. For example, what level of fluency do we require in order to count someone as an English speaker? You will no doubt be able to think of other problems too.

D7.1

If we compare the frequencies of a given form in two corpora and observe that in one corpus there are fewer instances of the form, all we can be sure of is that the form in question occurs less frequently as a proportion of one corpus than it does of the other. This does not necessarily tell us there has been a decline in usage. To be sure of this, we need to know that both corpora contain texts in which there is at least the opportunity for the form to exist. For example, imperative sentences turn up far more frequently in instruction manuals than in fiction. If we wanted to investigate whether imperatives were declining in English, we would need to compare corpora that contained the same kind of texts; e.g. we might compare a corpus of instruction manuals from the 1960s with an equivalent corpus of texts from 2019. That is to say, if we want to be sure that what we are observing is indeed a decline, we need to be confident that it is not simply a result of a poor text sampling strategy in our corpus design.

D7.2

Obviously, in corpus linguistic studies, the more data we have, the better. And one million words is not much by the standards of modern corpus linguistics. However, it is also important to consider the representativeness of the corpora in question and how well their constituent texts have been sampled (as in the commentary on Activity D7.1). Two very large corpora that are not representative and do not match each other in terms of sampling strategy will not make good comparators. And, of course, there is the added problem that for some periods of the history of English (e.g. Old English) we simply do not have a lot of data to work with.

GLOSSARY OF LINGUISTIC TERMS

accent A speaker's accent is the way that he/she pronounces their particular variety of the language that they speak. For example, the Birmingham accent differs phonologically from the Newcastle accent. A speaker's accent can indicate where he/she is from, what social class they belong to, how educated they are, etc. It is not uncommon to hear people speaking Standard English with a regional accent, though it would be unusual to hear someone speaking a regional dialect using Received Pronunciation. (See also *dialect*).

adjective Adjectives can either function as the head of an adjective phrase ('I am *very hungry*') or as modifiers in a noun phrase (The *large brown* cow). Most adjectives are gradable and have a base form, a comparative form and a superlative form. It is often possible to tell whether a word is an adjective by seeing if you can make a comparative or superlative form, as in *tall* (base form), *taller* (comparative) and *tallest* (superlative). Usually, adjectives specify the properties of a noun and can be descriptive ('The *large brown* cow') or evaluative ('The *most beautiful* cow').

adverb Adverbs function as the head of an adverb phrase. Sometimes the head is preceded by modifiers, which are often adverbs of degree. Here are some examples (the adverb phrases are underlined and the head is in italics): 'The professor gesticulated <u>*wildly*</u>'; 'He shouted <u>exceptionally *loudly*</u>'; 'The students applauded <u>very *enthusiastically* indeed</u>'. Adverbs can also function as modifiers in adjective phrases (the adjective phrases are underlined and the modifying adverbs are italicised): I am <u>*extremely* hungry</u>; The professor was <u>*very* pleased</u>; It was <u>*too* hot</u>. Adverbs often end in -ly, but be careful – sometimes what looks like an adverb is actually an adjective, e.g. *friendly*. Some adverbs also have comparative and superlative forms (e.g. She danced *well/better/best*; He danced *gracefully/more gracefully/most gracefully*). Adverbs give more information about the action, process, state, etc. described in the verb phrase. Adverbs can express manner (*quickly, well*), place (*here, there, somewhere*), time (*now, then, last night, six weeks ago*), duration (*constantly, briefly, always*), frequency (*daily, weekly*) and degree (*hardly, rather, quite*).

conjunction Conjunctions link phrases and clauses and can be either co-ordinating (e.g. *and, but, or, either, nor, neither*) or subordinating (e.g. *although, when, after, because, since, whereby, while, unless, as, but*). There are more subordinating than co-ordinating conjunctions. Subordinating conjunctions introduce a clause within a sentence that is linked to the main clause but which cannot stand on its own, e.g. '<u>*Although* he tried hard</u>, the hungry linguist could not resist eating more cake.'

consonant A consonant is a speech sound that is produced when the outflow of air from the lungs is restricted in some way by the articulators (e.g. teeth, lips, tongue).

determiner Determiners introduce noun phrases (e.g. '_A_ tiger ate _the_ hunters'). The definite and indefinite articles (_the_ and _a_, respectively) are determiners, as are demonstratives like _this, that, those, these, my, your, all, any, some, most_.

dialect A dialect is a sub-variety of a particular language. Dialects differ in terms of words, grammatical structures and pronunciations. For example, speakers of Yorkshire dialect may use words or grammatical structures that are not used in other dialects of English. Similarly, their pronunciation will vary from that of speakers of other dialects. The term _dialect_ is considered by some people to have negative connotations. For example, non-linguists often think of dialects as corruptions of a standard form. To avoid these problems, linguists sometimes use the term _variety_ as a neutral alternative. Note that the term _dialect_ incorporates differences in pronunciation, while the term _accent_ refers solely to phonological characteristics. (See also _accent_.)

digraph A digraph is a two-letter combination that represents one phoneme. For example, the digraph <sh> represents the phoneme /ʃ/, as in the English word _ship_. A digraph is a type of grapheme. (See also _grapheme_ and _graph_.)

diphthong A diphthong is a long vowel that is composed of two distinct vowel sounds with a glide between them, e.g. /au/, as in _south_.

discourse If we think of the elements that make up language as being hierarchically structured, then morphemes combine to form words, words combine to form phrases, phrases combine to form clauses, and clauses combine to form sentences (see the introduction to section C for more details). In each case, the unit of language that we are dealing with is larger than the last. The term _discourse_ refers to the next level up in the hierarchy; i.e. language above the level of the sentence. _Discourse_ is language that is meaningful and unified; that is, it is coherent (either syntactically or pragmatically). _Discourse_ can refer to both written and spoken language. Additionally, _discourse_ is used to refer to dynamic, communicative interaction between speakers and hearers, and writers and readers.

grammar Grammar refers to the structures that govern the formation of meaningful words and sentences in a language. Grammar can be sub-divided into _morphology_ ('word grammar') and _syntax_ ('sentence grammar').

graph A graph is a single letter that represents a particular phoneme. So the graph <k> represents the phoneme /k/. A graph is a type of _grapheme_. (See also _digraph_.)

grapheme A grapheme is a symbol used to represent a particular phoneme. Graphemes are indicated by angle brackets. For example, in English the grapheme <sh> represents the phoneme /ʃ/ and the grapheme <p> represents the phoneme /p/. (See also _graph_ and _digraph_.)

graphology Graphology is the study of the appearance of language in its written form. It may be useful to think of graphology as the written equivalent of phonology. That is, while the phonological level of language comprises the speech sounds of that language, the graphological level comprises its visual characteristics. (See also *phonology*.)

inflection An inflection is a morphological ending on a word or change in the form of a word that affects its grammatical function. For example, <er> is an inflection that can be appended to the base form of adjectives to form a comparative.

lexis The term *lexis* is a technical term to refer to the vocabulary of a language. The related term *lexical item* (or *lexeme*) is a more precise way of describing what non-linguists might call a word. For example, linguists would say that *jumping*, *jumped* and *jumps* are all different forms of the same lexical item, *jump*.

monophthong A monophthong is a pure vowel; e.g. /æ/, as in *cat* (compare this with a *diphthong*).

morpheme A morpheme is the smallest meaningful unit of language. Note that phonemes combine to form morphemes. Morphemes can be free (e.g. 'chair, 'hunt') or <u>bound</u> ('chair<u>s</u>, 'hunt<u>ing</u>'). (See also *morphology*.)

morphology Morphology is the study of word structure and how morphemes can combine to form meaningful words. (See also *grammar* and *syntax*.)

noun Nouns can function as the head of a noun phrase, as in 'The bright blue racing <u>car</u>.' *Car* is the head of this phrase; without the word *car* this phrase is incomplete. However, the head of a noun phrase is not always the final word in the phrase. Sometimes the head word can be post-modified (as opposed to the pre-modification in the above example); consider 'The bright blue racing <u>car</u> that won the race.' Also, some noun phrases (NPs) can be just one word long, as in '<u>Cows</u> (NP) eat (VP) <u>grass</u> (NP)'. A good test for a noun is to see whether you can put the definite article (*the*) before it. If you can, it is likely to be a noun. You can sometimes recognise a noun by its suffix. Typical suffixes include: *lead<u>er</u>, rac<u>ism</u>, stat<u>ion</u>, happ<u>iness</u>, prosper<u>ity</u>*. Some nouns can also be pluralised by adding either <s>, <es> or <ies>. Nouns often refer to physical things; e.g. people, places, objects, substances. These are concrete nouns. However, nouns can also refer to abstract concepts. Abstract nouns include *happiness, love, anniversary, pain, thought*.

orthography Orthography refers to the spelling system of a language. The study of a language's orthography is therefore the study of spelling in that language.

phoneme A phoneme is the smallest unit of sound. This can be indicated by considering minimal pairs; that is, words that differ in just one phoneme. For example, the words *tip* and *tap* are distinguishable in meaning only because of their different vowel sounds. This means that the /ɪ/ and /æ/ must be distinct phonemes, because replacing the phoneme /ɪ/ in *tip* with /æ/ changes the meaning of the word. Compare, on the other hand, the phonemes /t/ and /ʔ/. Replacing the /t/ in *bottle* with the glottal stop does not change the meaning of the word (compare /bɒtl/ and /bɒʔl/); therefore, /t/ and /ʔ/ must be considered variants of the same phoneme, rather than distinct phonemes. (See also *phonology*.)

phonetics Phonetics is the study of speech sounds: how they are produced and received, and what their physical characteristics are.

phonology Phonology is the study of how speech sounds are organised systematically and how they pattern together.

pragmatics Pragmatics is the study of meaning and how context affects this. If a librarian in the university library asks me if I have my library card and I say 'Damn! I've forgotten my wallet!', it is likely that the librarian would infer my answer to mean 'no', on the basis of being able to infer that my wallet is where I usually keep it. But if, on entering the pub, I say 'Damn! I've forgotten my wallet!', whoever I happen to be with might understand me to mean 'Can you pay for the drinks?' (and I can guess what their answer would be!). Pragmatics tries to explain how meanings can be inferred that are different from the surface-level meaning of the utterance.

preposition Prepositions usually express relations of position in space and time. They are often followed by a noun phrase, e.g. 'Dorothy travelled _over_ the rainbow', 'I parked the car _outside_ the house'.

pronoun Pronouns can be used in place of a noun phrase. For example, in the sentence 'The exceptionally well-organised lecturer smiled warmly', we can replace the noun phrase (_The exceptionally well-organised lecturer_) with a pronoun, e.g. '_She_ smiled warmly'. Pronouns cannot be modified with determiners or adjectives.

semantics Semantics is the study of meaning, incorporating lexical meaning and structural meaning (e.g. phrases, clauses and sentences), and how this is generated in language. While _pragmatics_ considers the effects of context on meaning, semantics does not.

syntax Syntax is the study of sentence structure and the rules governing the formation of meaningful sentences in a language. Note that in this case, 'rules' means descriptive as opposed to prescriptive rules; see C4 for more details on this distinction. (See also _morphology_ and _grammar_.)

text We are used to thinking of _text_ as referring to written language but linguists often use the term in a technical sense. _Text_, in this case, is the product of discourse, either written or spoken. So, a transcript of an interview is a text, even though the original discourse was spoken language.

utterance An utterance is a unit of spoken language that may or may not have the formal characteristics of a sentence.

variety The term _variety_ can be used as a neutral alternative to _dialect_ to avoid any negative connotations that the latter term may have. Since non-linguists tend to think of dialects as being specifically regional forms of language (e.g. Scouse, Lancashire), _variety_ can be particularly useful to refer to non-geographical aspects of language variation (e.g. linguistic differences based on social class). _Variety_ is also used to refer to international variants of a language (e.g. Australian English, Indian English, etc.).

verb Main verbs function as the head of a verb phrase (VP). Sometimes the verb phrase will consist of just the main verb, and other times there may be auxiliary verbs before it. Here are some examples of VPs (underlined), with the main verb in italics: 'Cows _eat_ grass', 'I was _avoiding_ work', 'The mice must have _eaten_ all the cheese!' Verbs have five different forms (see the following table). For regular verbs, the past and past participle form are the same. For irregular verbs, these are different. Verbs can refer to physical actions (_run, jump_), states of being (_is_), mental processes (_think, believe, understand_), etc.

	Infinitive	Present	Past	Present participle	Past participle
Regular	walk	walk/s	walked	walking	walked
Irregular	drink	drink/s	drank	drinking	drunk
	give	give/s	gave	giving	given
	fly	fly/ies	flew	flying	flown

vowel A vowel is a speech sound that is produced when the airflow from the lungs is not impeded as it is in the production of consonants. Different vowel sounds are achieved by varying the shape of the mouth cavity.

TIMELINE OF EXTERNAL EVENTS IN THE HISTORY OF ENGLISH

The following is a select list of external sociopolitical and cultural events that have had some influence on the development of the English language. The events listed are drawn from section A of this book, with some additions. You will no doubt be able to think of more.

	55 BCE	Romans attempt invasion of Britain under Emperor Julius Caesar.
	43 CE	Successful Roman invasion of Britain led by Aulus Plautius under Emperor Claudius.
	61	Boudicca, Queen of the Celtic Iceni tribe, leads a failed uprising against the Romans.
	401	Last Roman legion leaves Britain.
Old English	449	Arrival of Angles, Saxons and Jutes.
	597	Christianity re-introduced to Britain by the Benedictine monk Augustine, who later becomes the first Archbishop of Canterbury.
	663	Oswald becomes ruler of Northumbria and begins the process of founding churches and monasteries, including those at Lindisfarne and Jarrow.
	731	The Venerable Bede completes his *Ecclesiastical History of the English People*.
	787	First Viking raid on Britain.
	793	Viking raid on the monastery at Lindisfarne.
	794	Viking raid on the monastery at Jarrow, home of Bede.
	865	Vikings Ivar the Boneless and Halfdan conquer East Anglia.
	871	Vikings attack Wessex; Saxon king Ethelred is defeated; Ethelred dies and is succeeded by Alfred who pays off the Viking attackers.
	876	Alfred wins a decisive victory over Guthrum, Danish King of East Anglia; Danes are pushed back from Wessex; Guthrum is baptised.
	886	Line of Danelaw established, dividing Saxon and Danish territory; Alfred becomes first King of the Anglo-Saxons.
	late 800s	Work begins on the annals (historical records) that will eventually form the *Anglo-Saxon Chronicle*, the first history of the Anglo-Saxons.
	937	Athelstan, grandson of Alfred, is crowned King of the Anglo-Saxons and Danes.
	991	Anglo-Saxon army led by East Saxon ealdorman Byrhtnoth is defeated by a Viking army led by Olaf Tryggvason, later King of Norway.
	994	Tryggvason and Svein Forkbeard, King of Denmark, continue attacks against the Anglo-Saxons.
	1002	Ethelred the Unready marries Emma of Normandy.

	1014	Svein Forkbeard drives King Ethelred (the Unready) into exile in Normandy and is crowned King of England.
	1016	Cnut succeeds his father, Svein Forkbeard, to the throne of England; Ethelred the Unready dies; Cnut marries Emma of Normandy.
	1035	Cnut dies; coronation of Cnut's son, Harold Harefoot.
	1040	Harefoot dies and is succeeded by his half-brother, Harthacnut, son of Cnut and Emma of Normandy.
	1042	Harthacnut dies and is succeeded by his half-brother, Edward (the Confessor), son of Ethelred the Unready and Emma of Normandy.
	1066	Edward the Confessor dies childless; Battle of Hastings is fought to determine the successor the English throne; William the Conqueror emerges victorious and is crowned King of England on Christmas Day.
	1086	Domesday Book is completed on the orders of William the Conqueror, providing a complete administrative record of the land and stock in England.
	early 1100s	Henry I establishes the Exchequer as a government department.
Middle English	1154	Last entry in the *Anglo-Saxon Chronicle*.
	1204	King John loses the Duchy of Normandy, a major territorial connection with France, to the French king Philip II.
	1215	King John signs *Magna Carta*.
	1337	Beginning of the Hundred Years War between England and France.
	1348	Bubonic plague wipes out around a third of the population of Britain.
	1382	The first translation of the Bible from Latin into Middle English is made by John Wycliffe.
	1387	Geoffrey Chaucer begins *The Canterbury Tales*.
	1476	William Caxton sets up England's first printing press at Westminster.
	1492	Christopher Columbus voyages to the Americas.
	1525	William Tyndale translates the Bible into English from the original Hebrew.
Early Modern English	1536	Act of Union between England and Wales.
	1539	Henry VIII commissions the first official Bible in English.
	1564	Birth of Shakespeare.
	1600	British East India Company founded.
	1604	Publication of first monolingual English dictionary, *A Table Alphabeticall*, by Robert Cawdrey.
	1607	An English colony is established at Jamestown, Virginia, paving the way for the English colonisation of North America.
	1611	Publication of the King James Bible.
	1691	Stephen Skinner produces *A New English Dictionary*, incorporating common words as well as 'hard' ones and providing etymologies for these.
	1707	Act of Union between England and Scotland; formation of Great Britain.

Late Modern English	1755	Samuel Johnson publishes *A Dictionary of the English Language.*
	1770	Captain James Cook and the crew of *HMS Endeavour* are the first Europeans to reach Australia, landing at Botany Bay.
	1773	Enclosure Act prevents the grazing of animals on common land.
	1775–83	American War of Independence sees Britain lose its American colonies.
	1800	Act of Union between Great Britain and Ireland; formation of the United Kingdom of Great Britain and Ireland.
	1819	Peterloo Massacre takes place at St Peter's Field, Manchester, as around 80,000 working-class protestors gather to demand parliamentary reform and the vote; 18 people are killed by cavalry and around 650 injured.
	1828	Noah Webster publishes *An American Dictionary of the English Language.*
	1837	Queen Victoria accedes to the throne and is crowned Queen of the United Kingdom of Great Britain and Ireland.
	1840	Introduction of the Uniform Penny Post to the UK.
	1870	Elementary Education Act makes education compulsory for 5 to 13 year-olds.
	1876	Alexander Graham Bell patents the telephone.
	1914–18	First World War.
Modern English	1917	Daniel Jones publishes the first edition of his *English Pronouncing Dictionary*, using RP as his model for describing the speech sounds of English.
	1921	Partition of Ireland into Northern Ireland and Southern Ireland; establishment of the United Kingdom of Great Britain and Northern Ireland.
	1922	Foundation of the BBC.
	1928	*Oxford English Dictionary* is completed.
	1932	BBC begins regular television broadcasts.
	1939–45	Second World War.
	1947	India becomes independent of the British Empire and is partitioned into two states: India and Pakistan.
	1948	*SS Empire Windrush* docks at Tilbury, near London, bringing over 1,000 passengers from the Caribbean and marking the beginning of Caribbean migration to the UK.
	1963	The Robbins Report to the UK Government's Committee on Higher Education recommends the expansion of the university sector via the addition of a large number of new universities.
	1969	ARPANET, the precursor to the internet, is developed by an offshoot research agency of the US Defense Department.
	1971	Ray Tomlinson develops email.
	1973	First mobile phone call, by Martin Cooper of Motorola.
	1989	Tim Berners-Lee invents the World Wide Web.
	1994	SMS text messaging between phones introduced.
	2001	UK Labour government announces a target of 50% of young adults in higher education or training by 2010.
	2005	Launch of YouTube.
	2009	WhatsApp launched.
	2016	Election of Donald Trump as US president; referendum on the UK exiting the EU.
	2020	The UK leaves the European Union.

FURTHER READING

This book is a starting point. It provides a broad overview of some of the major aspects of the history of English and my hope is that it will leave you wanting to explore this topic further. Below are some suggestions as to books, articles and other resources that you will find useful for investigating particular topic areas in more detail.

BOOKS, CHAPTERS AND JOURNAL ARTICLES

General histories of English

❑ Baugh and Cable (2002) has long been a standard introduction to the history of English and is particularly good on the external history of the language. Blake (1996) is a history of standard English that dispenses with the traditional division of the language into Old, Middle, Early Modern and Modern varieties and as such provides an interesting alternative perspective on the way that the history of English is often packaged, as does Crystal (2005). Watts and Trudgill (2002) contains articles examining alternative histories of English, and Wales (2006) looks specifically at the development of Northern English. For a focus on the social and cultural aspects of the history of English, as well as some of the debates surrounding these, try Knowles (1997). *The Cambridge History of the English Language* is a comprehensive six-volume series of books and is highly recommended.

❑ For more information on the internal history of the language, Pyles and Algeo (1993) provides considerable detail. Freeborn (2006) is a comprehensive and chronologically ordered survey that is especially good on the development of written English, and has a strong emphasis on the examination of primary sources. Fennell (2001) is an excellent and highly accessible textbook that combines both an internal and external history of the language, and is an ideal next step once you have read an entry-level textbook such as this one. So too is Van Gelderen (2014). For a summary of the methodological practices of historical linguistics, see Culpeper and McIntyre (2015).

❑ For a solid description of English at its various stages, see Smith (2005). Horobin (2009b) and Pons-Sanz (2014) are excellent introductions to Old, Middle and Early Modern English that take a thematic rather than chronological approach to the subject. Volume 5 of *The Cambridge History of the English Language* focuses on the development and history of English in Britain and overseas.

❑ Crystal (2010) was written to accompany a major exhibition on the history of the English language, curated by the British Library in London in 2011, and contains a wide range of illustrations of texts and artefacts.

Old English

❏ Two very accessible introductions to Old English language are McCully and Hilles (2005) and Hough and Corbett (2007). When you feel ready to tackle something at a higher level, Mitchell (1995) is an excellent and very readable account of Old English and also provides a good deal of contextual information about the Anglo-Saxon world. Mitchell and Robinson (2007) is an extremely thorough guide to Old English grammar.

❏ Volume 1 of *The Cambridge History of the English Language* (Hogg 1992b) provides in-depth coverage of English from its earliest origins up until 1066. Brinton and Bergs (2017a) is another comprehensive survey.

❏ An understanding of phonetics and grammar is undoubtedly of help when it comes to deciphering Old English. If you feel you need to brush up on the basics, Jeffries (2006) is an ideal introductory textbook focusing on the description of English at all linguistic levels. For a specialist text on phonetics and phonology, try Collins et al. (2019), and for grammar and vocabulary, Jackson (2002).

Middle English

❏ A standard textbook on Middle English, which also contains considerable discussion of Middle English literature, is Burrow and Turville-Petre (1996). Smith and Horobin (2005) is a good, general introduction to Middle English and Horobin (2007) is a very accessible account of Chaucer's variety. Machan (2003) provides a fascinating account of the status and use of Middle English during the Middle English period.

❏ Volume 2 of *The Cambridge History of the English Language* (Blake 1992) provides comprehensive coverage of English from the Norman Conquest to the advent of printing. Brinton and Bergs (2017b) is also an excellent high-level account of the English of the period.

Early Modern English

❏ A good descriptive account of Early Modern English is Barber (1997). Görlach (1991) is a detailed and comprehensive study, with a greater focus on the mechanisms for change and development in the language, as is Nevalainen (2006).

❏ For an insight into Early Modern English speech, see Culpeper and Kytö's (2010) comprehensive study. Key methodological issues in studying dialogue via written data are discussed in Culpeper and Kytö (1999 and 2000). Crystal (2016b) is a dictionary of original Shakespearean pronunciation.

❏ On the issue of standardisation see especially Wright (2000), Nevalainen and Tieken-Boon van Ostade (2006) and Pillière et al. (2018).

❏ For comprehensive coverage of the period see volume 3 of *The Cambridge History of the English Language* (Lass 1999b) and Bergs and Brinton (2017b).

Eighteenth-century English to the present day

❑ Volume 4 of *The Cambridge History of the English Language* (Romaine 1999) provides detailed coverage of many aspects of the language of this period.

❑ Bailey (1996) and Görlach (1999) are comprehensive overviews of nineteenth-century English. Beal (2004) is an excellent study of later modern English.

❑ Biber et al. (1999) is a comprehensive, corpus-based grammar of spoken and written Present Day English, while Leech (2003) and Mair and Leech (2006) examine recent grammatical developments in English.

World Englishes

❑ For an introduction to the notion of World Englishes, see Jenkins (2015) and Saraceni (2015).

❑ Crystal (2003) is a good introduction to some of the important themes concerning English as a global language, while Bailey and Görlach (1984) provides in-depth surveys of the development and spread of English around the world. Murphy (2018) explodes a number of myths about the relationship between British and American English and is highly readable.

❑ Volume 6 of *The Cambridge History of the English Language* (Algeo 2001) focuses particularly on the development of English in North America, and Tottie (2002) is an accessible introduction to the linguistic and sociolinguistic aspects of American English. Bergs and Brinton (2017b) is a comprehensive survey of varieties of English within the context of the history of the language.

ONLINE RESOURCES

Web-based dictionaries and corpora

Bosworth-Toller Anglo-Saxon Dictionary

www.bosworthtoller.com/about
An online version of the dictionary of Old English produced by Joseph Bosworth in 1898 and supplemented in 1921 by Northcote Toller.

Dictionary of Old English

www.doe.utoronto.ca/pages/index.html
The website of an ongoing project to produce a comprehensive online dictionary of Old English; includes a corpus of Old English texts.

English-Corpora.org

www.english-corpora.org
On online interface for searching a wide range of free corpora of English, including the British National Corpus (BNC) of contemporary English and the Corpus of Historical American English (COHA).

Linguistic Atlas of Late Mediaeval English

> www.lel.ed.ac.uk/ihd/elalme/elalme_frames.html
> A web-based version of *A Linguistic Atlas of Late Mediaeval English* (McIntosh et al. 1986), offering an excellent resource for Middle English dialectology.

Middle English Compendium

> https://quod.lib.umich.edu/m/middle-english-dictionary
> Includes a Middle English Dictionary, bibliography of primary texts and a searchable corpus of Middle English prose and verse.

Other useful websites

Glottolog

> https://glottolog.org
> Glottolog is a comprehensive survey of the world's languages.

Old English Translator

> www.oldenglishtranslator.co.uk
> A useful tool enabling translation from Modern English to Old English and vice versa.

Original Pronunciation

> www.originalpronunciation.com
> This site details David Crystal's project to promote the performance of works from early periods of English in accents that would have been spoken at the time.

Twitter

DARE

> @darewords
> DARE is the Dictionary of American Regional English based at the University of Wisconsin-Madison.

M. Lynne Murphy

> @lynneguist
> M. Lynne Murphy is Professor of Linguistics at the University of Sussex and tweets about the differences between British and American English.

Medieval Manuscripts

@BLMedieval
This is an account run by the British Library, tweeting about their collection of medieval manuscripts, with accompanying images.

Old English Wordhord

@OEWordhord
Each day, Hana Videen tweets a definition of an Old English word. This is a great resource for learning new Old English vocabulary.

Simon Horobin

@SCPHorobin
Simon Horobin is Professor of English Language and Literature at the University of Oxford. He tweets about etymology.

The OED

@OED
This is the Twitter account of the Oxford English Dictionary, featuring a word-of-the-day and related news.

REFERENCES

Adams, R. and Turville-Petre, T. (2014) 'The London book trade and the lost history of *Piers Plowman*', *Review of English Studies* 65: 219–35.

Aitchison, J. (2001) *Language Change: Progress or Decay?* 3rd edition. Cambridge: Cambridge University Press.

Aitchison, J. (2013) *Language Change: Progress or Decay?* 4th edition. Cambridge: Cambridge University Press.

Algeo, J. (ed.) (2001) *The Cambridge History of the English Language. Vol. 6. English in North America.* Cambridge: Cambridge University Press.

Allan, K. (2009) *A Diachronic Approach to Metaphor and Metonymy: How Target Concepts for Intelligence are Cognitively and Culturally Motivated.* Oxford: Blackwell.

Altendorf, U. (2003) *Estuary English: Levelling at the Interface of RP and South-Eastern British English.* Tübingen: Narr.

Archibald, E. (2010) 'Macaronic poetry', in Saunders, C. (ed.) *A Companion to Medieval Poetry*, pp. 277–88. Oxford: Wiley-Blackwell.

Arnold, T. (1871) *Select English Works of John Wyclif.* Oxford: Clarendon Press.

Bailey, R. W. (1996) *Nineteenth Century English.* Ann Arbor, MI: University of Michigan Press.

Bailey, R. W. and Görlach, M. (1984) *English as a World Language.* Cambridge: Cambridge University Press.

Barber, C. (1964) *Linguistic Change in Present-Day English.* Edinburgh and London: Oliver and Boyd.

Barber, C. (1976) *Early Modern English.* London: André Deutsch.

Barber, C. (1997) *Early Modern English.* 2nd edition. Cambridge: Cambridge University Press.

Barber, C., Beal, J. and Shaw, P. (2009) *The English Language: A Historical Introduction.* Cambridge: Cambridge University Press.

Barr, H. (2001) *Socioliterary Practice in Late Medieval England.* Oxford: Oxford University Press.

Bauer, L. (1994) *Watching English Change: An Introduction to the Study of Linguistic Change in Standard Englishes in the Twentieth Century.* London: Longman.

Baugh, A. C. (1967) *A Literary History of England.* 2nd edition. London: Routledge.

Baugh, A. C. and Cable, T. (1993) *A History of the English Language.* 4th edition. London: Routledge.

Baugh, A. C. and Cable, T. (2002) *A History of the English Language.* 5th edition. London: Prentice Hall.

Beadle, R. (1991) 'Prolegomena to a literary geography of later medieval Norfolk', in Reddy, F. (ed.) *Regionalism in Late Medieval Manuscripts and Texts: Essays Celebrating the Publication of 'A Linguistic Atlas of Late Mediaeval English'*, pp. 89–108. Cambridge: D.S. Brewer.

Beal, J. (2004) *English in Modern Times*. London: Hodder Arnold.

Bede (1990 [731]) *Ecclesiastical History of the English People*. Translated by Leo Sherley-Price and revised by R. E. Latham. London: Penguin.

Benskin, M. (2004) 'Chancery Standard', in Kay, C., Hough, C. and Wotherspoon, I. (eds) *New Perspectives on English Historical Linguistics: Selected Papers from 12 ICEHL, Glasgow, 21–26 August 2002. Vol. II: Lexis and Transmission*, pp. 1–40. Amsterdam: John Benjamins.

Benskin, M. and Laing, M. (1981) 'Translations and *Mischsprachen* in Middle English manuscripts', in Benskin, M. and Samuels, M. (eds) *So Meny People, Longages, and Tonges: Philological Essays in Scots and Mediaeval English presented to Angus McIntosh*, pp. 55–106. Edinburgh: Middle English Dialect Project.

Bergh, A. E. (1903) (ed.) *The Writings of Thomas Jefferson* (Vol. XIII). Washington, DC: The Thomas Jefferson Memorial Association.

Bergs, A. (2000) 'Social networks in pre-1500 Britain: problems, prospects, examples', *European Journal of English Studies* 4: 239–251.

Bergs, A. (2005) *Social Networks and Historical Sociolinguistics: Studies in Morphosyntactic Variation in the Paston Letters (1421–1503)*. Berlin: Mouton de Gruyter.

Bergs, A. and Brinton, L. (eds) (2017a) *The History of English, Volume 4: Early Modern English*. Berlin: Mouton de Gruyter.

Bergs, A. and Brinton, L. (eds) (2017b) *The History of English, Volume 5: Varieties of English*. Berlin: Mouton de Gruyter.

Biber, D., Johansson, S., Leech, G., Conrad, S. and Finegan, E. (1999) *The Longman Grammar of Spoken and Written English*. London: Longman.

Björkman, E. (1969) *Scandinavian Loan-words in Middle English*. New York: Greenwood Press.

Blake, N. (ed.) (1992) *The Cambridge History of the English Language. Vol. 2. 1066–1476*. Cambridge: Cambridge University Press.

Blake, N. (1996) *A History of the English Language*. Basingstoke: Palgrave.

Blank, A. (1999) 'Why do new meanings occur? A cognitive typology of the motivations for lexical semantic change, in Blank, A. and Koch, P. (eds) *Historical Semantics and Cognition*, pp. 61–89. Berlin: Mouton de Gruyter.

Bloomfield, L. (1933) *Language*. New York: Henry Holt.

Bourdieu, P. (1977) *Outline of a Theory of Practice*. Translated by Richard Nice. Cambridge: Cambridge University Press.

Breeze, A. (2002) 'Seven types of Celtic loanword', in Filppula, M., Klemola, J. and Pitkänen, H. (eds) *The Celtic Roots of English*, pp. 175–81. Joensuu: University of Joensuu.

Brinton, L. and Bergs, A. (eds) (2017a) *The History of English, Volume 2: Old English*. Berlin: Mouton de Gruyter.

Brinton, L. and Bergs, A. (eds) (2017b) *The History of English, Volume 3: Middle English*. Berlin: Mouton de Gruyter.

Brutt-Griffler, J. (2002) *World English: A Study of Its Development*. Clevedon: Multilingual Matters.

Bugaj, J. (2004) *Middle Scots Inflectional System in the South-West of Scotland*. Frankfurt: Peter Lang.

Burchfield, R. (ed.) (1994) *The Cambridge History of the English Language. Vol. 5. English in Britain and Overseas: Origins and Development*. Cambridge: Cambridge University Press.

Burnley, D. (1992) *The History of the English Language: A Source Book*. London: Longman.

Burridge, K. and Mulder, J. (1998) *English in Australia and New Zealand*. Oxford: Oxford University Press.

Burrow, J. A. and Turville-Petre, T. (1996) *A Book of Middle English*. 2nd edition. Oxford. Blackwell.

Bybee, J. (2003) 'Mechanisms of change in grammaticization: the role of frequency', in Joseph, B. D. and Janda, R. D. (eds) *The Handbook of Historical Linguistics*, pp. 602–23. Oxford: Blackwell.

Cameron, A., Amos, A. C., diPaolo Healey, A. et al. (2007) *Dictionary of Old English: A to G*. Toronto: Dictionary of Old English Project. https://tapor.library.utoronto.ca/doe/.

Cameron, K. (1996) *English Place Names*. London: Batsford.

Cannon, C. (2006) 'Chaucer and the language of London', in Butterfield, A. (ed.) *Chaucer and the City* (Chaucer Studies XXXVII), pp. 79–94. Cambridge: D.S. Brewer.

Carney, E. (1994) *A Survey of English Spelling*. London: Routledge.

Cassidy, F. G. (1984) 'Geographical variation of English in the United States', in Bailey, R. W. and Görlach, M. (eds) *English as a World Language*, pp. 177–209. Cambridge: Cambridge University Press.

Cawdrey, R. C. (1604) *A Table Alphabeticall*. London.

Christianson, C. P. (1989) 'A community of book artisans in Chaucer's London', *Viator* 20: 207–218.

Christy, T. C. (1983) *Uniformitarianism in Linguistics*. Amsterdam/Philadelphia: John Benjamins.

Clanchy, M. T. (1993) *From Memory to Written Record: England 1066–1307*. Oxford: Blackwell.

Clark Hall, J. R., with supplement by Merritt, H. D. (1960) *A Concise Anglo-Saxon Dictionary*. 4th edition. Cambridge: Cambridge University Press.

Close, J. and Aarts, B. (2010) 'Current change in the modal system of English: a case study of *must, have to* and *have got to*', in Lenker, U., Huber, J. and Mailhammer, R. (eds.) *English Historical Linguistics 2008: Selected Papers from the Fifteenth International Conference on English Historical Linguistics (ICEHL 15), Munich 24–30 August 2008, Vol. I: The History of English Verbal and Nominal Constructions*, pp. 165–81. Amsterdam: John Benjamins.

Coates, J. (1983) *The Semantics of the Modal Auxiliaries*. London: Croom Helm.

Collins, B., Mees, I. M. and Carley, P. (2019) *Practical English Phonetics and Phonology: A Resource Book for Students*. 4th edition. Abingdon: Routledge.

Collins, P. (2009) *Modals and Quasi-modals in English*. Amsterdam: Rodopi.

Cooke, D. (1988) 'Ties that constrict: English as a Trojan horse', in Cumming, A., Gagne, A. and Dawson, J. (eds) *Awareness: Proceedings of the 1987 TESL Ontario Conference*, pp. 56–62. Toronto: TESL Ontario.

Corbett, G. (1979) 'The agreement hierarchy', *Journal of Linguistics* 15, 203–24.

Corbett, G. (1991) *Gender*. Cambridge: Cambridge University Press.

Corbett, J., McClure, J. D. and Stuart-Smith, J. (2003) 'A brief history of Scots', in Corbett, J., McClure, J. D. and Stuart-Smith, J. (eds) *The Edinburgh Companion to Scots*, pp. 1–17. Edinburgh: Edinburgh University Press.

Croft, W. (2000) *Explaining Language Change: An Evolutionary Approach*. Harlow: Longman.

Croft, W. (2006) 'Evolutionary models and functional-typological theories of language change', in van Kemenade, A. and Los, B. (eds) *The Handbook of the History of English*. Oxford: Blackwell.

Crowley, J. P. (1986) 'The study of Old English dialects', *English Studies* 67: 97–104.

Crystal, D. (1994) *Rediscover Grammar*. London: Longman.

Crystal, D. (1995) *The Cambridge Encyclopedia of the English Language*. Cambridge: Cambridge University Press.

Crystal, D. (2000) *Language Death*. Cambridge: Cambridge University Press.

Crystal, D. (2001) 'The future of Englishes', in Burns, A. and Coffin, C. (eds) *Analysing English in a Global Context*, pp. 53–64. London: Routledge.

Crystal, D. (2003) *English as a Global Language*. 2nd edition. Cambridge: Cambridge University Press.

Crystal, D. (2005) *The Stories of English*. London: Penguin.

Crystal, D. (2007) *How Language Works: How Babies Babble, Words Change Meaning, and Languages Live or Die*. London: Penguin.

Crystal, D. (2010) *Evolving English: One Language, Many Voices*. London: British Library.

Crystal, D. (2012) 'Plurilingualism, pluridialectism, pluriformity', in Pilar Díez, M., Place, R. and Fernández, O. (eds), *Plurilingualism: Promoting Co-operation Between Communities, People and Nations*, pp. 13–24. Bilbao: University of Deusto.

Crystal, D. (2016a) 'My priority for the next 50 years: an online cultural dictionary', Abridged version presented to an online IATEFL-TESOL seminar, November 2016; full version to appear in Barry Tomalin (ed.), 2017. *Training, Language, and Culture* 1(1): 13–27.

Crystal, D. (2016b) *Oxford Dictionary of Original Shakespearean Pronunciation*. Oxford: Oxford University Press.

Culpeper, J. and Kytö, M. (1999) 'Investigating non-standard language in a corpus of early modern English dialogues: methodological considerations and problems', in Taavitsainen, I., Melchers, G. and Pahta, P. (eds) *Writing in Non-standard English*, pp. 171–87. Amsterdam : John Benjamins.

Culpeper, J. and Kytö, M. (2000) 'Data in historical pragmatics: spoken interaction (re) cast as writing', *Journal of Historical Pragmatics* 1(2): 175–99.

Culpeper, J. and Kytö, M. (2010) *Early Modern English Dialogues: Spoken Interaction as Writing*. Cambridge: Cambridge University Press.

Culpeper, J. and McIntyre, D. (2015) 'Historical linguistics', in Braber, N., Cummings, L. and Morrish, L. (eds) *Exploring Language and Linguistics*, pp. 245–73. Cambridge: Cambridge University Press.

Cunliffe, B. (2013) *Britain Begins*. Oxford: Oxford University Press.

Curzan, A. (1999) 'Gender categories in early English grammars: their message to the modern grammarian', in Unterbeck, B. and Rissanen, M. (eds) *Gender in Grammar and Cognition*, pp. 561–76. Berlin: Mouton de Gruyter.

Curzan, A. (2003) *Gender Shifts in the History of English*. Cambridge: Cambridge University Press.

Dahl, Ö. (1999a) 'Animacy and the notion of semantic gender', in Unterbeck, B. and Rissanen, M. (eds) *Gender in Grammar and Cognition*, pp. 99–115. Berlin: Mouton de Gruyter.

Dahl, Ö. (1999b) 'Elementary gender distinctions', in Unterbeck, B. and Rissanen, M. (eds) *Gender in Grammar and Cognition*, pp. 577–93. Berlin: Mouton de Gruyter.

Davidson, M. C. (2001) *Language-mixing and Code-Switching in England in the Late Medieval Period*. PhD thesis, University of Toronto, Canada.

Davies, N. (2000) *The Isles: A History*. Basingstoke: Papermac.

Davis, N. (1971) *Paston Letters*. Oxford: Oxford University Press.

Dennison, D. (1998) 'Syntax', in Romaine, S. (ed.) *The Cambridge History of the English Language, Vol. 4: 1776–1997*, pp. 92–329. Cambridge: Cambridge University Press.

Devitt, A. (1989) *Standardizing Written English: Diffusion in the Case of Scotland 1520–1659*. Cambridge: Cambridge University Press.

Dillard, J. L. (1985) *Toward a Social History of American English*. Berlin: Walter de Gruyter.

Dillard, J. L. (1992) *A History of American English*. London: Pearson Education.

Diller, H. J. (1997/1998) 'Code-switching in medieval English drama', *Comparative Drama* 31(4): 500–537.

Doyle, A. I. and Parkes, M. B. (1978) 'The production of copies of the *Canterbury Tales* and the *Confessio Amantis* in the early fifteenth century', in Parkes, M. B. and Watson, A. G. (eds) *Medieval Scribes, Manuscripts, and Libraries: Essays Presented to N. R. Ker*, pp. 163–210. London: Scholar Press.

Eagleson, R. (1984) 'English in Australia and New Zealand', in Bailey, R. W. and Görlach, M. (eds) *English as a World Language*, pp. 415–38. Cambridge: Cambridge University Press.

Eckert, P. (2012) 'Three waves of variation study: the emergence of meaning in the study of sociolinguistic variation', *Annual Review of Anthropology* 41: 87–100.

Eckert, P. (no date) 'Third wave variation studies' [cited 1 September 2015]. Available from http://web.stanford.edu/~eckert/thirdwave.html.

Eckert, P. and McConnell-Ginet, S. (1992) 'Communities of practice: where language, gender, and power all live', in Hall, K., Bucholz, M. and Moonwomon, B. (eds) *Locating Power: Proceedings of the Second Berkeley Women and Language Conference*, pp. 89–99. Berkeley, CA: Berkeley Women and Language Group.

Edwards, A. S. G. (2014) 'Review: *Scribes and the City: London Guildhall Clerks and the Dissemination of Middle English Literature 1375–1425*. By Linne R. Mooney and Estelle Stubbs. York: York Medieval Press. 2013', *The Library: The Transactions of the Bibliographical Society* 15(1): 79–81.

Ekwall, E. (1956) *Studies on the Population of Medieval London*. Stockholm: Almqvist & Wiksell.

Ekwall, E. (1960) *The Concise Oxford Dictionary of English Place-Names*. Oxford: Oxford University Press.

Ellis, A. J. (1869) *On Early English Pronunciation*. London: The Philological Society.

Faiß, K. (1989) *Englische Sprachgeschichte*. Tübingen: Franke.

Feagin, C. (1994) '"Long I" as a microcosm of southern states speech', Paper given at NWAV1994. Ms., Zurich University.

Fennell, B. (2001) *A History of English: A Sociolinguistic Approach*. Oxford: Blackwell.

Fisher, J. H. (1996) *The Emergence of Standard English*. Lexington, KY: University of Kentucky Press.

Fisiak, J. (1968) *A Short Grammar of Middle English*. London: Oxford University Press.

Fitzmaurice, S. (2000a) 'Coalitions and the investigation of social influence in linguistic history', *European Journal of English Studies* 4: 265–276.

Fitzmaurice, S. (2000b) 'The Spectator, the politics of social networks, and language standardisation in eighteenth-century England', in Wright, L. (ed.) *The Development of Standard English 1300–1800: Theories, Descriptions, Conflicts*, pp. 195–218. Cambridge: Cambridge University Press.

Fitzmaurice, S. and Taavitsainen, I. (2007) 'Introduction', in Taavitsainen, I. and Fitzmaurice, S. (eds) *Methods in Historical Pragmatics*, pp. 1–10. Berlin and New York: Mouton de Gruyter.

Foulkes, P. and Docherty, G. (eds) (1999) *Urban Voices: Accent Studies in the British Isles*. London: Arnold.

Foxe, J. (1563) *Actes and Monuments*. London.

Freeborn, D. (2006) *From Old English to Standard English*. 3rd edition. Basingstoke: Palgrave.

Fukuda, T. (2010) 'Japanese students' perception of American English', in Stoke, A. M. (ed.) *JALT2009 Conference Proceedings*. Tokyo: JALT.

Gil, A. (1619) *Longonomia Anglica*. (2nd edition, 1621). London: Beale.

Godden, M. R. (1992) 'Literary language', in Hogg, R. M. (ed.) *The Cambridge History of the English Language. Vol. 1. The Beginnings to 1066*, pp. 490–535. Cambridge: Cambridge University Press.

Görlach, M. (1991) *Introduction to Early Modern English*. Cambridge: Cambridge University Press.

Görlach, M. (1994) *Einführung ins Frühneuenglische*. Heidelberg: Winter.

Görlach, M. (1999) *English in Nineteenth-Century England*. Cambridge: Cambridge University Press.

Green, L. J. (2002) *African American English*. Cambridge: Cambridge University Press.

Grund, P. (2017) 'Sociohistorical approaches', in Bergs, A. and Brinton, L. J. (eds) *English Historical Linguistics*, pp. 218–44. Cambridge: Cambridge University Press.

Gullberg, M., Indefrey, P. and Muysken, P. (2009) 'Research techniques for the study of code-switching', in Bullock, B. E. and Toribio, A. J. (eds) *The Cambridge Handbook of Linguistic Code-switching*, pp. 21–39. Cambridge: Cambridge University Press.

Gumperz, J. J. (1968) 'The speech community', in Sills, D. L. (ed.) *International Encyclopedia of the Social Sciences*, pp. 381–86. New York: Macmillan.

Gumperz, J. J. (1982) *Discourse Strategies*. Cambridge: Cambridge University Press.

Guzmán-González, T. (2003) 'Revisiting the revisited: could we survive without the Great Vowel Shift?', *Studia Anglica Posnaniensia* 39: 121–31.

Guzmán-González, T. (2005) 'Out of the past: a walk with labels and concepts, raiders of the lost evidence and a vindication of the role of writing', *International Journal of English Studies* 5: 13–32.

Halmari, H. and Regetz, T. (2011) 'Syntactic aspects of code-switching in Oxford, MS Bodley 649', in Schendl, H. and Wright, L. (eds) *Code-Switching in Early English*, pp. 115–53. Berlin and New York: De Gruyter Mouton.

Hamers, J. and Blanc, M. (2000) *Bilinguality and Bilingualism*. Cambridge: Cambridge University Press.

Hamilton, T (1833) *Men and Manners* (Vol. I). Edinburgh: William Blackwood.

Hart, J. (1551) *The Opening of the Unreasonable Writing of Our Inglish Toung.* Unpublished Ms.

Haugen, E. (1966) 'Dialect, language, nation', in Dil, A. S. (ed.) *The Ecology of Language: Essays by Einar Haugen,* pp. 237–54. Stanford, CA: Stanford University Press, [1972].

Healey, A. (2006) 'Straining words and striving voices: polysemy and ambiguity and the importance of context in the disclosure of meaning', in Walmsley, J. (ed.) *Inside Old English: Essays in Honour of Bruce Mitchell,* pp. 74–90. Oxford: Blackwell.

Held, D., McGrew, A., Goldblatt, D. and Perraton, J. (1999) *Global Transformations: Politics, Economics and Culture.* Cambridge: Polity Press.

Hock, H. H. (1991) *Principles of Historical Linguistics.* 2nd edition. Berlin and New York: Mouton de Gruyter.

Hogg, R. M. (1992a) 'Introduction', in Hogg, R. M. (ed.) *The Cambridge History of the English Language. Vol. I.: The Beginnings to 1066,* pp. 1–25. Cambridge: Cambridge University Press.

Hogg, R. M. (2016) *The Standardiz/sation of English.* Linguistics Association of Great Britain Educational Committee, 2016 [2000]. Available from http://lagb-education.org/wp-content/uploads/2016/01/SEhogg.pdf.

Hogg, R. M. (ed.) (1992b) *The Cambridge History of the English Language. Vol. I:. The Beginnings to 1066.* Cambridge: Cambridge University Press.

Hope, J. (2000) 'Rats, bats, sparrows and dogs: biology, linguistics and the nature of Standard English', in Wright, L. (ed.) *The Development of Standard English, 1300–1800: Theories, Descriptions, Conflicts,* pp. 49–56. Cambridge: Cambridge University Press.

Horobin, S. (2003) *Language of the Chaucer Tradition.* Woodbridge: Boydell and Brewer.

Horobin, S. (2007) *Chaucer's Language.* Basingstoke: Palgrave.

Horobin, S. (2009a) 'Adam Pinkhurst and the copying of British Library, MS Additional 35287 of the B version of *Piers Plowman', Yearbook of Langland Studies* 23: 61–83.

Horobin, S. (2009b) *Studying the History of Early English.* Basingstoke: Palgrave.

Horobin, S. (2011) 'Mapping the words', in Gillespie, A. and Wakelin, D. (eds) *The Production of Books in England 1350–1500,* pp. 59–78. Cambridge: Cambridge University Press.

Hough, C. and Corbett, J. (2007) *Beginning Old English.* Basingstoke: Palgrave.

Howe, S. (1996) *The Personal Pronouns in the Germanic Languages: A Study of Personal Pronoun Morphology and Change in the Germanic Languages from the First Records to the Present Day.* Berlin: Walter de Gruyter.

Huber, M. (2007) 'The Old Bailey Proceedings, 1674–1834: evaluating and annotating a corpus of 18th- and 19th-century spoken English', in Meurman-Solin, A. and Nurmi, A. (eds) *Annotating Variation and Change.* Helsinki: University of Helsinki. Available at: www.helsinki.fi/varieng/series/volumes/01/huber/

Hudson, A. (1981) 'A Lollard sect vocabulary?' in Benskin, M. and Samuels, M. (eds) *So Meny People, Longages, and Tonges: Philological Essays in Scots and Mediaeval English presented to Angus McIntosh,* pp. 15–30. Edinburgh: Middle English Dialect Project.

Hunt, T. (2011) 'The languages of medieval England', in Baldzuhn, M. and Putzo, C. (eds) *Mehrsprachigkeit im Mittelalter: Kulturelle, literarische, sprachliche und didaktische Konstellationen in europäischer Perspektive*, pp. 59–68. Berlin and New York: de Gruyter.

Hunter Blair, P. (1962 [1956]) *An Introduction to Anglo-Saxon England*. Cambridge: Cambridge University Press.

Hymes, D. (1974) *Foundations in Sociolinguistics: An Ethnographic Approach*. Philadelphia: University of Pennsylvania Press.

Ingham, R. (2011) Code-switching in the later medieval English lay subsidy rolls', in Schendl, H. and Wright, L. (eds) *Code-Switching in Early English*, pp. 95–114. Berlin: de Gruyter.

Jackson, H. (2002) *Grammar and Vocabulary: A Resource Book for Students*. London: Routledge.

James, E. (2001) *Britain in the First Millennium*. London: Arnold.

Jansen, S. (2018) 'Predicting the future of English: considerations when engaging with the public', *English Today* 34(1): 52–5.

Jefferson, J. A. (2013) 'Scribal responses to Latin in the manuscripts of the B-version of Piers Plowman', in Jefferson, J. A. and Putter, A. (eds) *Multilingualism in Medieval Britain (c. 1066–1520): Sources and Analysis*, pp. 195–208. Turnhout: Brepols.

Jeffries, L. (2006) *Discovering Language: The Structure of Modern English*. Basingstoke: Palgrave Macmillan.

Jenkins, J. (2015) *Global Englishes: A Resource Book for Students*. 3rd edition. Abingdon: Routledge.

Jespersen, O. (1909) *A Modern English Grammar on Historical Principles. Vol. I: Sounds and Spellings*. London: Allen and Unwin.

Johnson, F. R. (1944) 'Latin versus English: the sixteenth century debate over scientific vocabulary', *Studies in Philology* 41(2): 109–35.

Johnson, S. (1755) *A Dictionary of the English Language*. London.

Johnston, P. A. (1992) `English vowel shifting: one great vowel shift or two small vowel shifts?', *Diachronica* 9: 189–226.

Johnston, P. A. (1997) 'Older Scots phonology and its regional variation', in Jones, C. (ed.) *The Edinburgh History of the Scots Language*, pp. 47–111. Edinburgh: Edinburgh University Press.

Jones, D. (1917) *English Pronouncing Dictionary*. London: Dent.

Jones, M. A. (1995) *The Limits of Liberty: American History 1607–1992*. Oxford: Oxford University Press.

Judd, E. L. (1983) 'TESOL as a political act: a moral question, in Handscombe, J., Orem, R. A. and Taylor, B. P. (eds) *On TESOL '83*, pp. 265–73. Washington, DC: TESOL.

Kachru, B. (1982) 'Models for non-native Englishes', in Kachru, B. (ed.) (1992) *The Other Tongue: English Across Cultures*, 31–57. Urbana, IL: University of Illinois Press.

Kachru, B. (1984) 'South Asian English', in Bailey, R. W. and Görlach, M. (eds) *English as a World Language*, pp. 353–83. Cambridge: Cambridge University Press.

Kachru, B. (1985) "Standards, codification and sociolinguistic realism: the English language in the outer circle', in Quirk, R. and Widdowson, H. (eds) *English in the World: Teaching and Learning the Language and Literature*, pp. 11–30. Cambridge: Cambridge University Press.

Kachru, B. (1992a) 'The second diaspora of English', in Machan, T. and Scott, C. (eds) *English in Its Social Contexts: Essays in Historical Sociolinguistics*, pp. 230–52. Oxford: Oxford University Press.

Kachru, B. (1992b) 'World Englishes: approaches, issues and resources', *Language Teaching* 25(1): 1–14.

Kastovsky, D. (1992) 'Semantics and vocabulary', in Hogg, R. M. (ed.) *The Cambridge History of the English Language. Vol. I.: The beginnings to 1066*, pp. 290–408. Cambridge: Cambridge University Press.

Kay, C. (2000) 'Metaphors we lived by: pathways between Old and Modern English', in Roberts, J. and Nelson, J. L. (eds) *Essays on Anglo-Saxon and Related Themes in Memory of Dr Lynne Grundy*, pp. 273–85. London: King's College London Medieval Studies.

Kay, C. (2015) 'Old English: semantics and lexicon', in Bergs, A. and Brinton, L. J. (eds) *English Historical Linguistics*, pp. 313–25. Berlin: De Gruyter.

Kerby-Fulton, K. (1997) 'Langland and the bibliographic ego', in Justice, S. and Kerby-Fulton, K. (eds) *Written Work: Langland, Labor, and Authorship*, pp. 67–143. Philadelphia: University of Pennsylvania Press.

Kerby-Fulton, K. and Justice, S. (1998) 'Langlandian reading circles and the civil service in London and Dublin, 1380–1427', in Scase, W., Copeland. R. and Lawton, D. (1998) *New Medieval Literatures 1*, pp. 59–83. Oxford: Clarendon Press.

Kerby-Fulton, K., Hilmo, M. and Olson, L. (2012) *Opening Up Middle English Manuscripts: Literary and Visual Approaches*. Ithaca, NY: Cornell University Press.

Kibbee, D. (1991) *For to Speke Frenche Trewely. The French Language in England 1000–1600: Its Status, Description and Instruction*. Amsterdam: John Benjamins.

Kleparski, G. A. (1990) *Semantic Change in English: A Study of Evaluative Developments in the Domain of HUMANS*. Lublin: University Press of the Catholic University of Lublin.

Knappe, G. (1997) 'Though it is tough: on regional differences in the development and substitution of the Middle English voiceless velar fricative [x] in syllable coda position', *Zeitschrift für Dialektologie und Linguistik* (Special issue on Language in Time and Space: Studies in Honour of Wolfgang Viereck on the Occasion of his 60th Birthday, ed. by Ramisch, H. and Wynne, K.) 97: 139–163.

Knowles, G. (1997) *A Cultural History of the English Language*. London: Arnold.

Kopaczyk, J. and Jucker, A. H. (eds) (2013) *Communities of Practice in the History of English*. Amsterdam: John Benjamins.

Krapp, G. P. (1910) *Modern English*. New York.

Krapp, G. P. (1925) *The English Language in America*. New York: The Century Company.

Krug, M. (2003a) '(Great) vowel shifts present and past: meeting ground for structural and natural phonologists', *Penn Working Papers in Linguistics (Selected papers from NWAVE 31 at Stanford)* 9(2): 107–22.

Krug, M. (2003b) 'Frequency as a determinant in grammatical variation and change', in Rohdenburg, G. and Mondorf, B. (eds) *Determinants of Grammatical Variation in English*, pp. 7–67. Berlin and New York: Mouton de Gruyter.

Kytö, M. and Walker, T. (2006) *Guide to a Corpus of English Dialogues 1560–1760*. Uppsala: Acta Universitatis Upsaliensis.

Labov, W. (1966) *The Social Stratification of English in New York City*. Washington, DC: Center for Applied Linguistics.

Labov, W. (1972a) *Language in the Inner City*. Philadelphia: University of Pennsylvania Press.

Labov, W. (1972b) *Sociolinguistic Patterns*. Philadelphia: University of Pennsylvania Press.

Labov, W. (1978) 'On the use of the present to explain the past', in Baldi, P. and Werth, R. N. (eds) *Readings in Historical Phonology*, pp. 275–312. Pennsylvania: Pennsylvania State University Press.

Labov, W. (1994) *Principles of Linguistic Change. I: Internal Factors*. Oxford: Blackwell.

Labov, W. (2001). *Principles of Linguistic Change: Social Factors*. Oxford: Blackwell

Ladefoged, P. and Maddieson, I. (1996) *The Sounds of the World's Languages*. Oxford: Blackwell.

Laing, M. and Lass, R. (2007) *A Linguistic Atlas of Early Middle English, 1150–1350* Edinburgh: University of Edinburgh.

Lakoff, G. and Johnson, M. (1980) *Metaphors We Live By*. Chicago: University of Chicago Press.

Lass, R. (1976) 'Rules, metarules and the shape of the Great Vowel Shift', in Lass, R. (ed.) *English Phonology and Phonological Theory: Synchronic and Diachronic Studies*, pp. 51–102. Cambridge: Cambridge University Press.

Lass, R. (1992) 'Phonology and morphology', in Blake, N. (ed.) *The Cambridge History of the English Language. Vol. 2. 1066–1476*, pp. 23–155. Cambridge: Cambridge University Press.

Lass, R. (1997) *Historical Linguistics and Language Change*. Cambridge: Cambridge University Press.

Lass, R. (1999a) 'Phonology and morphology', in Lass, R. (ed.) *The Cambridge History of the English Language. Vol. 3. 1476–1776*, pp. 56–186. Cambridge: Cambridge University Press.

Lass, R. (ed.) (1999b) *The Cambridge History of the English Language. Vol. 3. 1476–1776*. Cambridge: Cambridge University Press.

Lass, R. (2006) 'Phonology and morphology', in Hogg, R. and Denison, D. (eds) *A History of the English Language*, pp. 43–109. Cambridge: Cambridge University Press.

Lave, J. and Wenger, E. (1991) *Situated Learning: Legitimate Peripheral Participation*. Cambridge: Cambridge University Press.

Lawton, D. (2003) 'Mapping performance', in Scase, W., Copeland. R. and Lawton, D. (1998) *New Medieval Literatures 1*, pp. 1–9. Oxford: Oxford University Press.

Leech, G. (2003) 'Modality on the move: the English modal auxiliaries 1961–1992', in Facchinetti, R., Krug, M. and Palmer, F. (eds) *Modality in Contemporary English*, pp. 223–40. Berlin and New York: Mouton de Gruyter.

Leech, G. and Smith, N. (2006) 'Recent grammatical change in written English 1961–1992: some preliminary findings of a comparison of American with British English, in Renouf, A. and Kehoe, A. (eds) *The Changing Face of Corpus Linguistics*, pp. 185–204. Amsterdam: Rodopi.

Leech, G., Hundt, M., Mair, C. and Smith, N. (2009) *Change in Contemporary English: A Grammatical Study*. Cambridge: Cambridge University Press.

Leith, D. (1997) *A Social History of English*. 2nd edition. London: Routledge.

Lenker, U. (2000) 'The monasteries of the Benedictine reform and the "Winchester School": model cases of social networks in Anglo-Saxon England?' *European Journal of English Studies* 4: 225–38.

Luick, K. (1896) *Untersuchungen zur englischen Lautgeschichte*. Strassburg: Truebner.

Lusignan, S. (2009) 'French language in contact with English: social context and linguistic change (mid-13th–14th centuries)', in Wogan-Browne, J., Collette, C. and Kowalski, M., et al. (eds) *Language and Culture in Medieval Britain: The French of England c. 1100–c. 1500*, pp. 19–30. York: York Medieval Press.

Machan T. W. (1994) 'Language contact in *Piers Plowman*', *Speculum* 69(2): 359–85.

Machan, T. W. (2003) *English in the Middle Ages*. Oxford: Oxford University Press.

Machan T. W. (2006) 'Medieval multilingualism and Gower's literary practice', *Studies in Philology* 103(1): 1–25.

Machan, T. W. (2011) 'The visual pragmatics of code-switching in late Middle English literature', in Schendl, H. and Wright, L. (eds) *Code-Switching in Early English*, pp. 303–336. Berlin: de Gruyter.

Machan, T. W. (2016) 'Snakes, ladders, and standard language', in Machan, T. W. (ed.) *Imagining Medieval English: Language Structures and Theories, 500–1500*, pp. 54–78. Cambridge: Cambridge University Press.

Madhawi, A. (2018) 'How to monetise your home – the ugly message of Netflix's new show', *The Guardian*, 28 October.

Mair, C. (2006) *Twentieth-century English: History, Variation and Standardization*. Cambridge: Cambridge University Press.

Mair, C. and Leech, G. (2006) 'Current changes in English syntax', in Aarts, B. and McMahon, A. (eds) *The Handbook of English Linguistics*, pp. 318–42. Malden, MA and Oxford: Blackwell.

Marckwardt, A. H. (revised by J. L. Dillard) (1980) *American English*. Oxford: Oxford University Press.

Marckwardt, A. H. and Rosier, J. L. (1972) *Old English Language and Literature*. New York: W. C. Norton and Co.

Marshall, P. (2017) *Heretics and Believers: A History of the English Reformation*. New Haven, CT: Yale University Press.

Martinet, A. (1952) 'Function, structure and sound change', *Word* 8(1): 1–32.

McCully, C. and Hilles, S. (2005) *The Earliest English: An Introduction to Old English Language*. London: Longman.

McMahon, A. (1994) *Understanding Language Change*. Cambridge: Cambridge University Press.

McMahon, A. (2006) 'Restructuring Renaissance English', in Mugglestone, L. (ed.) *The Oxford History of English*, pp. 147–77. Oxford: Oxford University Press.

McMahon, A. (2007) 'Who's afraid of the vowel shift rule?', *Language Sciences* (Issues in English Phonology) 29(2–3): 341–59.

Mencken, H. L. (1921) *The American Language: An Inquiry into the Development of English in the United States*. 2nd edition. New York: A. A. Knopf.

Mendoza-Denton, N. (2011) 'Individuals and communities', in Wodak, R., Johnstone, B. and Kerswill, P. (eds) *The SAGE Handbook of Sociolinguistics*, pp. 181–91. Los Angeles: Sage Publications.

Meyerhoff, M. (2008) 'Communities of practice', in Chambers, J. K., Trudgill, P. and Schilling-Estes, N. (eds) *The Handbook of Language Variation and Change*, pp. 526–48. Oxford: Blackwell.

Mills, A. D. (1998) *A Dictionary of English Place Names*. 2nd edition. Oxford: Oxford University Press.

Millward, C. M. (1996) *A Biography of the English Language*. 2nd edition. Boston, MA: Wadsworth.

Milroy, J. and Milroy, L. (1999) *Authority in Language: Investigating Standard English*. Abingdon: Routledge.

Milroy, L. (1987) *Language and Social Networks*. Oxford: Blackwell.

Milroy, L. (2002) 'Social networks', in Chambers, J. K., Trudgill, P. and Schilling-Estes, N. (eds) *The Handbook of Language Variation and Change*, pp. 549–72. Oxford: Blackwell.

Mitchell, B. (1995) *An Invitation to Old English and Anglo-Saxon England*. Oxford: Blackwell.

Mitchell, B. and Robinson, F. C. (2007) *A Guide to Old English*. 7th edition. Oxford: Blackwell.

Modanio, M. (2017) 'English in a post-Brexit European Union', *World Englishes* 36(3): 313–27.

Mooney, L. R. (2008) 'Locating scribal activity in late-medieval London', in Connolly, M. and Mooney, L. R. (eds) *Design and Distribution of Late Medieval Manuscripts in England*, pp. 183–204. York: York Medieval Press.

Mooney, L. R. and Stubbs, E. (2013) *Scribes and the City: London Guildhall Clerks and the Dissemination of Middle English Literature, 1375–1425*. York: York Medieval Press.

Mufwene, S. S. (2001) *The Ecology of Language Evolution*. Cambridge: Cambridge University Press.

Mufwene, S. S. (2008) *Language Evolution: Contact, Competition and Change*. London: Continuum.

Murphy, L. (2018) *The Prodigal Tongue: The Love–Hate Relationship Between American and British English*. London: Penguin.

Nelson, G., Wallis, S. and Aarts, B. (2002) *Exploring Natural Language: Working with the British Component of the International Corpus of English*. Amsterdam: John Benjamins.

Nevalainen, T. (2000) 'Mobility, social networks and language change in Early Modern England', *European Journal of English Studies* 4: 253–64.

Nevalainen, T. (2012) 'Variable focusing in English spelling between 1400 and 1600', in Baddeley, S. and Voeste, A. (eds) *Orthographies in Early Modern Europe*, pp. 127–66. Berlin: Walter de Gruyter.

Nevalainen, T. and Tieken-Boon van Ostade, I. (2006) 'Standardisation', in Hogg, R. and Dennison, D. (eds) *A History of the English Language*, pp. 271–311. Cambridge: Cambridge University Press.

O'Grady, W. and de Guzman, V. P. (1996) 'Morphology: the analysis of word structure', in O'Grady, W, Dobrovolsky, M. and Katamba, F. (eds) *Contemporary Linguistics: An Introduction*. 3rd edition, pp. 132–80. London: Longman.

Ogura, M. (1987) *Historical English Phonology: A Lexical Perspective*. Tokyo: Kenkyusha.

Pennycook, A. (2001) 'English in the world/the world in English', in Burns, A. and Coffin, C. (eds) *Analysing English in a Global Context*, pp. 78–89. London: Routledge.

Phillipson, R. (1992) *Linguistic Imperialism*. Oxford: Oxford University Press.

Pillière, L., Andrieu, W., Kerfelec, V. and Lewis, D. (eds) (2018) *Standardising English: Norms and Margins in the History of the English Language*. Cambridge: Cambridge University Press.

Platzer, H. (2005) 'The development of natural gender in Middle English, or: sex by accident', in Ritt, N. and Schendl, H. (eds) *Rethinking Middle English: Linguistic and Literary Approaches*, pp. 244–62. Frankfurt am Main: Peter Lang.

Pliny (77–79 CE) *Naturalis Historia*.

Pons-Sanz, S. (2014) *The Language of Early English Literature: From Cædmon to Milton*. Basingstoke: Palgrave.

Poplack S (1980) 'Sometimes I'll start a sentence in Spanish y termino en español: toward a typology of code-switching', *Linguistics* 18(August): 581–618.

Price, O. (1668) *English Orthographie*. Oxford: Henry Hall.

Puttenham, G. (1589) *The Art of English Poesie*. London: Richard Field.

Putter, A. (2009) 'The French of English letters: two trilingual verse epistles in context', in Wogan-Browne, J., Collette, C., Kowalski, M., Mooney, L., Putter, A. and Trotter, D. (eds) *Language and Culture in Medieval Britain: The French of England c. 1100-c. 1500*, pp. 397–408. York: York Medieval Press.

Putter, A. (2011) 'Code-switching in Langland, Chaucer and the Gawain poet: diglossia and footing', in Schendl, H. and Wright, L. (eds) *Code-Switching in Early English*, pp. 281–302. Berlin and New York: de Gruyter Mouton.

Pütz, M. (1994) *Sprachökologie und Sprachwechsel: Die deutsch-australische Sprechergemeinschaft in Canberra*. Frankfurt/M: Lang.

Pyles, T. and Algeo, J. (1993) *The Origins and Development of the English Language*. 4th edition. Fort Worth, TX: Harcourt Brace Jovanovich.

Quirk, R., Adams, V. and Davy, D. (1975) *Old English Literature: A Practical Introduction*. London: Edward Arnold.

Quirk, R., Greenbaum, S., Leech, G. and Svartvik, J. (1985) *A Comprehensive Grammar of the English Language*. London and New York: Longman.

Reaney, P. H. (1960) *The Origin of English Place Names*. London: Routledge.

Reddy, M. (1979) 'The conduit metaphor', in Ortony, A. (ed.) *Metaphor and Thought*, pp. 284–324. Cambridge: Cambridge University Press.

Reed, C. E. (1967) *Dialects of American English*. Amherst, MA: University of Massachusetts Press.

Roberts, J. and Kay, C. (1995) *A Thesaurus of Old English*. 2 vols. London: King's College Centre for Late Antique and Medieval Studies.

Roberts, J. and Kay, C., with Grundy. L. (2000) *A Thesaurus of Old English*. Amsterdam and Atlanta: Rodopi.

Romaine, S. (1982) *Socio-Historical Linguistics*. Cambridge: Cambridge University Press.

Romaine, S. (1988) *Pidgin and Creole Languages*. London: Longman.

Romaine, S. (ed.) (1999) *The Cambridge History of the English Language. Vol. 3. 1776–1997*. Cambridge: Cambridge University Press.

Rothwell, W. (1994) 'The trilingual England of Geoffrey Chaucer', *Studies in the Age of Chaucer* 16: 45–67.

Samuels, M. L. (1963) 'Some applications of Middle English dialectology', *English Studies* 44: 81–94.

Samuels, M. L. (1972) *Linguistic Evolution*. Cambridge: Cambridge University Press.

Sandved, A. O. (1981) 'Prolegomena to a renewed study of the rise of Standard English', in Benskin, M. and Samuels, M. (eds) *So Meny People, Longages, and Tonges: Philological Essays in Scots and Mediaeval English presented to Angus McIntosh*, pp. 31–42. Edinburgh: Middle English Dialect Project.

Sandvold, S. N. (2010) *Scribal variation in a legal document: a study of the bounding of Barmston (1473)*. MA thesis, University of Stavangar, Norway.

Saraceni, M. (2015) *World Englishes: A Critical Analysis*. London: Bloomsbury.

Sasse, H-J. (1993) 'Syntactic categories and subcategories', in Kastovsky, D., Kaltenböck, G. and Reichl, S. (eds) *Proceedings of Anglistentag 2001, Universität Wien*, pp. 35–46. Trier: Wissenschaftlicher Verlag.

Scase, W. (ed.) (2007) *Essays in Medieval Geography: Vernacular Manuscripts of the English West Midlands from the Conquest to the Sixteenth Century*. Turnhout, Belgium: Brepols.

Schendl, H. (1997) 'To London fro Kent / Sunt predia depopulantes': code-switching and medieval macaronic poems', *Vienna English Working Papers* 6(1): 52–66.

Schendl, H. (2000a) 'Syntactic constraints on code-switching in medieval texts', in Taavitsainen, I., Nevalainen T, Pahta, P. and Rissanen, M. (eds) *Placing Middle English in Context*, pp. 67–86. Berlin and New York: Mouton de Gruyter.

Schendl, H. (2000b) 'Linguistic aspects of code-switching in medieval English texts', in Trotter, D. A. (ed.) *Multilingualism in Later Medieval Britain*, pp. 77–92. Cambridge: DS Brewer.

Schendl, H. (2001) 'Code-switching in medieval English poetry', in Kastovsky, D. and Mettinger, A. (eds) *Language Contact in the History of English*, pp. 305–35. Frankfurt/M: Lang.

Schneider, E. (1997) 'Chaos theory as a model for dialect variability and change?', in Thomas, A. A. (ed.) *Issues and Methods in Dialectology*, pp. 22–36. Bangor: University of Wales, Department of Linguistics.

Schützler, O. (2009) 'Unstable close-mid vowels in Modern Scottish English', in Prado-Alonso, C., Gómez-García, L., Pastor-Gómez, I. and Tizón-Couto, D. (eds) *New Trends and Methodologies in Applied English Language Research: Diachronic, Diatopic and Contrastive Studies*, pp. 153–82. Bern: Peter Lang.

Scragg, D. G. (1974) *A History of English Spelling*. Manchester: Manchester University Press.

Seargeant, P. (2012) *Exploring World Englishes: Language in a Global Context*. Abingdon: Routledge.

Sebba, M. (1997) *Contact Languages: Pidgins and Creoles*. Basingstoke: Palgrave.

Sebba, M. (2012) 'Researching and theorising multilingual texts', in Sebba, M., Mahootion, S. and Jonsson, C. (eds) *Language Mixing and Code-Switching in Writing: Approaches to Mixed-Language Written Discourse*, pp. 1–26. New York and London: Routledge.

Serjeantson, M. S. (1935) *A History of Foreign Words in English*. London: Routledge and Kegan Paul.

Siemund, P. (2008). *Pronominal Gender in English: A Study of English Varieties from a Cross-Linguistic Perspective*. London: Routledge.

Simpson, D. (1986) *The Politics of American English, 1776–1850*. Oxford: Oxford University Press.

Smith, A. H. (1933) *Three Northumbrian Poems*. London: Methuen.

Smith, J. and Horobin, S. (2005) *An Introduction to Middle English*. Edinburgh: Edinburgh University Press.

Smith, J. J. (1988) 'The Trinity Gower D-Scribe and his work on two early *Canterbury Tales* manuscripts', in Smith, J. J. and Samuels, M. L. (eds) *The English of Chaucer and His Contemporaries*, pp. 51–69. Aberdeen: Aberdeen University Press.

Smith, J. J. (1996) *An Historical Study of English: Function, Form and Change.* London: Routledge.

Smith, J. J. (2005) *Essentials of Early English.* London: Routledge.

Smith, J. J. (2007) *Sound Change and the History of English.* Oxford: Oxford University Press.

Smith, J. J. (2013) 'Mapping the language of the Vernon manuscript', in Scase, W. (ed.) *The Making of the Vernon Manuscript: The Production and Contexts of Oxford Bodleian Library, MS Eng. poet. a.1*, pp. 49–70. Turnhout, Belgium: Brepols.

Smith, N. (2003) 'Changes in the modals and semi-modals of strong obligation and epistemic necessity in recent British English', in Facchinetti, R., Krug, M. and Palmer, F. (eds) *Modality in Contemporary English*, pp. 241–66. Berlin: Mouton de Gruyter

Sonntag, S. K. (2003) *The Local Politics of Global English: Case Studies in Linguistic Globalization.* Lanham, MD: Lexington Books.

Stenbrenden, G. F. (2003) 'On the interpretation of early evidence for ME vowel-change', in Blake, B. J. and Burridge, K. (eds) *Historical Linguistics 2001: Selected Papers from the 15th International Conference on Historical Linguistics, Melbourne, 13–17 August 2001*, pp. 403–15. Amsterdam and Philadelphia: John Benjamins.

Stenroos, M. (2016) 'Regional language and culture: the geography of Middle English linguistic variation', in Machan, T. W. (ed.) *Imagining Medieval English: Language Structures and Theories, 500–1500*, pp. 100–25. Cambridge: Cambridge University Press.

Stenroos, M. (in preparation) 'Determiner systems and gender change in Early Middle English texts of the Southwest Midlands.'

Stenton, F. M. (1955) *The Latin Charters of the Anglo-Saxon Period.* Oxford: Clarendon Press.

Stockwell, P. (2007) *Sociolinguistics: A Resource Book for Students.* 2nd edition. Abingdon: Routledge.

Stockwell, R. (1972) 'Problems in the interpretation of the Great Vowel Shift', in Estellie Smith, M. (ed.) *Studies in Linguistics in Honor of George L. Trager*, pp. 344–62. The Hague: Mouton.

Stockwell, R. (2002) 'How much shifting actually occurred in the historical English vowel shift?', in Minkova, D. and Stockwell, R. (eds) *Studies in the History of the English Language: A Millennial Perspective*, pp. 267–81. Berlin and New York: Mouton de Gruyter.

Stockwell, R. and Minkova, D. (1988) 'The English vowel shift: problems of coherence and explanation', in Kastovsky, D., Bauer, G. and Fisiak, J. (eds) *Luick Revisited*, pp. 355–94. Tübingen: Gunter Narr.

Stuart-Smith, J. (2003) 'The phonology of Modern Urban Scots', in Corbett, J., McClure, J. D. and Stuart-Smith, J. (eds) *The Edinburgh Companion to Scots*, pp. 110–37. Edinburgh: Edinburgh University Press.

Sweetser, E. E. (1990) *From Etymology to Pragmatics: Metaphorical and Cultural Aspects of Semantic Structure.* Cambridge: Cambridge University Press.

Swift, J. (1712) *A Proposal for Correcting, Improving and Ascertaining the English Tongue.* London.

Symons, V. (2016) *Runes and Roman Letters in Anglo-Saxon Manuscripts.* Berlin: De Gruyer.

Thomas, E. R. (2006) 'Vowel shifts and mergers', in Brown, K. (ed.) *Encyclopedia of Language and Linguistics*, pp. 484–94. 2nd edition. Amsterdam: Elsevier.

Thompson, J. J. (2007) 'Mapping points west of West Midlands manuscripts and texts: Irishness(es) and Middle English literary culture', in Scase, W. (ed.) *Essays in Medieval Geography: Vernacular Manuscripts of the English West Midlands from the Conquest to the Sixteenth Century*, pp. 113–28. Turnhout: Brepols.

Tieken-Boon van Ostade, I. (2000) 'Social network analysis and the history of English', *European Journal of English Studies* 4: 211–16.

Timofeeva, O. (2017) 'Aelfred mec heht gewyrcan: sociolinguistic concepts in the study of Alfredian English', *English Language and Linguistics Online*: 1–26.

Todd, L. (1974) *Pidgins and Creoles*. London: Routledge and Kegan Paul.

Todd, L. (1984) 'The English language in West Africa, in Bailey, R. W. and Görlach, M. (eds) *English as a World Language*, pp. 281–305. Cambridge: Cambridge University Press.

Toomer, G. J. (1984) *Ptolemy's Almagest*. London: Duckworth.

Toon, T. E. (1984) 'Variation in Contemporary American English', in Bailey, R. W. and Görlach, M. (eds.) *English as a World Language*, pp. 210–50. Cambridge: Cambridge University Press.

Toon, T. E. (1992) 'Old English dialects', in Hogg, R. (ed.) *The Cambridge History of the English Language. Vol. 1. The Beginnings to 1066*, pp. 409–51. Cambridge: Cambridge University Press.

Tottie, G. (2002) *An Introduction to American English*. Oxford: Blackwell.

Trapp, J. B., Gray, D. and Boffey, J. (2002) *Medieval English Literature*. 2nd edition. Oxford: Oxford University Press.

Trim, R. (2007) *Metaphor Networks: Comparative Evolution of Figurative Language*. Houndmills, Basingstoke: Palgrave Macmillan.

Trudgill, P. (1974) *The Social Differentiation of English in Norwich*. Cambridge: Cambridge University Press.

Trudgill, P. (1999) *The Dialects of England*. 2nd edition. Oxford: Wiley and Sons.

Trudgill, P. and Hannah, J. (2008) *International English: A Guide to the Varieties of Standard English*. 5th edition. London: Hodder Education.

Van Gelderen, E. (2014) *A History of the English Language*. Amsterdam: John Benjamins.

Wales, K. (1996) *Personal Pronouns in Present-Day English*. Cambridge: Cambridge University Press.

Wales, K. (2006) *Northern English: A Cultural and Social History*. Cambridge: Cambridge University Press.

Wallis, S. (forthcoming) 'Z-squared: the origin and use of χ^2', *Journal of Quantitative Linguistics*. www.ucl.ac.uk/english-usage/statspapers/z-squared.pdf.

Watts, R. and Trudgill, P. (eds) (2002) *Alternative Histories of English*. London: Routledge.

Webster, N. (1789) *Dissertations on the English Language*. Boston, MA: Isaiah Thomas.

Webster, N. (1806) *A Compendious Dictionary of the English Language*. Hartford: Sidney's Press.

Webster, N. (1828) *An American Dictionary of the English Language*. New York: S. Converse.

Wehrle, W. O. (1933) *The Macaronic Hymn Tradition in Medieval English Literature*. PhD thesis, Catholic University of America: Washington, DC, USA.

Weinreich, U., Labov, W. and Herzog, M. (1968) 'Empirical foundations for a theory of language change', in Lehmann, W. and Malkiel, Y. (eds) *Directions for Historical Linguistics*, pp. 95–195. Austin, TX: University of Texas Press.

Wenger, E. (1998) *Communities of Practice: Learning, Meaning and Identity*. Cambridge: Cambridge University Press.

Wenzel, S. (1994) *Macaronic Sermons. Bilingualism and Preaching in Late-Medieval England*. Ann Arbor, MI: University of Michigan Press.

White, A. (2019) 'The new *Joker* movie provides a depressing glimpse at the future of cinema', *The Guardian*, 2 September.

Williams, J. M. (1975) *Origins of the English Language*. New York: The Free Press.

Wogan-Browne, J. (2009) 'General introduction: What's in a name: the 'French' of 'England', in Wogan-Browne, J., Collette, C., Kowalski, M., Mooney, L., Putter, A. and Trotter, D. (eds) *Language and Culture in Medieval Britain: The French of England c. 1100–c. 1500*, pp. 1–13. York: York Medieval Press.

Wolfe, P. M. (1972) *Linguistic Change and the Great Vowel Shift in English*. Berkeley, CA: University of California Press.

Wolfram, W. and Thomas, E. R. (2002) *The Development of African American English*. Oxford: Blackwell.

Wright, L. (1994) 'On the writing of the history of Standard English', in Fernandez, F., Fuster, M. and Calvo, J. J. (eds) *English Historical Linguistics 1992*, pp. 105–15. Amsterdam: John Benjamins.

Wright, L. (1996) 'About the evolution of Standard English', in Tyler, E. M. and Toswell, M. J. (eds) *Studies in English Language and Literature: 'Doubt Wisely', Papers in Honour of E. G. Stanley*, pp. 99–115. London: Routledge.

Wright, L. (ed.) (2000) *The Development of Standard English, 1300–1800: Theories, Descriptions, Conflicts*. Cambridge: Cambridge University Press.

INDEX